Studies in English Legal History

Studies in English Legal History

T.F.T. Plucknett

THE HAMBLEDON PRESS

Published by The Hambledon Press
35 Gloucester Avenue, London NW1 7AX
1983

ISBN 0 907628 11 7

History Series 14

British Library Cataloguing in Publication Data

Plucknett, T. F. T.
Studies in English legal history. – (History series; 14)
1. Law – England – History and criticism
I. Title
344.2 KD608

This book contains 352 pages

Printed and bound in Great Britain by
Robert Hartnoll Ltd., Bodmin, Cornwall

CONTENTS

ACKNOWLEDGEMENTS

The articles collected here were originally published in the following places and are reprinted by the kind permission of the original publishers.

I	Economic History Review, Vol. VI (1935).
II	Columbia Law Review, Vol. XXXI (1931).
III	Harvard Law Review, Vol. XLII (1928-9).
IV	Harvard Law Review, Vol. LI (1938).
V	The Creighton Lecture, 1953 (Athlone Press, London).
VI	Politica, Vol. II (1937).
VII	Transactions of the Royal Historical Society, 4th Series, Vol. XXXII (1950).
VIII	T. R. H. S., 5th Series, Vol. 1 (1951).
IX	T. R. H. S., 5th Series, Vol. 2 (1952).
X	T. R. H. S., 5th Series, Vol. 3 (1953).
XI	Law Quarterly Review, Vol. 64 (1948).
XII	American Historical Review, Vol. XXX (1924).
XIII	Law Quarterly Review, Vol. 60 (1944).
XIV	Harvard Law Review, Vol. XL (1926).
XV	Cornell Law Quarterly, Vol. XXVII (1942).
XVI	Columbia Law Review, Vol. 61 (1961).
XVII	*Studies Presented to Sir Hilary Jenkinson*, ed. J. Conway Davies (London, 1957).
XVIII	Cornell Law Quarterly, Vol. XIV (1929).
XIX	Law Quarterly Review, Vol. XLVIII (1932).
XX	New York University Law Review, Vol. 26 (1951).

I

BOOKLAND AND FOLKLAND

THESE two words have engaged the attention of historians of Anglo-Saxon law for at least three centuries, and for the last hundred years have been surrounded by considerable controversy. The recent appearance of two fresh contributions to the discussion affords an opportunity for briefly reviewing the literature.[1]

Beginning with bookland, it is evident that it is land held in connection with a book or charter. Of these charters many hundreds have come down to us from dates extending over several centuries. That bookland was in contrast to other land is as evident to us as it was to contemporaries, but as soon as we ask what the characteristics of bookland were, difficulties immediately appear. The charters themselves are too conventional in form to be very communicative, and so we are left to rely largely on speculation. At first sight one would naturally think that a charter was merely a method of transferring land, and that once the transfer was completed, the matter was at an end. Things were not so simple as this, however, and there is a general opinion that transfer by book went farther, and impressed an indelible mark on the property. Thus Brunner and Vinogradoff held that the charter was (*a*) a sort of private statute which governed the devolution, devisability, and alienability of the land, and that (*b*) subsequent alienations could be effected merely by delivery of the original charter without drawing up a new one.[2] No doubt many charters did contain clauses limiting the devolution of the property along particular lines, and a passage in the Anglo-Saxon laws expressly states

[1] Access to the older literature can be had from Stubbs, *Constitutional History*, 1876, ch. v; Pollock, *The Land Laws*, 1883, p. 190; and *Essays in Anglo-Saxon Law*, by Henry Adams, H. Cabot Lodge and others, Boston, Mass., 1876. The modern works include notably Vinogradoff, " Folkland," *English Historical Review*, vol. viii, p. 1, 1893, reprinted in his *Collected Papers*, vol. i, p. 91; Vinogradoff, " Romanistische Einflüsse in Angelsächischen Recht: Das Buchland," *Mélanges Fitting*, vol. ii, p. 501, 1908, reprinted in his *Collected Papers*, vol. i, p. 168; Vinogradoff, " Transfer of Land in Old English Law," *Harvard Law Review*, vol. xx, p. 532, 1907, and in his *Collected Papers*, vol. i, p. 149; Brandileone, " Anglo-Saxon Documents of the Eighth and Ninth Centuries," *Wigmore Celebration Essays*, p. 384; Maitland, *Domesday Book and Beyond*, 1897, pp. 226-317; Hazeltine, Introduction to Whitelock, *Anglo-Saxon Wills*, 1930; Turner, " Bookland and Folkland," in *Historical Essays in Honour of James Tait*, 1933; Jolliffe, "English Book-Right," *English Historical Review*, vol. l, p. 1, 1935.

[2] Vinogradoff, *Collected Papers*, vol. i, p. 99, approving Brunner. *Zur Rechtsgeschichte der römische und germanischen Urkunde*, 1880, p. 166 *ff.*; Pollock and Maitland, *History of English Law*, 1898, vol. ii, p. 87 accept this view with obvious hesitation.

that such limitations are to be observed.[1] The further claim that the first charter was a document of title whose delivery from hand to hand sufficed to transfer the property is much more difficult to accept; Mr. Turner has assailed it vigorously,[2] and other scholars have introduced modifications in the hope of rendering it more convincing. There is little inclination at the present day to maintain that all after-dealings with the land could be effected by mere delivery of the original charter; indeed, opinion tends to doubt whether the charter was dispositive[3] even on the first occasion of its use. Thus Professor Hazeltine regards the charter as a form analogous to the *wed*, and so "the Germanic peoples, adding the document to their long list of more ancient symbols, transformed the Roman *traditio* of a dispositive *carta* into the symbolic *traditio per cartam*."[4] The actual charter would be merely evidence, although evidence of a particularly valuable kind. Mr. Turner expresses some sympathy with Professor Hazeltine's view,[5] but would emphasise still more the importance of seisin. Some of Mr. Turner's propositions on post-Conquest conveyancing seem open to debate, but we can agree with him when he doubts whether even formalities sufficed to convey land in the Anglo-Saxon period. It was not early Germanic law, nor was it post-Conquest law. How then should this temporary aberration have come about? Is it an answer to say (with Vinogradoff) that we are in the presence of "Roman influence"?

It is unnecessary to discuss Roman influence until we have first ascertained the state of the Anglo-Saxon law of charters. This is a hazardous undertaking, and we are far from certain on many important matters. The theory that the original charter represented the land seems to us particularly uncertain, and we agree with Mr. Turner in abandoning it. So refined and artificial a notion that a document could represent a thing was certainly reached in the sixteenth century by commercial lawyers when they decided that bills of lading and warehouse receipts could be transferable,[6] and in the fifteenth century when the common law held that chattels could pass by deed without delivery.[7] The dispositive deed to convey land is a still more modern device whose remotest origins are as recent as the sixteenth century.[8] The ceremonies with which the old

[1] Alfred, 41 (*c.* 892), in Stubbs, *Select Charters*, 1905, p. 63. Turner's dissent (*op. cit.*, p. 264) from Brunner's and Vinogradoff's view that the book changes the "descent" is merely one of terminology: it is only long after the Conquest that the rule arose that "only God can make an heir," and that the holders of estates under successive limitations do not "inherit" from their predecessors.

[2] Turner, *op. cit.*, pp. 362-5.

[3] "A written document may stand in one of two relations to a legal transaction. On the one hand it may itself be the transaction: that is to say, the act of signing, or of signing and delivering, the document may be the act by which certain rights are created or transferred. On the other hand, the instrument may be but evidence of the transaction." Maitland, *Domesday Book and Beyond*, p. 262. In the one case the charter is "dispositive" and in the other it is "evidentiary."

[4] Hazeltine, *op. cit.*, p. xxxii.

[5] Turner, *op. cit.*, p. 358 n.

[6] Sanborn, *Origins of Commercial Law*, New York, 1930, pp. 123-4, 214-15.

[7] The first decision to this effect was in 1468, Holdsworth, *History of English Law*, vol. iii, p. 357.

[8] Holdsworth, *History of English Law*, vol. vii, p. 354 *ff.*

English decorated their legal transactions are inevitably difficult to evaluate. Mr. Turner goes to the root of the matter when he suggests that no charter or ceremony by itself could effect a complete and final transfer of land unless there were an actual change of seisin. This was certainly the law after the Conquest, and it was a widespread principle on the Continent. Ought we to assume that England was an exception, and that when the idea of seisin came to us it was " Norman and new " ?[1] No proof has yet been offered on either side, and so we are left with a choice between two possibilities ; at present, we are inclined to prefer the one which involves the fewest sudden changes in legal thought,[2] and to accept the general theory of Mr. Turner that neither charters nor ceremonies were completely effective until there had been a real (and not merely fictitious) change of seisin. As for the ceremonies, it was no doubt (and still is) gratifying to a benefactor to deliver an imposing document amid speeches and rejoicing ; the layfolk still like to see their alms offered up at the altar, and we have heard recently of mortgage deeds being publicly burnt. Such ceremonies are the proper expression in ritual form of emotions natural to the occasion, but we must beware of treating them as legally necessary or legally operative. Moreover, it has recently been suggested that a charter might not be made until a considerable time after the gift had become in fact effective.[3]

Besides these two propositions advanced by Brunner and Vinogradoff, there is a third which was emphasised by Maitland. To him the most important fact about bookland was that it generally (perhaps invariably) enjoyed privileges. Very frequently there was no physical land at all, the subject of the grant being entirely incorporeal rights. The nature of the privileges Maitland described as mainly revenues, partly jurisdiction, and partly greater devisability and alienability.[4] Mr. Turner objects to this view also, but his reasons are not easy to discover, and it seems to us that Maitland's argument, so far as it goes, has not been refuted : it is necessary to remember, however, that Maitland was only considering certain features of bookland and that his exposition is not, and was not intended to be, a discussion of bookland in all its aspects. One matter which has received little attention is the position of bookland in criminal law, where the unusual liability to forfeiture seems a natural counterpart to the privileges which often attached to it.[5]

Mr. Turner's own explanation is disconcertingly simple. Bookland is merely " land which is capable of transfer by book or charter with livery of seisin. It is land which after the Norman Conquest passed by charter and livery of seisin and became generally known as freehold land."[6] In

[1] Hazeltine, *op. cit.*, p. xxxiii.

[2] Thus Pollock and Maitland, vol. ii, p. 87, postulate the disappearance of seisin (under " Roman influence "), and its return in consequence of " some external force " at the Conquest.

[3] Galbraith, " Foundation Charters," *Cambridge Historical Journal*, vol. iv, p. 205.

[4] Maitland, *Domesday Book and Beyond*, pp. 231 *ff*, 243 *ff*.

[5] *Ibid.*, p. 295.

[6] Turner, *loc. cit.*, p. 369.

an interesting digression, Mr. Turner shows examples from the late fifteenth century onwards until the present day of " charterland " and " indentureland " being contrasted with copyhold. When it is asked how certain land came to be put into this class, Mr. Turner replies that it is unnecessary to enter the mists of antiquity—bookland is immemorially old: " transfer of land by charter and livery of seisin was already an ordinary and usual practice in the days of the earliest royal charters that still survive.[1] So simple and sweeping a theory has no difficulty in taking the high jump at the year 1066. The Anglo-Saxon holder of bookland appears after the Conquest as the holder of a manor " and other lands which, though not expressly so described, were of the same character. The holders of these manors were thegns,"[2] and thus " bookland is the land of the thegn, the land of the manorial lord."[3] In a word, bookland was just ordinary freehold land. No privileges were involved; the " book " had no more magical properties than the post-Conquest charter of feoffment; the ceremonies of which we hear were not in themselves operative; the need for a real change of seisin continued without interruption from a remote past until the Statute of Uses; there is no dichotomy between bookland and folkland or any other sort of land[4]; and incidentally the spectre of " Roman influence " is exorcised.

Such utter simplicity is likely to strike the historian of Anglo-Saxon society as unnatural, and even suspicious; and the contemporary references to bookland can hardly be read, we think, without receiving the impression that there must be more behind them than this. Just twelve months after Mr. Turner's startling contribution came an article[5] by Mr. Jolliffe, which seems to be an answer, although the author contrived to avoid mentioning either the heretic or the heresy,[6] confining himself to a mere exposition, richly documented, but not controversial.

Mr. Jolliffe easily makes his first point—that bookland was a product of the national conversion to Christianity, and that " the English charter grew not from the daily concerns of small proprietors, but in national councils."[7] We feel compelled to accept this view in the absence of evidence for Mr. Turner's dictum that charters were in common use from the beginning.

Originally proceeding from the king, the landbook to the last retained its close dependence on the monarch, and even when the grantor is a subject, the king is made a party to the grant; even an under-king's grant needs the collaboration of his over-king. No doubt Mr. Jolliffe is too rash when he asserts that " it is the crown and not the individual ruler who must act,"[8] but in general he is reviewing familiar evidence and drawing an irresistible conclusion when he urges that there must be a reason for this royal intervention even in private grants. " It is because the king is doing something his subjects cannot do. The land,

[1] Turner, *op. cit.*, p. 368.
[2] *Ibid.*, p. 383.
[3] *Ibid.*, p. 385.
[4] *Ibid.*, p. 368.
[5] Jolliffe, " English Book-Right," in *English Historical Review*, vol. l, p. 1, 1935.
[6] He makes a veiled reference, however, *ibid.*, p. 19.
[7] Jolliffe, *op. cit.*, pp. 5-6.
[8] *Ibid.*, p. 7.

it is true, is not the king's, if land has in fact passed between the parties; but he has given something: he has given privilege."[1] This conclusion obviously follows from the evidence which Mr. Jolliffe has marshalled; Mr. Turner's only way of escape is to predicate the existence of a legal doctrine distinguishing corporeal from incorporeal hereditaments, which should include a rule that charter evidence of the latter had to be preserved although not of the former, and so to provide an explanation for the disappearance of the numerous hypothetical charters which he claims were current in a remote age.[2] Such a doctrine was, we believe, a novelty when Edward I propounded it in his *quo warranto* proceedings,[3] and the assumption that a doctrine typical of the age of the year books can be transplanted to a period five or six centuries earlier is in itself highly improbable. Nor is it convincing to argue that documents of a particular class were very numerous, but have one and all disappeared, although rarer documents of the same age have survived by hundreds. It, therefore, seems to us unescapable that the ecclesiastical and royal origin of the Anglo-Saxon charter is proved beyond a reasonable doubt.

The nature of the privilege is a more difficult matter. Mr. Jolliffe agrees with Maitland that the devolution of bookland was different from that of other land, and that herein lies the explanation of those curious charters in which the king "books" land to himself.[4] He abandons the subtleties of Brunner without regret,[5] and would also jettison "those rights of tax and plea which came to be a concomitant of book-right in the tenth century. Royal charters came at last to be issued with sake and soke, with freedom from all secular dues, often with specified royal pleas also, but such immunity is not of the essence of book-right, or cannot be proved to be so. Many, the majority," he thinks, "of the earlier books make no such pretences."[6]

The condition of bookland, in Mr. Jolliffe's view, is thus characterised by its alienability, and also by another factor which he is the first to discuss in detail, although Henry Cabot Lodge hinted at it sixty years ago.[7] This important contribution concerns the forum and the mode of proof appropriate to litigation over bookland.[8] As to the forum, Mr. Jolliffe finds that "case after case in which a charter can be produced is tried before the witan, and the few cases where there is none are tried before the shire."[9] As for proof, the production of a charter was wellnigh conclusive as a defence; at the worst, the holder could only be required to swear his right by a decisory oath. The demandant who is claiming against a charter had not the right to support his claim by oath—a rule which survived a thousand years, in the form that wager of law will not lie against a deed under seal. This seems to us an important contribution,

[1] Jolliffe, *op. cit.*, p. 7. [2] Turner, *op. cit.*, p. 366.

[3] He soon had to abandon it in part: Statute of *Quo Warranto*, 18 Edw. I (1290).

[4] Jolliffe, *op. cit.*, p. 12. [5] *Ibid.*, p. 19. [6] *Ibid.*, p. 19.

[7] *Essays in Anglo-Saxon Law*, Boston, 1876, pp. 111-12.

[8] For a long discussion of Anglo-Saxon procedure in real actions see *Essays in Anglo-Saxon Law*, pp. 227-62. [9] Jolliffe, *op. cit.*, p. 15.

which a fuller investigation of Anglo-Saxon procedure would very probably confirm.

We must now turn to the problem of folkland. The general current of opinion from the sixteenth century onwards[1] has been that bookland was in a special position because it was held by book or charter, while folkland was held without charter and subject to the ordinary rules of customary folk law. This view was challenged by John Allen,[2] in 1830, who argued that folkland was something entirely different—that it was land owned by the folk, the nation. This view seems to have had an extraordinary fascination, and was adopted by English and foreign historians almost immediately. Not until 1893 was it questioned, when Vinogradoff published his famous essay in which he restated the older theory.[3] Allen's view lost support almost as suddenly as it had gained it; Stubbs[4] alone showed reluctance to abandon the public lands of the Anglo-Saxon state.

Vinogradoff approached the problem from the point of view of a controversy which had occupied many scholars in the middle of the nineteenth century. They realised that bookland was something exceptional; but if that was so, what was the normal form of land holding? More particularly, what was it called? Scholars found this problem so baffling that they were reduced to the dangerous expedient of inventing a technical terminology for Anglo-Saxon law. Kemble[5] proposed to call this ordinary and normal land *ethel*. Lodge suggested the still more impressive word *yrfeland*,[6] although he finally agreed that neither word had contemporary authority, and that, therefore, both were dangerous; he, therefore, declined to venture into pseudo-Anglo-Saxon and contented himself with the expression "family land."[7] To this Sir Frederick Pollock proposed "heir land" as an amendment.[8] Reviewing this controversy, Vinogradoff realised that there was no need to manufacture a word, for the authentic word was there in the documents: folkland. Restoring folkland to its meaning of normal customary land necessarily meant the abandonment of Allen's theory that folkland was the property of the nation. And so Vinogradoff rediscovered what Lambard, Coke,[9] Spelman,[10] and the other old antiquaries knew several centuries ago.

There things rested until Mr. Turner's recent article. The biggest of all the surprises in that exciting essay is the last—he invites us to return

[1] Lambard, Αρχαιονογμια (1568), f. 48, translates *folcland* by *terra sine scripto possessa*.

[2] Allen, *Rise and Growth of the Royal Prerogative in England*, p. 143 *ff*.

[3] *English Historical Review*, vol. viii, p. 1; *Collected Papers*, vol. i, p. 91.

[4] See the passage (*Constitutional History*, 1897, vol. i, p. 81) cited by Turner, *op. cit.*, p. 381.

[5] Kemble, *Saxons in England*, 1849, vol. i, p. 289.

[6] *Essays in Anglo-Saxon Law*, p. 76 (*cf.* Vinogradoff, *op. cit.*, vol. i, p. 96, no. 2); Pollock, *Land Laws*, 1883, uses *yrfeland*.

[7] *Essays in Anglo-Saxon Law*, pp. 68-9.

[8] Pollock, *Land Laws*, 1883, p. 191.

[9] Coke, *Institutes*, 1628, vol. i, p. 58a.

[10] Spelman, *Archæologus*, 1626, p. 101; *cf.* his *Glossarium*, 1664, p. 84, and *Reliquiæ*, 1696, p. 12.

to Allen's theory that folkland is land owned by the nation. A second time he comes to the thorny hedge of 1066, and again he clears it with apparent ease : folkland is nothing but the ancient demesne of Domesday Book.[1] The few and obscure texts upon which Mr. Turner, like his opponents, has to rely cannot be considered here. There are questions of philology—and the Anglo-Saxons contrived to make Latin almost as elusive as their native tongue ; there are questions of genealogy—and a family which had something to conceal ; questions, too, of topography. The one great text is the famous passage in the laws of Edward the Elder (*c.* 900)[2] which clearly divides bookland from folkland ; the former must be sought before the king, the latter in the shire-moot. At this point Mr. Jolliffe's procedural approach at once provides the answer. Folkland is litigated in folk moots and so amenable to folk right.

One last point may be mentioned in this brief review of a tangled and highly technical controversy. One of Vinogradoff's most emphatic conclusions was that bookland was free from certain restrictions which lay upon folkland ; restrictions which rendered it wholly or partly inalienable. Bookland, on the contrary, could be either freely alienable and devisable, or its devolution could be directed along certain channels at the fancy of the grantor. Kinsmen had some rights in folkland which could not be defeated ; only when royal or ecclesiastical authority had erected it into bookland were the interests of the heirs extinguished, or limited strictly (as Alfred decreed) to the limitations expressed in the charter. This point seems to us of equal importance to the procedural aspects which Mr. Jolliffe has stressed. Unfortunately, he feels some difficulty in accepting this view. Summarising and criticising Vinogradoff's exposition, Mr. Jolliffe writes thus : " The freedom is one of alienation. Bookland is without value, therefore, except in so far as all land held in folk-right is inalienable. It is meaningless without a vast background of kindred and kindred-bound land as a foil, and such a picture is difficult to accept within historical time. I do not think that we can avoid the conclusion that such a bond of inheritance could be broken by the book. From continental analogy or from hints in the books themselves, I am convinced that this was one of the functions of the book in the days when book-right was in process of formation. I am not prepared to admit that it was still a vital matter in the tenth or eleventh centuries. . . . The folk-moots are busy with grant and witness. In making his conflict of bookland with folkland one between alienability and the primitive birthright,

[1] Turner, *op. cit.*, p. 375.

[2] I Edward 2 : " Further we have declared what [penalty] he is liable to, who withholds from another his rights either in bookland or folkland. And with regard to the folkland [we have declared] that he [the plaintiff] shall appoint a day when he [the defendant] shall do him justice in the presence of the reeve. If however he [the plaintiff] does not obtain his rights either in bookland or in folkland, he who withholds the rights shall forfeit a fine of 30 shillings to the king, and 30 shillings also on the second occasion, and on the third occasion the fine for insubordination to the king, that is 120 shillings, unless he has already desisted [from his wrong-doing]." (Attenborough, *Laws of the Earliest English Kings*, p. 117.)

Vinogradoff was committing himself to a picture of England impossibly archaic."[1]

We can find no grounds for these objections, based as they are on the view that the system of "birthrights" became extinct at an early date in our history. In fact, it is easier to argue that they were "not waning but waxing."[2] It was against heirs that the charters hurl their choicest curses, but for all that, heirs succeeded in banishing the will of lands from the common law. It is not necessary to assume that folkland was absolutely inalienable; it seems nearer the truth to hold that an ancestor could not entirely defeat the expectations of his closest kin. If we look at the treatise called Glanvill, which was written a hundred years after Domesday Book, we shall find a most illuminating passage. Setting aside military land, which has rules of its own, Glanvill describes the régime of other free land which retains ancient customs. It is not freely alienable; new acquisitions (technically "conquests") are easier to give than "heritage"; if a man has both, he can alienate the conquest, but not the heritage (save a "reasonable" amount for his daughters' marriage portions, or for a faithful servitor); if he has nothing but conquests he must reserve a reasonable part for his heir.[3] Glanvill will not define a "reasonable" part, but the very vagueness of the principle must have made it very troublesome. When Glanvill says these customs are ancient, he will easily carry us back three generations to Domesday Book and thence to the last years of the Anglo-Saxon age, which is the date at which Mr. Jolliffe raises this difficulty. From this and other evidence we suggest that Vinogradoff's picture of family restraints on alienation is by no means "impossibly archaic"; it seems indeed to be well established. Such a conclusion, moreover, adds one more reason to those given by Mr. Jolliffe for the fact that bookland became steadily more desirable as the Anglo-Saxon age proceeded.

We may end with a few conclusions drawn from this intricate controversy. Whether the Anglo-Saxon charter was evidentiary or dispositive, or what position it occupied between the two, is only important to those whose concern is with legal metaphysics; if pressed for an answer, we should be inclined to doubt its dispositive effect. The view that it for ever after represented the land need no longer detain us. Mr. Turner's emphasis on seisin brings us back to a more probable position, but positive proof is hardly to be expected from the sources at our disposal. As for the characteristics of bookland, we may safely agree with Maitland that it frequently enjoyed fiscal and judicial privileges, and may often have been entirely incorporeal seignorial rights; that this was always the case may well be open to question, as Mr. Jolliffe remarks. The procedural

[1] Jolliffe, *op. cit.*, p. 20.

[2] Pollock and Maitland, *History of English Law*, vol. ii, p. 255.

[3] Glanvill, *De Legibus* (ed. Woodbine), lib. vii, p. 1. Compare the discussion in Pollock and Maitland, *History of English Law*, vol. ii, p. 308, where it is shown that it was the spread of primogeniture downwards from military fees which finally extinguished the system of birthrights and brought with it complete freedom of alienation. Many borough customs illustrate the older system.

advantages of bookland deserve close attention. Its forum was before the king, and it was immune from the jurisdiction of the folk-moots. In matters of proof, too, it enjoyed enormous advantages, both in attack and in defence. In an environment when most land was subject to restraints upon alienation, bookland was conspicuously free. Often the charter made it alienable and devisable ; sometimes the charter created successive interests, and in the latter case they were enforceable. As to folkland, we believe that Vinogradoff's view is the right one. The proper forum is the folk-moot, the procedure is folk-right. It was ordinary unprivileged land, and the normal type of property. In it members of the family had expectations protected by folk-right, with the result that it was difficult to alienate, in some cases, perhaps, impossible. From this condition only the stately charter with its crosses and curses, and its mention of king, bishop and witan, could avail to set it free.

II

CASE AND THE STATUTE OF WESTMINSTER II

If there is one single action to which we can point as the most fruitful in the growth of the common law, it is the action of case. From it is derived the action of *assumpsit* and a large part of our law of simple contract; another line of development gave us trover and the opportunity of developing, somewhat tardily, our law of personal property; the main line, moreover, flourished exceedingly and served as the medium of a good portion of our law of tort. When at length the common lawyers decided that there must be somewhere in their armory a remedy for every legal wrong, it was to case that they most often turned. Some thought that it should be regarded as the great action of final resort, and propounded the doctrine that case should therefore lie only where there was no other legal remedy, but soon this limitation was denounced and case competed in many points with other actions. Others, still more imaginative, would have made case as wide as a general equitable remedy to be administered through common law forms, and it was only after a struggle that conservative forces checked this daring innovation. So although case may have missed its brightest destiny, nevertheless, its career through the books is the story of five hundred years of honorable service in enlarging the scope of the common law.

The origin of the action of case is therefore a matter of more than ordinary interest. Was it developed by judicial liberals from the bench, or was it imposed upon the law by the heavy hand of the legislator? Is there any great name or any great statute to which it can be accredited?

I. The Modern Theory

On this question there is a very general consensus of opinion at the present moment. Practically all the authorities agree in pointing to the famous Statute of Westminster the Second and its provision in the twenty-fourth chapter concerning the formulation of writs in new cases which are similar to old ones, as the origin of the action.[1] Thus, Sir William Holdsworth[2] observes that this statute "was principally used to extend the scope of trespass," while Professor Jenks[3] concedes that there is a close connection between this chapter and "the great and undeniable development of the action of case which followed swiftly upon the passing of the statute," although he warns us that "it is easy

---

[1] Westminster II, (13 Edw. I) c. 24 (1285); the best text is in 1 Statutes of the Realm (1810) 83. For a new translation, see *infra*, p. 789.

[2] 2 Holdsworth, History of English Law (1923) 365.

[3] Jenks, Short History of English Law (1924) 78.

to exaggerate both the importance and the failure of this celebrated *consimili casu* clause."

On at least two occasions Roman analogies have been invoked. Dr. George Bowyer in his very suggestive *Readings delivered before the Honorable Society of the Middle Temple in the Year 1850* ventured to place before that distinguished body his observations, as a civilian, upon the principles of the common law, illuminating both systems with the light of general jurisprudence and natural law. In the course of his remarks[4] on the nature of the judicial power he cites our statute, compares the action of case with the action *praescriptis verbis in factum,* and sends us to the Digest[5] for "a law very similar to the English statute" and to Papinian[6] for a maxim which has a modern counterpart in the French *Code Civil.*[7] More recently, Sir William Holdsworth[8] has compared the formless remedy of case with the *Lex Aquilia,* both seemingly wide remedies at their inception, only to be outgrown as the law increased in scope.

Maitland[9] has expressed, perhaps unconsciously, a latent hesitation: "It is regarded as the statutory warrant for the variation of the writs of trespass so as to suit special cases"—words in which we seem to find the shadow of a doubt characteristically expressed, although classroom conditions did not permit him a lengthy examination of the question.

Mr. T. A. Street[10] is another thoughtful writer who has found difficulties in the traditional view, and so offers a theory of his own to account for a seeming inconsistency between the facts and accepted history. He observes that the statute was at first interpreted very rigidly, and its general words strictly limited to the special circumstances which precede them, in accordance with what we now refer to as the *ejusdem generis* rule. Then there came a change. After the lapse of about a century "the common law began to feel the full effect of the important provision in the Statute of Westminster II which authorised the issuance of writs *in consimili casu* with the established forms." This liberal construction continued, and finally became so wide that in the end the action of case was used in circumstances, such as slander, which were not "similar" to any old common law action. As we shall see later, Mr. Street has come very near discovering the weakness of the traditional doctrine.

---

[4] BOWYER, READINGS (1851) 89.
[5] D.19.5.13.
[6] D.22.5.13.
[7] CODE CIVIL FRANÇAIS, *Titre Préliminaire,* art. 4.
[8] 2 HOLDSWORTH, *op. cit. supra* note 2, at 454.
[9] MAITLAND, EQUITY AND THE FORMS OF ACTION (1910) 345.
[10] 3 STREET, FOUNDATIONS OF LEGAL LIABILITY (1906) 249.

These doubts are not universally held, however, and some recent writers have tended to ignore them. Mr. Sutton,[11] for example, in his admirable treatise on personal actions, unhesitatingly regards the statute as the origin of the action of case, and goes so far as to entitle his treatment of case with the words "The Writ *in Consimili Casu*." The more general rule, however, is to find that the older books are more emphatic than the moderns. Ames is a typical example of those historians who place the whole of the development of the action of case and its subsidiaries to the credit of the legislature.

> "They were all the product of a few lines in a statute written near the end of the thirteenth century. . . . This beneficient statute of Edward I, the origin of all our actions of trespass on the case, has been the great reforming agency in supplying the defects of the common law."[12]

Earlier still the learned and industrious Reeves subscribed to the opinion that case was developed by using the liberties permitted by the statute upon the action of trespass, although he notices that the development did not appear until the middle of Edward III's reign, and then only after a good deal of hesitation by the courts.[13] When we get back to Blackstone, we find the theory stated in terms as large and general as those used by Ames.

> "This statute accounts for the very great variety of writs of trespass on the case to be met with in the Register; whereby the suitor had ready relief according to the exigency of his business, and adapted to the specialty, reason, and equity of his very case."

Indeed, Blackstone goes much further than any other of our authors in maintaining the importance of the statute, for he holds that if it had been properly construed there would have been little need for a separate jurisdiction of equity:

> " . . . which provision (with a little accuracy in the clerks of the Chancery, and a little liberality in the Judges, by extending rather than narrowing the remedial effects of the writ) might have effectually answered all the purposes of a court of equity; except that of obtaining a discovery by the oath of the defendant."[14]

But if the common lawyers refused to avail themselves of the benefits of the act, the chancellors were wiser in their generation, and the

---

[11] Sutton, Personal Actions at Common Law (1929) 24.
[12] Ames, Lectures on Legal History (1913) 442.
[13] 2 Reeves, History of English Law (1869) 394.
[14] 3 Bl. Comm. *51.

craftiest of them, John of Waltham, Bishop of Salisbury,[15] "by a strained interpretation of the above-mentioned statute of Westm. 2 devised the writ of *sub poena*." If this were true, then our statute would be not merely the basis of a great part of the common law, but also the origin of the whole of equity.

The words in which Blackstone attributes the action of case to the beneficent policy of the Statute of Westminster are in fact almost a direct quotation from Lambard's *Archeion,* which first appeared in 1635, although it was written in 1591.

> "Yea, it is probable also that either then, or soone after, it rested in the Chancellor's power to devise any writ for the direction of suits at the common law, for remedie in cases where no proper helpe was formerly knowne. The doing whereof (conformed to the authoritie of the Roman Praetors) was extraordinarie and speciall: and was therefore then, and yet is, called the action or writ upon the case: as by the benefit whereof the suitor in law might have readie reliefe according to the exigencie of his businesse, and fitting to the specialtie, Reason, and equitie of his very case. And here it is that our Register affordeth so plentifull varietie of writs upon the case warranted by the statute of Westminster the Second."[16]

This publication of the year 1635, is the earliest we have found which attributes the action of case to the statute. Sir Edward Coke, that great father of legends, is at least innocent of this one. On several occasions he discussed both the action and the statute, but as far as we have discovered, never suggested any connection between them.[17] Fitzherbert, writing a century before the publication of *Archeion,* never hints at it in his *New Natura Brevium.*[18] There is good ground for concluding therefore that the theory of the statutory origin of the action of case was first propounded by Lambard, and popularised by Blackstone. Had it not been for the Vinerian Professor's classical treatise, it might indeed have never emerged from the obscurity of the *Archeion,* for most succeeding authors seem unaware of the theory. Sheppard,[19] for example, makes no mention of it, and Barrington,[20] who set out to comment upon the great statutes, does not even include

---

[15] Waltham was never in fact Chancellor, although he was a very able Treasurer. On his death in 1395, "the king showed his affectionate regard for his memory by burying him 'among the kings' in the Confessor's chapel at Westminster . . . setting the first precedent of burial in the Abbey as a recognition of exceptional merit." 3 TOUT, CHAPTERS IN MEDIAEVAL ADMINISTRATIVE HISTORY (1928) 461.

[16] LAMBARD, ARCHEION (1635) 61.

[17] CO. LIT. § 67; 2 INST. 407.

[18] The first edition was in 1537; PUTNAM, EARLY TREATISES ON THE JUSTICE OF THE PEACE (1924) 34 n. 4.

[19] ACTION UPON THE CASE FOR SLANDER (1662); ACTION UPON THE CASE FOR DEEDS (1663).

[20] BARRINGTON, OBSERVATIONS ON THE MORE ANCIENT STATUTES (1766).

chapter 24 among the portions of the statute of Westminster the Second which he deemed worthy of discussion.

Our theory, then, first appears more than three centuries after the making of the statute, if we can judge from the legal text-writers. It now remains to examine the early cases in order to see whether they contain any reasonable grounds for the conjecture which Lambard ventured to make.

II. The Form of the Action Examined

First of all it must be observed that writs which derived their validity from statutes are fairly common, and the Year Books give us some glimpses of the attitude towards them of lawyers and the courts. This attitude, in general, was to insist upon a close correspondence between the writ and the statute. This was naturally most marked in those cases where the statute contained a specific form of words, but even when no form was prescribed in the statute, we find a steady policy of restricting the scope of the writ by a close interpretation of the statute.[21] Moreover, it was the general practice for writs to rehearse, or at least to allude to, the statute in their preambles, with a conclusion charging the defendant with having acted "contrary to the form of the provision aforesaid," *i.e.,* the statute.[22] Fairly soon the reasonable rule was established that there was no need to rehearse a statute which had set forth a form of writ; but where no form was prescribed, then rehearsal of the provisions of the statute was necessary.[23]

In any case, even when the statute is not rehearsed in the writ, it is necessary to mention it in the declaration as being the authority upon which the action is based;[24] but it is significant that neither the writ nor the count[25] in the action of case makes the slightest reference to the statute with which tradition has connected it for the last three hundred years.

But even if the writ and the count fail to allude to the statute, it is hardly possible that actions of case could be established, after hesitation and in face of doubts and opposition, without some references being made in the course of argument to the statute which authorised their establishment. Statutes were freely invoked in Year Book argu-

[21] See in general Theloall, Digest des Briefs Originals (1687).

[22] Registrum Omnium Brevium (1634) f. 97b ff.; Plucknett, Statutes and their Interpretation (1922) 146-148.

[23] 2 Inst. 336.

[24] Theloall, *op. cit. supra* note 21, *lib.* 10, c. xxviii.

[25] Numerous specimens are to be found in the books of entries of Coke, Rastell, and others. *Cf.* Townesend, Tables to most of the Printed Presidents of Pleadings (1667).

ments whenever parties saw an advantage in so doing, and if this action had been regarded as in any way dependent upon the statute we should expect to find numerous references to the circumstance in the Year Books. In the course of an examination of all the early examples and many of the later ones, we have failed to find a single reference to the statute. Once again we must insist that the first suggestion of any connection between the action on the case and the Statute of Westminster is to be found in Lambard's *Archeion,* a little book written in 1591 and published posthumously in 1635, three hundred years after the statute, and more than two hundred years after the action of case became of frequent occurrence.

The historian naturally feels a reluctance to base conclusions upon "negative" evidence, but in the present circumstances such a course is unavoidable. The Year Books are of considerable bulk, and the number of examples of actions on the case is likewise considerable; the discussions are fairly long, and counsel are never loath to cite a statute if they see an advantage—even when that advantage takes the form of obscuring the points really involved. Yet no instance has been found of a writ of trespass on the case being supported or attacked by a reference to the statute. The conclusion can hardly be avoided: The action of case is unrelated to the statute.

III. The Interpretation of the Statute by the Courts

The problem has so far been examined from the side of the action on the case, but it is obviously possible to approach it from the side of the statute, and so, in the hope of obtaining a completer proof, we shall trace the history of the interpretation of the statute through the Year Book cases with a view to finding some clue to the real significance of what is, at present, a somewhat enigmatic text.

The first appearance of our statute in the Year Books is in 1294, when Bereford used it, in the eyre of Middlesex, to illustrate his point that there might well be a right even although there were no remedy.[26] Another case in the same eyre shows us an attempt to argue that since an anomalous writ brought by the plaintiff had in fact issued out of the chancery, that therefore it had the authority of the statute;[27] we are told of no decision, but clearly the acceptance of such a proposition would have deprived the common law courts of all right to pass upon the validity of the writs brought before them. Ten years later we again find the statute alluded to by a serjeant who objected that a traditional writ ought not to be used in a novel situation, "for in a novel case the

[26] Anon. v. Waltham, Y. B. 21 & 22 Edw. I, 322 (1294).
[27] Anon. v. Earl of Warren, Y. B. 21 & 22 Edw. I, 528 (1294).

statute says there ought to be a novel remedy." The objection was overruled and the case continued.[28]

So far, the cases cited have only been concerned with the general principle mentioned in the statute concerning rights and remedies, but in this same year 1304 we find the first reference to the *consimili casu* clause which is our immediate concern here. The Statute of Gloucester[29] had provided that in certain cases an heir should not be barred from demanding his mother's heritage by reason of his father's deed. We now find it argued that the *consimili casu* clause could be applied to this rule with the complementary result that an heir ought not to be barred by his mother's deed from demanding his father's heritage. Bereford admitted that the cases were exactly similar, but did not discuss the *consimili casu* clause, and the court therefore held that the plaintiff was without remedy.[30] Here, it would seem, was a clear case for the application of the *consimili casu* principle, and the court was evidently in sympathy with the demandant; yet he was sent away without a remedy, and the attempt to invoke the liberality of the statute seems to have aroused no debate of interest to the reporter. Three years later another case arose wherein a demandant claimed a forfeiture as remainderman under an entail in circumstances which the statute of Gloucester[31] covered only as to reversioners after a doweress. This time both statutes were examined by the court, which reached the conclusion that a remainder is not "similar" to a reversion.[32]

Not until 1310 do we find the first example of the application of the statute—a quarter of a century after its enactment—when a statutory remedy for guardians in chivalry[33] was extended to guardians in socage. The plaintiff's claim in this case that his writ had been delivered to him in the chancery is identical with that of the other plaintiffs mentioned above, and taken by itself would mean that a writ was necessarily good if it bore the great seal. But Brabazon, C. J., adds a material detail, apparently out of his own knowledge: "This writ is given by the statute *Ne Querentes*[34] by common counsel of the clerks in Chancery. . . . And so the writ is good."[35] This seems to be the

[28] Maltalent v. Romyley, Y. B. 32 & 33 Edw. I, 226, 230 (1304).

[29] 6 Edw. I, c. 3 (1278).

[30] Tawney v. St. Omers, Y. B. 32 & 33 Edw. I, 282, 286 (1304). As it was a writ of right and a hard case, the court declined to give judgment against the plaintiff, and merely non-suited him.

[31] 6 Edw. I, c. 7 (1278).

[32] St. Michael v. Beauchamp, Y. B. 33 & 35 Edw. I, 426 (1307).

[33] 20 Hen. III, c. 6 (1236); Westminster II (13 Edw. I) c. 35 (1285).

[34] These words are clearly a reference to the *consimili casu* clause.

[35] Frowyk v. Leuekenore, Y. B. 2 & 3 Edw. II, 157, 161 (1310). According to another version, "Since the statute says *quod querens non recedat sine remedio de cancellaria,* and since this writ is given by common counsel of the chancery in accordance with the facts of the case . . . we award the writ good";

necessary clue; the *consimili casu* clause can only be effectually employed after a formal conference of the chancery clerks, as in fact the statute expressly requires. We believe that the cases here collected will show that this formal conference was always held before the statute was applied to any new situation,[36] and naturally such conferences would attract the attention of the profession.

The best known example is, of course, the series of events leading up to the formation of the writ of entry *in consimili casu*—the only form of action which derives its name from the statute. The story is too well known to need detailed treatment here. The first attempt[37] at establishing a writ of entry *in consimili casu* was not successful, as we have seen, for the writ had been based on the statute of Gloucester, and clearly the case was not covered by it. In 1310 another case[38] shows us a remainderman trying to combine the two statutes so as to regain land alienated by the life tenants, and still unsuccessfully; he had used a writ of entry *in casu proviso* and it was clear that he was not in the case provided, although he certainly was in a similar case. The next term an attempt[39] was made by a reversioner to regain land alienated by a tenant by curtesy, and with the same lack of success. In both of these cases the demandants (or their legal advisers) learned a lesson which was to benefit other litigants, although it was too late to mend their own affairs. In both cases, moreover, Denom was counsel for the demandants, and it may be at his suggestion that protests were carried to the clerks of the chancery, who in consequence conferred together with the Chief Justice, Bereford. As a result of this conference a form of writ was drafted which satisfactorily met the difficulties felt by the court. In this way the statutory requirement of deliberation by the chancery clerks was fulfilled, and the writ of entry *in consimili casu* was created.

The establishment of this writ seems to complete the tale of our statute's exploits. A few insignificant references to the statute occasionally appear in the books, as noted below,[40] but its principal results have now been placed before the reader.

---

ibid., at 160. This, of course, does not mean that we have here an action on the case in the modern sense, for the proceedings were brought in the King's Bench, and the writ alleged force and arms and breach of the peace, for which the defendants were committed to prison.

[36] In the guardian's case, *supra* note 33, this is not quite clear.

[37] *Supra* note 32.

[38] Devereux v. Tuchet, Y. B. 3 Edw. II, 18 (1310).

[39] Stirkeland v. Brunolfshead, *ibid.*, at 106 (1310).

[40] In Anon., Y. B. 6 & 7 Edw. II, 12 (1313) the tenant pleaded the statute of Marlborough (52 Hen. III, c. 9) (1267) which benefits "those who are enfeoffed by charter for a certain service, such as *(veluti)* for the free service of so many shillings payable annually for all service." The tenant held in fact by free alms, but the court was of opinion *(entendrent)* that he was entitled

IV. The Legal Consequences of the Statute

It is now possible to draw some conclusions about those strictly legal results which can be safely ascribed to the operation of this statute. That they might have been of the gravest consequence no one can doubt. The principle that rights precede remedies[41] is of theoretical and historical interest, expressing succinctly the history and mission of the royal common law since its foundation. The implication of this principle in the statute was of great practical importance at the moment, for it enabled the courts of common law to expand their system until it was as broad and varied as the interests of the growing public which looked to it for protection. By the middle of the fourteenth century a conservative reaction had set in,[42] and there can be little question that the general words of this statute served as a useful reminder that the formulary system of the law was not necessarily complete. In the hands of so vigorous a judge as Bereford a maxim like this was a powerful weapon, but as a matter of historical fact it must be confessed that his successors used it but rarely and timidly.

Lesser minds, however, found in the general words of the statute some other principles which the courts wisely declined to accept. It would have been a serious step, for example, to have established the doctrine that a writ was unexceptionable merely because it had issued from the chancery;[43] the result would probably have been to measure the common law, as was said later of equity, by the length of the chancellor's foot. In any case, the initiative, in consequence of such a rule, would have definitely passed to the chancery, which at this time was a purely administrative office, and the common law courts would have lost the veto upon innovation which was their traditional privilege.[44]

to the benefit of the statute "since the word *veluti* would attract the statute in similar case." This reference to Westminster II can only be read into the case by some such emendation as *atirereit* for *atorereit;* but this is very conjectural. However, if *atorereit* stands for a word having the sense of "enlarge," then it would be unnecessary to take the text as referring to Westminster II: "the word *veluti* would enlarge the statute to [include] similar cases." Obviously the words "such as" in a statute are an invitation to extend it to similar cases, and this seems by far the most probable construction. (It is unlikely that the record or the preceding reports are connected with this case). With this suggested interpretation of *veluti* compare that of *simili modo* in Anon., Y. B. 18 & 19 Edw. III, 26 (1344).

In R. v. Prior of St. John, Y. B. 16 Edw. III, ii. 276, 282 (1342) it was argued that a statute which mentioned tithes could be used also for oblations, reference being made to the statute *in consimili casu* and its effect upon the writ of ravishment of ward (see Frowyk v. Leuekenore, *supra* note 35). The crown's pleadings base the action on the ground that they are *in consimili casu quo remedium per idem statutum* (Westminster II, c. 5) *ordinatum est.* No decision is reported or recorded.

41 *Supra* p. 783.

42 Plucknett, *op. cit. supra* note 22, at 121.

43 *Supra* p. 783.

44 Bracton, f. 414; *cf. infra* p. 793.

Nor need we regret the prompt denial of the position that the statute forbade the development of a new remedy save by chancery.[45] Such a doctrine would have kept the common law in that rudimentary stage of development from which it was by now emerging. Anonymous chancery officials had done splendid work in laying down the foundations of the register of writs, but the continued development of the system into a semblance of logic and symmetry was destined to be the task of the courts and not of the civil service.

Considerations such as these almost amount to saying that the most important thing about the statute was its failure to achieve sweeping results—if indeed such was its object (as to which we shall speak later).[46] The consequences directly flowing from the enactment, as we have seen, were but slight. Nothing whatever on so grand a scale as the action of trespass on the case can be traced to it. The writ of entry, of course, was of practical importance within its own narrow limits, and had the useful general effect of maintaining the policy of emphasising the similarities instead of the differences between the various particular estates. Then, too, the extension of the writ of ravishment of ward[47] may have helped to maintain the dignity of socage tenure as a social and legal equal of tenancy by chivalry, and to prevent distinctions of tenure becoming distinctions of class. Allowing all due credit for these achievements, however, the fact remains that the results of the statute were few, strikingly few compared with the large claims which have been made for it.

From the preceding cases it will be seen that the courts were inclined to pay most respect to the *consimili casu* clause when its application had been settled by a conference of chancery clerks, as the statute expressly required. If the statute had been regularly observed, we should expect to find a fairly long series of such conferences among the memorials, or at least, among the traditions of the profession. Indeed, if this practice had accompanied the theory that novelties could only be initiated in this manner, then our legal system might have developed along rather curious lines. We should have had the common law courts reduced to the role of trying cases upon writs whose scope was beyond their criticism. The expansion of the law would have taken place, not in the courts, but in the chancery which alone could settle the form of a writ in unusual circumstances, and the chancery's decision would be conclusive as to the existence of a right of action in a given state of facts and as to the appropriate form in any doubtful

---

[45] *Supra* pp. 783-784.
[46] *Infra* pp. 791-796.
[47] *Supra* pp. 784-785.

case. The constant use of this procedure would perhaps have given rise to the severance of the judicial process into two different functions performed by two different bodies—the settlement of the formula, and the trial and conclusion of the case on the basis of that formula. The theoretical implications of such a system must not detain us now, interesting as they are, for the statute was soon systematically ignored, and the bench proceeded to exercise those mingled powers which from the fourteenth century until today have defied analysis. Occasional conferences no doubt took place, for traces, more or less clear, have survived.[48] For our purposes, however, the most important consideration is that no trace of a conference has been found which suggests that the action of trespass on the case owes its origin or its legality to the operation of the statute.

V. An Examination of the Statute

Thus far we have found that there is no evidence discernible in the action on the case, nor in the contemporary interpretation of the statute, to support the modern theory that the statute was the basis of the action. We have likewise seen that the statute has left little mark upon the position of the common law courts, and that the generalities contained in it were prudently ignored in the thirteenth and fourteenth centuries. It is now time, therefore, to examine the text and to see what the statute really does say, remembering always that the interpretation of a document six hundred years old must necessarily proceed as much from its external history as from a study of the precise words it contains. It would be rash indeed to venture an opinion upon the significance of a statute based solely upon its text, without a thorough consideration of its appearances in the older books.

That portion of the Statute of Westminster the Second which soon became known as chapter 24 consists of several provisions, loosely connected by the laws of association rather than of logic. The text printed in the Statutes of the Realm is probably as good as any, for it is drawn from the great roll of the statutes which was most probably a semi-official compilation. The general clumsiness of the Latin appears to be original, for there is no reason to suppose that the text of the roll represents a degeneration from any earlier or better form. The translation printed by the commissioners is illiterate and even unintelligible; we shall therefore expand the text of the statute roll and place beside it a new translation.

---

[48] Registrum Brevium (1634) f. 200, for example.

In casibus quibus conceditur breve in cancellaria de facto alicujus, de cetero non recedant querentes a curia regis sine remedio pro eo quod tenementum transfertur de uno in alium et in registro de cancellaria non est inventum aliquod breve in illo casu speciale, sicut de domo, muro, mercato conceditur breve super eum qui levavit et si transferatur domus, murus, et hiis consimilia in aliam personam, breve denegatur; set decetero cum in uno casu conceditur breve et in consimili casu simili remedio indigente, sicut prius, fit breve: Questus est nobis A quod B injuste etc. levavit domum, murum, mercatum et alia que sunt ad nocumentum: si huiusmodi levata transferantur in aliam personam decetero fiat breve sic: Questus est nobis A quod B et C levaverunt etc.

In cases where a writ is granted in chancery concerning an act done by one person, let not the plaintiffs depart from the king's court without remedy merely because the tenement has been transferred from that person to another, and no writ fitting that special case is to be found in the register of chancery. For example, a writ is granted against one who levies a house, wall or market; but if the house, wall, market or the like is transferred to another person, the writ is denied. Henceforth, therefore, when a writ is granted in one case, but a corresponding remedy is lacking in a similar case (as above said) let there be a writ. [Thus] "*A* has complained to us that *B* unjustly, etc., levied a house, wall, market, etc., to the nuisance, etc."; but if the things so levied are transferred to another person, then the writ henceforward shall be thus: "*A* has complained to us that *B* and *C* have levied, etc."

Eodem modo sicut persona alicujus ecclesiae recuperare potest communiam pasture per breve nove disseisine, eodem modo decetero recuperet successor super disseisitorem vel ejus heredem per breve quod permittat, licet hujusmodi breve prius a cancellaria non fuit concessum.

Likewise, just as a parson of a church can recover common of pasture by a writ of novel disseisin, so henceforth let his successor against the disseisor or his heir by a writ of quod permittat, although such a writ has not been granted heretofore by the chancery.

Eodem modo sicut conceditur breve utrum aliquod tenementum sit libera elemosina alicujus ecclesie vel laicum feodis talis, decetero fiat breve utrum sit libera elemosina talis ecclesie vel alterius ecclesie, in casu quo libera elemosina unius ecclesie transfertur in possessionem alterius ecclesie.

Likewise, where a writ is granted to enquire whether *(utrum)* a tenement is the free alms of a church or the lay fee of a certain person, henceforth let there be a writ to enquire whether it is the free alms of one church or of another church, in cases where the free alms of one church have been transferred into the possession of another church.

Et quotienscunque decetero evenerit in cancellaria quod in uno casu reperitur breve et in consimili casu cadente sub eodem jure et simili indigente remedio, concordent clerici de cancellaria in brevi faciendo, vel atterminent querentes in proximo parleamento et scribant casus in quibus concordare non possunt et referant eos ad proximum parleamentum, et de consensu jurisperitorum fiat breve, ne contingat decetero quod curia diu deficiat querentibus in justicia perquirenda.

And whensoever henceforth it shall happen in the chancery that a writ is found in one case, but none is found in a similar case falling under the same law and requiring a similar remedy, let the clerks of the chancery agree in making a writ; or let them adjourn the plaintiffs into the next parliament, and write down the cases in which they could not agree and refer them to the next parliament, and let a writ be made by those learned in the law so that for the future it shall not befall that the court fail in doing justice to complainants.

It will be noticed that the statute gives us three examples of "similar cases," followed by a general recommendation to follow them in suitable circumstances, with a provision designed to avoid leaving an absolute veto with the chancery clerks; their refusal to exercise discretion henceforth will not be final, for the question can be brought before the legal experts in parliament. All three of the examples given in the statute are of the same character, namely, cases where actions have been denied because the land involved has been alienated since the cause of action arose. The remedies provided in all three cases are just as similar, that is to say, the extension of actions for and against the successors in title of those who would originally have had the right to bring them. In the first instance, the assize of nuisance, subsequent owners of the offending property are to be joined as co-defendants with him who originally erected the nuisance. In the second, the disturbance of a parson's common of pasture, it is provided that *quod permittat* shall lie between the parson's successor and the disseisor or his heir. In the third case, the writ of *Utrum* is launched upon its curious and obscure career as "the parson's writ of right." All three examples are of real property actions. All of them extend swift remedies to cases where only slower ones had previously been available, and so no change in substantive law was made.

These are not the only statutory examples, however. It has so far escaped the attention of historians that this same problem had been attacked three years previously in the Statute of Gloucester, and that the same principle was there laid down. The situation was indeed even more remarkable in that instance, for the statute assures us that the king himself was having difficulties in bringing *quo warranto* proceedings against usurpers of franchises who demanded an original writ before being put to answer. The statute[49] therefore provided a form of writ for use in certain cases, with this significant provision:

> "And let the forms of the writ be changed according to the diversity of the franchises and of circumstances, according to the discretion of the chancery and the justicery."[50]

The king himself had therefore suffered from the same inconveniences as his subjects, and the remedy he gave the people was the same as he provided for himself. Moreover, it is clear that the Statute of Gloucester foreshadowed the treatment which this problem was soon to receive in a more generalised form in the Statute of Westminster the Second.

---

[49] St. of Gloucester (6 Edw. I) preamble (1278).

[50] The word *justicerie* is worth noting; if ever we need a ministry of justice, here is a good common law name for it, dating from the golden age of legal language.

If we compare these statutory examples with the cases found in the Year Books, we see immediately that the cases, like the statute, are all concerned with real property matters. The statute and the cases therefore concur in their general outlines. On the other hand, it is clear that the extensions set out in the statute as being typical of its policy are less radical than some of the Year Book cases which profess to follow in its steps. To extend the writ of ravishment of ward from military to non-military tenures, and to extend the relief originally provided for reversioners after tenants in dower to reversioners and remaindermen after other life estates, is a rather more serious matter than the provision of remedies between the successors in title of parties who themselves were qualified to sue and be sued. Consequently the hesitation of the chancery clerks and judges must be regarded as well justified. Such considerations make it all the more evident how remote is the action of trespass on the case from the words and the policy of the statute.[51]

VI. The Political Aspects of the Statute

One other aspect of the statute remains to be considered, and that is its place in administrative and constitutional history. The problem is commonly discussed in the form of two questions: Was it the intention of the statute to enlarge or to diminish the powers of chancery? Was its object attained? Opinion is divided upon all this. Coke regards the statute as a restriction upon chancery, and so does Professor Baldwin.[52] On the other side, Blackstone and Professor Jenks see in it an enlargement, or, at least, a revival of chancery activity.[53] Somewhere in between these two views is the position taken by Maitland:

> "In Edward's day we find it admitted that new writs cannot be made without the action of the national assembly—they must be sanctioned by statute; indeed, so strict has this rule become that in 1285 it requiries a statute to permit the clerks in the king's chancery to vary the old writs slightly so as to fit new cases as they arise, but only new cases which fall under rules of law already established and which require remedies which are already given. Henceforth the sphere for judge-made law is hemmed in by the existing remedies, the writs that have already been made; to introduce a new form of action requires a statute. Henceforth for nearly two centuries the growth of unenacted law is very slow indeed."[54]

---

[51] It is only comparatively late that case became available for matters connected with real property, such as waste, easements, commons, *etc.*

[52] Co. Lit. § 67; Baldwin, King's Council (1913) 238-9.

[53] 3 Bl. Comm. *50-51; Jenks, *op. cit. supra* note 3, at 46.

[54] Constitutional History (1913) 105. The reader will note that Maitland foresaw the results of our detailed discussion in Part V and had already reached the conclusion that the statute was only concerned with points of detail. His last sentence, however, is difficult to reconcile with the marked contrast be-

By way of preliminary to this question something must be said about the general history of the office of chancellor. Chancery was much slower than the exchequer in becoming a state bureau separate from the royal household, and the power of such great chancellors as St. Thomas Becket (1155-1162), William Longchamp (1189- *c.* 1197), and Hubert Walter (1199-1205) must be attributed to their close personal contact with the king, rather than to the inherent importance of their office, which was in fact still a mere department of the household. The growth of an office organization, however, was inevitable and it is not surprising that the bureau becomes more powerful as the personality of the chancellors becomes more striking. The baronial magnate who was the typical chancellor in the reigns of Henry II and his sons, Richard and John, was apt to be a dangerous rival to the monarch, especially when (as happened on several occasions) he bought the office for life from an impecunious king and made substantial profits out of it. In 1238, however, Henry III succeeded in breaking the line of baronial chancellors, and began the long series of "inglorious chancellors," men of humble standing who administered the well-organised bureau on something like civil service lines, although it still remained in close touch with the wardrobe.[55] The baronage, on the other hand, aspired to re-establish the practice of appointing distinguished and powerful chancellors representative of their order as a check upon the crown, and to set up the chancery organization on an independent basis like the exchequer. This was one of several issues which combined to produce the baronial rebellion in the middle of the thirteenth century.

In the midst of this troubled period Bracton was writing his treatise, which he ceased to revise to any notable extent after 1256. The description which he gives us of the nature of the writ and the functions of the writ-issuing office will therefore be seen to apply to the period during which the chancery was under royal control as part of the household establishment. Bracton observes that:

> "There are some writs based upon certain circumstances which are *de cursu;* these are granted and approved by the common counsel of all the realm, and cannot be changed in any way without their will and consent.

tween the Year Books of Henry VII and the treatise of Britton. The great development of the law during this period is undeniable, and it is clear that comparatively little of the new material was of statutory origin, most of it having, in fact, been effected by enlarging the scope of actions on the case and their derivatives.

[55] TOUT, PLACE OF EDWARD II (1914) 58-9; 1 TOUT, ADMINISTRATIVE HISTORY (1920) 186-7. The office of chancellor "was suspended for forty years under Philip Augustus, and for nearly a hundred years after 1227. . . . Similarly the office of papal chancellor came to an end in the last years of Innocent III." 1 TOUT, at 15 n.

There are others which are called magistral, which are often modified according to the variety of different cases, deeds, and complaints, being sometimes real, personal, or mixed."[56]

It will be noted that the term "magistral" is not familiar in the common law; it is probably an invention of Bracton.[57] In any case, he makes it clear that any writ, however "magistral" it be, will have to undergo the scrutiny of the courts:

"A writ will abate if it has been brought against the law and custom of the realm *(contra jus)* especially the charter of liberties. . . . If the writ is without warrant from the law *(praeter jus),* it shall be sustained as long as it is consonant with reason and not contrary to law, provided that it has been granted by the king and approved by his council. Such a writ should be personal, and granted only as a special favor; but it is immaterial that the magnates have not given their express assent, as long as they have not expressly dissented, for unless sufficiently good reason has been shown against such a writ, it pertains to the king to provide a competent remedy for the suppression of every wrong."[58]

Bracton's program is therefore a free issue of new writs by the king and his council in special circumstances, subject to protests by the magnates. We can now compare this with the baronial declarations made during their assumption of power.

The petition of grievances presented by the barons to the Oxford parliament in June, 1258, contains no complaint of the undue issue of original writs, but the Provisions of Oxford made at that meeting contain a form of oath to be taken by the chancellor (among others) binding him to co-operate with the revolutionary committee of twenty-four, which for practical purposes was to supersede Henry III.

"*The Chancellor of England shall swear this.*

"That he will not seal any writ save writs of course without the command of the king and those of his council who shall be present; nor will he seal a grant of wardship, nor a grant of . . . [59] nor of escheat without the assent of the great council or a majority of it; nor will he seal anything against the ordinance made or to be made by the twenty-four or a majority of them. . . . And a colleague shall be provided for him as the council shall provide."[60]

A consideration of this text will show that there is nothing in it inconsistent with the principles stated by Bracton. Writs not of course

---

[56] BRACTON, f. 413b.

[57] It must not be connected with the masters in chancery, for it is certain that this office was not yet in existence; 3 TOUT, at 211.

[58] BRACTON, f. 414b.

[59] Hiatus in the original.

[60] STUBBS, SELECT CHARTERS (1913) 380; *cf. ibid.,* at 382.

will need the consent of the king and small council, as he had recommended. Indeed, apart from this one passage, there is no reference to the question of the issue of extraordinary writs. In curbing the power of the chancellor it is not writs, but the disposal of patronage and property which excites the interest of the insurgents. From our point of view, therefore, the Provisions of Oxford make no new contribution; the question of novel writs was not in issue, and the general writ-issuing power of the chancellor was left as Bracton stated it.

Coming to the reign of Edward I, we find a significant change in the chancery. The "inglorious chancellors" come to an end, and in their place we find a man of first-rate abilities and high distinction filling the office for eighteen years, not, however, as a baronial nominee, but as the trusted friend and confidant of the king. Above all, he was the author, or at least the inspirer, of the statute now under discussion. Robert Burnell, later Bishop of Bath and Wells, from his early youth had served Edward at home and abroad, meanwhile amassing a considerable fortune. On Edward's accession and return to England in 1274 Burnell became chancellor and held the seal until his death in 1292. His term of office therefore coincides with the statutes of Westminster the First and of Bigamists (1275), Gloucester (1278), Mortmain (1279), Acton Burnell (enacted in 1283 at the chancellor's ancestral home, where he played host to the king and parliament), the Statute of Wales (a re-statement of English law made in 1284), the Statutes of Merchants, Westminster the Second, and the Statute of Winchester (all in 1285), Quia Emptores and Quo Warranto in 1290—to mention only the more important. No later chancellor has rivalled Burnell's record until Lord Birkenhead. Lawyers today are so little acquainted with Burnell's fame, that we shall quote at some length from the estimate of his work and character written by the late Professor T. F. Tout:

> "It is hard to determine Burnell's precise share in the great legislative acts of Edward I's time. But his constant and intimate association with his master, the strong bonds of personal friendship that plainly united the sovereign and minister, and the facts that Burnell's elevation to the chancery marks the beginnings of Edward's legislative reforms, and that after his death few more great statutes were passed, combine to suggest that Burnell largely shared in the glory of the work. But not in law-making only was Burnell's influence felt. His resolution in 1280 to settle the chancery, which had hitherto followed the court, at London as a fixed place where suitors could always find a remedy for their grievances, marks an important epoch in the history of that court. . . .
>
> "The private habits of the chancellor were not such as to satisfy even the low standard of ecclesiastical decorum then exacted, and may well have barred him from the archbishopric. An unpleasant feature of his character

was his insatiable greed. . . . On his death he was in possession of estates in nineteen counties, and the holder in whole or in part, of eighty-two manors. . . .

"Burnell's faithfulness, wisdom, and experience must be set against the greediness and the licentiousness and the nepotism that stained his private character. His kindness of heart, his liberality, affability, love of peacemaking, and readiness in giving audience to his suitors brought him a good share of hs master's popularity. The intimate friend of Edward I could hardly have been lacking in some elements of justice. The confidential minister of the greatest of the Plantagenets was almost necessarily a great statesman. . . . The monk of Worcester was fully justified in saying that his peer would not be found in those days."[61]

Let us for a moment examine the problem of the issue of original writs from the chancellor's point of view. He is the head of a bureau which by this time has attained a high degree of organization. True, it is still necessary for a writer of Burnell's time to classify the chancery among the other household departments such as the steward, marshall, chamberlain, clerk of the market, the usher, and the clerks of the kitchen, pantry and butlery. Likewise it must be admitted that this author, Fleta, here describes the chancery as an "office" and withholds from it the more solemn title of "a court which the king has," thus distinguishing it from the exchequer, for example.[62] But for all that, the chancery is an office of considerable importance with a large establishment. Its clerks are sworn to the king, honest and circumspect, well grounded in the law. Some of them deserve the title of "preceptors"; a lower grade are in the nature of "examiners"[63] who examine writs from the standpoint of legal experts; then there are the prothonotaries who, like all the rest, are the *familiares* or household dependents of the king, fed and liveried by him; while lower still are the learners, the quill-drivers. This can only be the description of a large organization. Now it is a perennial characteristic of government offices that they should become more conservative as they grow in size. The constant contact of civil service clerks working regularly together, each in his appointed place in the official hierarchy, naturally tends to increase the inertia of the whole machine and to confine its effectiveness to the performance of routine duties. This, in fact, is precisely the criticism of the chancery which our statute admits in its prologue and attempts to remedy. Such a criticism brought to the ears of such a chancellor as Burnell must have engaged his serious attention. Was his solution

[61] 7 Dict. of Nat. Biography (1886) 386-9.

[62] Fleta, *lib.* II, c. 13. In c. 2 he seems to treat chancery as a court; but the whole of that chapter looks rather like an expanded list of chapter headings referring to the extended discussions which follow.

[63] It was the "examiners in chancery" who conferred with Bereford over the problem of Stirkeland v. Brunolfshead, *supra* note 39.

the enlargement or the restriction of the powers of his official establishment? We believe that Burnell was too wise to adopt either course. So experienced an administrator must surely have seen that a numerous body like the chancery would be closely bound by its traditions, and that the faithful performance of familiar tasks was all that he could expect from his clerks. The exercise of discretion in framing new forms for new cases required a smaller body and a different outlook. And so Burnell's solution was to leave the chancery just as it was, save for the addition of one little mechanism. In such obvious cases as those given in the statute, the clerks may modify their old forms slightly if they can agree together; but if they cannot agree, then Burnell provides them with a procedure which he applied to several other similar situations. They were required to write down the circumstances of the case and to signify their failure to act, and then adjourn the whole matter to parliament. This was Burnell's device to circumvent the fatal tendency of a large office to avoid its difficulties by simply declining to move. Henceforth the complainant was to get either his original writ to proceed in the common law courts, or else a case stated and a day in parliament for its discussion. As parliaments at this time were generally held several times a year,[64] this procedure caused the slightest possible delay. Parliament, moreover, consisted at heart of a small band of intimate royal councillors, having within call all the other official and aristocratic advisers ready for consultation as occasion required at a moment's notice.[65] Burnell had therefore found the machinery for giving practical effect to the principles laid down by Bracton and repeated at this very moment by Fleta. His use of Parliament as a regular means of solving legal difficulties created by the particularism of a department is typical of his whole chancellorship, which is in fact a long succession of parliamentary reforms. Our statute certainly gives point to Fleta's contention that Parliament's business is to provide new remedies for new wrongs, and, indeed, it would almost seem that Fleta had this chapter in mind when he wrote his famous passage upon Parliament.[66]

Burnell's use of the case stated in writing becomes the more significant when it is placed beside some similar examples of its use in other legislation passed during his term of office. Thus, *c.* 31 of this same statute deals with a somewhat analogous situation existing in the common law courts. Litigants who had put forward exceptions which the court overruled were sometimes surprised to find that on examining the

[64] Richardson and Sayles, *Early Records of the English Parliaments* (1928) 5 Bull. Inst. Hist. Research 129.
[65] Baldwin, *op. cit. supra* note 52; c. XII.
[66] Fleta, *lib.* II, c. 2.

enrolment of the case no trace of their exception was to be discovered. Proceedings in error were therefore impossible, for the error which they sought to have corrected was not on the record. The bench consequently had wide arbitrary power not merely of overruling a party's exception, but also of preventing their decision from being reviewed by the simple device of keeping it off the roll. The law courts were therefore open, like the chancery, to the charge that they denied justice to litigants by refusing to act. The remedy provided by the statute was characteristic. The proponent of an exception which was overruled could write it down on a slip of parchment and require any justice present to put his seal to it; if it were found that the exception did not appear on the roll when it was brought up on a writ of error, then the sealed memorandum should serve as if it were the record.[67] Here we have a complete parallel to the requirement in *c.* 24 of a written statement by the chancery of the cases in which it refused to issue an original writ. In both examples, moreover, the writing was to be the basis of proceedings in a superior jurisdiction. Both of these reforms appear in the same statute and their close resemblance strongly suggests a common authorship.

If any further evidence is needed to show that the stated case under *c.* 24 and the bill of exceptions under *c.* 31 are part of a deliberate policy, we submit the following example drawn from another statute passed during Burnell's chancellorship. The grievance this time was the failure of justice in ecclesiastical courts as a result of parties obtaining prohibitions from the crown forbidding the spiritual court to proceed; when the plaintiff had no remedy at common law, and the defendant served a prohibition on the ecclesiastical court, the result was a real failure of justice. The reader will recognize a familiar style in the statutory remedy provided for this situation and will admire the economy of the machinery used—the plaintiff simply shows the original libel to the chancellor or to the chief justice, and if it appears that the libel contains nothing determinable at common law, either of them may write to the ecclesiastical judge to proceed notwithstanding the prohibition.[68]

VII. Summary and Conclusions

As a result of the foregoing study we believe that we are justified in reaching these conclusions. First, the modern theory that the action of case was deliberately created by, or at least was the actual result of,

[67] The courts strongly resented this procedure; PLUCKNETT, *op. cit. supra* note 22, at 67-8.

[68] STATUTE OF CONSULTATION (18 EDW. I, 1290). For the use of the sealed bill as a check upon dishonest sheriffs, see WESTMINISTER II, c. 39 (*cf. c.* 8 and WESTMINSTER I, c. 18).

the Statute of Westminster II cannot be traced earlier than 1591, when it was originated by William Lambard. Although Lambard's book was printed in 1635, his view was not accepted, nor even discussed, by other writers until Blackstone adopted it and gave it currency in an extreme form. Thenceforward it has been accepted doctrine that the action of case is the product of the statute, Ames' exposition being a typical example of this view. The difficulties felt by Maitland, and openly expressed by Street, left no mark upon orthodox teaching. We are therefore bound to admit that the current view is based primarily upon a tradition which arose for the first time more than three hundred years after the event, which depends upon Blackstone for its popularity, and which has so far been accepted unexamined. This alone is sufficient to raise doubts and to compel further enquiry.

The further enquiry which we have carried out, has shown that actions of case bear no trace of connection with the statute. The original writ and the declaration have never at any period of history made the slightest reference to the statute of Westminster or any other statute; nor do the Year Books report any mention of the statute in arguments upon actions of case. In view of the policy of our mediaeval courts in emphasising the statutory origin of those actions which were in fact based upon statutes, this silence is significant. We therefore feel forced to the conclusion that case is entirely unrelated to the statute; the traditional doctrine is the speculation of a text-writer with no foundation in the full and abundant sources which exist for the history of the action of case.

Confirmation has been found in another line of investigation, starting this time with the statute. The conclusions suggested by this mode of approach are that the statute was not regarded by the courts as making any radical departure from current practice. Attempts to build sweeping theories upon its general words were repressed almost immediately, thus concentrating attention upon its detailed provisions. We have seen, moreover, that these provisions were carried out in close adherence to the letter as well to the spirit of the act. The changes in the law attributable to the statute were few and unimportant, and certainly not comparable in significance to the action on the case. Furthermore, an examination of the statute in the light of the Year Books shows that the contemporary interpretation was easily deducible from the text. The statute and the reports concur in showing that the "similar cases" contemplated were of a definite type, and that the action on the case was not of that type.

One point comes out with great clearness during this portion of the investigation, and that is the importance of the political machinery provided by the statute; and so we come to the last stage of the investigation, namely, the political and constitutional aspect of Westminster II. Beneath its legalisms and technicalities we seem to feel the presence of a personality which we have ventured to identify with Edward I's great chancellor, Robert Burnell. The question of the proper power to issue novel writs was of old standing, but only a minor one in comparison with the political questions surrounding the office of chancellor. The writ-issuing power is therefore only a very slight factor in the constitutional controversies of the thirteenth century. There was, nevertheless, a problem, and we are inclined to give Burnell the credit for solving it by means of a neat device which appears several times in legislation during his term of office. This consisted of a bill or memorandum to be drawn up when a lower jurisdiction could not or would not act, and designed to serve as a mechanism for automatically carrying the case to a higher jurisdiction. The real significance of the famous twenty-fourth chapter is thus brought to light. It did not create the action on the case, either directly or indirectly; nor did it enlarge or restrict the writ-issuing power of chancery to any serious extent; but it did make a new step forward in administrative technique, and above all, it called into play the youthful powers of the newest of the common law courts, parliament.

And so Lambard's unlucky guess about the origin of case, and all that has been based upon it during the last three hundred years, need no longer disturb us. We are free from the necessity of believing that case is "similar" to debt, account, trespass, or anything else. But if the statute is no longer to be regarded as the base and origin of the action, where is that origin to be sought? That is a question to which we hope to return on another occasion.

III

NEW LIGHT ON THE OLD COUNTY COURT

BAFFLED historians have often derived consolation from the thought that the possibilities of discovery are limitless, and that problems which for the moment must be laid aside as insoluble may at any time be reopened and reëxamined in the light of some lucky discovery of new evidence. Very recently there has happened a striking confirmation of this hope, and as a result it will be possible to draw a picture of the old county court in much firmer lines than would have been warranted by the evidence available only three years ago. This does not mean that this ancient institution was altogether beyond the reach of patient and scholarly research; far from it. Masses of archives in the Public Record Office throw light on its place in local and national administration, and from sources of this description much has already been learned.[1] But historians felt that if only some record of the county court itself were available, it would be possible to speak with much more confidence of its activities, which so far could only be traced through their chance appearance on the records of other institutions. In short, the greatest need was the discovery of some roll or other memorandum of its proceedings kept by the county itself. Whether any such document ever existed was felt to be problematical. There is a long tradition that the county was not a court of record,[2] and when it seemed to "bear record" in higher courts in connection with proceedings in error, it was perfectly easy to assume that its memory was its record.[3] A faint ray of hope appeared in the earliest printed

1 2 STUBBS, CONSTITUTIONAL HISTORY (1875) c. xv; 1 POLLOCK AND MAITLAND, HISTORY OF ENGLISH LAW (1898) 532–56; ADAMS, COUNCIL AND COURTS IN ANGLO-NORMAN ENGLAND (1926) *passim*; MORRIS, EARLY ENGLISH COUNTY COURT (1926).

2 2 CO. INST. cap. lv.

3 Note the ambiguity in the use of the Latin verb *recordari*, for it could be employed in two senses, first, to remember, and secondly, to recall in a solemn and legal manner — to record in the modern sense of the word. Consequently it does not necessarily imply the use of a written record. The recorder of London, for example, when he bears record, must do so by word of mouth and not with the aid of written memoranda — although he has forty days in which to search his memory. Y. B. 17–18 Edw. III, 555–56, 564 (1344). Indeed, one man's memory may be better than another man's rolls, 1 ROTULI PARLIAMENTORUM (1292) 84. For the pro-

Year Book where we find a case in which Justice Cave explained that "in this case the roll of the county does not bear record, but the whole body of the county and the suitors and coroners do."[4] These few words were welcome evidence that once there had existed rolls of some sort, and whatever their conclusiveness as records in the strictest legal sense, the historian would gladly have seen one of them. But none were extant,[5] and it was generally denied that rolls were ever kept.[6]

There things rested until 1923 when the first number of the *Cambridge Historical Journal*[7] contained the announcement by Mr. Hilary Jenkinson that fragments of county court rolls had just been discovered in the Public Record Office. This time interest was thoroughly aroused in the subject, and finally it transpired that some eighteen years ago Mr. Stewart-Brown had identified a number of rolls in the Record Office as being in fact county court rolls for Chester, and these, the richest find of all, are now published in calendar form by the Chetham Society.[8] For the first time we are able to read a series of several rolls of a county court, and the flood of new light thrown upon this ancient institution is of the highest importance to constitutional and legal history. The latest news is better still: a county roll of Bedfordshire belonging to the descendant of a former coroner, is now being edited *in extenso* (a very necessary step) by Dr. G. Herbert Fowler, for the Bedfordshire Historical Record Society, and this volume will be

---

cedure of *recordari facias loquelam,* whereby county proceedings were enrolled in the common pleas, see 1 POLLOCK AND MAITLAND, *op. cit. supra* note 1, 536–37.

[4] Y. B. 20 & 21 Edw. I, 236 (1292).

[5] Twenty years ago, it is true, a few fragments of county court rolls were actually printed — for the first time — in Miss Putnam's valuable study, THE ENFORCEMENT OF THE STATUTES OF LABORERS (1908) 162, n.1, *391–92. Mr. G. J. Turner thought of preparing a volume on the subject for the Selden Society, but the matter was not pursued further.

[6] This case in the Year Books seems very little known, and Maitland had once asserted that no such rolls were kept. See 1 SELECT PLEAS OF THE CROWN (1887) xxi. In 1 SELECT PLEAS IN MANORIAL COURTS (1888) xv, however, he revised this opinion and expressed the hope that some rolls might be found. Dr. Bolland later denied this possibility against Maitland and against a similar passage in 1 Eyre of Kent (1313–14) in 43 SELDEN SOCIETY (1909) 23; see (1920) 36 L. Q. REV. 58–60; (1921) 37 L. Q. Rev. 311.

[7] (1923) 1 CAMB. HIST. J. 103 *et seq.*

[8] CALENDAR OF COUNTY COURT, CITY COURT AND EYRE ROLLS OF CHESTER, 1259–1297 (Manchester: printed for the Chetham Society, 1925).

awaited with great interest.[9] The object of the present paper will be to describe the more salient features which appear from the rolls, especially those of interest to legal historians, leaving to others the task of reconstructing other aspects of the county court both from the old sources and the new.

First of all, a short description of the rolls must be given. Of those mentioned by Mr. Jenkinson little can be said at present for they are unpublished, and so their text is not yet available, but some interesting facts relating to them have already appeared in the *Cambridge Historical Journal.* The first roll [10] is a single membrane relating to the county of Oxfordshire for the first year of Richard II (1377), and was discovered in the company of the well-known collection of letters and papers of the Stonor family.[11] The second fragment [12] is of the same year and concerns Berkshire, which at this date was united with Oxfordshire under the same sheriff. The third fragment [13] seems to have come into the national archives in the course of business; it is earlier — 1333 is its date — and longer, and contains particularly detailed information upon the financial side of medieval justice — the *magnum emolumentum* which the age constantly associated with the administration of the law. The word *probatur* (which is medieval Latin for O.K.) several times occurs upon it, and the conclusion is irresistible that the sheriff of Cornwall had brought it to Westminster and handed it in as a voucher to his account for the profits of the county, although the usual practice was to enroll accounts separately.[14] We therefore may conclude that the Record Office is not the natural place for county rolls to rest. Two of them are

---

9 For a description, see Jenkinson, *Rolls from a Sheriff's Office in the Fourteenth Century* (1928) 43 ENG. HIST. REV. 21, 27. For a short extract, see *infra* pp. 668–69.

10 It is officially known as Chancery Miscellanea 37/19.

11 Most of the Stonor papers seem to have reached the public archives in consequence of the attainder of Sir William Stonor for his part in Buckingham's Rebellion in 1483. A few extracts from the roll are printed in (1923) 1 CAMB. HIST. J. 106, and in KINGSFORD, SUPPLEMENTARY STONOR LETTERS AND PAPERS (Royal Hist. Soc. Camden Miscellany, vol. xiii) 1–2.

12 Court Rolls 153/62.

13 It is known as Court Rolls 161/74 and has recently been printed in part by MORRIS, COUNTY COURT (1926) 181–97.

14 CHESTER COUNTY COURT ROLLS 7/47, 10/66 and 24/166, 167, 25/179. (This mode of citation will be observed throughout this paper, namely a reference to the page, followed by the number of the entry).

there simply as part of a collection of private papers which chance brought to the state archives; the third owes its presence there, it seems, to a rather different sort of accident. Their proper resting place is therefore the private muniment room of families whose ancestors have at some time served as sheriffs, but they seem almost never to have survived in private collections.[15]

But there is another circumstance which may result in the preservation among public archives of documents essentially private in their nature. The king was not only the political head of the nation enjoying property and revenues as of his crown, but was also a rich landowner in his private capacity. Not only are the courts at Westminster the king's; there are also throughout the country numerous manors which belong to the king and which he administers upon exactly the same lines as any other landed proprietor would. He therefore has just the same sort of muniments — deeds, accounts, and court rolls — and these muniments are now in the Public Record Office. Among them are numerous rolls and other manuscripts relating to the county of Chester among which the greatest discovery of all was made — a lengthy series of county court rolls. From 1237 the county of Chester has belonged to the Crown, and so all its archives have become part of the general archives of the country.[16] The fortunate result is that there survives a series of county court rolls which would almost certainly have been lost had the county remained in private hands.

The volume published by the Chetham Society contains the five earliest known rolls of the county of Chester, and of these the first is remarkably early, covering the period from November, 1259 to August, 1260. The second runs from December, 1281 to September, 1282; the third, fourth, and fifth together extend from December, 1286 to September, 1289. The text most unfortunately is not printed, but a very full calendar, amounting almost

[15] On the puzzling completeness with which county archives have vanished, see the remarks of Jenkinson, *Rolls from a Sheriff's Office of the Fourteenth Century* (1928) 43 ENG. HIST. REV. 21–22.

[16] On questions of the history and jurisdiction of the palatinate, see Stewart-Brown, *The End of the Earldom of Chester* (1920) 35 ENG. HIST. REV. 26–54; 1 HOLDSWORTH, HISTORY OF ENGLISH LAW (1922) 117–32; Tout, *The Welsh Shires* (1888) 9 Y CYMMRODOR 201–26; TOUT, PLACE OF EDWARD II (1914) 374 *et seq.*

to a translation, supplies its place. Moreover, there has appeared in Professor Morris' monograph on *The County Court in the Thirteenth and Fourteenth Centuries*[17] an interesting collection of documents among which are to be found extracts from the Cornwall roll already mentioned, and four rolls containing financial details of the counties of Kent, Essex, Devon, and Yorkshire.

One more preliminary question must be mentioned before we begin to describe the contents of the rolls, and this is a point of considerable importance. The county of Chester was peculiar in its privileges, and so it becomes necessary to inquire how far the rolls of the county court of Chester are typical of the average English county. This is not an easy matter to discuss for the average county has so far left us no rolls by which to judge its work. In the course of time, moreover, Chester developed an elaborate judicial organization closely modelled upon that of the kingdom and so reached the full stature of a county palatine. As far as this paper is concerned, it may be safely assumed that most of this development is still in the future; there was, it is true, already a Justiciar in Chester, who is perhaps a little more than an ordinary sheriff, but nevertheless it seems that the two jurisdictions were not yet separated into that of the county and that of the Justiciar. Thus as late as 1287, we have a most illuminating case where it was said that " though the plea was before Luke as Justiciar, yet the decision was really with the *judicatores* of the county court, who were acting in the faith and peace of the king," and this contention seems clearly borne out by the judgment of the court.[18] It thus seems patent that whatever the future of the office of Justiciar is going to be, in 1287 he was still only the presiding officer of the county court and that the jurisdiction was essentially that of the county court. For further light on this problem, recourse may be had to the general sources for county court history and chief among them, to the second book of Fleta, which is contemporary with our rolls, and is also the earliest systematic attempt to describe the judicial organization of England.[19] The

---

[17] Published in 1926.

[18] CHESTER COUNTY COURT ROLLS 60/51.

[19] FLETA (1647) lib. II, c. 43, at 94. Unfortunately the only remarks in Bracton are incidental to other discussions.

anonymous author of this work has been slighted ever since Selden dismissed him as a mere abbreviator of Bracton, and used him as a peg upon which to hang a learned but irrelevant *Dissertatio*. Succeeding writers have continued the same attitude until finally in our own day he seems to be hardly ever used.[20] That legal history is the worse for its neglect of him, the following pages will show. Fleta's second book is an estimate of the extent of the jurisdiction of the crown, by a contemporary who shows numerous evidences of intimate knowledge of the machinery of government. His exposition is all the more striking since he has built it round a significant formula: "Now the King has his court" is the constant declaration with which the author opens his discussion of all sorts of tribunals from parliament down to the sheriff's tourn. Courtier as he surely was (probably also a judge) and convinced in his views on the centralization of jurisdiction, nevertheless he also understood the local institutions of justice as he may have seen them in operation during the numerous commissions into the country on which justices were constantly sent.

Fleta opens his discussion in these terms:

"*Concerning the King's Court in the County*. There is really a twofold court in the county. For the King has his court and his Justice (that is to say the sheriff) when jurisdiction is delegated to him by writ, thus enabling him to have a record, for it is to him and not to the suitors that the command is given *quod juste deduci facias*. But there is also a court which partakes of the nature of a court baron (or royal) such as is held in some of his manors, where the sheriff is only a bailiff or farmer

---

20 1 POLLOCK AND MAITLAND, HISTORY OF ENGLISH LAW (1911) 210, have the inadequate remark that, "Fleta is little better than an ill-arranged epitome of Bracton; what its author has not borrowed from Bracton he has for the most part borrowed from some of those little tracts on husbandry and the economic management of manorial affairs which were becoming popular,"—and this in spite of the fact that Maitland had previously made effective use of Fleta in MEMORANDA DE PARLIAMENTO (1893) lxxxi *et seq.* 2 HOLDSWORTH, HISTORY OF ENGLISH LAW (1923) 321–22, and WINFIELD, CHIEF SOURCES OF ENGLISH LEGAL HISTORY (1925) 262–63, are equally summary. The constitutional historians have used this one chapter quite frequently (notably Pollard in England and Baldwin in America), and Tout has some references to the description of the household in his CHAPTERS IN MEDIAEVAL ADMINISTRATIVE HISTORY (1920–26), and suggests with reason that a new edition is necessary. 1 *id.* 38; 2 *id.* 34 *et seq.* But the lawyers have been content to write the history of the courts without the aid of Fleta.

of the king, the judgment proceeding from the suitors, so that they and not the sheriff are punished if they give judgment irregularly." [21]

These few words of Fleta are full of historical significance. The old county court was in fact a double institution, drawn from the combination of two very different ancestries. From most ancient times the shire-moot had been an institution of wide powers and fundamental importance. The weighty words of Stubbs still stand as he wrote:

"If the shire be the ancient under-kingdom, or the district whose administrative system is created in imitation of that of the under-kingdom, the shire-moot is the folk-moot in a double sense, not merely the popular court of the district, but the chief council of the ancient nation who possessed that district in independence." [22]

Naturally, an institution with so ancient a history preserved numerous relics of the former age, and so it is characteristic of this *original* jurisdiction of the county court that the proceedings should be conducted by the suitors, accompanied, doubtless by the antique modes of proof by ordeal and oath.[23] But after the conquest great changes took place, more especially, the imposition upon the county of a sheriff who differed from his Saxon predecessor in that his powers were based not on the county, but on the administrative connection with the crown.[24] The change was curious, however, for it consisted in the addition of new machinery without the abrogation of the old, for the ancient county court survived the conquest and pursued its course without a break. There are consequently the two sorts of proceedings which Fleta says must be distinguished: those which were con-

---

[21] FLETA lib. II, c. 43, at 94. The text is unsatisfactory and the translation given above of the last clause is conjectural. An alternative translation might run thus: "so if they give judgment without the sheriff irregularly, they shall not be punished." *Cf.* HENGHAM, MAGNA SUMMA (1660) c. 4.

[22] 1 STUBBS, CONSTITUTIONAL HISTORY OF ENGLAND (1874) 116. These well-known words of Stubbs are confirmed as to essentials by MAITLAND, CONSTITUTIONAL HISTORY (1913) 39–42. See also the suggestive remarks of the late G. B. Adams on the tangle of jurisdictions in the earlier period. ADAMS, COUNCIL AND COURTS IN ANGLO-NORMAN ENGLAND (1926) 148 *et seq.*

[23] As to this, see FLETA lib. II, cc. 44–47, 53.

[24] See MORRIS, THE MEDIAEVAL ENGLISH SHERIFF (1927) 73.

ducted *by* the county court, and those which were conducted by the sheriff *in* the county court.

The powers of the sheriff to adjudge were therefore rather unusual and depended for the most part upon delegations made *ad hoc*. The powers of the county, on the other hand, were ancient and very extensive, and in the early Norman age seem to have been without limit. Pleas civil and criminal, common and royal, were all within its jurisdiction.[25] Strangely enough the process by which this omni-competence was gradually taken away has never been traced, and we can only offer at present the barest outlines. The rule that a man need not answer for his freehold without a royal writ, must have undermined its civil business very seriously; [26] it seems to have been on the point of surrendering its power over the greater crimes to the sheriff, when *Magna Carta* forbade him from holding pleas of the crown,[27] which henceforth were dealt with judicially by commissioners of various sorts, and only administratively and financially by the sheriff.[28] Such a drastic centralization of justice in Westminster, however, had to be modified sooner or later, and a compromise was found in the frequent visits of commissions of eyre, *oier* and *terminer,* assize, gaol delivery, and *nisi prius,* and eventually by the institution of the commission of the peace — all of these new expedients being in the nature of substitutes for, rather than restorations of, the ancient power of the county court.

But the loss of its original jurisdiction was to some extent compensated by the fact that the remnants still in its hands were capable of expansion. The *actio furti* was still within its competence in Bracton's day,[29] in spite of the recent accession of larceny to the list of pleas of the crown.[30] Debt, detinue, and covenant seem also to have remained within the jurisdiction of the old

---

25 1 Holdsworth, History of English Law 8.

26 Maitland, Forms of Action (1910) 315, suggests that this rule originated in some ordinance of Henry II; as late as 1390 it was a matter of tradition that the rule was statutory. Y. B. 13 Rich. II, Hil. 8 (1390). The latest research has suggested that the rule may come from Henry I. See Mrs. Stenton, *England: Henry II* (1926) 5 Camb. Mediaeval Hist. 586.

27 Magna Carta c. 24 (1215); *id.* c. 17 (1225).

28 For the difference between "holding" and "keeping" pleas of the crown, see McKechnie, Magna Carta (1914) 307–09.

29 Bracton, De Legibus (1640 ed.) f. 150b.

30 2 Pollock and Maitland, History of English Law (1911) 495.

county court,[31] together with an indefinitely large field of trespass which was for the first time limited to cases involving forty shillings in 1278.[32] Finally, there had already commenced the practice of allowing the sheriff to hold pleas which were beyond his ordinary competence, by furnishing him with authority *ad hoc* by means of the writ *justicies*.[33] As a result, there soon grew up a fairly long list of causes which could be heard in the county court, some as part of the court's original jurisdiction, others as part of the office of the sheriff, and still others as being viscontiel, that is to say, within his power if they are brought by a special form of writ containing the *justicies* clause. That all these proceedings in the same court should soon become mingled is only natural, and hence their different histories were soon forgotten. The process had begun in Fleta's day and was complete by the time of Crompton and Coke. For the future the only practical distinction was between those cases which did and those which did not require a writ.

"But first of all," says Fleta, "let us see some examples of those things which are properly pleaded before the sheriff himself." The first action is that of withernam which our author describes in minute detail, explaining that by the force of circumstances somewhat summary powers have to be entrusted to the sheriff.[34] This description, already long, leads into a general discussion of unlawful distress,[35] and thence by a natural transition to the action of mesne which he treats in a long chapter rich in procedural detail.[36] Next he comes to the writ of naifty and cognate matters[37] which were not infrequently brought in the county court.[38] Finally, he adds,

"there are many pleas which can be pleaded in the county and before the sheriff such as pleas concerning medleys, assaults, wounds and such like personal actions where process is by attachment and distress; unless,

---

31 1 Holdsworth, History of English Law 72.

32 Statute of Gloucester, 6 Edw. I, c. 8 (1278).

33 The writ of *justicies* occurs as early as the reign of King John; Maitland, *The History of the Register of Original Writs* (1889) 3 Harv. L. Rev. 112.

34 Fleta lib. II, cc. 43–44, 47, 49.

35 *Ibid.* cc. 45–46, 48.

36 *Ibid.* c. 50.

37 *Ibid.* c. 51.

38 *Cf.* Chester County Court Rolls 26/195, 42/56.

however, the plaintiff alleges a breach of the king's peace in which case the plea must be in the king's Bench or in the Bench at Westminster. So too with pleas of customs and services, debts and countless other pleas and wrongs." [39]

The substantial accuracy of Fleta's essay on the jurisdiction of the county court can be established from an important official source, the Statute of Wales,[40] made in 1284, which had for its object the transference of the English county organization into that country and therefore had to describe with some detail the essentials of the system.

With the period after the death of Edward I we are not strictly concerned here, since the rolls of the county of Chester have not been printed for later years than 1289, although it is stated that a long series exists in the Public Record Office extending through the fourteenth century. We shall therefore make only one brief remark on the later history of the county court. It is the unanimous opinion of the historians that the county court fell into the utmost decay by the close of the middle ages and never recovered. This seems to be somewhat exaggerated. It is worth remembering that county courts did not all have the same ultimate origins and that they preserved some traces of individuality even very late in their history — Chester, for example, was intent on preserving the writs of *justicies* from falling into desuetude [41] — and that therefore the decline of all county courts did not proceed at the same pace or to the same extent. One at least was active enough to produce a little book of practice as late as the year 1818 with this interesting title:

" A Guide to the Practice of the County Court of Somerset: containing a variety of Precedents of Declarations, and other Pleadings, Tables of Costs, &c. &c. at present in general Use, and allowed in this Court. By W. Baker. Sherbourne: printed by J. Langdon and Son."

---

39 FLETA lib. II, cc. 21, 51. This last phrase recalls HENGHAM, MAGNA SUMMA (1660) c. 2, where the treatment of the county court is very brief. Hengham's most interesting contribution is his fourth chapter where he enumerates the matter which the court may be called upon to record — many of them being procedural details of litigation which takes place in the superior courts.

40 12 EDW. I (1284).

41 1 HOLDSWORTH, HISTORY OF ENGLISH LAW 188–89.

The dedication is dated December 1, 1818, and the volume consists of eighty-four pages devoted to an explanation of the procedure of the court, illustrated with numerous examples.[42]

The foregoing remarks, we hope, will serve at least as an indication of the problem which awaits the historian who would define the jurisdiction of the county court and trace the various lines of development which have contributed to its formation. The documents which have just come to light already make important contributions to our knowledge of the institution, and doubtless will soon be followed by others. The crucial problem, however, will have to be solved without much assistance from this direction. It is in the Norman age and the early thirteenth century that the great changes were taking place, and from so early a period there is no likelihood of finding any rolls. The *Leges Henrici Primi,* Glanvill, charters, chronicles, and the financial records of the central administration contain practically all the available information and constitute a mass of material as refractory and difficult to handle as any to be found in English history.

We must pass on, therefore, to a brief description of the more salient features of the rolls, and so the remainder of this paper will be devoted to a few topics upon which definitely new light is shed by the newly discovered documents.

First as to the rolls themselves. Why should it be that when the king's courts require a record of proceedings in the county court, the county has to resort to such ancient methods as sending four knights, who may even have to undertake to maintain the truth of their record by means of battle? [43] Why did it not suffice to send a transcript of the roll? In short, why were the rolls not considered as records, and the court as a court of record? This is a difficult question, and particularly so during our period, for as yet the idea of record was hardly defined. In fact the curious modern definition

---

[42] Lest this should be thought an isolated example, the following list of practice books on the county court is submitted to the reader: SHEPPARD, SURVEY OF THE COUNTY JUDICATURES (1656), commonly called the County Court, Hundred Court, and Court Baron. WILL. GREENWOOD, Βουλευτηριον OR A PRACTICAL DEMONSTRATION OF COUNTY JUDICATURES (1659). By 1730 this treatise had reached its ninth edition. DALTON, OFFICE AND AUTHORITY OF SHERIFFS (1623, 1662, 1670, 1682, 1700) (and an abridgment by the author, 1628); this work contains a fair section on the county court. SWEET, THE PRACTICE OF THE COUNTY COURTS (2d ed. 1835).

[43] For an example, see SELECT PLEAS OF THE CROWN (1887) No. 192.

of a court of record as being one which can fine and imprison [44] is itself evidence that the term "court of record" has had a tortuous history. The origin of the definition may perhaps lie in the rules for pleading various sorts of judicial memoranda, the word record being appropriated to those whose existence it had become customary to establish by the inspection of, or the mere production of an official copy of the original, and not by witnesses or by averment to the country.[45] All this, however, is for our purposes still in the future.

What degree of authority was attributed to the rolls of the county in the later thirteenth century? As early as 1166 there were occasions when the sheriff ought to make a written memorandum, but for more general purposes it sufficed for him at that date to send two lawful men to bear the record of the county and the hundred to the king's justice when suspected criminals are called before him.[46] In 1275 it was required by statute [47] that sheriffs have rolls duplicating the rolls kept by the coroners, so as to serve as a check upon the latter officials who of late had been "mean persons and undiscreet." This enactment therefore specified that certain matters ought to be enrolled by sheriffs, but it did not establish a new class of archive, nor materially modify existing enrollments. Indeed an examination of those of our Chester rolls which are earlier than the statute will show that they are already full of this sort of information, while earlier still, in 1243, we learn that the suitors of Sussex were fined "because they had no record." [48] Indeed, every sort of matter, whether it be the business of the county or the sheriff, is to be found in these documents — and here let it be observed that the rolls attempt no distinction between the different classes of jurisdiction exercised by or in the county court.[49] All sorts of matters that seem memorable are enrolled without distinction or arrangement. Once made, it is moreover clear that reference was made to the enrollments for various purposes; in 1288 we get a clear case of a party vouching the roll in support of his contention that a previous suit had been settled in a

---

44 *Per* Lord Holt in Groenvelt v. Burwell, 1 Ld. Raym. 454, 467 (1697).

45 Co. LIT. 117b.

46 Assize of Clarendon (1166) cc. 4, 18.

47 STATUTE OF WESTMINSTER I, 3 EDW. I, c. 10 (1275).

48 (1922) 1 CAMB. HIST. J. 105.

49 The peculiar treatment of pleas of the crown in the earliest rolls is hardly more than a temporary exception to this general rule. See *infra* pp. 667, 669.

particular way and losing his case because upon examination the roll did not bear him out.[50] It is not easy to distinguish such an enrollment from a true legal record, and it may be that the county court came near to having a record, at least within its own jurisdiction.

Whether the king's court would accept its enrollment is, of course, quite another matter. It cannot be denied that there is some difficulty in reconciling this case on the Chester roll with the recital in a statute of 1285 [51] that a tenant can disclaim in a county court holding land of his lord with perfect impunity as the county is not a court of record. Perhaps other counties did not keep their rolls as methodically as Chester did [52] (although the Cornwall roll of 1333 which Professor Morris has printed seems in every way as full); or more likely, the crown deliberately adopted the policy of depressing the local institutions which might otherwise hinder that centralization upon which the expansion of the common law was dependent. Certainly the county court never quite succeeded in establishing the authenticity of its rolls outside it own jurisdiction, and the old methods of *recordari facias loquelam*, *pone*, and false judgment remained the proper methods of evoking or reviewing its proceedings.[53] In one respect only was it conceded that a county court could have a record, and that was in outlawry, which was regularly returned to the superior courts under *certiorari.*[54] One of the documents printed by Professor Morris shows a still more curious method of ascertaining what went on in the county; a chancery clerk was sent out with instructions to inquire of a liti-

---

[50] CHESTER COUNTY COURT ROLLS 94/165; *cf. ibid.* 60/51; this latter passage is significant, for it shows that not only acts done *in* the county court, but also acts done *by* the county court, can appear on the rolls. There is no distinction of the various jurisdictions.

[51] STATUTE OF WESTMINSTER II, 13 EDW. I, c. 2 (1285). Line 9 of the translation in 1 STAT. REALM 72 (1810), can be made more intelligible (if not more graceful) by reading " aught " for " ought." For a disclaimer in the county court, see CHESTER COUNTY COURT ROLLS 29/220.

[52] The care with which the entries were made can be seen from such passages as CHESTER COUNTY COURT ROLLS 3/7, where a long addition was made (apparently in a blank space purposely left) some twenty-six months after the principal entry.

[53] The forms of these writs may be seen in the following places: *Recordari facias loquelam* (frequently called *re. fa. lo.*), in REGISTRUM BREVIUM ORIGINALIUM (1687) f. 166; *Pone* f. 141, in MORRIS, COUNTY COURT 168; false judgment in REGISTRUM BREVIUM ORIGINALIUM f. 15.

[54] FINCH, Νομοτεχνια (1613) f. 116, with which compare STAUNDFOUND, PLEES DEL CORONE (1607) 64b. Such a *certiorari* is printed in MORRIS, COUNTY COURT 169.

gant whether she had put herself upon the grand assize, or whether battle had been waged, and wrote back to say that she had put herself on the assize by attorney.[55] The firm hand maintained by the crown over the sheriffs may also have had something to do with the peculiar treatment of their rolls. The sheriff was not allowed to separate his official from his private capacity, and so the whole of his personal fortune was regarded as a guarantee of his official responsibility to the crown and to the people. Hence the necessity of selecting men of substance to undertake the heavy liabilities of the office. Nor did the sheriff's responsibilities cease with his term of office, nor even with his life, for his heirs may still be called before the justices in eyre to produce his rolls and answer for his deeds. In this way his rolls and other archives are reduced to the position of family papers, and it was long before it became a regular practice for one officer to hand them over to his successor.[56]

Whatever the legal authority possessed by these rolls, there can be no doubt that they bear matters of the gravest importance, some of which seem to rise to the dignity of county legislation. Let us take an early example. It comes from the year 1260 and deals with a situation which had steadily become more serious, and for which no general solution was found until the statute *Quia Emptores* settled the matter once and for all in 1290.[57] The problem was to prevent subinfeudation or substitution without the consent of the lord of the fee and the satisfaction of his lawful demands—for it must be remembered that alienation is not yet free.[58] Subinfeudation frequently meant a serious loss to the lord, and as early as 1217 *Magna Carta* had contained a general prohibition of the practice, without, however, giving the lord any remedy.[59] It seems

[55] MORRIS, COUNTY COURT 167; in line 10 read *deforciantem* instead of *deforciatam*. There are several more minor errors as well.

[56] "Up to 1885 . . . when the Lord Chancellor went out, his secretaries destroyed or took with them any official records which they had kept. . . . The tradition of regarding the office records as the personal property of the Lord Chancellor of the day . . . continued until quite recently." MINISTRY OF RECONSTRUCTION: REPORT OF THE MACHINERY OF GOVERNMENT COMMITTEE (1918) (Cd. 9230) 70–71; *cf.* HALL, STUDIES IN ENGLISH OFFICIAL HISTORICAL DOCUMENTS (1908) 7. A sheriff's active files, of course, were handed over, seemingly by indenture. Jenkinson, *Plea Rolls of Medieval County Court* (1922) 1 CAMB. HIST. J. 105.

[57] 18 EDW. I (1290); 1 STAT. REALM (1810) 106.

[58] See in general 3 HOLDSWORTH, HISTORY OF ENGLISH LAW 76–87.

[59] MAGNA CARTA (1217) c. 39.

that a bad case of this sort of thing arose, and that the county combined two functions in one operation by laying down a general rule to govern the situation, and at the same time giving judgment on the specific case before the court.[60] They therefore declare that none should enter a lord's fee without satisfying him for his dues; anyone who enters otherwise can be ejected and can have no remedy by the assize of novel disseisin (this, no doubt, being already customary); and finally, they "ordain" that the recent trick of conveying by lease and release must be defeated. This form of conveyance was employed in order to avoid the forty-day rule. A tenant under a lease for years would enter, and then accept a release of the fee without the consent of the lord, who, moreover, could not eject him since he had been in for more than forty days. The county now proceeds to enact that if a lord suspects a termor of having secretly accepted a release, he may distrain him to appear in the county court and there disclose what title he claims, and if he has received the fee by release, the lord may eject him: "witness the Abbot of Cumbermere who by this was compelled to acknowledge in full court that the toll he held from Richard of Wilburgham was for a term of ten years; and Richard's charters which he had for the said toll, he renounced." The conclusion seems irresistible that this piece of legislation and the case of the *Abbot of Cumbermere*[61] are closely connected. Exactly what the connection is, it is less easy to say. Two suggestions may be ventured and left to the reader's judgment. It may be that we have here the same sort of procedure which we find in the case of *Butler v. Hapeton*[62] which was decided in parliament

60 CHESTER COUNTY COURT ROLLS 5/29.

61 *Ibid.*

62 1 ROTULI PARLIAMENTORUM (1292) 79; 1 STAT. REALM 109; PLUCKNETT, STATUTES AND THEIR INTERPRETATION (1922) 22–23. The practice was widespread and the following example will illustrate its use nearly three hundred years later in the city of Winchester. During a period of shortage, Robert Bagger "had great plentye and abundance of malte redye in his howse to have byn brewed and made in ale for the releiffe and great comfort of the Kynges leige people . . . and wold not brewe the same malte . . . but lefte brewynge utterlye . . . to the extreme famyshement of the Kynges leige people of the same cyte; It is therefore enacted at the same assemble uppon the ripe and mature consideracion of the ungentill and unnaturall behavior of the sayd Robert Bagger in the premisses . . . that the sayd Robert Bagger shall not frome hensforthe be admitted to brewe . . . and that everi brewar frome hensforthe leike so offendinge shall leike wyse be dischargid frome ony further brewinge. . . ." BLACK BOOK OF WINCHESTER (Bird ed. 1925) 181–82. The entry is dated 1550.

and duly entered on the parliament roll as a law suit between two private individuals, and which soon after was treated (and finally printed), as a "statute of Waste." Or, as an alternative hypothesis, we may suggest that it may have something to do with a peculiar rule on the application of statutes which we shall consider later.[63] In any case, we find a few months later that one Hugh of Venables was accused by his lord of alienating his fee "contrary to the provision of the whole county," and came into the county court where he disclaimed all tenure of the lord.[64]

As we have seen, the court "ordained" the rule mentioned above, and a few months later this ordinance is styled a "provision" — an alternation of terms which is by no means unusual at this period, for neither had a specialized meaning.[65] But our rolls contain another name for legislation which is less often found, that of "*judicium* (judgment)." The word *judicium* already had the meaning of a decision by a court upon litigation before it — the writ *de falso judicio* is an obvious example, to which may be added countless passages in Bracton and his successors. But the use of the word to mean a general rule intended to apply to all cases of a particular class is unusual enough to deserve comment. It was possible to use the word in some curious senses: the English versions of the Bible speak constantly of the "judgments of the Lord"[66] which can hardly be regarded as anything but the broadest and most general commands; when "judges judged Israel"[67] it is clear that they fulfilled all the functions of government which those turbulent times demanded, notably that of conducting military operations; the duties of justices of the peace were by no means entirely judicial; while finally it is to be remembered that "Lords Justices were frequently appointed to govern England during the reigns of William III and even the first two Georges, when the King was abroad, and Lords Justices have governed Ireland for considerable periods of its history."[68] It is worthy of note

---

63 *Infra* p. 658 *et seq.*

64 CHESTER COUNTY COURT ROLLS 29/220.

65 PLUCKNETT, *op. cit. supra* note 62, at 33. But see the remarks of Professor Powicke, *The Baronial Council* in ESSAYS IN MEDIAEVAL HISTORY PRESENTED TO THOMAS FREDERICK TOUT (1926) 130. It would appear that this entry was also described as a "judgment." See *infra* note 69.

66 PSALMS cxix, 108, etc.

67 JUDGES, iii, 10, iv, 4, etc.

68 POLLARD, EVOLUTION OF PARLIAMENT (2d ed. 1926) 63; *cf.* Turner, *The Lords Justice of England* in (1914) 29 ENG. HIST. REV. 453. Sardinia had been ruled for

that the word *judicium* is occasionally found elsewhere in this same sense of a local by-law.[69]

Upon the same roll as the provision just mentioned, we find what seems to be one of these *judicia*. It was to the effect that a lord need only present his steward once to the Justiciar; if there is a change in Justiciars, it is not necessary to present the steward again. We are not told whether this statement was made only in these general terms, or whether it is a generalization reached by means of a specific piece of litigation, but we are given some other details which add considerable interest to the entry. "William de Boydel," we are told, "dissented, but the county said that his opposition should not hold unless he gave security to prosecute." [70] We are not informed what, or whom, the minority should prosecute, still less what the method of the prosecution should be, but clearly there are here some interesting problems for the historian of the majority principle.[71] The difficulty of translating the word *judicium* by any modern term of political science can be seen from examples such as this:

> "*Judicium* — The county decided that Sir Roger de Venables who sold the wardship of the land lately Richard de Doun's, must sustain the part of Richard's children which the guardian ought to sustain, because by his sale he received full compensation for the wardship of the land." [72]

Here the word *judicium* seems applied (as far as the obvious inadequacy of the calendar allows one to judge) to some application of equity to an unusual case, perhaps with the suggestion that a rule for the future could also be laid down at the same time.

---

five centuries by *judices* (later hereditary), until their title was changed in 1403 to that of marquis.

[69] In the city of Exeter, for example, "Adjudicatum fuit in plena curia" that butchers should pay certain customs (c. 1264). ANGLO-NORMAN CUSTUMAL OF EXETER (Schopp and Easterling ed. 1925) c. 20. Compare also the famous *Judicia Civitatis Londoniae* in the reign of Athelstan.

[70] CHESTER COUNTY COURT ROLLS 6/37; *cf. Leges Henrici Primi VII*, 7.

[71] A summary of what is known on the matter will be found in 2 REDLICH, PROCEDURE OF THE HOUSE OF COMMONS (1908) 261–64; Gierke, *Uber die Geschichte des Majoritätsprinzips* in ESSAYS IN LEGAL HISTORY (1913) 312–35. The idea of "prosecution" naturally suggests a comparison with ancient Greek practice where novel legislation had first to undergo a regular judicial trial; an excellent summary of this method is given by the late Sir John Sandys in 12 ENCYCLOPAEDIA BRITANNICA (1911) 503; *cf.* 2 VINOGRADOFF, HISTORICAL JURISPRUDENCE (1922) 133–34.

[72] CHESTER COUNTY COURT ROLLS 16/111.

Sometimes these *judicia* lay down rules of law of considerable importance. For example in 1260 we find the enactment of a novel kind of theft — the impounding of stray animals by public officers without observing certain prescribed forms[73] — which does not involve that *animus furandi* which Bracton so much insisted on.[74]

One other piece of weighty legislation must be considered. Provision was made with the assent of the whole county and in the presence of the Justiciar and other notables, that an alienee of land could sue a writ, and be entitled to the same judgment, as his alienor, and such suit could be brought by the alienee in his own name.[75] The significance of this depends largely on the date, which is September 21, 1260, thirty years before *Quia Emptores*.[76] It would require a detailed study of the very obscure history of the fee simple during this period to bring out all the meaning of this provision; suffice it to say here that it seems to anticipate the policy of Edward's statute which finally made it the law of the whole land that the alienee stood exactly in the place of his feoffor.

There was one other way of achieving the ends of legislation and this was with the concurrence of the royal justices in eyre. On these solemn occasions the county met the commissioners for the transaction of all sorts of business and to undergo a merciless inquisition into all that had happened since the last visitation.[77] The rolls of Chester do not as yet afford an example of this procedure, but a precedent from Kent illustrates the method. Jurors presented to Hugh le Bigod, Justiciar in Eyre, that a certain custom had been followed in the county,[78] whereupon " it was ordained and established on the King's behalf " that the custom should cease throughout the county save in merchant burghs.[79]

---

73 *Id.* 25/180.

74 " Sine animo furandi non committitur." BRACTON, DE LEGIBUS f. 150b.

75 CHESTER COUNTY COURT ROLLS 31/228.

76 18 EDW. I (1290).

77 See in general BOLLAND, THE GENERAL EYRE (1922).

78 This presentation of a custom, almost an indictment of it, is remarkably paralleled by Greek legislative forms, whereby a law could be attacked on a variety of grounds, both of general fitness and of constitutionality. *Cf.* Sandys, *loc. cit. supra* note 71.

79 Attention was first drawn to this document by Mr. H. G. Richardson in The London Times Literary Supplement, Jan. 1, 1925, at 9; the text was first printed in (1925) 41 L. Q. REV. 252, with a note by Mr. Richardson; while a still fuller treatment of the whole subject of this eyre, including this incident, will be found in

Extensive as were the powers of county courts to legislate, national statutes nevertheless had become a necessity, and with them came the problem of their reception and interpretation. For the history of this great achievement, the county rolls are a new and valuable source, for they give us some of our earliest examples of the interpretation of statute law, even the latest of them being three years earlier than the earliest printed Year Book. Although the Provisions of Merton are frequently invoked to aid the enclosure movement,[80] the most interesting questions arose out of the first and second Statutes of Westminster. The interpretation of these famous enactments may well have puzzled the local lawyers, for even the sergeants in the Court of Common Pleas found them baffling. But whatever vagaries we find in the county rolls in the treatment of statutes, one thing is quite certain, and that is the unquestioned validity of statutes in the palatinate. At a later date, in the fifteenth century, this point will appear open to argument.[81]

Occasionally we find interesting questions of principle raised and these will first be mentioned, for they have considerable general interest. *The Abbot of Cumbermere v. Saunford*[82] was an assize of novel disseisin brought by virtue of a recent statute[83] which for the first time extended the assize to this sort of subject. The abbot asserted that he had been disturbed by constant distresses whenever he attempted to exercise his right to take estovers in a certain wood. The defendant's main objection was that the plaintiff's writ was a novelty unheard of until the new statute two years before gave remedy by assize for the first time. Now the disturbance complained of had taken place before the statute, and on this ground the defendant alleged that no action lay by this writ, since the plaintiff was not seised (and therefore could not have suffered a disseisin) since the statute. This construction regards the statute as creating a new right which in the circum-

---

JACOB, BARONIAL REFORM AND REBELLION (8 Oxford Studies 1925) 69, 351–52; *cf.* 1 POLLOCK AND MAITLAND, HISTORY OF ENGLISH LAW 555.

80 20 HEN. III, c. 4 (1236); CHESTER COUNTY COURT ROLLS 6/33, 34; *id.* 15/100; *id.* 20/142; 100/230 (for which see also STATUTE OF WESTMINSTER II (1285) c. 46).

81 CROMPTON, L'AUTHORITIE ET JURISDICTION DES COURTS (1594) f. 138b.

82 CHESTER COUNTY COURT ROLLS 68/120 (1287).

83 STATUTE OF WESTMINSTER II, 13 EDW. I, c. 25 (1285).

stances the plaintiff had never enjoyed. The situation looks rather different, however, when it is remembered that apart altogether from the statute the plaintiff could have had recovery by a writ *de estoverio rationabili* which is in the form of a *quod permittat* and may be brought in the county by *justicies*.[84] All this is perfectly consistent with the preamble of the statute which explains that the assize is conspicuous among all actions for its swiftness and convenience, but that its scope has been so far limited to "free tenements"; wherefore it is enacted that estovers and a variety of other rights of similar nature shall be triable by assize and deemed to be "free tenements." Whatever may have been the intention of the legislature, there can be no doubt that the mode of interpretation in the present case is in accord with several other cases which all exhibit the same feeling with regard to statutes, their operation being restricted to cases in which every material fact occurred after the statute.[85] As Chief Justice Bereford explained, in words which have a strangely modern sound, one never knows when a new statute is going to change the law;[86] and the same idea appears in the present case — at the time of the disseisin the disseisors did not know that a future statute would render them liable to an assize as well as to the much more leisurely proprietary action.[87] They ought therefore not to be prejudiced by the statute. That the court shared this view is evident from the fact that the abbot finally accepted the issue on his seisin both before and after the statute.[88]

The following case throws additional light upon one of the most curious theories of statute law which have come before the courts — the theory that a statute should not be applied in the ordinary course of adjudication unless it has already been applied before.

---

84 Bracton, De Legibus f. 231.

85 Several such cases are collected in Plucknett, Statutes and their Interpretation (1922) 118–20.

86 Rote v. Anon., Y. B. 32 & 33 Edw. I, 480 (1304).

87 The presence of a marked criminal element in the assize adds weight to this contention.

88 The defendant raised another point of more special interest when he argued that the reason of the statute was to give a remedy to tenants of particular estates. There is no support for this interpretation in the text of the statute, nor has the proposition been put forward subsequently. There may, however, be some truth in it.

The statute in question in our present case had enacted in 1278 that:

"... Similarly let not the heir of a woman, after the death of his father and mother, be barred from his action on account of his father's charter, if he demands by a writ of entry the inheritance or the marriage portion of his mother which his father alienated during her lifetime, unless it were alienated by fine levied in the King's Court." [89]

We must first point out a very common misconception that this statute created a new form of action, entry *cui in vita* or entry *sur cui in vita* as the case may be.[90] Both these actions existed before the statute as may be conclusively proved by the rolls in which they are recorded.[91] Nevertheless, our case assumes that the action was created by the statute as was frequently believed at the time.[92]

Now in 1287 Henry Brodheht brought a writ of entry *sur cui in vita* against Urian de St. Pierre and the case proceeded thus:

"And the aforesaid Urian comes and defends tort and force . . . and says that he ought not to answer to such a writ, nor to such a form of entry as is alleged in the demand, forasmuch as the heir of a woman whose tenements were alienated by her husband during her lifetime is not entitled to an action by a writ of entry, but only to a writ of right; nor has a writ of entry such as this ever before issued out of the chancery, and he prays judgment.

"And the aforesaid Henry says that the lord King in his statutes issued at Gloucester established that an action by writ of entry was available to the heir of the woman in the case proposed, and so he prays judgment similarly.

---

89 STATUTE OF GLOUCESTER, 6 EDW. I, c. 3 (1278).

90 If the woman survives her husband she may recover lands of her inheritance alienated by him (other than by fine with her assent) by entry *cui in vita*; if she does not do so, her heir can recover by entry *sur cui in vita*.

91 Entry *cui in vita* is common in MAITLAND, BRACTON'S NOTE BOOK (1887); *sur cui in vita* occurs there but once. *Id.* 22, 60.

92 In 1309, Claver suggested Westminster II, c. 3 (not c. 40 as in Maitland's note) with "Gloucester" as a variant reading in one manuscript, as the origin of Y. B. 2 & 3 Edw. II, 150 (1309). In 1311 Hengham asserted, and all the rest assumed that he was right, that the Statute of Gloucester, c. 3, was the origin of the action. Y. B. 4 Edw. II, 169 (1311).

" And the aforesaid Urian says that although the statute is as Henry has alleged, nevertheless no such writ of entry has so far issued out of chancery under the statute, and so he prays judgment." [93]

The court thereupon adjudged that the plaintiff had no recovery by this writ, but could sue a writ of right if he cared to. In the meantime he is amerced for his false claim.

This case is now the third known instance in which this theory is expressed and it will be well to place it beside the other two for the purposes of comparison. They are both considerably later in point of date, one of them being from the year 1345 and the other from 1410. In the case of 1345 Justice Thorpe remarked that " some people hold that statute to be of no value to foreclose the King, for it was never put into operation." Chief Justice Scot agreed and ordered the defendant to plead something else.[94] In 1410 Norton prefaced his plea to an action on the Statute of Provisors with the words " saving to us this advantage, that that statute has not heretofore been put into effect. . . ." Nothing more appears as to this point, and from the fact that Norton continued to argue on the statute and made no further use of the " advantage " we may conclude that he had little faith in the point.[95]

When first we had occasion to discuss this curious theory, it seemed that perhaps it was peculiar to statutes subtracting from the royal authority; [96] the case of 1410 would place penal statutes in the same category, the common element being the need to exercise special caution and strictness in their interpretation. The newly discovered case in the Chester rolls, however, no longer permits either of these suppositions, but makes it clear that the notion was applicable to all sorts of statutes whether they be penal or otherwise and whether they restrain the crown or not. In two out of the three cases known where the point is raised, the court definitely accepted the proposition, and that without remarking on its

---

[93] Chester County Court Rolls 75/196.

[94] Rex v. Bishop of Lincoln, Y. B. 19 Edw. III, 170 (1345). The statute was that of 14 Edw. III, stat. 4, c. 2 (1340), and its working and history and the remarkable circumstances of its repeal are described in Plucknett, *Execrabilis in the Common Pleas: Further Studies* (1921) 1 Camb. L. J. 64.

[95] Rex v. Bishop of St. Davids, Y. B. 11 Hen. IV, f. 39b (1410).

[96] Plucknett, Statutes and their Interpretation (1922) 143–44.

rarity or indeed commenting on it in any way. There are obvious questions to ask — what procedure was adopted in order to obtain the first application of a statute? What authority had the privilege of enforcing a statute for the first time, if this could not be done by the courts in the ordinary course of adjudication? Could this authority withhold its permission and thus exercise a virtual veto on statutes which had already been approved by King, Lords, and Commons? These questions are impossible to answer at the present stage of our knowledge; to the first of them alone will we hazard a suggestion. There is one case in which a statute recently made was brought into the court under the great seal, and perhaps this precaution was directed against possible objections of the nature under discussion. One other scrap of evidence may be adduced, although its bearing upon the problem is not quite so certain. In 1304 Hengham laid down a rule of process and formally called the attention of all the clerks of the bench to what was evidently an innovation. The Year Book duly narrates all this with the curious addition: "And this was done judicially a short time after in this term." [97] Can it be that the same idea prompted this note, and that the reporter regarded it as material to the validity of the rule that not only did Hengham state it in general terms to the clerks, but also that it had been applied judicially for the first time by the court? [98]

So much, then, for legislation both royal and local. It now remains to consider the nature of the common law observed in the county and the mode of its administration. It is here that the rolls of the county court make their most striking contribution to our knowledge of medieval law, for they supplement the evidence of the royal plea rolls. The view derived from the study of the national courts at Westminster must not be taken too confidently as being true also of the administration of justice throughout the country, for recourse to the king's court must still have been the exception rather than the rule, and in any case can only be regarded as typical of the capitalist class. The few exceptional entries which have been found upon the rolls of the Westminster

---

[97] Y. B. 14 Edw. III, 138 (1340).

[98] Y. B. 33 & 35 Edw. I, 16 (1307). Some curious 18th century parallels are noted in Plucknett, *Bonham's Case and Judicial Review* (1926) 40 HARV. L. REV. 30, 56–58.

courts have only served to emphasize the contrast between the territorial magnate who is deliberately sought by the royal courts and the lesser men who hardly ever get to Westminster Hall. For the latter, the county court is the natural resort, and there can be little doubt that the litigation of the great bulk of the people never proceeded further than the county town. Our rolls therefore show us the working of the provincial system of legal administration as it dealt with the affairs of the smaller local gentry and of the poorer classes. It here becomes clear that the problem of the unification of England had a double aspect. One phase is familiar — the growth of central institutions and the eventual subjection of all persons and causes to their jurisdiction; the other is less easy to trace and consists in the penetration of the common law even into those courts which had hitherto withstood the encroachments of the great tribunals of Westminster Hall. It is only in such sources as the rolls of the county courts that we can hope to find the details of this history. We shall therefore briefly summarize under a few broad headings the more remarkable material which throws light upon the substantive law administered within the county jurisdiction.

Real Property

Interesting light on the administrative side of the crown's prerogative rights comes from a case of 1289. Warin de Meynwaring held several manors in Cheshire of mesne lords, but in the county of Norfolk he had some lands held of the crown in chief; consequently the wardship of all his properties was due to the crown in virtue of its prerogative. It was doubtless to avoid part of this burden that on his death bed he conveyed two manors in Cheshire to John de Arderne who was seised of them on the 28th and 29th of May, 1289. The escheator (whose office it was to watch the royal interests) showed remarkable zeal. He seized one of the manors on the 30th and the other early on the 31st merely in anticipation of the death of Warin which in fact did not occur until the evening of the 31st. John's protest against this indecent haste and the irregularity of the whole proceeding resulted in an inquiry which elicited the foregoing facts, and the crown withdrew its claims against the manors; as the inquest shows, Warin did not die seised of them. The incident gives a striking picture of the thoroughness with which the administration watched the interests of the crown.[99]

Nor were the subjects of the English Justinian less tenacious of their rights; we find assizes of novel disseisin brought for "two-thirds of one-third of a piece of waste 30 feet by 13 feet,"[100] and for "a heath 10 feet by 2 feet."[101] In the latter case the writ was adjudged insufficient as a doweress and several other interested persons were not joined as defendants, the plaintiff being in mercy—but he is "pardoned by the justiciar because he is poor."[102] How small these claims really were is not so clear; it may be that there were valuable appurtenances and common rights attached to these holdings; in one case a plaintiff demanded a piece of land four feet by three feet and when the defendant made out a strong title accepted a settlement which looks strange—the plaintiff grants ten acres of land to the defendant in return for an acknowledgment by the latter of his title to the plot in dispute.[103]

The rolls show us a fair selection of the more usual forms of action, and occasionally give us some learned discussion about them; the famous controversy of the correct moment to tender the demi-mark in a writ of right, for example, which was "a great question in the law" in 1701, was already a matter of dispute in 1282.[104] In spite of the complexity and rigidity of the real actions, the public seem in general to have valued their privilege of not answering for their freeholds save to a royal writ,[105] and then they reproduce all the features of an action in the highest courts of Westminster. Nevertheless there are a few occasions on which we find that a different rule of law is applied in Chester from that followed in the royal courts. Thus we find certain defendants arguing that "when a tenement was assigned in dower without a plea the growing crops on the land were not included according to the rule in the county" whereupon judgment was given for them. Westminster Hall constantly adhered to the contrary.[106]

---

99 CHESTER COUNTY COURT ROLLS 147/286.

100 *Id.* 145/271.

101 *Id.* 138/191.

102 *Ibid.*

103 *Id.* 80/5.

104 *Id.* 41/47. BOOTH, REAL ACTIONS (folio, 1701) 98.

105 CHESTER COUNTY COURT ROLLS 66/104.

106 *Id.* 30/222 with which contrast BRACTON, DE LEGIBUS f. 96; *cf.* Dyer 316a and 2 CO. INST. 81.

An interesting example of one of the several medieval equivalents for a mortgage is to be found in the case of *Holm v. Bircheles*[107] where the plaintiff demanded a messuage and land by a writ of entry *ad terminum* alleging that the defendant was his lessee for a term of years which had now expired. The defendant claimed the fee in virtue of the plaintiff's charter and so the plaintiff was forced to admit that he had made the charter, but said that it was as security for a sum of money borrowed of the defendant, that the charter had been delivered to one Robert le Blake, and that the defendant had refused to accept the money when tendered to him and had obtained the charter by bribing Blake. Both parties accept trial by jury, and in due course a verdict is returned to the effect that the charter was made under these circumstances, but that the plaintiff defaulted and so the defendant entered.[108] This arrangement is really a variant of the form of gage described by Glanvill and Bracton[109] suitably modified to escape the theoretical difficulties of the shifting fee, and placing a mutual friend of the parties in the position of the court with power to enforce the forfeit by delivering the charter. It is unfortunate that the roll does not record what judgment was given upon the verdict. The use of a written deed delivered in escrow to a neutral party was quite common, and also went a long way towards supplying the lack of a more suitable procedure for actions on contract.[110]

Personal Property

The obscurity which reigns over the early history of the law of personal property has compelled historians to conclude that the solution lies in the proceedings of the local courts. The present rolls, however, contain little that is absolutely new, although they do give useful confirmation of impressions derived from other sources. The old real action for chattels was still in existence as may be seen from such passages as the editor has summarized thus:

---

107 Chester County Court Rolls 36/10.

108 *Ibid.*

109 Glanvill, De Legibus (1780) x, 6; *cf.* Bracton, De Legibus f. 268b.

110 Numerous references to the medieval use of escrows will be found in Corbin, *Conditional Delivery of Written Contracts* (1927) 36 Yale L. J. 443, 450.

"Roger son of Stephen came to claim his ox which he found in the hands of Thomas son of Nicholas of Northwich. Thomas said he bought it in the open market at Northwich in clear day, and paid toll. Roger accepted this statement but the ox was adjudged to him. Thomas was acquitted of any offence." [111]

This and similar cases amply confirm the statements of Bracton. Withernam, which is just on the point of turning into replevin, is frequently represented on the rolls, and in 1288 we find some interesting remarks on its nature occasioned by a daring attempt to use replevin as a means of trying title to land.[112]

Another case of replevin which has peculiar interest occurred in 1333 when a lord brought replevin for the taking of beasts from divers "of his free tenants whom he is bound to defend." [113] There is reason to believe that a lord could bring replevin for the beasts of his villein "although he claims no property in them," [114] but this case seems the only one where a lord brought it in respect of the beasts of his free tenant. It was, however, an extremely ancient principle that a lord should assist his tenant in litigation, and was probably one of the most valuable incidents of the homage-relationship.[115]

Contract

Acknowledgments of debt are frequently made in open court, and often with the covenant that the debtor shall be liable to distraint by the sheriff or the king's bailiffs if he defaults. Equally common is the covenant to forfeit 20*s* if such distress is made; in some cases this sum is to go to the bailiff "for his trouble," [116] while in others it is promised as a "penalty" to the barons of the exchequer.[117] Apparently it was the regular charge for the privilege, for whether the debt is 76 marks or only 5 marks, the penalty is still the same sum, 20*s*,[118] which in the latter case amounts to thirty

---

111 Chester County Court Rolls 77/222.

112 *Id.* 98/200.

113 Morris, Early English County Court (1926) 184 (from the county court roll of Cornwall, 1333).

114 Fitzherbert, New Natura Brevium (1534) 159f.

115 1 Pollock and Maitland, History of English Law 300.

116 Chester County Court Rolls 44/82.

117 *Id.* 39/36.

118 *Id.* 108, 109.

per cent of the original debt. In one case we find that a grant of a life annuity is subject to the sanction of distress by the sheriff (although in this case there is no provision for the 20*s* penalty).[119] An enigmatic entry — at least that is all that can be inferred from the calendar — in 1289 seems to show that this device could be used in a building contract. Richard de Swetenham was responsible for the repair of the chancel of the church [120] of Tarpeley and had engaged the carpenter Richard de Neuhall to do the work; Swetenham then bound himself in the cost of the work (without specifying any obligee) and submitted all his lands and chattels to distress by the sheriff if the roof remained unfinished by Christmas through the carpenter's default.[121]

There is a considerable quantity of matter about arbitration, but in every case it seems that the agreement to arbitrate was made in the course of litigation already begun and with the leave of the court; [122] consequently we find nothing of the formal submission and the bond to abide by the award, their place being supplied no doubt by the entry on the roll.[123]

The Cornwall roll shows one example of an action upon a simple contract. The text is not altogether free from ambiguities, but its sense is as follows:

> " The inquisition was not prosecuted between Peter Blundel querent by attorney, and Richard Bras of Merther and Sochius of Tregemunyon respondents by their attorneys, in a plea of covenant brought because they had agreed with him to keep safely his boat while they used it for fishing; which covenant they had broken, to his damage of one hundred shillings. Adjourned." [124]

---

119 *Id.* 58/50.

120 By the common law of the church this burden should fall upon the rector, but in England the parishioners were generally liable by custom. LYNDWOOD, PROVINCIALE (1679) 53, gl. *reparacione.*

121 CHESTER COUNTY COURT ROLLS 151/318. In one case a bailiff had not merely distrained, but had levied and paid the debt. This was held illegal in Wolfe v. Martone, Y. B. 3 & 4 Edw. II, 145–46 (1310). According to one manuscript the deed actually gave him power to do so, but the court still refused to recognize it. Y. B. 4 Edw. II (1311).

122 *Cf.* Woodbine, *The Origins of the Action of Trespass* (1924) 33 YALE L. J. 799, 802 *et seq.*

123 CHESTER COUNTY COURT ROLLS 27/196, 33/237, 43/71, 82/27, 124/67.

124 MORRIS, EARLY ENGLISH COUNTY COURT 185.

The case is a useful reminder that as late as 1333 the action of covenant still had the general character ascribed to it in the Statute of Wales[125] where we read that the action of covenant can be brought for moveables or immoveables, as well as for damages, and that since the contracts in covenants are infinite and cannot be mentioned specifically, the juries shall find the facts in every case with or without the help of documents. It will be noted that in the present case there is no assertion (nor denial by the defendants) of the existence of a sealed writing; nor is it at all likely that a promise to use care in handling a borrowed boat would be embodied in a deed under seal.

Tort and Crime

The period of our rolls has not quite succeeded in distinguishing these two branches of law. It was natural in the existing state of society that most of the wrongs commonly occurring should be treated as crimes, and it was an old tradition that one form of action could serve the double end of punishing the offender and compensating the injured. What the division comes, the line is drawn somewhat arbitrarily between the pleas of the crown and pleas that are common. Then it is possible to treat a trespass as though it were a common plea simply by omitting the words "against the peace of the King." Consequently there is hardly any separate thought peculiar to either of these two categories. Liability in tort, for example, is scarcely distinguished from criminal liability.

Pleas of the crown appear on our county rolls of Chester owing to its peculiar jurisdiction; ordinarily they are put on the rolls of the coroners, and kept for trial by royal commissioners. Among those mentioned in the Chester rolls are some which seem in curious company: "That a dog of Robert of Thelewall's bit a boy dangerously. He made fine." This brief entry is sandwiched between two felonies among the pleas of the crown, and seems to have been treated as a crime, for the owner is fined and no mention is made of damages.[126]

One of the most important cases yet discovered in a county roll,

125 12 Edw. I, c. 10 (1284).

126 Chester County Court Rolls 24/174.

however, came to light since the calendar of the Chester County Court rolls were published. It is contained in a roll for the county of Bedford dated September 27, 1333, now in private hands, a description of which by Mr. Hilary Jenkinson, of the public record office, recently appeared in the *English Historical Review*.[127] He informs us that the roll is to be published by Dr. G. H. Fowler in the Transactions of the Bedfordshire Historical Record Society, and has been kind enough to revise our transcript of the case in question. The text[128] may be translated as follows:

" COUNTY OF BEDFORD HELD ON MONDAY AFTER THE FEAST OF ST. MATTHEW THE APOSTLE IN THE SEVENTH YEAR OF THE REIGN OF KING EDWARD THE THIRD AFTER THE CONQUEST [Sept. 27, 1333]. . . .

" John, son of Robert atte Mor of Ampthill, senior, complains of John, son of Ralph atte Mor of Ampthill by a plea of trespass. William le Taillour and John, son of Robert atte Mor junior[129] are pledges for prosecuting.

" And the aforesaid John, son of Ralph, is attached to answer by John Herm and Maur de Ronhale. And thereupon the aforesaid John, son of Robert, complains that the aforesaid John, son of Ralph, on [February 5, 1332] Wednesday next after the feast of the Purification of the

---

127 See note 9, *supra*.

128 The text is as follows:

COMITATUS BEDFORD' TENTUS DIE LUNE PROXIMO POST FESTUM SANCTI MATTHAEI APOSTOLI ANNO REGNI REGIS EDWARDI TERCII A CONQUESTU SEPTIMO. . . . Johannes filius Roberti atte Mor de Ampthull' senior queritur de Johanne filio Radulphi atte Mor de Ampthull' deplacito transgressionis. Et sunt plegii de prosequendo; Willelmus le Taillour et Johannes filius Roberti atte More junior. Et predictus Johannes filius Radulphi attachiatus est quod respondeat per Johannem Herm' ęt Maur de Ronhale Et vnde predictus Johannes filius Roberti queritur quod predictus Johannes filius Radulphi die Mercurii proximo post festum Purificacionis beate Marie anno regni Regis Edwardi nunc sexto vocavit ipsum Johannem filium Roberti apud Hampthull' falsum hominem et infidelem per quod idem Johannes filius Roberti perdidit credenciam versus Johannem de Morteyn. de xl. s. quos ab eo ex mutuo habuisse debuit a predicto die Mercurii usque diem Jovis proximo post festum Annunciacionis beate Marie proximum sequentem vt dicit quod deterioratus est ad dampnum xxti. s. et amplius Et inde producit sectam Et predictus Johannes filius Radulphi venit et defendit omnem vim et injuriam et quicquid &c et quod in nullo est inde culpabilis &c Et hoc paratus est facere legem et est ad ad [*sic*] legem &c. Plegii de lege Ricardus Tyuill' et Willelmus Archier.

129 Note that Robert atte Mor has two sons, both named John; the elder is the plaintiff, and the younger is one of his pledges for prosecuting. See the remarks of Dr. Bolland on Y. B. 6 Edw. II (1313) pt. II, at xxiii.

Blessed Mary in the sixth year of the present King Edward at Ampthill called this same John son of Robert a false and faithless fellow: whereby the same John son of Robert lost credit with John de Morteyn concerning forty shillings which he would have borrowed of him, from the said Wednesday until [March 26, 1332] Thursday after the feast of the Annunciation of the Blessed Mary next following whereby [130] he says that he has suffered loss to the damage [131] of twenty shillings and more, and thereof he brings his suit.

"And the aforesaid John, son of Ralph, comes and defends all tort and force and whatever &c and denies that he is in anywise guilty thereof. And of this he is ready to make his law. And he is at his law. Pledges for his law: Richard Tyvill and William Archier." [132]

Maitland has long ago given proof that defamation was a fairly frequent complaint in manorial courts and in hundred courts in private hands,[133] but this case for the first time shows that the county court was also prepared to give a remedy to the slandered. The mode of trial in the county as well as in the manorial courts is by wager of law; where the manorial courts give trial by inquest it seems to be usually as a privilege.[134]

The more purely criminal side of the county's work is very much in evidence; obviously the maintenance of peace and order is largely dependent on the activity of local organizations. Consequently the rolls are particularly full of interesting material on the subject. The roll at times professes to distinguish the pleas of the crown from other pleas, but examination shows that the practice was soon abandoned; for example, the heading "Pleas of the Crown" on page six of the Chester volume does not apply to all the cases following, some of which are real actions, nor are all the felonies separated from civil actions.

---

130 Reading *unde* for *ut*. See note 128, *supra*.

131 The clerk has condensed the more usual phrase "unde deterioratus est et dampnum habet ad valenciam. . . ." See note 128, *supra*.

132 We have omitted from the text and translation certain letters and figures interlined in the original which indicate the essoins cast by the parties.

133 See the references in 2 POLLOCK AND MAITLAND, HISTORY OF ENGLISH LAW 538 n.2, to which may be added 1 BATESON, BOROUGH CUSTOMS (1904) 78–80.

134 In one case the privilege is bought with sixpence. SELECT PLEAS IN MANORIAL COURTS (1888) 170. In another with one-half a sextary of wine (*id.* 190); in another jury trial is ordered to ascertain the truth of the charges which the defendant had circulated against the plaintiff (*id.* 95 — the defendant had craved a jury).

The appeal of larceny is common; the following case is in typical form and illustrates the action admirably; it will be noted that the victor himself has the duty of hanging the vanquished (who, it would seem, was already dead):

> "Adam de Witeby appealed John de Albo Monasterio [Oswestry] for stealing his mare from the common pasture of Witeby and offered proof by his body during the day time, giving gage and finding pledges, Lawrence de Stoke and Henry de Sutton. A day was appointed at the next county; they appeared in open county duly armed and properly equipped and by the oath aforesaid; and on the field of battle Adam defeated and slew John and by judgment of the county hanged him and led away the mare which he had demanded." [135]

When one thief turned approver against another, it seemed to be his duty also to execute the sentence of the court upon his old accomplice.[136] One enigmatic entry tells us that "Elis, servant of Sir Roger de Montalt, accused Philip, the clerk of Chester, for unjustly taking his lord's chattels." [137] This brings us to the famous controversy over the history of the law of bailment, and every new case which is discovered deserves careful scrutiny. It has been said that "a bailee can, and always could, sue one who has taken goods from . . . his possession as though he were owner." [138] That he has an acton is true; that the action is an appeal, which a true owner can also use, is likewise true; but it does not follow that a bailee is in the position of an owner. This case is one of several cases where an appeal is brought by a bailee, and the appellant expressly states his position and gives the name of the bailor to whom he ascribes ownership, although it is the bailee himself who prosecutes the appeal.[139] Further into this matter we cannot go; but lawyers will remember that new light may confidently be expected when more of the county court rolls are published.

The question of the ownership of stolen goods has been intimately connected with the law of forfeiture:

---

[135] Chester County Court Rolls 23/162.

[136] *Id.* 18/121.

[137] *Id.* 24/171.

[138] 3 Holdsworth, History of English Law 327.

[139] Select Pleas of the Crown (1887) no. 126; *cf.* Maitland, Bracton's Note Book 824.

"Men will begin to say that the thief has property in the stolen goods and that this is the reason why the king takes them. As a matter of history we believe this to be an inversion of logic: — one of the reasons why the thief is said to have property in those goods is that the king has acquired a habit of taking them and refusing to give them up." [140]

Our rolls do not show us the king as a receiver of stolen goods, for the procedure was still by appeal rather than indictment, and the practice was perhaps still in the future: tradition points to the eyre of Northampton of 1329 as being the source of many of the burdensome extensions of the law of forfeiture,[141] but the publication of the eyre of Kent of 1313 shows that some were already in existence at the earlier date. The Chester rolls show us nothing that can be called oppressive, although the forfeitures were strictly enforced. Where the accused had fled, security was taken from one to whom he had delivered some chattels, doubtless in order that they should be forthcoming if he were subsequently convicted.[142] Another case seems to suggest that if a felon were executed outside of the jurisdiction of Chester, his chattels in the hands of bailees within the jurisdiction might be forfeited.[143] To despoil the house of one who had fled (and who is therefore a prospective outlaw) seems to be a plea of the crown.[144] To be found in possession of stolen or suspicious goods, even if there was no one to claim them, was a perilous thing, especially for a suspicious character, for it might land him in prison.[145] In Chester the penalty seems to have been adjuring the county if the offender was a young person,[146] while for an adult the matter would doubtless have been more serious.

Every medieval court was constantly reminded of the fact that

---

140 2 POLLOCK AND MAITLAND, *op. cit. supra* note 133, 166.

141 FITZHERBERT, CORONE (1516) 284–373.

142 CHESTER COUNTY COURT ROLLS 15/107.

143 *Id.* 24/175.

144 *Id.* 7/45.

145 THE COURT BARON (Maitland ed. 1890) 64.

146 CHESTER COUNTY COURT ROLLS 27/199. It will be noted that the county of Westmorland claimed to have a custom of compulsorily putting suspected persons upon an inquest of the four neighbouring vills; if the party could not find pledges for his appearance while this procedure was in progress, he was committed to gaol until the arrival of a commission of gaol delivery. See the extract from an assize role of 1278 in MORRIS, EARLY ENGLISH COUNTY COURT 158.

within the realm there was a foreign competing jurisdiction — that of the Church. The county was no exception, and we naturally find on its rolls reflections of the religious conditions of the times, and traces of the conflict of jurisdiction between Church and State. It is well known that one of the principal motives in the struggle for the celibacy of the clergy was the fear of the feudalization of ecclesiastical benefices. The danger was pressing, and the tendency to make parish churches hereditary was obstinate; as late as 1287 we find on the Chester rolls a plea which discloses the fact that a certain church had had four hereditary incumbents.[147]

As for the conflict of jurisdiction, the war was waged along a front stretching from the king's court in Westminster to the county and even to the manorial court, although it was not necessarily a war of laity against clergy. We find, for example, that an abbot, prelate though he be, will fine his tenants for pleading before the archdeacon instead of in his own lay, manorial court.[148] There is, however, this difference: the king can use particularly drastic measures, prohibiting both the judge of the church and the parties from proceeding; yet in the county and inferior courts there seems no remedy by prohibition but only an action of trespass.[149]

Procedure and Constitution

Some day it will be possible to reconstruct the proceedings in a typical county court; at present only occasional hints are available, but they are sufficient to show that there is important matter hidden in its history. For example, the courts at Westminster were singularly late in admitting the evidence of witnesses and in developing that law of evidence which is so prominent an element of the common law. Yet it is clear that borough and mercantile courts employed witness proof, and the Chester rolls now reveal its existence in the county court. We read that " Gilbert de Wilmis-

147 Chester County Court Rolls 59/51.

148 Select Pleas in Manorial Courts (1888) 113. *Cf.* Addy, Church and Manor (1913) 167 *et seq.*, and Makower, Constitutional History of the Church of England (1895) § 22, for further material.

149 Chester County Court Rolls 42/57. One must be careful not to allege that this was in contempt of the king, or the case will be put beyond the competence of the county and within that of the courts at Westminster. Morris, Early English County Court 196.

lawe and Jordan de Shotiswall are to be summoned to show why they did not come to give witness "[150] and that "Richard de Sudington was amerced for false witness before the Justiciar."[151] Careful thought over such facts as this will accentuate the strangeness of the attitude adopted by the superior courts, and show the need for a careful search for the explanation. No doubt it was a peculiarity of the county of Chester that it had the "liberty and custom" of correcting its own erroneous judgments in a subsequent county court.[152] All the same, it is equally clear that error would also lie from the county to the "Lord Edward in council" who sat at London.[153] It is clear, too, that the defense by "thwertnic" was originally a privilege of the men of Chester, rather than a survival of primitive ideas of pleading.[154] Nevertheless other jurisdictions enjoyed the same privilege, and here as in many other cases, what was originally a rare local custom or privilege later on became the general right of a much wider public. Of the county in its administrative aspects, we shall say nothing; the study is already in the hands of competent scholars with special equipment in administrative history.[155] To them we may leave the distinction between full counties and rear counties,[156] and the application of mathematical analysis to the dates upon which various counties held their sessions.[157] As to the matter of doomsmen or *judicatores*, which is more the concern of legal historians, the

[150] CHESTER COUNTY COURT ROLLS 99/205.

[151] *Id.* 96/192. It is most unfortunate that these two entries give us no clue to the nature of the evidence involved, nor whether the offenders were transaction-witnesses, witnesses to a deed or charter, or witnesses in the more general sense of the word.

[152] *Id.* 94/167.

[153] *Id.* 31/225.

[154] Stewart-Brown, *Thwert-ut-nay and the Custom of "Thwertnic" in Cheshire* (1925) 40 ENG. HIST. REV. 13–21.

[155] Professor Morris' latest study, THE MEDIEVAL ENGLISH SHERIFF TO 1300 (1927), contains much material on the administrative aspect of the county, while Miss M. H. Mills (who has already published notable studies on the sheriffs' accounts) has examined the Lord Treasurer's Remembrancer's Miscellaneous Rolls, bundle 5, where financial documents are to be found which are intimately connected with the county court rolls.

[156] Morris, *Plenus Comitatus* (1924) 39 ENG. HIST. REV. 401; CHESTER COUNTY COURT ROLLS xxii *et seq.*; MORRIS, THE COUNTY COURT 97–100.

[157] Alexander, *The Dates of Early County Elections* (1925) 40 ENG. HIST. REV. 1–12; Alexander, *The Dates of County Days* (1925) 3 BULL. OF INST. HIST. RESEARCH 89–95.

Chester rolls enable a little addition to be made to our knowledge on the subject. The view of Stubbs and Maitland that all the suitors were doomsmen will require modification. It must now be said that although it may be true in the general sense that all suitors are answerable for the judgments given in their court, nevertheless there are certain people who are in a more special way responsible for judgments; and, as Mr. Stewart-Brown observes, this function seems to have become hereditary, probably because it has been attached to particular pieces of land. Indeed, there is a Year Book case which has so far escaped the historians of the matter, which asserts as much: John de Tornerghe, we are told, owed suit to the court of Dalton and was bound to come to the aid of the suitors at every court when a thief was to be judged, when a writ of right was pending, or when there was a difficult judgment to be done.[158] This, together with the other instances already known, is concerned with an inferior court in private hands, and it is to the Chester rolls that we owe the information that there were doomsmen as well as suitors in the county court.

At this point we must leave the matter. When more evidence becomes available (as it surely will), the picture can be drawn with firmer lines and richer detail. In the meantime we can only wait, and search, and above all, publish the recent discoveries in carefully edited texts. Already the main outlines of the county's history are appearing, and they merit all the historian's art and skill. Of all English institutions, save the crown alone, the county is the most ancient, and for a long time it was the most significant. Throughout that period when it was the largest institution in regular constant action, it must have been foremost in men's minds as the most powerful organ of government with which they were usually in contact. Consequently, like every active, flourishing institution, it must have reflected to a large extent the political and juridical thought of the people. The time has not yet come when one can justly weigh the relative importance of the various factors which produced its decline and ultimate fall; the great question whether the rise of the royal courts was the cause or the result of the county's fall, must

---

[158] Tornerghe v. Abbot of Furness, Y. B. 15 Edw. III, 107 (1341). In modern times suitors faced with a difficult point would take counsel's opinion.

receive careful consideration in the light of much more evidence than is before us at the present moment. However interested we may be in the beginnings of the royal courts at Westminster, we must remember that they were intruders upon territory which was already occupied by a more ancient system. A reading of Glanvill leaves the impression that the royal court was well aware of this, and that it had not yet entertained that dazzling vision of the crown, through the machinery of the future common law, becoming supreme over all persons and causes. Indeed, Glanvill shows us a court which is rather anxious to limit itself and to avoid as many problems as it can. In Bracton we find a different atmosphere: science, speculation, criticism, all combine to prove the vigorous expansion of the new common law. But for a long time still, that common law will bear traces of its political and administrative origins, and appear almost reluctant to assume the responsibilities of a national legal system of general application. The control of the land was a political necessity, and the royal courts never for one moment relaxed their grip on the soil of England. But beyond that, there is hesitation, almost indifference, and whole fields of law are left to the local courts, the Church, and the fairs. While this state of things continued, the county court must have remained of great importance, and in its rolls we must look to find the deficiencies of the royal jurisprudence supplied. We have now the satisfaction of knowing that such rolls did once exist, that some have survived, and that the few specimens already available have proved of great and varied interest.

IV

THE HARVARD MANUSCRIPT OF THORNTON'S *SUMMA*

THE fate of a book which is too good for its public is often well worth studying. It has been several times suggested that Bracton's monumental treatise was such a book, and that the compilations of Britton, Fleta and Hengham are evidence that the lawyers of the reign of Edward I found old Bracton too massive, and took to the degenerate device of shortening his text as well as modernising it.[1] That reign was indeed a critical moment in English legal literature; the broad sweep of Bracton's work was very probably too broad, too erudite and too cosmopolitan, for the busy lawyers who were building fortunes and getting offices in the last years of the thirteenth century. Writers were feeling their way towards a new type of legal literature. Even when they took their stand on the past and made Bracton's text the basis of their works, they nevertheless introduced novel experiments of their own. Britton hit upon the extraordinary idea of a draft code in the vernacular; Fleta (whoever that was) surveyed the law from the standpoint of the crown, the royal household, and royal legislation. Even the unlucky Hengham succeeded in producing his effect — albeit a depressing one — by concentrating on the dismal intricacies of process. Any one of these experiments might have succeeded. Edward I might have taken to Britton's book as enthusiastically as the public had done; on the other hand, the public might have given a welcome to Fleta's royalist doctrine; or Hengham might have founded a school of scientific procedurists such as the canonists and civilians had. In fact none of these possibilities came about. Britton's code was never enacted, Fleta's book was never multiplied, and common-law process remained for centuries unhonoured and incognoscible. Thoughtful and laborious as all these ventures were, the future lay with a completely different sort of law book — with those scrappy, ver-

[1] See in general, 1 POLLOCK AND MAITLAND, HISTORY OF ENGLISH LAW (2d ed. 1898) 206–10; 2 HOLDSWORTH, HISTORY OF ENGLISH LAW (3d ed. 1923) 236–43, 319–27, where all these works are discussed.

nacular, informal notes which at this very moment were beginning to turn into Year Books.

There was in fact yet another venture in the field of legal literature during the reign of Edward I. The author was Gilbert de Thornton,[2] who had succeeded Hengham as chief justice of the king's bench in 1290. He wrote a book of which his contemporaries took no heed, although its ghost has haunted the history books for the last three hundred years. From the time when Thornton wrote it, about 1290, until 1647, his book remained unknown. None of his contemporaries mention it, and the succeeding three centuries and a half contain not the slightest allusion to it. Its existence was not even suspected until John Selden published his long and discursive *Dissertatio Historica* as a pendant to the first edition of *Fleta*.[3] In that essay he mentions, almost incidentally, that he had acquired a manuscript of Thornton's book, that he had neither seen nor heard of any other copy, that his copy was a handsome one, illuminated, but disastrously mutilated with the loss of many leaves.[4] Selden gives us the impression that Thornton is an interesting book, but for the purpose he had in mind it was not necessary to discuss the matter at great length. His circumstances did not incline him to compose an erudite tract, for he was merely obliging a bookseller, "as owing to a slight indisposition of some days' duration, I had an uninterrupted period of domestic leisure incompatible with more extensive studies or more weighty affairs." [5]

In this casual way Thornton makes his first public appearance in Selden's disappointing essay, only to sink back into oblivion for another two centuries and a half. Of Selden's manuscripts and books, many went to the Bodleian library at Oxford, others to Lincoln's Inn, and the remainder were stored in the Temple until they perished in the conflagration of 1679 (if they had indeed

[2] For Thornton's life see Foss, A Biographical Dictionary of the Judges of England (1870) 656; Turner's article in 46 Dictionary of National Biography (1898) 300, and 1 Sayles, Select Cases in the Court of King's Bench (55 Selden Society, 1936) lvii.

[3] Selden, Fleta seu Commentarius . . . Subjungitur etiam Joannis Seldeni ad Fletam Dissertatio Historica (1647). This dissertation is now cited from the edition with translation and notes by Ogg, Ioannis Seldeni ad Fletam Dissertatio (1925).

[4] Selden, Dissertatio (Ogg's ed. 1925) 9, 15–23.

[5] *Id.* at 3.

survived an earlier fire in 1677, and the Great Fire of 1666). Selden's manuscript of Thornton is not at Oxford, nor at Lincoln's Inn. In all probability therefore it remained with the unlucky remnants in the much-burnt Temple. Thornton's book, a fragment, but unique, had perished.[6]

It seemed that all we could hope to know about Thornton's work was what we found in Selden's *Dissertatio Historica,* and that the unique manuscript was irretrievably lost. Nearly thirty years ago, however, Professor Woodbine[7] built up a brilliant conjecture to the effect that a certain volume in Lincoln's Inn might be a Thornton, but it differs so widely from Selden's description that he expressed himself with great caution and reserve. That attitude was justified, for there now reposes a magnificent manuscript in the Harvard Law Library which is indubitably a copy of Thornton's long lost work, as magnificent as Selden's manuscript was, and immensely more precious, for the Harvard one is complete. Indirectly Professor Woodbine may have contributed to its discovery, for the dealer who sold it had carefully studied that article in the *Law Quarterly Review* of 1909.

The Harvard codex is a handsome folio of 104 leaves measuring on an average 13½″ by 8″; although these dimensions leave very fair margins around the text (the bottom margin is always more than 2″) the book was once considerably wider, judging by the extent to which some of the marginal notes have been cut in the course of re-binding. The present binding in full vellum is old, but certainly not mediaeval in appearance, and this is confirmed by the fact that *marginalia* in a fine italic hand have been cropped in order to reduce the volume to the dimensions of the present covers. There are but few marks of ownership. A hand of the end of the fifteenth century has left a few notes, and the italic hand just mentioned has left a few more, especially on ecclesiastical points, both of them writing in Latin. There may be some significance in this, for it seems to show that the volume never received any close attention from a common lawyer, for we miss the Law-French comment which is inevitable when a book has been studied by a mediaeval member of the profession. Two whole

---

[6] For the fate of Selden's library, see MACRAE, ANNALS OF THE BODLEIAN (2d ed. 1890) 110.

[7] Woodbine, *The Summa of Gilbert de Thornton* (1909) 25 L. Q. REV. 44.

leaves at the end have been cut out, no doubt because they were blank. A third, bearing at the top the last three lines and the *Explicit* of the treatise, has also been shorn of the whole of the blank space below the text, leaving only the narrow horizontal label of the original leaf at the top. As this seemed untidy, the narrow label was later mounted upon a sheet of parchment which thus replaces the abstracted portion of the leaf; this substituted sheet is pasted to the remaining narrow hinge of the original as well as to the label which bears Thornton's concluding sentences. The thrifty owner who cut out the blank portion of the leaf did not replace it with another blank — such an operation would have been pointless — but with an old parchment document which had doubtless lost its value with the passage of the years. This was a notarial act passed before John Smith, notary, on the 11th October, 1506 at Styrley, Yorkshire; it attests that Tilffridus Brynnesley has appointed John Brynnesley junior to be his proctor for taking the oath of canonical obedience to the Archbishop of York required by law before entering upon the rectory of half of the church of Trowell, Nottinghamshire.

Only one owner has left his name upon the volume. This was Sir Thomas Gargrave, Kt., whose autograph appears on folio 1 and folio 103b. Gargrave[8] was a lawyer who spent his life in the difficult task of ruling the North during the reign of Elizabeth. He became a member of the Council of the North in 1539, was knighted in 1547, became Vice-President of the Council in the North in 1560, and held that onerous position until his death in 1579. He was several times a member of parliament, and was once Speaker. Dr. Reid has expressed a high opinion of Sir Thomas and his work.[9] That work was mainly political, although it did include a number of important legal reforms. Nevertheless, Gargrave once modestly pleaded twenty-eight years of government service as an excuse for having forgotten whatever law he knew. Clearly he had little opportunity for studying this precious volume, which contains no other marks from his hand. The house which he founded came to a disastrous and tragic end after a few generations. The owner, Gargrave or another, who ordered the existing binding was apparently unaware of the principal interest

---

[8] For Gargrave's life, see 20 DICTIONARY OF NATIONAL BIOGRAPHY (1889) 435.

[9] REID, THE KING'S COUNCIL OF THE NORTH (1921).

of the book, however, for he had it lettered on the back "Bracton".

The first thirteen folios seem to have been copied for a former owner from the original beginning; folio 14 shows heavy damp stains and it may be presumed that the beginning of the work was even more severely damaged and had to be replaced in consequence. This task was carried out in a stiff, heavy, angular hand, of ecclesiastical aspect, much taller than the original, and occupying therefore more space. Its date must be the end of the fifteenth century. It leaves off at the foot of folio 13b, its catch-word referring to the top of folio 14 where the original hand of the book first appears.

The bulk of the volume, ff. 14–104, is all in the same excellent hand, compressed, but very clear and regular. Its date is obviously the fourteenth century, and the carefully cloven tops of *b*, *h*, and *l* seem to indicate the earlier portion of the century. Perhaps the reign of Edward II is the most likely date, judging from the palaeographical evidence (as to which the present writer, however, claims no particular skill). There are on an average forty-six lines, six inches long, to the page.

We have already said that it is a sumptuous volume, and the decoration merits special attention. Each of the "books" into which the work is divided begins with an initial in gold, filled up with line work in blue and red; each chapter begins with an initial in blue decorated with line work in red (alternate chapters reversing this colour scheme), both types of initial having loops and spirals which extend for considerable distances into the margins. The numerous paragraph divisions are indicated by the conventional signs alternately in blue and red. The numbers of the chapters are in the margin in blue and red, and the headings of the books and chapters are written in red. The original hand left pencil directions on these details for the guidance of the rubricator which are still to be seen in many cases. The division of the treatise was therefore the object of great care at every stage. Of less moment for our purposes, although they add to the gaiety of an already very brilliant page, are the numerous grotesques which adorn the margins, drawn in brown and touched with a pale brown wash, sometimes too with red or blue.

The loss of the first thirteen folios is much to be regretted;

the first initial of the whole work may very well have been an exceptionally fine piece of illumination.[10] The later hand which replaced the damaged leaves took some pains, but made no attempt to vie with the original in lavish decoration. He wrote the general title of the whole work in a dark and dirty red, and to indicate the beginning of a new chapter generally used a large capital of the same unpleasant colour, of heavy design, extending into two or more lines of the ruled page. Unlike his early model, he did not number the chapters in the margin, although he did write their headings in red. Now there are twenty of his large chapter initials, indicating twenty chapters. But there ought to be twenty-one, for the original hand resumes the tale with chapter twenty-two. This little discrepancy is easily resolved, however, for it is clear that on f. 7 the copyist used a small capital where he ought to have used a large one. His blunder is hard to excuse, since he has himself written in red ink the lengthy heading of the *capitulum* (" chapter "). The twenty tall capitals added to this undecorated *capitulum* thus make up the required tale; hence not only is the text of the volume complete at this point in spite of the change of hands, but the implied numeration of the chapters is likewise continuous.

This matter of the numbering of the books and chapters is of importance for the identification of the manuscript, as will appear when we compare it with what we know of Selden's manuscript.

Selden tells us that his manuscript of Thornton was divided into eight books of which he gives us the list and headings. The Harvard manuscript corresponds exactly to this description. More than that, Selden was at pains to tell us the number of chapters in each of the books.[11] Here too the correspondence is almost complete. Books II (19 chapters), III (31 chapters), IV (26 chapters), V (18 chapters), VI (21 chapters) and VIII (14 chapters) present no problems for the correspondence is exact. As for Book I, the discrepancy is only apparent. Selden's copy contained 58 chapters. The Harvard manuscript, as we have seen, has really

---

10 Selden's manuscript contained a very elaborate first initial, as may be seen from the engraving of it in the 1647 edition of his Dissertatio ad Fletam, 462 (not reproduced in Ogg's ed.).

11 Selden, Dissertatio (Ogg's ed. 1925) 15–17.

21 unnumbered chapters in the late hand, and continues with chapters 22 to 58 in the original hand. The number of chapter 56 has been cut away from f. 26b, possibly by some vandal who took a fancy to one of the grotesques in the margin, but we may be sure that a chapter division occurred there, for the penciled direction in the margin has partly survived. For a moment the scribe seems to have thought of making a new chapter out of the latter part of chapter 48, but changed his mind in time. The correspondence of the Selden and the Harvard manuscripts in Book I is therefore quite established. Book VII raises a different problem. Selden's copy had 15 chapters, although he tells us that there ought to have been 25. His copy seems to have had a table of contents from which he derived this information, but there is the possibility that the table itself was inaccurate, or that Selden misread it. The Harvard manuscript has no gap, and the text is continuous, but it has only 15 chapters. The evidence all indicates that Book VII ought to have 15 chapters only, and that Selden was mistaken in believing that there ought to have been 25. It is abundantly clear that the Harvard and Selden manuscripts are different, for Selden's lacked chapters 43 to 58 in Book I, 10 to 19 in Book II, 9 to 19 in Book III and 1 to 15 in Book V; all these portions duly appear in the Harvard manuscript.

So much, then, for the structure of the book and its external aspect. The only evidence Selden had for thinking his manuscript was a copy of Thornton's *Summa* was the title of his manuscript. Now the title of the Harvard manuscript is in substantially the same words (although we must allow for the fact that the substituted beginning of the Harvard volume was the work of a not-too-thoughtful scribe who was copying a much damaged and obliterated original). Here is the title of the Harvard manuscript (referred to as *H*), collated with that of Selden's (referred to as *S*):

Incipit summa de legibus et consuetudinibus Anglie [12]quam composuit Magister Henricus de Britonia[12] tempore Henrici regis[13] filii regis Johannis, quam quidam[14] summam Dominus Gilbertus de Thorntona [15]cum capitalibus justic'[15] Domini regis [16]Edwardi filii regis Henrici [16]

---

[12] a magistro Henrico de Bryctona composita — S.

[13] *om.* — S.

[14] quidem — S.

[15] tunc capitalis justiciarius — S.

[16] in Anglia — S.

secundum [17] leges Anglicanas [18] in presenciarum [18] usitatas [19] ac comodum posteriorum [19] abbreviavit [20] An. . . .[21] regis Edwardi primi [22] vicesimo. Et ipse idem Gilbertus tempore illo sna[23] bonitatis [24] et mansuetudine floruit eleganter.

The copyist's task must certainly have been difficult, but it cannot be said that he brought to it much patience or care for the niceties of Latin grammar. He sees no difference between *quidam* and *quidem*, or between *cum* the adverb and *cum* the preposition. In spite of all his blunders, however, it is clear that he was copying a title which was substantially the same as the title to Selden's manuscript, and that title ascribes the work to Gilbert of Thornton. The loss of Selden's mutilated manuscript need no longer hamper us, for there is now a complete Thornton among the many other treasures in Langdell Hall.

And now we come to the mystery. Almost thirty years ago Professor Woodbine contributed an article [25] to the *Law Quarterly Review* in which he put forward the claims of a manuscript in Lincoln's Inn (where it is catalogued as Hale 135) to be identified as a text of Thornton's lost *Summa.* His general conclusion was expressed thus: [26]

> " This evidence will appeal to different minds in different ways. To some it will seem reasonable to consider Thornton the author of Hale 135. Others will answer the question with a big ' perhaps.' But we can say this — that the Hale manuscript, which can no longer be considered a mere abridgement of Bracton, has more and better claims than any other manuscript which is now accessible to be considered a copy of Gilbert de Thornton's Summa."

Until the discovery of the Harvard manuscript this conclusion was unassailable. The relative force of the different arguments by

[17] statuta et — *add.* S.
[18] tunc — S.
[19] ad utilitatem posterorum diligenti studio postmodum — S.
[20] sub compendio — *add.* S.
[21] *illegible* — H; anno regni — S.
[22] filii regis Henrici — S.
[23] sciencia — S.
[24] bonitate — S.
[25] Woodbine, *The Summa of Gilbert de Thornton* (1909) 25 L. Q. REV. 44.
[26] *Id.* at 52. The argument is necessarily a series of inferences. Hale 135 contains neither title nor colophon.

which Professor Woodbine reached that result may be differently estimated, however, by different readers. The first argument is in fact an answer, by anticipation, to an inevitable objection. The arrangement of the Lincoln's Inn manuscript bears no resemblance to that of Selden's. To Professor Woodbine's argument that this discrepancy is immaterial we shall return later. The second argument is based on the general resemblance of the readings of the Lincoln's Inn manuscript to those of Selden's in the few passages of which Selden gave us a text. These passages are so few, and the results so insignificant, that we have relegated them to the Appendix of this article. If the collation shows anything, it is that the Harvard manuscript is nearer to Selden's. A third argument rests on the memoranda scribbled on the fly-leaves of the Lincoln's Inn manuscript. They relate to the financial transactions of one Alan de Thornton. He had money to invest with some merchants and was lending numerous sums to his neighbours. Now this Alan seems to have held land in Caburne, Lincolnshire, where we know that Gilbert also had property. More than that, Alan's dated memoranda begin the year after Gilbert's death. There is therefore good reason for believing that Alan and Gilbert were both members of the same family; indeed, it seems quite probable that Alan may have been the son of Gilbert. If that were so, it would be reasonable to suppose that the Lincoln's Inn manuscript may once have belonged to Gilbert (but this, of course, does not mean that Gilbert was therefore the author of it). The fourth argument is of extraordinary interest. The Lincoln's Inn manuscript contains a passage referring to a case which may be rendered thus: [27]

> By transmitting cases to ecclesiastical courts it often happens that bastards inherit, and concubines of rectors and priests recover their dower; so it happened with Margaret Stryke, concubine of Stephen Sybri all the time he was rector of the church of West Rason, Lincolnshire, who recovered her dower in the common pleas about the 10th or 12th year of Edward I.

The validity of her marriage having been questioned in the common pleas, that court evidently sent to the church courts for their ruling; they no doubt applied the principle which the author criti-

[27] For the Latin text, see *id.* at 49.

cises, namely, that the wife of a married man who has become a priest since his marriage is nevertheless entitled to her dower. Their subsequent cohabitation is no doubt reprehensible, but has no bearing on the rights of the woman who, after all, is a lawful wife. This curious story owes its great significance to the fact that Thornton undoubtedly had local knowledge of the matter. He acquired lands in the neighbourhood by a charter to which " Stephen Sybri of West Rasen " was a witness. Stephen the rector must have been dead when the action for dower was brought, and as the charter is dated later still, Stephen the witness is almost certainly that " Stephen son of Stephen Sybri " of whom we have mention in another connection. Here then is a most teasing link which seems to connect Thornton with the Lincoln's Inn manuscript. Professor Woodbine's conclusion is that " the insertion of this case does not prove that Thornton wrote the *Summa* in which it occurs, but the assumption that Thornton did write the contents of the Lincoln's Inn manuscript would explain the insertion of this unique case."

It is extremely difficult to draw any conclusion save that in the second half of this sentence. Still, the circumstance is curious in the extreme, and it will naturally be wondered whether the undoubted manuscript of Thornton's *Summa* now in Harvard throws any light on the matter. It does. The case duly appears in the Harvard manuscript, and in a slightly better text.[28] In other words, Thornton's authorship of the Harvard text amply explains the use there of a case which was certainly within Thornton's personal knowledge. It does not so easily explain the use of the case in the Lincoln's Inn manuscript, however. If that manuscript had stood alone, it would be possible to argue that several other lawyers might just as well have come across Margaret Strike's (or Styrke's) case. It is queer that the author of the Lincoln's Inn manuscript was so uncertain of the date (the Harvard manuscript, as one would expect, is more precise on this point). To answer this question would in fact be to solve the

[28] It occurs on folio 89*b*. The first word 'vero' of the Latin text printed by Woodbine *supra*, note 27 from the Lincoln's Inn manuscript does not make good grammar, but the Harvard manuscript reads 'per huiusmodi' which is obviously right. For 'Strike' the Harvard text has 'Styrke' (a very common sort of metathesis), and it gives the date as 'circum annum decimum' (omitting the 'vel duodecimum' of the Lincoln's Inn manuscript).

identity of the Lincoln's Inn manuscript, and it is no part of our purpose to undertake that difficult enterprise. There is one point only which we will advert to on this occasion. It has already been mentioned that the arrangement of the Lincoln's Inn manuscript bears no resemblance to that of Selden's copy, and that Professor Woodbine urges that this discrepancy has no significance — citing the fact that some manuscripts of Bracton would hardly be recognised as his work if we had to rely solely upon a table of contents for our knowledge of the normal form of his treatise. The two situations, we suggest, are hardly comparable. Bracton's work was widely used for a century; many manuscripts survive, and many more must be lost. The possibility of disarrangement increases greatly with the number of texts in circulation. When a work in the middle ages became famous and widely used, any careful reader might constitute himself editor and assume wide powers of revising, enlarging, abbreviating and rearranging the text. His aim in preparing a copy for his own use was not to preserve the *ipsissima verba* of the master, but to put between one pair of covers all of the original which seemed to him valuable, plus such additions and corrections as his learning suggested. If he felt that he could use the work better with a different arrangement, then he forthwith rearranged it. Now if we take such a work as Britton, we see that its circulation was considerably less than that of Bracton; fewer texts have survived, and fewer divergencies occur in the arrangement. When we come to Fleta and Thornton we are dealing with works which never had a public, and which remained practically unknown to the contemporary profession. Neither was ever heard of until Selden printed the one, and described the other, three and a half centuries after they were written. There is but one mediaeval manuscript of Fleta, and only two of Thornton, one of which has since been lost. If the Lincoln's Inn manuscript should prove to be a third copy, its serious divergencies in arrangement would be most surprising, and would need explanation. However, the problem of the Lincoln's Inn manuscript may well be left for Professor Woodbine to determine; it is he who first discovered it, and the skilful conjectures of his article of 1909, and the noncommittal conclusions drawn from them, will we hope be replaced by more certain deductions now that the Harvard manuscript of Thornton's *Summa* is available as a sure basis of comparison.

Fascinating as they are, these questions are merely preliminary to the larger topic of Thornton's place in legal history. So far, he is principally known to historians as the crown's most active prosecutor of the *quo warranto* proceedings. With his text before us, we may be able to get a clearer view of his attitude towards the law and its problems. We know that he occasionally drew upon his own legal experience — the West Rasen case is an example; there may be others (such as the curious case of an island born in the sea which came before him in his official capacity).[29] We may soon be able to form a more accurate estimate of his real aim in writing. Selden conjectured that he wanted to depict Bractonian law, rather than the law of his own day.[30] He seemed not to have set out, as Britton and Fleta did, to bring Bracton up to date. But he abridged him drastically, reducing the bulk it seems to something below half of a full-length Bracton. It may well be that the best approach to Edwardian law in Thornton's day was through Bracton (it still is, in fact), but Thornton's interest in that fact seems to show him especially preoccupied with a problem of legal education. That also raises long vistas of possibilities. More than this we ought not to say at the present time, but a fuller appreciation of many questions raised by the great outburst of legal writing under Edward I may perhaps result from the studies now being carried on around the Harvard manuscript of Thornton.

---

29 1 Calendar of Inquisition, Miscellaneous, Chancery (1904) no. 1512. The case was in 1290.

30 Selden, Dissertatio (Ogg's ed. 1925) 15.

APPENDIX I

SOME TEXTUAL POINTS

Besides the title (discussed above) Selden gives the following extracts from his manuscript, which are here collated with the Harvard manuscript (H) and the Lincoln's Inn manuscript (L).

I

SELDEN, DISSERTATIO (Ogg's ed.) 17.
Ego talis animum induxi. — S.

Selden is here obviously in error; no known manuscript of Bracton has *induxi*, and it may well be doubted whether Selden's manuscript of Thornton did. The Harvard and Lincoln's Inn texts, like the Bractons, have *erexi.*

II

SELDEN, DISSERTATIO (Ogg's ed.) 20.
Lex gravem poenam infligit iudici corrupto per munera sordida, ut C. ad legem milit. l. omnes, ubi dicitur quod omnes cognitores et iudices a pecuniis manus abstineant ne alienum iurgium putent suam praedam. — S.

In order to make this passage tally with Bracton and L, Woodbine has found it necessary to accuse Selden of twice misquoting (" apparently he abbreviated this passage intentionally. . . . He certainly was not quoting without additions of his own " — 25 L. Q. REV. 46). The additions by Selden according to this view are (*a*) the obvious *inquit Thorntonius* and (*b*) the equally obvious parenthesis pointing out that the *milit.* in the citation should be *Juliam, quae est repetundarum* (*i.e.* Cod. 9.27.3).

The omissions in question are certain passages which Woodbine thought must have been in Selden's copy (although he did not quote them) because they were in fact in L. These passages peculiar to L are the useless expansions which one commonly finds in mediaeval glosses. Thus L reads *sordes, id est per* after the *per* in the first line of the extract, thus introducing a meaningless tautology; and after the *ut* in the same line adds *si judex pacificatur cum litigore ad tertiam partem, ut.* Other weak points in the text of L are the addition of *humana* after the first word, and the reading *neque* for *ne.*

The Harvard manuscript clears up the matter, for it agrees with Selden's text almost exactly; the only difference is that H adds *autem* after *lex* (H, f.30b line 22). H is thus much closer to S than L is, and incidentally Selden's minute accuracy need no longer be doubted.

III

SELDEN, DISSERTATIO (Ogg's ed.) 22.
Here there are several scrappy extracts from S. Where S has *multae* and *sancimus* (both of which are correct), L has *multo* and *senctimus.* H has *multo* and *sanctimus.* H and L, like most English manuscript scribes, were baffled by civilian citations and by words (such as *sancimus*) which are not used by common lawyers. Where Fleta had *inhibitioni* H agrees with S in reading *constitutioni.*

IV

SELDEN, DISSERTATIO (Ogg's ed.) 26.
Cum lex regia. — S.

The Harvard manuscript agrees with S (which is correct): L and many Bracton manuscripts have *lege* or *legia*.

V

SELDEN, DISSERTATIO (Ogg's ed.) 182.
Here Selden quotes a passage from his manuscript which alludes to a statute of " Edward II " which authorised the writ of novel disseisin for a corody: since Thornton died about 1295 Selden concluded that the passage was an interpolation. The words *temporibus . . . tenemento* of S are omitted by H and by L. There was something in the appearance of S which suggested to Selden that the passage was " potius librarii glossema "; but there is nothing inherently impossible in Thornton's having written it, for the reference is obviously not to a statute of Edward II, but to the statute of Westminster II, c. 25 (1285). Selden has noticed in other places that Thornton refers to Edward I as " Edward II " on several occasions in S; H has the same peculiarity.

APPENDIX II

FORM AND CONTENTS OF THE HARVARD MANUSCRIPT

The volume measures 34 x 20.5 cms.

Folio 2: -dala et eos qui faciunt.

Collation. a^6, b^6 (*6 do tibi), A^{10}, B^6, C^4 (*4 cum fuit), D^{10}, E^4 (*4 fedi firmarius), F–G^8, H^{10}, K–M^8, N^8 (–6, 7, 8) = 104.

Contents. The following is the list of books and chapters as they occur in the manuscript. The general scheme was for the headings of books and chapters to be written in red, and the number of the chapter to appear in the margin. The later hand which wrote the first thirteen folios, however, made no attempt to number the chapters, although he did (with one exception) use a large capital to begin a chapter. He also wrote the heading of the chapter in red, except in a few cases where his original was apparently too damaged to read.

In the following table square brackets enclose the conjectural numbers of the first 21 chapters of book 1, and also the English indication of the contents of a chapter in those cases where the manuscript does not give a Latin heading.

[BOOK I] 1a
[i]. [On law in general] 1a
[ii]. Consideranda sunt hec 1a
[iii]. Leges et consuetudines jubent 1b
[iv]. Quid sit jurisprudentia 2a
[v]. Quot sunt precepta juris 2b
[vi]. De jure privato 2b
[vii]. De jure naturali gentium et civili 2b
[viii]. De jure civili 3a

V

THE MEDIAEVAL BAILIFF

HISTORY in our day has divided into many special branches, with the disadvantage that they easily lose touch with one another and fail to profit as they might from one another's discoveries. Indeed, there is grave risk that partial instead of complete views of institutions and problems may be the result, unless deliberate attempts are made to transcend the boundaries which now divide the broad field of historical science.

As an example, let us consider the mediaeval bailiff. In the straight-forward political history of the old masters, he does not figure at all. To the student of constitutional history he will be remembered as appearing in *Magna Carta* and a few other texts as a petty, but incorrigible oppressor of the common people. A rather different picture is formed in the minds of students of economic history. There we find a clear, intelligible account in Walter of Henley telling us exactly what a bailiff does and how he prepares those accounts which exist to this day by the thousand. That of course is much too good to be true, and Mr H. S. Bennett long ago warned us that 'bailiffs' in books may turn out to be reeves when we get down to earth.[1] But when we have made a note of all that, the search for the mediaeval bailiff must be pressed still further, until it is carried into another realm of history—the most dessicated of them all—legal history. Here we observe that the statutes throw a sinister light upon the bailiff and his accounts; the reeve vanishes completely; instead, we learn that the law regards as 'bailiffs'

[1] 'The reeve and the manor in the fourteenth century', *English Historical Review* (1926), xli. 358. This article in an enlarged form constitutes chapter vii of his *Life on the English Manor*.

several classes of people who have not so far come into the subject—partners, agents, factors, carriers and others. The word itself turns out to be ambivalent: the very human 'bailiff' must now be considered in more abstract terms as 'bailee'.

It is only in text-books that constitutional, economic and legal history are set apart from one another. In real life they are simultaneous, and one man lives all his histories concurrently. Let us therefore fix our attention on a bailiff of the Middle Ages, and try to see him as he saw himself, and as his contemporaries saw him, in the midst of his daily work.

The Bailiff and Agricultural Management

The best known, and possibly the central function of the bailiff is to act as general manager of a manor or agricultural estate. The accounts of this fundamental aspect of the bailiff's work given by *Fleta*[1] and Walter of Henley[2] during the reign of Edward I are manifestly related, but which of them is original and which derivative, need not be determined at this moment.

Fleta describes the organization of a big business with a large administrative staff; smaller concerns no doubt doubled some of the parts and omitted many more. He requires the bailiff to rise early and work hard; he must be everywhere and see everything; the major agricultural operations must be conducted under his eye. He must do a certain amount of trading on his lord's behalf and for his lord's profit, and let him beware the day of judgement when his account is rendered. Clearly, the bailiff's duties lie principally in the fields, in the barns, among the ploughmen and labourers, and *Fleta*'s remark that the bailiff does not eat at the lord's table but provides his own food out of a fixed daily wage, emphasizes the fact that the bailiff is essentially occupied out-of-doors, dealing directly with the tillers of the soil.

[1] *Fleta, seu commentarius juris Anglicani* (ed. J. Selden, 1647), lib. ii, c. 72 (*de officio communis seneschalli*), c. 73 (*de officio ballivi*), c. 76 (*de preposito*).

[2] *Walter of Henley's Husbandry, together with an anonymous Husbandry, Seneschaucie, and Robert Grosseteste's Rules* (ed. E. Lamond and W. Cunningham).

Moreover, *Fleta* provides the bailiff with a superior above him, as well as with subordinates. In general command is the lord's steward. A paragon of virtues,[1] the steward must be a fund of expert knowledge, the framer of policy, and the dispenser of justice. He is to know the resources of each manor, to be personally acquainted with the bailiffs and other officers, to find out whether the estate is making a profit, and to ascertain the lord's legal rights both in labour services and in wardships and marriages. For this he must be knowledgeable in the laws and customs of the region. We must picture him surrounded by extents, court rolls and indentures. But he does not handle money, nor does he render account, although he is expected to take responsibility for the orders he has given. On the other hand, however, he receives daily accounts from the household servants. There seems little doubt that the steward was primarily engaged in office work, and only to a secondary degree (at least in *Fleta*'s view) with household management.

When we come to the bailiff's subordinates, and especially the reeve, we come to the heart of the agricultural economy. At dawn he musters the labour force, all day he watches to see that a full day's work is done by man and beast, and before nightfall he sees that the horses and oxen are properly fed and that nobody steals their fodder.

All this is part of the familiar, age-old story of the works and the days of agricultural life and labour. It is the division of duties which concerns us here, and the significance of that division will appear all the more clearly if we place *Fleta*'s description beside that of an older tract of eleventh-century date, written in Anglo-Saxon, and entitled *Gerefa*, 'The Reeve'.[2]

Under that one title the author describes an office which

[1] *Fleta* makes nicely graduated demands upon the morals and characters of the officers, down to the reeve of whom nothing is asked save that he be not lazy or sleepy.

[2] Text in F. Liebermann, *Gesetze der Angelsachsen*, i. 453–5; the text is reproduced with an English translation by W. Skeat, in W. Cunningham, *Growth of English Industry and Commerce: the Middle Ages*, as an appendix.

combines the functions of the steward, the bailiff and the reeve as portrayed by *Fleta*. The very first sentence of *Gerefa* requires the sagacious reeve to know the law as well as agricultural routine and the weather. He must also be a good manager of men, and know every detail of the estate he is entrusted with—down to the last mouse-trap, we are told. He is to keep his lord's goods, and from the list of them it is clear that he is concerned with the household as well as the farm. Indeed, if he has time to spare, he is told that he can clean and tidy up the house lest he be idle. In short, the work of the three officers described by *Fleta* is done by one man in this tract, and he is called the 'reeve'.

We need not be surprised that these multifarious duties should come to be divided, nor that the division should have been made where *Fleta* makes it, or thereabouts. The central indispensable function is obviously the out-of-door work of supervision, of seeing that things are done in due season, and done well. Only a man who is constantly out on the land can do that effectively. With the growth of larger properties, exploited more intensely, and in a legal and social system of greater complication, the burden of the unspecialized reeve must have become impossible.

In two ways the burden could be lightened. First, so busy a man, immersed in daily detail, could be relieved of the responsibility of forming general policy. The making of extents, the estimating of proper yields, the broad financial aspect of the estate, and above all, the extremely important business of keeping courts and safeguarding the lord's complex legal rights over his tenants, bond and free, were things that could well be concentrated in the hands of a separate official. Those duties, moreover, are all indoor work, and it so happened that there was an indoor officer conveniently ready to take them over—the steward, who could easily combine them with his original domestic and household attributes into one office which was for the most part sedentary. One consequence followed inevitably:

the steward of a manor, like the steward of the king's own household, is close to his master, and therefore deep in his counsels, and therefore an informal partner of his power. The reeve was no doubt eased of some of his burden by the steward in consequence of some such process as this; but the steward was indubitably his superior, sitting in the house, conning his rolls and extents, holding courts and developing steadily into a lawyer-administrator, while the wretched reeve was left to tramp the fields and carry on the ungrateful but vital task of getting things done by unwilling, dishonest or even hostile peasants.

Secondly, the transfer to the steward of legal work and matters of high policy still left the reeve with an uncomfortable, perhaps even incompatible combination of duties. Economic and administrative developments soon made this clear. It was easy in the eleventh century to remind the *gerefa* that if he has been remiss in the cattle-store or on the threshing-floor, it will show in the barn at the end of the season. True enough, it will; but when the thirteenth century was drawing to its close, *Fleta* tells of a more accurate and searching test—the account. Again, the older treatise says simply that the reeve must 'keep' his lord's goods; when we come to *Fleta* we see how complicated and responsible that task has become. There is much buying and selling to be done. Surplus or unthrifty stock must be disposed of, more profitable or more desirable commodities must be acquired. From the rolls we see that the money economy has penetrated into the heart of the manor: 'works' may be converted into cash, and cash may be used to buy labour. Money is therefore circulating in such quantity that a large part of agricultural life can be conveniently expressed in figures, real or notional, as an account. The old injunction to 'keep' his lord's goods has now become a duty to trade with them on the lord's behalf. Once again, the only effective check upon such activities is a well-drawn account.

Such accounts have survived by thousands, and some of them

are exceptionally splendid rolls.[1] The reeve has thus become the creator of a vital series of records, although nothing compels us to believe that he himself indited them. They were presumably drawn up by clerks and accounting experts, but the reeve must have provided the detailed information.[2] Some of it may have been written, and some in the form of tallies, and much may have been stored in the astonishing memories which country-folk develop when they cannot write. However that may be, there can be no doubt that the application of business methods to the manor, and the brisker pace of trade in the countryside, added considerably to the burden of the reeve's office. Indeed, they added also to his private store. Chaucer tells us that his reeve always rode hinderest of the rout—and doubtless that was his proper place in such a company. Back in his village, however, he ruled with a rod of iron; the men feared him like death; none dared dispute his word; as he said, so was the reckoning, and no auditor could unravel his peasant cunning. His handsome house, shaded with trees, was known to contain a hoard of ill-won wealth which he would increase by lending to the lord the lord's own money.

In short, the reeve's duties were so multifarious that a further division of labour became desirable, at least on large and busy estates. Theorists of administrative method and business experts saw roughly where the division should be made. The reeve was to be confined to the humblest and most ancient function of his office, that of watching and directing the work in the fields, the cowsheds and on the threshing floor. On a large manor that was ample work for one man, and well within the competence of an experienced and intelligent villein.

The other duties—the trading, accounting, discipline of the labour force, rent-collecting and the like—seemed to call for a

[1] Such as that printed in W. Cunningham, *Growth of English Industry and Commerce*, i. 591–610.

[2] *Seneschaucie*, p. 101 says that the reeve ought to account annually with his bailiff.

different type of man, and to be sufficiently onerous to keep him busy. That other man was the bailiff. So we finally reach the classical hierarchy. At its head is the steward who becomes a lawyer-financier, surveying his lord's fortune as a whole. In the middle rank is the bailiff in charge of a manor or small group of neighbouring properties. At the bottom there is in each manor or estate, the reeve.

All that may be plausibly conjectured in the field of economic and administrative history, but before we take leave of the ancient office of reeve, we must mention the obscure and unsolved problems which surround him on the social and constitutional side. His office became compulsory, like so many others. More than that, it was often imposed upon villeins. So frequent was this, that the common law regarded liability to serve the office of reeve as raising a presumption of villeinage. More strangely still, in some places the reeve was elected, and villeins were ready to buy this privilege although it carried with it the corollary that they became liable to guarantee the reeve's account. As a variation of this, we sometimes find a community purchasing the immunity of all its members from the office of reeve.[1]

The reconstruction of manorial developments just put forward is based upon a consideration of functions, and must be regarded as largely *a priori* and hypothetical. It would be rash indeed to suggest that any particular manor, or any considerable number of manors, had in fact evolved along those precise lines—'we must beware of introducing order where all is disorder' as Mr Bennett properly reminds us; but there can be little doubt that these factors must have existed, and must have exerted pressure in the direction which I have supposed, although in any particular case their effect may have been modified by other factors, human, legal and geographical.

A brief analysis of the passages in *Fleta*, Walter of Henley, *Seneschaucie* and the anonymous *Hosebonderie* shows that there

[1] H. S. Bennett, *Life on the English Manor*, pp. 166 ff.

was some uncertainty as to the precise division of labour between the bailiff and the reeve. Thus, in *Fleta* it is the bailiff who is required to rise early and make daily rounds of the estate, performing a number of functions which duplicate those assigned to the reeve. In a number of cases the bailiff and the reeve are called upon to act together. When *Fleta* does make clear distinctions, the facts belie them; thus he mentions the bailiff's duty to account, and says nothing of the fact that reeves rendered accounts in a large number of cases. We must therefore beware of hastily associating particular functions too closely with particular offices. Again, *Fleta* attributes to the bailiff a vague duty to discipline the labour-force, which seems to be beyond the attributes of a reeve; yet *Seneschaucie* thinks it necessary to forbid a reeve to hold pleas[1]—an exalted function normally reserved for the steward, and as late as 1402 a manumitted serf was exempted from serving as 'bailiff' and from other servile obligations.[2] In other words, there is a possibility of the traditional reeve occasionally acquiring the style, although not the status, of the traditional bailiff.

Bailiffs and Manorial Courts

So much can be extracted from the early agricultural manuals. But they are by no means our only source of information, and there are other types of literature which illuminate aspects of the bailiff's work which otherwise would be unknown. The last years of Henry III saw the beginning of a new sort of law-book which is, for the most part, in the vernacular French instead of the more traditional Latin. If it represents on the one hand the decline of the scholarly Bractonian tradition, it nevertheless shows on the other hand the demands of a literate, but non-clerical class of society for legal instruction.

[1] *Seneschaucie*, p. 101.

[2] Historical Manuscripts Commission, *Middleton MSS.*, p. 101 cited by E. Hughes, 'The eighteenth-century estate agent', in *Essays in British and Irish History presented to J. E. Todd*, p. 187.

Some of these new readers meant to become professional practitioners of the common law in the king's courts, but others were content to remain on the outer fringe and to make their careers in local practices which consisted in giving legal advice generally, holding manorial and franchisal courts, making up accounts, and being generally useful to landowners. It is within that socially interesting group of lettered laymen that we seem to find our bailiffs and stewards, instructing themselves—perhaps even receiving formal instruction—by means of the growing vernacular literature of the law, court-keeping, accountancy and agriculture.

We have already noticed that the agricultural treatises ascribe to the bailiff a vague duty of maintaining discipline among the tenants, and counsel him to act discreetly in doing so. For a detailed account of this side of the bailiff's work we must look to the treatises which circulated under the title of the 'court baron', or similar words, which Maitland edited in the fourth volume of the Selden Society's publications.

The picture they show us is vivid and life-like. The bailiff appears in the role of public prosecutor in the lord's court, as well as its process-server and executive officer. We need not consider the higher sorts of franchise which could hear pleas of the crown, for the bailiff's duty is amply illustrated by the normal court baron. Nor would it be helpful to pursue the question whether the proceedings were civil or criminal, for clearly they are in a traditional form which was innocent of such a sophistication.

Cases began by the bailiff making a formal count narrating the misdeed, and concluding by saying that this was to the lord's damage of 40*s*. and to his shame of 20*s*. or some such sums. If the facts involve force, they are said to have been done against the peace of God and the lord—any mention of the peace of the king would of course take the case out of the jurisdiction of the lord and into the king's court. The opening stages therefore resemble a civil action for damages.

The defendant put in a plea (and occasionally we are told that he has a pleader beside him), which is sometimes prolonged into an altercation with the steward. The accused may plead guilty and at the same time urge that there were extenuating circumstances. Thus spake a poacher in the lord's pond:

> Sir, for God's sake take it not amiss that I tell you truly how I went the other evening skirting the bank of that pond, and watched the fish at play in the water, so beautiful and so bright, and because of the great longing I had for a tench, I laid me down on the bank, and with my hands alone, quite simply, and without any other device, I caught that tench and took it away.

An irresistible temptation, and a plea irresistible to all save a stony-hearted steward,[1] who hinted darkly at previous convictions.

The mode of trial was generally compurgation six-handed, occasionally by jury, and the judgement that the offender be amerced. We hear nothing of the lord getting the preposterous damages which the bailiff claimed on his behalf.[2]

The matters prosecuted by the bailiff are varied. The assize of bread and ale, of course; assault and battery on the bailiff himself; mowing the lord's stubble so that he could not thatch the cow-shed; cutting the freshest grass which is reserved for the lord's palfrey; sending a small boy to rob the lord's orchard; hurrying away from the mill with one's flour without paying toll and multure; selling every day and the whole year fish which is stinking, putrid and so corrupt that many have been made ill; and refusing to sell ale to the lord (who was entertaining visitors) although the bailiff earnestly and debonairely besought him and offered cash down. The brewer vehemently maintained that he had not a drop in the place—to which the

[1] *Court Baron*, pp. 54–5; several other touching defences, including the desire to indulge the fancy of an ailing wife, are given by different manuscripts printed there.

[2] *Court Baron*, p. 22 contains an obscure reference to the 'taxation' of these sums; probably they were usually merged in the amercement.

bailiff retorted that he had enough to serve the villagers. We may suspect some country malice here.

These cases seem all to have begun with the taking of pledges and thereafter with further attachments.[1] These procedures (which could be very damaging to a peasant, whether bond or free) were in the hands of the bailiff. The subsequent proceedings before the steward in court, were conducted by the bailiff. It needs little imagination to see the enormous power which this system placed in the bailiff's hands, and the ample opportunities it afforded for oppression, blackmail and vindictiveness.

One aspect of this problem received early attention, for it raised a general question of procedure which concerned many others besides bailiffs. In its broadest terms, it is this: is it right and fair that a public official should be able to put a man on trial—in jeopardy, as the Americans expressively put it—simply by his bare word alone?

The problem was being solved already, as between private litigants in civil proceedings. A bare claim could be met by a flat denial, and the denial was conclusive.[2] A claim supported by a suit of people, however, could only be successfully met by a denial supported by compurgators.[3] The most serious sort of claim, that based upon a deed under seal, will drive the defendant to prove his denial by recourse to a jury. A roughly similar system obtained in criminal procedure.[4] All that is perfectly reasonable and logical. The problem arises when we ask whether there is sufficient justification for departing from a well-balanced system of assertions and denials when the assertions are made by an official?

[1] So important was this process, that the treatise on court-keeping compiled by (or for) Sir John de Longueville bears for sole title the single word 'Attachiamenta': *Court Baron*, pp. 79 ff. Compare the similar, but much more extensive work in Scotland 'Quoniam Attachiamenta' edited by Lord Cooper for the Stair Society.

[2] *Bracton's Note Book* (ed. Maitland), no. 57; cf. *Brevia Placitata* (Selden Society, 66), pp.64–5.

[3] *Court Baron*, p. 84.

[4] Pollock and Maitland, ii. 606.

Evidence suggests that Henry II several times legislated on this point. By the year 1158 it was possible to say that a dean had transgressed 'the king's constitution' by proceeding against a woman for adultery without any other accuser than himself.[1] At that moment the king was in England, but in the following year he was in Normandy and by an ordinance of Christmas 1159 made at Falaise he prohibited deans from proceeding thus, and extended the principle to his own judges there.[2] Back in England in 1164 he renewed his prohibition and insisted that laymen be accused in church courts only by 'lawful and ascertained accusers and witnesses', without otherwise diminishing the powers of archdeacons, however.[3] In the same text the king proceeds further, and considers the common case when no accuser dares to come forward. For that very real difficulty Henry II provided a remarkable solution: on the bishop's request, the sheriff must summon a jury, and their presentment will supply the place of an accuser. Two years later, in 1166, he adopted the same device for royal criminal procedure, and so established the grand jury for centuries to come as a part of the common law system.

Both royal and ecclesiastical procedure in criminal matters were thus subjected to the great principle that the mere word of an official is insufficient to put a man upon his trial; there must be an individual accuser, or a presentment by a jury. There still remained the humblest sort of court, to which large masses of the population were subject, which Henry II had not seen fit to reform. It is nearly fifty years later that we find the first protest against the still untamed bailiff, in the Articles of the Barons, c. 28: the remedy swiftly followed in the Great Charter, c. 38 of King John:

[1] Fitz Stephen, in *Materials for the History of Thomas Becket* (Rolls Series), iii. 44–5; C. H. Haskins, *Norman Institutions*, p. 331. This constitution is no longer extant.

[2] Robert of Torigni (ed. L. Delisle), ii. 180; Haskins, p. 329.

[3] Constitutions of Clarendon, c. 6 (in W. Stubbs, *Select Charters*).

Henceforth, no bailiff shall put anyone to his law by his bare word, without the production of reliable witnesses.

These words, slightly expanded, appear in all subsequent issues of the charter.[1] It was of course impracticable in most manors to require the use of a grand or presenting jury; but it was possible to insist that the bailiff's word should be supported by suit or *secta*, and the model forms in the *Court Baron* show that this requirement was faithfully fulfilled.

For all that, the police powers of the bailiff were still formidable. He could arrest on suspicion;[2] constant reference is made to his duty of keeping the peace; in case of disturbance he could call out the homage and imprison a rebellious villein;[3] and all the time he is carrying out his daily duties of taking pledges, making attachments, levying distresses and collecting amercements. In those purely routine duties there possibly lurked the commonest and most tempting opportunities for oppression. On the comparatively rare occasions of a general eyre, the judges would sometimes make an example of an oppressive bailiff by putting him in gaol,[4] and of course there were civil remedies to be had in the court of common pleas by those entitled to pursue them—which did not include the unfree.[5] Nevertheless, a bailiff's life might have, extra-legally, its chastening moments; there is much in the rolls to tell of assaults, batteries, woundings, ambushes, and 'other enormities' committed against bailiffs.

The Bailiff and his Lord

In all this, we have been considering the bailiff principally within the environment of the manor or agricultural estate,

[1] Even before the Great Charter, Pontefract and Leeds already possessed a custom to this effect: G. Woledge, 'Medieval borough of Leeds', Thoresby Society, *Miscellany*, xxxvii. 308, no. 14. For the bearing of this upon the 'witnessmen', see R. Stewart-Brown, *Serjeants of the Peace*, p. 85.

[2] *Year Books of Edward II* (Selden Society), xxiv. 92–3.

[3] *Ibid.*, x. 236, xiii. 152.

[4] *Eyre of Kent* (Selden Society), i. 63, 132.

[5] The bailiff's defence would be to say that the plaintiff was his lord's villein.

with his duties of management and discipline as depicted in the tracts on husbandry and on procedure in courts baron. Taken together, they illustrate the bailiff's position as most of his peasant subjects must have seen it. Of course, that is only half the story. The bailiff's position with respect to his lord was equally, if not more important, for it was in fact the source of all his power. This brings us to the heart of the matter, namely, the nature and quality of the relationship of lord and bailiff.

What seems to be the oldest manifestation in the common law of this relationship, appears in the reign of Henry II when the terms of the assize of novel disseisin were settled. In that action the original writ[1] orders the sheriff to attach the defendant 'or if he himself is not to be found, then his bailiff'. Evidently, the policy behind the assize of novel disseisin was to bring the full force of the law to bear in the shortest possible time. It is the only real action which begins with an attachment (instead of the customary summons), and it is the only action of any sort which can proceed immediately against anyone save the defendant named in the writ. The object of this drastic procedure was to ensure that there should be someone in court immediately who could answer for an alleged disseisin—and herein we note that, from about 1166 onwards, the law regarded it as perfectly normal that if the lord of a piece of land could not be found, the sheriff could depend on laying his hands upon the lord's bailiff at fairly short notice, and that from the middle of the twelfth century lords could be assumed to have bailiffs.

This capacity of a bailiff to answer for a disseisin alleged against his lord[2] was a startling anomaly, but the rolls and year books show that for centuries it was in use. It soon became necessary to define the limits within which the bailiff was com-

[1] Glanvill, xiii. 33.

[2] For a rare example of a bailiff acting for a plaintiff (instead of a defendant) lord, see *Three Rolls of the King's Court* (Pipe Roll Soc., 14), p. 48 where in 1194 'Alexander, bailiff of Henry de Ver, complains that Hugh de Tileburi disseised his lord' of a rent.

petent to plead, and Bracton,[1] explaining the situation in his own day, tells us that the bailiff in general can use all the exceptions which would be open to his lord. Here we must beware of thinking of the bailiff as a sort of attorney. Novel disseisin was so strongly tinged with criminal characteristics that attorneys in this action, as in other criminal proceedings, were not permitted until, in the fourteenth century,[2] it had become predominantly a civil instead of a criminal remedy in general estimation. Bracton himself makes this point by describing the bailiff as a *responsalis* only, who is not authorized (as an attorney is) to confess the action, to compromise it, or to divide the disputed land, or to surrender it.[3] The bailiff's appearance is not the result of powers conferred upon him for that purpose by his lord, nor of his admission to that function by the king or his judges, but rests upon the fact that he stands in a particular relationship to his lord[4]—a relationship so close and so well known that it needed no definition and could be taken for granted.

The forcible disseisin of men from their land is a grave social evil which has sometimes driven governments into panic legislation—as in the later Roman Empire—with disastrous results to general legal conceptions.[5] That was not the case with

[1] Bracton, f. 212b.

[2] By statute 12 Edward II, c. 1 (1318). The statute expressly saves answering by bailiff, as heretofore used, if the tenants so desire.

[3] For the bailiff's answer in novel disseisin, see the statute of Westminster II. c. 25 (1285); *Y.B. 20 & 21 Edw. I* (Rolls Series), p. 414; *32 & 33 Edw. I* (Rolls Series), p. 48; *Y.BB. Edw. II* (Selden Society), i. 133, vi. 131, viii. 69, xv. 77, xix. 39. For ingenious subtleties, *Y.B. 11 & 12 Edw. III* (Rolls Series), p. 560. For a bailiff in 1219 who confessed a disseisin, see *Eyre Rolls of Lincolnshire* (Selden Society, 53), no. 788 and the disapproval of Bracton. ff. 182, 212*b*. For the *responsalis* see Woodbine's note in his edition of Glanvill, pp. 262–5 and Bolland's introduction to *Y.BB. Edw. II* (Selden Society), xv. pp. xi–xxi.

[4] In a famous page Roscoe Pound, *Interpretations of Legal History*, p. 57, contrasts this common-law approach with Roman law which looks primarily to the will of the parties.

[5] Cf. Ernst Levy, *West Roman Vulgar Law: Property*, p. 250.

Henry II, however, and his assize of novel disseisin has none of the marks of a desperate remedy, such as forfeiture and the death penalty. The issue of process against the bailiff in default of the lord was no frantic gesture, but merely a recognition of the current feeling that a bailiff stood in a particular relationship, not only to the lord, but also to the lord's land.

The most enduring illustration of this is the bailiff's power of leasing his lord's land—simply because he is bailiff. No doubt that power was somewhat abridged by the end of the Middle Ages to the grant of leases at will, and not for years,[1] but in the great days of the bailiff we find him not merely leasing but even alienating in fee.

Such an alienation was certainly tortious, but it was effective, until the lord succeeded in defeating it by means of a writ of entry against the alienee to recover land

> into which the said alienee had no entry save by a certain one, formerly the demandant's bailiff of such a vill, who demised that land to him without the will of the aforesaid demandant, as he says.[2]

This conception of the bailiff being, as it were, the bailee of his lord's land, and having in it so curious and dangerous an interest, suggests the need for investigating the history and associations of the word. The etymology of the word *ballivus* (and of *ballia* meaning the land, and the bailiff's interest in it) exercised the grim fancy of mediaeval scholars: did it not come from that Baal whom the Hebrew prophets denounced? The grave Ducange refutes that speculation, and leaves no doubt that the central idea is that which still survives in the modern English 'bailment'. It is a delivery of a thing from one person to another, not as a final gift, but for a time, or upon conditions. That

[1] Y.B. 2 Edw. IV, Pasch. no. 9 (1462); cf. Y.B. 10 Edw. IV, Pasch. no. 7 (1470). In 27 Ass. 5 (1353) a bailiff's pledge of his lord's chattels was upheld.

[2] Bracton, f. 323*b*. Cf. *Brevia Placitata* (Selden Society, 66), p. 199; Hengham, *Summa Parva* (ed. Dunham), p. 61.

sense of the word, even in connection with land, is common in England early in the thirteenth century. In 1219 'Henry comes and says that he does not hold that land, and claims nothing in it, save by the bailment (*per balliam*) of Robert de Percy'.[1] The king, who often had a subject's land in his hand, might make a temporary grant of it 'out of his bail' (*de baillia sua*) to a grantee who will 'have therein nothing save a bail'.[2] The records are sometimes so vague that it is difficult to see the exact nature of the bailment, as when we are told that Alice *tenet ex ballia et dono Willelmi*.[3] Sometimes the bailment is expressly at will,[4] or during pleasure.[5] In some cases it is clear that the bailment is for a term of years and is thus (in later terminology) a lease[6]—and it is relevant to note that the French for a lease today is still *bail*. Then, too, the feudal wardship of land in England is described as a *ballia*,[7] and in the custom of Paris *bail* became the technical name which distinguished the wardship exercised by collaterals from the *garde noble* exercised by ascendants.[8]

Bearing in mind this group of associations[9] of the word *ballia*, we can see more clearly the nature of the bailiff's position. A lord who commits a manor to the management of a bailiff, or

[1] *Eyre Rolls of Yorkshire* (Selden Society, 56), no. 355.

[2] *Ibid.*, no. 1151.

[3] *Eyre Rolls of Gloucestershire &c.* (Selden Society, 59), no. 127.

[4] *Ibid.*, no. 231.

[5] *Ibid.*, no. 1018.

[6] *Casus Placitorum* (Selden Society, 69), p. 28 no. 81 (with which compare *Casus et Judicia* in the same volume, lxxxi. no. 50); p. 32 no. 6.

[7] *Eyre Rolls of Gloucestershire &c.* (Selden Society, 59), no. 597. Just as a guardian of land may have a *ballia*, so a bailee of chattels has *custodia* of them; Bracton, f. 151.

[8] Olivier Martin, *Histoire de la coutume de Paris*, i. 166; see also Beaumanoir (ed. Salmon), §§ 506 ff. for other uses of the word in the custom of the Beauvaisis.

[9] There are others, notably the grant of powers by a gild or a community to persons who become its representatives for external relations, and its domestic rulers for internal affairs. That process gave rise to 'bailiffs' of a different sort, with which we are not here concerned. The bailiffs of liberties, of sheriffs and of courts are likewise excluded.

who makes over an infant tenant's property in his wardship to someone else who will exploit it, is thus making a *ballia*, a bailment, of the land. He may do so for a stated term of years, or he may express it during his pleasure, or at his will; he may make the arrangement gratuitously, or at a rent, or subject to an accounting for the profits. Essentially fragile and temporary, such a bailment may in practice last quite a long time so that the bailee begins to look like, and even to behave, like an owner.

The bailiff therefore succumbed to the temptation which had already overcome the guardian in chivalry and the married man (whose position was closely analogous[1]), and by his tortious feoffments compelled the true owners to bring their solemn, slow and complicated writ of entry to undo the mischief—for the common law gave no relief for fraud. As we have seen, the early registers of writs, Bracton, *Brevia Placitata*, and Hengham all give attention to the problem.

Then doubts appeared. After the middle of the thirteenth century lawyers began to analyse their concepts more precisely. Much of the law therefore became more logical and coherent; but some portions became difficult to explain, and lawyers (some of whom may have undergone the searching experience of trying to teach the law) encountered theoretical difficulties. The vague old notions of seisin were hardening into the dogma of 'seisin of a free tenement'[2]—with the result that guardians and bailiffs and termors no longer qualified as 'seised' in the sense which was now becoming classical; how then could they transfer to a tortious feoffee a seisin which they did not possess? Again, the list of estates of freehold in land was soon to be closed—and the *ballia* was not among them; it was left in the outer darkness with wardships and terms of years as merely a chattel real. All this, moreover, is reflected in a new precision in

[1] Pollock and Maitland, *History of English Law*, ii. 414.

[2] For the study of these questions the work of F. Joüon des Longrais, *La conception anglaise de la saisine* is fundamental.

technical terminology and a widening of the gulf between real and personal property, so that it became a shocking solecism to speak of the 'bailment' of land or the 'seisin' of chattels. English law was at last entering upon its 'classical' age.

The legislation of Edward I came in the full flood of this classicizing movement, and gave to it statutory expression. The Statute of Westminster II, c. 25 (1285) is very much in point here. In the course of a thorough reform and extension of the assize of novel disseisin, it enacts that the assize shall lie against a guardian or a termor who alienates in fee, and also against the alienee. As we have seen, the only remedy heretofore available was a writ of entry: without indicating whether the old remedy is abolished or retained, the statute now offers the speedy assize of novel disseisin, and treats both the alienor and the alienee as disseisors.[1] Moreover, the assize is made available immediately, while the old writ of entry (at least in the case of alienation by a guardian) had to await the heir's coming of age, or (in the case of a termor, it would seem) the expiry of the term. The statute in fact does not mention bailiffs.

On the face of it, the statute provided a much more speedy and effective remedy, and to contemporaries that was generally all they saw in it. Then, in 1310, there came the curious case of *Sampson* v. *Grenel*[2] which caught the famous Chief Justice Bereford in a reminiscent as well as an irascible mood. The demandant here brought the old common-law writ of entry,[3] and was immediately met by the objection that the statute gave him the assize of novel disseisin, and that if the statute gave a new remedy, it must be taken by implication to have abolished the old one.

[1] If either the disseisor or the disseisee died (so that novel disseisin would not serve), the statute permits 'remedy by writ of entry'. This was always construed as entry *sur* disseisin, and not what we have called shortly the 'old' writ of entry: *Y.BB. Edw. II* (Selden Society), iv. 113 *per* Stanton, J.

[2] *Y.BB. Edw. II* (Selden Society), iv. 112.

[3] Why he should have done so is not explained.

That raised a general problem of statutory interpretation[1] which we need not examine on this occasion, for Bereford found other grounds for holding that the old remedy was no longer available. The writ before him in this case was based upon an alienation by a guardian, but Bereford naturally equated the position of a guardian with that of a bailiff.[2] Putting together the three reports of the case which have come down to us, Bereford's view can be reconstructed thus: 'at common law, if my bailiff alienated I had my recovery only by a writ of entry; but that was not, and is not, good law, because the free-tenement was always in me (and not in the bailiff) until the alienation deprived me of it; the consideration[3] leading to the enactment of the statute was this, that the basis[4] of this writ was not founded upon reason.' When counsel remarked that 'at common law you shall have a writ of entry where a bailiff alienates in fee' Bereford replied (evidently with some warmth) 'I have been here fifteen years and have never heard of such a writ; if my companions were here,[5] I would not go hence to-day until you had judgement against you.' It was on the morrow that he was joined by Staunton, J. who delivered the judgement of the court: the old law was defective since it made the heir await his age before recovering from his guardian's alienee, and so the statute has amended it by a provision which accords with law and reason; hence the defective old remedy is abolished; 'and so this court awards that you take nothing by your writ.'

[1] It was similarly debated for some years whether mort dancestor could be used by a tenant in tail after the statute *De Donis* had set up formedon in the descender: *Y.BB. Edw. II* (Selden Society), xiii. 44, xx. 136, xxii, 39; cf. Fitzherbert, *New Natura Brevium,* 196 K for claims by a remainderman.

[2] The statute of Marlborough, c. 17 had already done so when it subjected the guardian in socage to the action of account—which so far had been used only against bailiffs.

[3,4] In both these places Bereford used the word *cause*, in the continental sense.

[5] For this, compare the introduction to *Y.BB. Edw. II* (Selden Society), iv. pp. xxviii–xxix.

We cannot forbear in passing, a word of appreciation for the boldness with which this case applies the 'relativity' of English mediaeval theory. Just as a writ of right in matters of property decides which of two rights is the more rightful, so here the court had to decide which of two laws was the more lawful. When the court decided in favour of the statutory remedy and went so far as to say (in spite of the statute's silence) that the old remedy was impliedly abolished, it seems to have done so without reference to the nature of statutes, and simply on the grounds that the statutory provisions were intrinsically 'more accordant with law'.

Much might be said of the philosophical significance of that phrase, but for the purposes of this enquiry we need only attend to one aspect of it. To say that the old law was not in accord with 'law' reveals a crisis in the course of which 'law' had rapidly changed. And clearly, 'law' there means 'general principles' or (as Maitland puts it in a footnote) 'sound doctrine'. The result of doctrine becoming more 'sound' was that the older law appeared to be against reason when it gave only a writ of entry upon the alienation of a guardian or bailiff. The statute does not enter into theoretical considerations, but it is significant that it deals only with alienations by termors and guardians, whom it treats as parties (with their alienees) to a disseisin. The ground for this is evidently that their position is to be sharply distinguished—and therein lies the novelty—from tenants for life who are seised of a free tenement.[1] It is they who, out of their seisin, can make a tortious feoffment; the termor, the guardian and the bailiff under the new doctrine have no such estate.

Bereford had just applied the same principle in another sort of case. In *Pateshull* v. *Bray*[2] a father had resorted to a question-

[1] Tortious feoffments by life tenants also needed a swifter remedy than the older writs of entry, and the combined operation of the statutes of Gloucester, c. 7 and Westminster II, c. 24 provided it, but not by novel disseisin; instead, recovery was by entry *in casu proviso* and *in consimili casu.*

[2] *Y.BB. Edw. II* (Selden Society), iii. 185, iv. 136.

able device, apparently to avoid the wardship of his infant heir. He enfeoffed the child of the land, and then 'bailed' the land to a friend to keep until the child came of age. The heir, having attained his age, brought a writ of waste against the friend. In accordance with the new doctrine Bereford abated the writ, saying that the remedy against a bailiff was an action of account and not of waste, thus again denying to the bailiff any real interest in the land—even to the exiguous extent that a guardian or a termor had.

The classical movement, enshrined in the Statute of Westminster II, brought about a declension in the power of the bailiff which is indeed remarkable. In the earlier part of the century the bailiff had held the manor much the same as the Anglo-Norman justiciar had held the kingdom; after Edward I the bailiff is a mere servant. Where formerly the bailiff enjoyed that 'beatitude of seisin' which enabled him to make a feoffment which could only be defeated by the solemnity of a writ of entry, the new doctrine denies any seisin in the bailiff, allows no effect to a feoffment by him, and treats him merely as an accomplice (with his alienee) in a disseisin of his lord. Hence the statute accords them no more ceremony than the summary and semi-criminal assize of novel disseisin.

There remains yet one other aspect of the bailiff for consideration, and that is his accountability to his lord.[1] This is indeed the most conspicuous feature about bailiffs as far as the year books and early reports are concerned, where actions of account are fairly frequent. Its early history, so important for the purposes of this study, is nevertheless obscure. Glanvill does not mention it; it does not appear in the earliest registers of writs;[2] Bracton (who intended to write about personal actions) did not

[1] Bailiffs were occasionally appointed, by deed, quit of account: *Y.BB. Edw. II* (Selden Society), x. 3 (1311); *Y.B. 12 & 13 Edw. III* (Rolls Series), 6 (1338).

[2] It must be remembered that there may be special reasons, *e.g.* the famous 'Irish' register (British Museum, Julius D. II) only professes to give writs 'of course'.

live to do so; the post-Bractonian treatises generally refuse to venture into a field which the master had not surveyed before them. From the law treatises therefore one would not suspect the existence of the action. Yet we can learn from the plea rolls[1] that it occurs in the king's court as early as 1200, and it appears occasionally during the next fifty years or so thereafter, although it is still decidedly rare. The natural inference therefore would be that account is a comparatively late development. The remarkable study of G. J. Turner, however, shows how false such a deduction may be.[2] In the thirteenth century the bulk of the nation's litigation did not take place in the king's court, but in the county courts upon writs cast in the peculiar form called *justicies*. The earliest annotated collections[3] of writs in fact give only the *justicies* form of the writ of account, and so the absence, or rarity, of the action cannot be deduced from an examination of the plea rolls. Although rare in the king's court, actions of account may well have been frequent, by writs of *justicies*, in the county courts. The proved existence of the action of account from the very beginning of the thirteenth century merits some attention. The very idea of accounting suggests business and trade, and we are bound to ask whether account may be a commercial practice which was only later applied to agricultural affairs. The reverse seems to have been the case. In its early history account is found only as between lord and bailiff, and so we have the interesting spectacle of an important remedy which later on was to concern agents, factors and partners evolving from the manorial economy, instead of being imported directly from the international fund of general commercial law.

By the end of the thirteenth century an important development had taken place which doubled the scope of the action of account. As we have seen, the bailiff is essentially a bailee, and

[1] *Curia Regis Rolls*, i. 191, 249.
[2] In his introduction to *Brevia Placitata* (Selden Society, 66), pp. li, lvii ff.
[3] *Brevia Placitata* (Selden Society, 66), pp. 23, 68, 176.

the lord alleges in his count that 'he bailed to him 40 librates of land to take care of (*à garder*)'.[1] In its original form the action charges the bailiff in respect of what the lord himself had bailed, be it land or chattels. In practice, the bailiff's activity came to be more extensive; particularly, he may receive the lord's rents from the hands of tenants, or the lord himself may sell something, saying to the purchaser 'pay my bailiff'. Since there was here no bailment by the lord to the bailiff, the situation did not at first fall within the formula of the writ of account. It was thus a momentous advance when the law allowed lords to charge bailiffs not only as bailees but also as receivers; quite often a writ will contain both charges, and sometimes the defendant is charged only as a receiver and not as bailiff.[2]

Among the difficult and delicate situations which inevitably presented themselves in actions of account, some were the result of employing trial by compurgation, 'wager of law', which itself is an indication of the ancient origin of the action. This concerned, particularly, transactions between the lord and bailiff which often were extremely informal and took place in private conversations of which a jury, even in theory, could not be supposed to have any knowledge. If a lord alleged that the defendant had received money from the lord himself, the defendant could deny it and wage his law; receipt from the hands of a stranger would be tried by jury.[3] In their endeavours to limit wager of law, the courts applied this principle strictly. Thus wager of law was not permitted as a denial of receipt at

[1] *Brevia Placitata* (Selden Society, 66), p. 177.

[2] Such cases seem at first non-manorial and to concern agents for the sale of goods as in *Y.BB. Edw. II* (Selden Society), ii. 34 (1308–9), merchants who have received from the plaintiff money to trade with, as in *ibid.* vi. 3 (1311), and agents to receive money from third parties as in *ibid.* xix. 71 (1315) where the distinction is well drawn. In the first two cases the objection that the defendant should be charged as bailiff was overruled for reasons not stated and difficult to surmise.

[3] *Y.BB. Edw. II* (Selden Society), xvi. 104–5 (1314); *Y.B. 14 Edw. III* (Rolls Series), p. 172 (1340).

the hands of the lord's predecessor as abbot,[1] his wardrobe clerk,[2] or his wife.[3] Plaintiffs naturally sought to avoid being met by the defence of wager of law, and even resorted to fictitious pleadings for that purpose.[4] The converse, however, was also true; thus when a defendant alleged that he had paid some of the money to his lord and had tallies to show it, the lord was allowed to wage his law in denial.[5]

Legislation throws a sinister light upon the bailiff, for it devotes anxious consideration to the problem of the bailiff who absconds without discharging his debts to his lord. Even those who did not flee were beyond the effective reach of the law if they did not themselves own land, for process in the action of account ran against the defendant's land only. The statute of Marlborough (1267), c. 23 allowed the arrest of the landless bailiff, but the statute was easily evaded by acquiring a few penn'orth of land which the law had to accept as security for debts of hundreds of pounds.[6] It will be noticed that the landless bailiff is now a pressing problem; he is a man who has nothing but his managerial and commercial aptitudes to furnish him a living, a phenomenon for which the common law was quite unprepared. The situation was so desperate that in 1285 it was enacted that the absconding bailiff be outlawed[7]—the first occasion when outlawry was applied in civil procedure.[8] When the bailiff was at last brought to account, he was imprisoned forthwith (and without any application to a court) if

[1] *Y.BB. Edw. II* (Selden Society), xvi. 185 (1314).

[2] *Ibid.*, xxiv. 146 (1319); judgement is not recorded.

[3] *Y.B. 16 Edw. III* (Rolls Series), ii. 262–4 (1342).

[4] *Ibid.*, ii. 26 (1342).

[5] *Y.B. 20 Edw. III* (Rolls Series), i. 448 (1346).

[6] *Y.BB. Edw. II* (Selden Society), iii. 91–2 (1310), also reported *ibid.*, vi. 137, overruling the decision of Hengham, C. J. in *Y.B. 33–35 Edw. I* (Rolls Series), 6 (1305).

[7] Statute of Westminster II (1285), c. 11. For further details see Plucknett, *Legislation of Edward I*, pp. 152 ff. and *Statutes and their Interpretation*, pp. 84, 101, 134.

[8] Bracton, f. 440*b* merely says that it would be good if outlawry were possible in a mitigated form in certain violent trespasses.

he did not discharge his liabilities then and there. Only by using the heaviest artillery of the law was the bailiff at long last tamed.

Henceforward the bailiff is visibly on the defensive, and the cases show the sort of perils which beset him. There was some danger that he might be called upon to account twice,[1] for the lord seems to have been under no obligation to give his bailiff a formal discharge.[2] In practice, a rule had been evolved that when the account is closed, the bailiff should hand over to the lord or his auditors the rolls and tallies concerned with it; hence a lord who has these documents in his possession cannot demand an account. Whether this was also a rule of law, is less certain. The point was often raised, and once it was held that a lord who had invaded the bailiff's house *vi et armis* and made off with the rolls, was not entitled to an account;[3] but later cases seem less certain.[4] A further hazard was that a bailiff may have rashly accounted before the wrong auditors, whom the lord disavowed,[5] or that when the bailiff got the case removed into the exchequer (as was possible by statute[6]) he would there be confronted by other rolls than those on which the case had originally been brought.[7]

Although in general a man who is described as a 'bailiff' is liable to the action of account, it was not invariably so. As we have already noted, a bailiff may be appointed with the express provision that he shall not be accountable,[8] and there may even

[1] *Y.B. 20 & 21 Edw. I* (Rolls Series), p. 180 (1292).

[2] Technically the bailiff needed none; even when he was appointed and made accountable by deed, he could always aver, without producing a deed, that he had accounted: *Y.B. 11 & 12 Edw. III* (Rolls Series), p. 388 (1338).

[3] *Y.BB. Edw. II* (Selden Society), xxiv. 134–5 (1319).

[4] *Y.B. 14 Edw. III* (Rolls Series), p. 38 (1340); cf. the earlier case in *Y.B. 20 & 21 Edw. I* (Rolls Series), p. 180 (1292).

[5] *Y.B. 11 & 12 Edw. III* (Rolls Series), pp. 298–300 (1337).

[6] Statute of Westminster II (1285), c. 11.

[7] *Y.B. 17 & 18 Edw. III* (Rolls Series), p. 547 n. col. 1 (1344).

[8] *Supra*, p. 22 n. 1.

be cases where a 'bailiff' may succeed in showing that the burden of accountability ought to be cast on someone else—apart altogether from the terms of his appointment. This brings us to the situation considered by Mr Bennett, which was mentioned at the outset of this study, namely, that many of the surviving manorial accounts are submitted by reeves and not by bailiffs. The year-books afford further confirmation of that fact. Thus we find a bailiff successfully pleading that it was not he, but the reeve, who actually managed the manor and handled its issues, but since he was not very skilful, the lord asked the bailiff to keep an eye on what was being done.[1] A generation later another bailiff took issue on the allegation that the reeve, and not himself, was accountable.[2]

Bailiffs were doubtless handled somewhat roughly at times. The statute of 1285 actually required that the defaulting accountant should be put in irons. Thus in 1295 Peter Jakes[3] (although he was not accountable, so he said), was compelled to pursue his lord, the bishop of Bath, from Northumberland to London, having had the reeve's rolls[4] copied for the purpose. Lengthy and costly proceedings followed, and finally he spent a year in irons in the Fleet. Another complaint against the same redoubtable bishop was that no allowance was made for these heavy expenses, nor for his outlays in the course of his duties.

This was an important matter with which the courts had only occasionally to deal. The result of a successful action of account was simply that the defendant should account. The examination of the rolls and striking a balance was a subsequent stage, con-

[1] *Select Cases on Law Merchant* (Selden Society, 46), ii. p. xc (1304).

[2] *Y.B. 11 & 12 Edw. III* (Rolls Series), p. 488 (1338); at the top of p. 490 for 'foreman' read 'reeve'; it is an instructive case on pleading in actions of account. Cf. *Y.B. 15 Edw. III* (Rolls Series), p. 188 (1341) where the defendant raising this point is driven to take the general issue.

[3] *Select Cases before the King's Council* (Selden Society, 35), p. 11.

[4] In the second line of the translation *op. cit.*, p. 12 for 'manor' read 'reeve'.

ducted out of court, before auditors appointed by the lord,[1] and it was for the auditors to decide what allowances to make in favour of the bailiff. Such questions might be difficult, but seem very rarely to have been raised in court. The statute of 1285 authorized aggrieved accountants to appeal from auditors to the barons of the exchequer, and it is probably there, rather than in the common pleas, that law and practice developed; unfortunately too few plea rolls of the exchequer are in print to throw much light upon the proceedings there.[2] Certainly by 1319 it was settled that the liability of a bailiff in account was less onerous than that of a bailee at common law;[3] as Bereford, C. J. explained in words that need close attention:[4]

> A plea of account shall not be conducted by common law, but by equity and reason; for a man can be discharged in an account etc., where at law he would remain charged. Thus the answer that you give does not lie here before us, but before the auditors etc.

It will be observed that 'reason and equity' have their place not 'before us' (the judges of the common pleas), but 'before the auditors' where the common sense of experienced business men was working out principles based upon the natural and customary relationships between lord and bailiff or receiver. Those principles, whether 'equitable' or not, were only directly examined by the common pleas on rare occasions; indirectly, however, they had the sanction of the common law, because the final balance due upon an accounting could be recovered by an action of debt. It was in such an action that Bereford's words were repeated and expanded by Stonor, J. in a case where (as sometimes happened) the bailiff turned out to be a creditor instead of debtor on balance[5]:

[1] In the vast majority of cases accounting took place without having to use the action of account; but if the accounting was by judgement, the court might itself appoint the auditors.

[2] The case of Bogo de Clare may have reached the exchequer in this way: *Select Cases in the Exchequer of Pleas* (Selden Society, 48), no. 170 (1286).

[3] E. G. M. Fletcher, *Carrier's Liability*, p. 19; Coke, *On Littleton*, p. 89a.

[4] *Y.BB. Edw. II* (Seldon Society), xxiv. 147 (1319).

[5] Y.B. Hil. 19 Edw. II (Maynard edn.), f. 656 (1326).

Account shall be conducted by equity and not by the rigour of the law, as by allowing things which ought to be allowed and by disallowing things which ought to be disallowed; wherefore, since it is found before the auditors that he [the bailiff] had used his own money for the profit of the manor, and that allowance was given to him for this in the account, it seems that is enough to entitle him to be answered. Moreover, it was seen in the time of Sir Ralf de Hengham[1] that in a writ of account it had been found before the auditors that upon the account the plaintiff owed the defendant a certain sum, and by judgement execution was awarded to the defendant against the plaintiff.[2]

The fruitfulness of the action of account in introducing unfamiliar elements into the old common law is strikingly shown in such cases as this, and it has long been recognized that to the action of account we also owe the action 'for money had and received'.[3] Nor is it quite fanciful in that connection to link these fourteenth-century remarks on the 'equitable' features of the old action of account with the eighteenth-century pronouncements of Lord Mansfield that the count for money had and received rested upon *aequum et bonum*, and was equivalent to a bill in equity.[4]

So far, all this has been the law and practice of a peculiar institution, and did not apply to the public generally. Thus in 1318 a writ against one who had received money on behalf of another was abated because the defendant, although he had received, was not the plaintiff's 'common receiver';[5] and in the

[1] Hengham, C. J. left the bench in 1309 in consequence (it has been surmised) of the hostility of Piers Gaveston, and was succeeded by Bereford who was closely allied with the favourite: W. H. Dunham, *Radulphi de Hengham Summae*, pp. lviii–lix.

[2] The recovery by this means of moneys voluntarily laid out by a bailiff for the benefit of his lord merits attention. Later cases are concerned to protect lords from having extravagant expenditure imposed upon them by their bailiffs.

[3] J. B. Ames, *Lectures on Legal History*, pp. 119–21.

[4] P. H. Winfield, *Province of the Law of Tort*, pp. 127 ff; C. H. S. Fifoot, *Lord Mansfield*, pp. 141 ff; R. M. Jackson, *History of Quasi-Contract*, pp. 117 ff; Holdsworth, *History of English Law*, xii. 542 ff.

[5] *Y.BB. Edw. II* (Selden Society), xxii. 264.

next year Bereford declared 'the main point of this matter is that you were his receiver, and that is an office as much as a bailiffship, and is open to the cognizance of the country.'[1] By the end of the fourteenth century these limitations were being relaxed, and the action was allowed against persons who were not constituted bailiffs and receivers, but merely casual bailees or receivers, and notably against factors who for the purposes of the action were long described as 'bailiffs'.[2]

It has long been remarked that from the close of the Middle Ages (when this sort of question began to be agitated) until early in the eighteenth century the law consistently ascribed title in the goods to the factor, as it had done also to his historical predecessor, the bailiff.[3] Here we have a parallel in the matter of chattels with the bailiff's interest in his lord's land mentioned above. As we have seen, the bailiff lost that interest by 1285; by 1733 he and his successor (the factor) likewise lost his title to the goods entrusted to him.[4] At long last the law thus abandoned the most ancient survival of the mediaeval bailiff's legal status,[5] and was free to re-state the whole mass of rules in the modern language of agency.

The Bailiff's Place in History

In the course of this hasty scamper over varied and broken country, our object has been to keep the mediaeval bailiff always in view and to follow the trail of his activities wherever it

[1] *Y.BB. Edw. II* (Selden Society), xxiv. 147 (1319).

[2] Cases are cited in Plucknett, *Legislation of Edward I*, p. 151 n. 4.

[3] J. B. Ames, *Lectures on Legal History*, pp. 116–17.

[4] *Godfrey* v. *Furzo*, 3 P. Wms. 185.

[5] Unless it be (and this is, as yet, but pure conjecture) that the undisclosed principal is centuries older than *Scrimshire* v. *Alderton* (1743) 2 Str. 1182, and derived from the status of bailiff. If that is so, then the difficulties of this case would be clearly ascribable to the new fashion of stating the problem in terms, not of status, but of contract; hence the trouble encountered in searching for the 'consideration'. Alternatively, the fact that this case is only ten years after *Godfrey* v. *Furzo* may be a clue to this famous mystery. For a different view, see Müller-Freienfels, 'The Undisclosed Principal', *Modern Law Review*, xvi. at pp. 308–9.

may lead. The story necessarily began with the reeve, and it would be a falsification if we tried to disentangle the reeve from the bailiff, whom history itself has so intimately joined together. The Anglo-Saxon reeve had the same vast scale of activity as the bailiff; in both cases the word might mean anything from the foreman of a farm, to a key position in a large organization. In time the native English word was reserved for the humblest and most servile variety, and the more exalted took the French name of bailiff. There is no suggestion of a breach of continuity, but the new name may nevertheless have imported some change in the nature of the office; indeed, the word bailiff may be the result of a deliberate attempt to define the legal nature of the relationship as being essentially that of a bailment. It was a good beginning, and put the emphasis in the right place: the bailiff was indeed bailee (and even something more) of his lord's land and chattels, subject to the duty of account. In fact, he enjoyed wide and even dangerous powers which in the vague and untutored thought of the time looked somewhat like an interest in the land or chattels.[1] These powers were curbed earliest, as one would expect, where they concerned land. It is a measure of the bailiff's great importance that he should have made the lawyers think so hard and so long upon the vital question of the rights and duties of a man who is in control of property owned by another. The reeve, on the other hand, being unfree, had his problems settled for him summarily in his lord's domestic or manorial jurisdiction.

We need not be surprised that the courts found the bailiff a serious problem—so baffling as to drive them to the desperate remedy of talk about 'equity'—for we have seen what sort of man it was who entered the adventurous company of bailiffs. He was often without roots, and that in an age when the law hardly knew how to reach a landless defendant, but nevertheless he was keen-witted, literate but lay, acquisitive,

[1] For the 'haziness in the conception of ownership' see Pollock and Maitland, ii. 153, 177, 229.

harsh to his peasants, none too honest with his lord, whose misdeeds called down upon him some of the most stringent legislation of the Middle Ages. One thinks of Robert Carpenter (*ob. c.* 1267) whose 'treatise is unique, in that it gives explicit and illuminating instructions for "cooking" accounts'.[1] It is a fact of some significance that this pursuit of the bailiff has led us into legal history and the beginnings of the law of factors and agency; hitherto those who have written of the early history of agency—Holmes, Maitland, Holdsworth—have done so without considering the bailiff; the exceptions are Ames and Würdinger.[2] In the course of his history the bailiff has therefore covered a great deal of ground. We first made his acquaintance as the key man in the country's greatest industry, agriculture, and we have seen him trading with his lord's goods and receiving his lord's moneys on so vast a scale that the common law was compelled to make room for him by giving the action of account, and by cautiously accepting the principles which lords, bailiffs and auditors were working out in the less formal atmosphere of rendering account out of court. Just as the action of account was to become the remedy for the professional merchant and his partners, so the principles which it embodied served the purposes of the trader and the factor.

In the story of this ceaseless activity by bailiffs, there has been no lack of teasing and difficult problems; some things which seemed clear before, may now even seem obscure—but that is a common result when one proceeds further into a complicated matter. The thing to remember is that life is not simple, and that a simple picture of it is likely to be false. Nor must the investigator be deterred by 'technicalities'; after all, a technicality is nothing but a statement made with unusual brevity and exactness, and that is what a historian should prize most in his sources. In any case, they are inescapable, for the historian

[1] N. Denholm-Young, *Collected Papers on Mediaeval Subjects*, p. 100.

[2] Ames, in the *Lectures*, and Hans Würdinger, *Geschichte der Stellvertretung (agency) in England* (1933).

must use all the sources which can throw light upon his subject, and when that subject is so busy a man as the mediaeval bailiff it becomes apparent that the social, economic and legal sides of life are inseparable, and that legal history, like all the rest, is part of that history, one and indivisible, which we all profess.

VI

THE RISE OF THE ENGLISH STATE TRIAL

Recent events in several countries have drawn attention to the state trial. Whatever the political régime in force, such trials seem to be inevitable, although their frequency may well be taken as an index of the political health of the country in which they occur. The study of state trials and their history seems to have been seriously neglected, however. The English lawyer is apt to dismiss the subject on the ground that the courts, the law and the procedure of "state" trials differ in no way from those applicable to any other trial; this most happily is true of the present time and place, but it has not always been true, even of English state trials. The political historian often succumbs to the temptation of regarding their outcome as inevitable —like the other things which did happen, and so probably had to happen—and hence of concluding that they were little more than political vindictiveness veiled under legal forms. If the older disciplines of law and political history have neglected the state trial, there are newer studies which might well examine it, especially in relation to the modern mysticisms which prevail in so many countries to-day.

It is no exaggeration to say that the state trial is part of the technique of politics in some countries, combining art and science in the service of the all-important object of preserving the established government. The nature of a state trial inevitably implies some of these developments. Its aim, like the aim of all trials, is not to find facts but to present facts before an audience. Normally the audience is a judge or jury whose function is to test the facts and ascertain their legal consequences. At all periods, however, governments have had a larger audience in mind. Mediæval chroniclers often give detailed accounts of state trials which evidently were supplied from official quarters; the sentence on the Despensers was so widely circulated that most manuscript collections of statutes contain it.[1] Narratives of many state trials were circulated by the printing press in the seventeenth and eighteenth centuries, and the recent development of broadcasting and filming such proceedings is only a natural adaptation. The end in view is clearly to confirm the political faith of the public, and to create an impression of the government's strength and stability. Rather different is the variation which goes to the opposite extreme of secrecy. The secret trial is at least as old as the inquisition, and was originally the product less of policy than of a confusion of the two processes of fact-finding (which like all criminal investigation must take place in private) and adjudication. The use of written minutes of evidence instead of evidence given orally in court naturally led to adjudication likewise being carried out in private, for the consideration of a large mass of written matter can hardly take place in the presence of a crowd of bystanders. The result was a more or less secret trial wherever this written procedure was followed—and it was followed (in civil matters) in our chancery as well as in the criminal procedure of the mediæval inquisition. Once established, secret trials were found to have a strong psychological effect, creating fear akin to terror. The present tendency seems to be for state trials to be either very secret, or very public. Added to this, is a tendency, strongly marked at the present moment, for these trials to be conducted by special courts instead of in the ordinary tribunals. This seems to be the result of the modern practice of erecting institutions merely to illustrate an ideology.

The history of the English state trial is a comparatively sober affair, but neverthess worthy of attention. The fact that this history has never been systematically explored is due in part to the general considerations already mentioned—a state trial at the present day is merely a more sensational criminal trial which has political implications. Historians of criminal law have therefore dismissed those cases which do not conform to the general type of a common-law trial as irregular and as perversions of judicial forms for political ends. This attitude is surely open to question. A government generally tries to create the impression that its opponents are being lawfully and justly tried; it will do its best to escape the charge of arranging a flagrant judicial murder by conceding all it can to the sentiment

[1] It duly appears, even in printed editions, e.g. *Statutes of the Realm*, I, 181.

of the public. Any procedure which to us looks unfamiliar ought to be carefully scrutinised in order to see whether it is really a perversion, or a procedure which was in fact legitimate for the purpose at that time. There is also a more special reason for the neglect of the subject, in that the materials have not been collected, although they are certainly voluminous. The series generally called *The State Trials*[1] is far from satisfactory. It contains hardly any material before the seventeenth century, and the large mass of matter for the Stuart period which it presents is largely a reprint of unofficial pamphlets which themselves came from interested sources. Indeed, it has been forcibly argued[2] that the collection owes its origin to the enterprise of bookseller-politicians whose aim was to blacken the memory of the Stuarts after the Revolution.

The seventeenth-century state trial, therefore, raises preliminary problems of historical evidence which yet await solution. The mediæval sources, on the other hand, are in a state which enables us to use them with some confidence, and hence to lay the foundations for a study of the earlier state trials as a whole. There is one fundamental contrast between a mediæval and a modern trial which must be emphasised at the outset. At the present day, the public, lay and professional, expects a trial to be substantially fair. That is to say, we expect an open trial, with opportunities for preparing a defence, and for putting it before the court. We expect evidence to be presented orally, and to be subject to searching criticism. In short, we look primarily to the problem of proof. In the middle ages, legal development had hardly reached this stage. We know very little of how the problem of proof was handled in jury trials; in all probability its importance had hardly yet been realised. There was certainly very little that a modern lawyer would regard as a law of evidence. It may very well be that even jury trial was still regarded as something like an ordeal, an appeal to a body which reached decisions by means which defied investigation. Consequently, the emphasis rested not on the problem of proof, but upon the orderly conduct of the proceedings as a whole. A mediæval critic would demand that the procedure of a trial should be flawless, that all the "delays" should be accorded, that the writs and rolls should be scrupulously accurate, that there

[1] Edited in 34 volumes by Cobbett and Howell, 1809–1823. There is a continuation in eight more volumes by Sir John Macdonell, 1888–1890.

[2] J. G. Muddiman, *State Trials: the need for a new and revised edition* (Edinburgh, 1930).

should be no " error on the record." In taking this attitude, the mediæval lawyer was concentrating upon a problem which he knew was within his competence, and which was for centuries to be fundamental. A rigidly settled procedure is the first requirement for the development of a legal system, and the middle ages achieved it.

Procedure can be written down in technical terminology with a high degree of precision, and so the mediæval records are easier to use in reconstructing the essentials (as they were then understood) of a state trial, than are the attempts to give verbatim reports of oral evidence in the seventeenth century trials. It is therefore in a study of mediæval procedure that we can trace the development of the English state trial and watch the gradual supersession of archaic by more modern ideas. The earliest period, for which chroniclers are the main source, is naturally difficult to handle briefly, but the murder of Piers Gaveston by Thomas of Lancaster in 1312 began a feud which dominated our history for some two hundred years, and the state trials which marked its progress are to be found in abundance upon the endless series of rolls which still survive. The following remarks are confined to a very few of the cases available, and do not pretend to offer a final conclusion; they do claim, however, to establish the fact that the state trial deserves careful study from the constitutional, legal and social points of view.

The series begins with two cases which show a striking contrast, one of them—*Berkeley's case* (1330)—presenting an appearance of sweet reasonableness which has convinced every modern historian that the government intended to spill whitewash rather than blood. The recorded procedure suggests an oral altercation cast into the form of rather unusual pleadings. Thomas of Berkeley appeared in custody before the lords in parliament, and it was said to him that he had been the custodian of the deposed Edward II, who had been murdered in Berkeley castle; how would he acquit himself of that death? Thomas answered that this was the first he had heard of the murder, and that he had had nothing to do with it. The point was then put to him that since he was Edward's custodian, he ought to excuse himself. Berkeley had his excuse ready—he was ill at the time, and was not in the castle when the crime was alleged to have been committed. The court then put a further proposition: Berkeley appointed his own servants, was he not responsible for them? To this he answered that he trusted his servants as himself, and so finally pleads not guilty. Seven weeks later a jury of fellow knights found him not guilty, but parliament reserved the legal point of his liability for his servants.[1]

It is a curious case. Modern historians have destroyed Berkeley's *alibi* from his own household accounts[2]; his claim to have heard nothing of the rumoured murder until his trial is quite incredible; his deep complicity in the mysterious end of Edward II is beyond doubt. It is the procedure, however, which concerns us. He was brought before a regular court, parliament; he was accused (although not indicted); he was invited to defend himself, and did so, both by pleading facts, and denying (by implication) a point of law; his plea of not guilty was tried by a jury of knights who were his peers. The main outline of the case is reasonable and looks quite modern compared with others which we shall have to consider, but its most striking feature is the novel rule of law which Berkeley had to meet, namely, that an employer (or, in any case, a gaoler) was criminally responsible if his servant murdered a prisoner. The point seems not to have been decided, but we must note the important fact that a state trial in the early fourteenth century may involve rules of law which are not yet established in the ordinary criminal law.

Only eight years earlier, in 1322, very different proceedings had resulted in the condemnation of Thomas, Earl of Lancaster. Taken prisoner at the battle of Boroughbridge, this turbulent peer was brought immediately into the presence of the king, seven other earls, and an unspecified number of barons and magnates. Thereupon the king "recorded" a long (but by no means exhaustive) list of Lancaster's misdeeds, and notably that he had burnt and slain and had offered resistance to the king in warlike array with his (Lancaster's) banners flying, "which treasons, homicides, arsons and hostile wars are manifest and notorious to the earls, barons and other magnates, and to the people of the realm. Wherefore it is adjudged that the said earl Thomas be drawn for the treasons, hanged for the homicides, robberies and arsons, and beheaded for the flight."[3] His sentence was richly deserved, but the manner of his

[1] *Rot. Parl.*, II, 57 (16).

[2] The latest discussion is in Tout, *Collected Papers*, III, 174.

[3] The proceedings were put on the close and patent rolls (printed in Rymer, *Fœdera* (1818), II, 478) and were recited verbatim in the reversal of the judgment in 1327 (*Rot. Parl.*, II, 3, printed from the close roll).

condemnation raised highly important questions. The body which tried him made no pretence of being a court, regular or irregular. Contemporaries seem to have thought that it was an example of military justice. However that may be, the record clearly bases the procedure upon the principles of record and notoriety. These deserve examination, for at all periods the non-lawyer is apt to be impatient when he is asked for a formal proof of events which he regards as self-evident: at times there is the further temptation to regard the statement of an important personage as conclusive. These tendencies are not confined to state trials, whether mediæval or modern.

The irrefutable record of the king was a royal prerogative from quite early times. At the end of the seventh century we find that the king's unsworn word was nevertheless incontrovertible[1]; after the conquest this is expanded into the statement that things done in his presence cannot subsequently be denied[2]; in 1224 we have a note that the testimony of the king, whether oral or by charter, surpasses all other proof.[3] Nor is Lancaster's case merely an example of an archaism, for the following reign still shows us a judge stating that "when the king records anything of his own view, that record shall never be annulled; but when he records on the information of others, that record may be defeated."[4] Further examples are to be found in two statutes which deserve more attention than they have yet received. The first enacted that when one or more justices of the peace are informed that a "forcible entry" has been committed, they may take the *posse comitatus* and verify the fact, and put the offenders in the county gaol "there to abide convicted by the record of the said justice or justices."[5] That was in 1391. Early in the next century the same principle was applied to riot when it was enacted that two or more justices of the peace, and the sheriff or under-sheriff, should have power to arrest rioters and "to record what they shall find done in their presence against law," and that offenders so taken should be regarded as convicted.[6]

[1] Wihtred 16.

[2] Leis Willelme 24. This principle was then extended to the king's courts: see the able discussion of these matters by Thorne, "Notes on courts of record in England," *West Virginia Law Quarterly Review*, XL, 347.

[3] *Bracton's Note Book*, 239 (cf. 226 margin).

[4] Y.B. 12–13 Edw. III, 101 (1338); cf. 183.

[5] 15 Rich. II, c. 2.

[6] 13 Hen. IV, c. 7 (1411). A different procedure is provided where the offenders are not arrested on the scene of the riot.

The above examples are sufficient to show that the peculiar force of the king's record was well known both before and after Lancaster's case, and that the notion of a conviction summarily following such a "record" was even extended to justices of the peace who could record the participation in a riot of such persons as they arrested *flagrante delicto.*[1]

The king did not rely entirely upon the efficacy of his oral record against Earl Thomas, for he further alleged that the earl's offences were manifest and notorious to his judges and to all the realm. This concept of "notoriety" has played a large part in the development of criminal procedure and deserves examination. Thus the hand-having and back-bearing thief was led to instant execution—the *maynour* rendered his guilt so evident and notorious that no denial could be allowed.[2] Between "obvious" facts, and beliefs strongly held, the line is thin, and confusion was often made between the two. Hence punishment will fall upon the one who is "suspected," *malecreditus*, of ill-repute, *diffamatus*, who may soon be called a "common malefactor." Our grand jury acted upon such local reputation—that was its function, and the trial jury too must often have judged by the same means in the centuries before the rise of the modern practice of informing the jury by oral testimony. At first, perhaps, it was thought that such notorious ill-fame amounted to proof, but the better (and perhaps later) opinion was that it was a specific and different offence.[3] Thus, to be a heretic was an ecclesiastical offence, and to be suspected of heresy was another and still very serious offence.[4] We can sometimes see the transition, especially when the mode of proof imposed upon a suspect is so difficult and dangerous that it comes to be regarded, not as a hazardous defence open to a suspect, but as a punishment for being suspected.[5]

Such, then, is the general character of Lancaster's trial.

[1] Other legislation of the period shows that this procedure was made necessary by the fears of grand juries who dared not indict rioters.

[2] Pollock and Maitland, *History of English Law*, II, 496. Whether the practice was followed in the royal courts (as Maitland held, *ibid.*, 579–580) is not so clear. The common enrolment *non potest dedicere* seems to mean that the accused had in fact no defence to offer, rather than that he was debarred by law from presenting a defence even when he had one. Many presentments of misdemeanour in local courts were not traversable in the thirteenth century, as Maitland, *op. cit.*, 653 shows, although they were traversable from the early fourteenth century before justices of the peace.

[3] Eighteenth century vagrancy legislation (some of which is still with us) makes suspicious conduct an offence merely because it is suspicious.

[4] Lyndwoode, *Provinciale* (ed. 1679), 290 gl. *pugnaverit.*

[5] The language of the gloss by Lyndewoode cited in the last note strikingly illustrates this transition.

It was by no means unique, nor is it difficult to find cases very near it in date which present variations in detail. One which may be recalled here is the trial of Andrew Harclay, Earl of Carlisle, in 1323. His trial took place before special commissioners (an earl, three lords of parliament, a household official, and Geoffrey Scrope, who a few months later became a judge). These persons were given two documents : a commission to degrade and judge Harclay according to a certain form, and the " form " in question. The record of their proceedings enrolled on the King's Bench roll[1] shows that they recited their commission, and pronounced judgment in the very words of the " form." That document contained a statement of Harclay's treasonable correspondence with Bruce, and a list of his other treasons " which are notorious and known in the realm, and which our lord the king records." Once again we find the two elements of notoriety and royal record which together exclude the accused from any defence.[2]

Widespread as was the use of this procedure, to contemporaries it seemed that there was something distinctively military about it, and there are examples of its use in the court of the constable and marshal against some of Lancaster's fellow rebels—Roger Damory, for example[3]—as well as several examples closely following Harclay's case. This very question was raised when Henry of Lancaster brought a petition in the parliament of 1327 for the reversal of the judgment against his brother.[4] The writ of error and the proceedings upon it were in normal form, and procedurally there is nothing in the case which calls for comment. The points raised in the pleadings, however, are of the highest constitutional and legal interest.

The first error assigned is that Earl Thomas was condemned " without arraignment and without answer." Much has been written about arraignment[5] : in later times a mere ceremony, it nevertheless came to be the symbol of a common law trial, for its original signification was the putting of a

[1] The case also illustrates the pitfalls created by the lack of a collected edition of mediæval state trials. The late L. O. Pike in Y.B. 12 & 13 Edw. III, xxxii, congratulated himself on having discovered the record on the plea roll, thanks to a clue in the Petyt MSS. He was unaware that the record had been printed in full over sixty years earlier in Palgrave, *Parliamentary Writs*, II, ii, app. 262.

[2] The same procedure was used against the Mortimers (see the record rehearsed later, in *Cal. Pat.* (1327–1330) 141–143).

[3] Palgrave, *Parliamentary Writs*, II, ii, app. 261.

[4] *Rot. Parl.*, II, 3 (printed from the close roll).

[5] Pike, introduction to Y.B. 19 Edw. III, xxxvi ff. ; Hale, *History of the Pleas of the Crown*, II, 216.

prisoner to answer, and inviting him to make his defence. A further error assigned was stated in the form of a principle: the king ought not to "record" the guilt of a person in time of peace, the implication being that that procedure is legitimate in war time. Lancaster put forward a most interesting suggestion on the test to be applied in order to distinguish peace time from war time. The earl's offences, and his capture and trial took place in peace time, he urged, mainly "because the chancery and other places of the king's court were open and administering justice in the accustomed manner to all who sought it throughout that period, nor did the king ride with banner displayed during that period." A subject therefore may raise a revolt in warlike array without necessarily creating a state of war, and the principal test for recognising the existence of a state of war is the suspension of the normal work of the courts.

The importance of these pleas can be realised by comparing them with the Petition of Right three hundred years later, which asserted equally well that martial law was inapplicable in time of peace. Henry of Lancaster's claim of 1327, however, is more developed than that of the men of 1628, for the Petition of Right did not attempt a definition of time of peace. That definition was well known, however, for Coke stated it[1] in 1628 and cited Lancaster's Case as the authority, and the rule was also to be found in the Year Books of Edward III.[2] The judgments against the Mortimers (which followed the model of that upon Andrew Harclay) were reversed at the same time as Lancaster's, and for the same reasons.[3]

These cases therefore became ultimately of great constitutional importance, and might have become immediately a turning point in the history of English state trials. Party passion however seems to have been stronger than legal theory, and the main principle of these cases of 1327 was abandoned shortly afterwards, in 1330, when the younger Mortimer was again on trial.[4] This time the record is on the parliament roll, and the trial took place in parliament, possibly in view of Lancaster's objection that he ought to have been tried by his fellow peers. Nor did the king

[1] Co. Lit., 249b.
[2] Y.B. 14 Edw. III, 140.
[3] *Cal. Pat.* (1327–1330), 141–143. They had not been executed: the uncle died in prison and the nephew escaped.
[4] *Rot. Parl.*, II, 52.

venture to "record" the guilt of the accused. If (as contemporaries seem to have thought) that procedure was essentially a military one, there could be no ground for using it against Mortimer: he had not rebelled, but was the victim of the young king's *coup d'état.* His crimes were not "recorded," therefore, but the king claimed that they were "notorious," and the proceedings went forward on that assumption. The entry on the roll concludes with some narrative passages, but the beginning is obviously a transcript of a document headed "These are the treasons, felonies and crimes committed by Roger Mortimer and his accomplices against our lord the king and his people." Fourteen counts follow, and conclude with a charge by the king "to you earls and barons, peers of his realm . . . that you make a right and lawful judgment such as one ought to have who is guilty (as he believes) of the above crimes, which are notorious and known to be true to you and all the people of the realm." Whether these last words are part of the document, or a report of an oral accusation matters little. The peers retired, returned with a message that the charges were notorious, and as judges of parliament adjudged with the king's assent that Mortimer be drawn and hanged. The earl marshal was charged with the duty of arranging for the execution. At the same time, and apparently by a similar procedure, Sir Simon Bereford was condemned and executed, and some others were condemned in their absence. One point only gave rise to misgivings: the peers protested that they were under no duty to adjudge by these methods persons who were not members of their order.

At least some of the points raised by Henry of Lancaster were confirmed in Mortimer's Case. There was indeed no "record" of conviction, but the element most wholeheartedly adopted was the insistence on peerage. Unlike Lancaster, Mortimer was judged by all his peers, and the peers took the opportunity to insist on the peculiarities of their order, and carried out their sentence through their own officer, the earl marshal. Some of the worst features of the proceedings in 1322 were retained. The principle that "notorious" facts need no proof and admit of no defence was accepted, and consequently there was no arraignment.

Nevertheless, it was almost the last great case where such procedure was used, and by this time "record" and "notoriety" must have begun to look archaic. Edward III "recorded" the treason of David Marshall,[1] but shortly afterwards discovered that he was innocent.[2] Notoriety serves a more reasonable function when it is stated that it may suffice to put the accused upon his trial,[3] just as *maynour* itself will take the place of an indictment,[4] neither of them now operating as a conviction. The old scope of "record" was openly denied in Marshall's Case where Sjt. Birton said that "it is ordained by statute that the king ought never to record save by due process"—words full of future significance.[5] The editor was unable to identify the "statute," but it seems to have been an allusion to parliament's reversal in the Lancaster Case. The condemnation of Mortimer was finally reversed in parliament nearly a quarter of a century later when it was held to be erroneous forasmuch as he had not been put to answer.[6] Notorious facts, therefore, like facts recorded by the king, will no longer suffice for a conviction without defence—and it is noteworthy that the knights of the shire and all the other commons participated in the judgment (1354). For the future, even in parliament, notorious facts will be merely ground for putting the accused upon his trial (although the process may be abbreviated, and contumacy result in a specially rapid outlawry.)[7]

In the end, therefore, the two reversals, Lancaster's and Mortimer's, established the rule that arraignment and hence an opportunity for defence were essential to a valid trial. Both cases moreover illustrated the need for peers to be judged by all their fellow peers, and so parliament comes into great prominence as the court for state trials. Even commoners were tried there (although under protest), and the commons joined with the lords in reversing Mortimer's condemnation. It is difficult to escape the conclusion that parliament was already laying claim to be the proper court for state trials. This view was expressed with great clearness when Archbishop Stratford maintained that peers who were also ministers of the crown could only be tried

[1] Y.B. 12 & 13 Edw. III, 101.

[2] *Ibid.*, cii.

[3] Ex-Chief Justice Willoughby on his trial objected to the absence of an indictment: "the king is informed by the clamour of his people" was the answer he received. Y.B. 14 & 15 Edw. III, 259 (1340).

[4] Y.B. 17 Edw. III, 215 (1343).

[5] Y.B. 12 & 13 Edw. III, 101. Willoughby, C. J., disputed this (above, footnote 3), but clearly tried to make the old theory tolerable by adding a qualification to it.

[6] *Rot. Parl.*, II, 255–6.

[7] *Rot. Parl.*, III, 316–7 (1393) is an illustration.

for official misconduct in parliament and nowhere else.[1] For the remainder of the middle ages, state trials are largely parliamentary trials, the rival jurisdictions of the constable, marshal and steward competing fitfully but unsuccessfully. The procedures based on " record " and " notoriety " were not essentially parliamentary in their origin, and their abandonment still left parliament with a choice between the common law type of procedure (of which Berkeley's case has already been cited as an example), and other modes of action more peculiarly its own. Of these, impeachment and attainder came to be the most conspicuous, and their development deserves investigation. In effect, we had created special procedures for state trials, and had come very near to confining them to a special court, parliament, by the end of the fourteenth century. In drawing attention to the problem of the " Origin of Impeachment " the late Miss M. V. Clarke has done good service.[2] Starting from the accepted point of view that " the impeachments of 1376 were a daring novelty," she examined the antecedent legislation and cases, stressing most properly the inherent contradictions which they contained. Jealousy of the council and chancery had in fact provoked the opposition to exalt the Great Charter as the palladium of legal liberties. Trial by due process was their watch-word.[3] But their only device to guarantee due process was the threat of a state trial in parliament of those who had offended.[4] In other words, justice according to the common law was to be protected by means of extraordinary proceedings in parliament. The inevitable results were the proscriptions of the fifteenth century and the triumph of conciliar law enforcement under the Tudors. So desperate a remedy was clearly the product of a psychological crisis. The Walton Ordinances of 1338 had resulted in " a new efficiency " in administration ; taxation was heavy ; the war was failing ; subsidies to foreign allies were costly and ineffectual ; king and people suspected the embezzlement of public funds. John of Gaunt, who should have been the leader of the opposition, had always belied the

[1] 15 Edw. III, stat. 1, c. 3 (1341). Certain officials, not being peers, were also made justiciable in parliament by c. 4. A full narrative is given by Dr. Lapsley in *English Historical Review*, XXX, 6 ff, 193 ff. For Edward's withdrawal of the statute because his assent to it was " feigned," see Richardson and Sayles in *Law Quarterly Review*, L. 550.

[2] In *Oxford Essays in Medieval History presented to H. E. Salter*, reprinted in Clarke, *Fourteenth Century Studies*, 242–71.

[3] 5 Edw. III, c. 9 (1331); 25 Edw. III, st. 5, c. 4 (1351); 28 Edw. III, c. 3 (1354); 42 Edw. III, c. 3 (1368).

[4] 15 Edw. III, st. 1, cc. 1 and 3 (1341).

great name of Lancaster. As the situation grew worse, the sense of frustration which oppressed the public grew deeper, and more desperate measures came to be discussed.

However "novel" the proceedings of 1376, there were precedents for most of the separate elements which composed them, although not, perhaps, for their combination into the form of impeachment. Miss Clarke's essay is somewhat discursive, and unhappily uses the word "indictment" in a number of senses, but her view of the main course of events seems fairly clear. She points out that criminal proceedings before the council were begun by a bill, "suggestion," or "information," instead of by indictment as at common law. Now council and parliament were intimately connected, and the earliest "impeachments" may have taken place largely before the council. Here, then, she suggests is a clue to the origin of the new procedure. Moreover, the commons in parliament on several occasions presented petitions complaining of official misconduct, and a judicial enquiry by the council sometimes was the result. Miss Clarke cites, as a good example, the petition of William Latimer in 1368 complaining of the oppressions he had suffered at the hands of Sir John de la Lee.[1] As a result Lee was brought before the king, lords, and some of the commons, and the petitions of Latimer and of some other (unspecified) persons were set forth against him by the chief justice of the common pleas. Lee gave an explanation which the lords regarded as insufficient, and Lee was committed to the Tower. From the Tower he was brought before the great council and further examined, after which the council gave specific relief to Latimer and others who had lost lands to Lee, ordered the restitution of several deeds, and the cancellation of others.

The case is interesting since it had a marked political aspect (Lee was steward of the household), but we venture to suggest that it will not bear the interpretation which Miss Clarke put upon it when she wrote: "Though the details of the procedure are obscure, it seems clear that Lee was tried on information laid in parliamentary petitions and in the presence of certain of the commons," and that "it is not too much to conclude that the petition is beginning to take on the appearance of an indictment." The petition was to the council; there is nothing to connect it with the commons for it was the individual complaint of Latimer

[1] *Rot. Parl.*, II, 297; Clarke, *Fourteenth Century Studies*, 258–59.

himself. The other petitions are nowhere associated with the commons and were doubtless of the same nature. The proceedings in parliament took place after the king's farewell dinner to the commons, who had just voted supplies. The roll does not connect the commons with the proceedings in any way, save by the fact that some of them were present. The whole case is typical of the relief which the council gave, and of the council's procedure, and the effective decisions were reached by the lords and the council, who combined (in a way typical of council proceedings) criminal and civil equity. The petition is still far from an "indictment." It is still more difficult to see the connection of William of Windsor's case with the development of impeachment, for the charges of which he was tried by the council were based upon indictments regularly taken in Ireland.

We suggest as an alternative hypothesis that the material discussed earlier in this paper contains a more likely clue. The characteristics of impeachment are that the trial is in parliament, by the lords, and is initiated by the exhibition of articles by the commons, and without indictment. Such lists of charges we have seen preferred by the king in the earlier part of the century.[1] They were at first a terrible weapon, being "of record," and containing "notorious" matter, and operated as an immediate conviction. We have seen that these practices were rejected in calmer moments, but only in part. "Notoriety" was still enough to put Sir Richard Willoughby, an ex-chief justice, upon his trial before a royal commission of oyer and terminer in 1340, without an indictment[2]—the king "was informed by the clamour of his people." Willoughby's case, moreover, contains another element of great significance for our purpose, for the proceedings continued with the reading of "several bills which were not affirmed by pledges."[3] In one of these, the "commune" of the county of Nottingham complained of divers extortions; another bill came from the "commune" of the county of Lancaster. Here we have one of the most characteristic features of impeachment, namely, the accusation by a "commonalty" instead of by an individual. It is rare for proceedings before commissions of oyer and terminer to appear in the Year Books, and

[1] It was proceedings of this sort which led Charles I to believe that it was still possible for the Crown as well as the commons to initiate an impeachment.

[2] Y.B. 14–15 Edw. III, 258.

[3] That is to say, they were not put in by an individual complainant who had given security for prosecuting.

very little is known of how cases were tried before them. Whether this case of 1340 is unique or not, it is impossible to say at present, but in any case its significance seems clear.

How short was the step from this communal accusation before the commissioners, to an accusation[1] by the commons in parliament, will be seen by examining the two earliest cases of "impeachment" (in 1376) as they are reckoned by modern historians. They began with a London merchant and financier, Richard Lyons, who "was impeached and accused by the commons of divers deceits, extortions and other misdeeds" which were described in some detail (principally levying taxes without the assent of parliament, and embezzling the proceeds), and "notoriously taking unto himself royal power." Some oral evidence was heard, Lyons made his defence, and he was sentenced "according to the quantity and horriblety of the trespass"; which did not prevent the lords imposing another sentence a little later—or Alice Perrers procuring him a full pardon later still. The next case was that of William, Lord Latimer, who "was impeached by the clamour of the said commons" upon a long and detailed list of articles "whereof a bill was delivered into parliament." Then, "forasmuch as no individual person would openly accuse the said lord of these matters in parliament, save the commons who were ready to maintain the accusations in common," Lord Latimer was heard in his defence, to which both commons and lords replied. Next William Ellis was impeached "by the surmise of the commons" (supplemented in the course of the proceedings by bills brought by several injured parties). A number of other cases followed, many of them described as impeachments: one case was promoted by the commons on behalf of the Prior of Ecclesfield, but the prior was told to bring his bill and proceed in the ordinary way. An attempt by the bishop of Norwich to have a judgment of the common pleas reversed in parliament was firmly stopped by the decision that he must first pass by the King's Bench.

The proceedings in these cases were orderly, much evidence was heard, and due limits observed. The impeachment was kept fairly distinct from proceedings upon bill by individuals, the original and the appellate jurisdictions of parliament

[1] An intermediate stage may be the participation (noted above) of the commons in the reversal of Mortimer's' Case in 1354.

were kept clearly separate. The function of the commons was described as being to accuse when no private prosecutor dared come forward. The basis of their role was notoriety, clamour, surmise. The process of impeachment is therefore a combination of familiar elements rather than a new invention. If notorious facts no longer mean a conviction out of hand, they are still potent enough to put the offender upon his trial, and if the commons of Nottingham and the commons of Lancaster could put Willoughby to answer in 1340, the commons of the land could fairly accuse Lyons, Latimer and the rest in 1376, for parliament's original criminal jurisdiction was undoubted throughout the middle ages.

The most awkward question was whether this was really "due process." Parliament had so often and so recently asserted that proceedings could only be begun by original writ, by appeal, or by indictment, that the contrast is unescapable. It is this contrast which makes 1376 a turning point in the history of the English state trial. In spite of the roots of every detail in the past, the procedure as a whole was new, and the contrast with common law principles had to be admitted and expressed in a new dogma. The fourteenth century seems to have been full of strange projects. A new theory of peerage was taking shape with especial emphasis upon the hereditary officers of the crown. A pamphlet exalting the powers of the Lord High Constable made its appearance[1]; another magnified the Lord High Steward[2]; we have already noted a significant reference to the Earl Marshal; parliament itself was the subject of the mystifying *Modus Tenendi Parliamentum*, which most scholars attribute to the period of Richard II.[3] Still more serious was the action of the lords appellant in 1388. Appeals of treason, often involving trial by battle, have been brought at various dates in the court of king's bench, and now they spread to the court of the constable (where procedure was alleged to be according to civil law) and thence—for the first time—to parliament. This proceeding, unprecedented in parliament, at once raised the crucial question of which body of law should apply. The judges, serjeants and civilians were asked to advise, and answered that in either

[1] In *Black Book of the Admiralty* (ed. Twiss), I, 301–30.

[2] In L. W. V. Harcourt, *His Grace the Steward*, 164–67 (the date is possibly close to that of the *Modus*).

[3] In M. V. Clarke, *Medieval Representation and Consent*, 374–84 (her argument that the *Modus* is as early as Edward II has not been generally accepted).

event the appeals were invalid, both at common law and by civil law. This politic report gave an obvious opportunity of quashing the appeals and shelving the question, but that was not what the lords wanted. They over-ruled the judges and placed upon their rolls an extraordinary statement[1] which represents the high-water mark of their pretensions. With the king's consent, and by common accord, they resolved as follows :—

> "In a crime so high as that alleged in this appeal touching the king's person and the state of all his realm, committed by persons who are peers of the realm together with others, the case shall be conducted in parliament and nowhere else, and in accordance with no other law but the law and course of parliament ;
>
> and it pertains to the lords of parliament, and to their franchise and liberty by ancient custom of parliament, to be the judges in such cases, and to judge them with the assent of the king ;
>
> and thus it shall be done in this case by award of parliament, forasmuch as the realm of England has never heretofore been ruled or governed by the civil law, and it is not the intention of the king and the lords of parliament that it ever shall be ;
>
> nor is it their intent to rule or govern so high a cause as this appeal (which shall not be tried or determined elsewhere than in parliament as aforesaid) by the course, process and order used in any inferior court or bench within the realm, for such courts and benches are merely the administrators [*executours*] of the ancient laws and customs of the realm, and of the ordinances and establishments of parliament ;
>
> and in the opinion of the lords of parliament, and with the king's assent, this appeal was sufficiently well and duly brought and affirmed, and the process thereupon was good and effectual according to the law and course of parliament, and such they award and adjudge it to be."

The hasty and well-meaning measures of the Good Parliament of 1376 led inevitably to this ominous declaration of the Merciless Parliament of 1388. Henceforward we were to have state trials in the special sense of the words —trials of a political character before a special tribunal, parliament, and unfettered by the common law, or any

[1] *Rot. Parl.*, III, 236.

other law save the "law and course of parliament." That result was the work of the fourteenth century, and the present study, confined as it is to a few cases, and to the procedure employed in them, might well have been amplified by fuller reference to the political factors, to other procedures besides impeachment (notably attainder, which still awaits investigation), and to the important questions of substantive law involved, which contributed to this result. No doubt, three centuries later the state trial was tamed, and indeed set a good example to the common law, but in the meanwhile it proved to be a fearful weapon in the battles of political factions. The creation of such an institution, so contradictory to the tradition of the common law, and openly denying the middle age's noblest conception, the rule of law, is well worth study; but that study can hardly be placed upon a firm basis until we have a comprehensive collection of mediæval state trials.

VII

DEEDS AND SEALS

One of the more pleasant aspects of academic life is the informal chat between a professor and a young historian when they plan together a very necessary and illuminating book. It will be agreed that the subject is of high interest from several points of view, that the material is adequate—indeed, abundant, and that it might well prove to be a *magnum opus* upon which a respectable reputation could be built. Some of the main problems of the subject will be briefly indicated, some daring guesses will emerge (of course, suitably qualified with the remark that 'there may be nothing in it, but it might be worth looking into'), and a wealth of references will be given to the more obscure foreign periodicals.

After a pleasant hour the young inceptor withdraws, half flattered, half frightened at the prospect before him, and finishes up, as often as not, in politics or a bank. (My experience, as you know, is mainly from schools of law and economics.) The master has long been used to that sort of thing and comforts himself with the thought that in any case he has been sowing good seed, and it only needs luck for some of it to fall on propitious soil. Occasionally the book actually comes into existence, but the chances are that the subject has taken a new shape, that the sources fail at the critical moment, and that instead of solving the problems which interested the proposer, it raises others which attract him less. Most frequently, however, he is spared that disappointment, and rests with the feeling that at least the good seed was sown, and that sowing seed is a graceful gesture (as French postage stamps used to remind us), and not at all strenuous.

The remarks I am about to lay before you are very much of the sort just indicated, at least in this respect, that they will suggest a book which ought to be written. No doubt it is obvious that most Fellows of the Society are already busy with other books on other subjects; nevertheless, I venture to hope that somehow, someone may be moved directly or indirectly by a consideration of my plea, which is this: there ought to be a thick volume (or better still, several) which would merit the title of *Manuel de diplomatique anglaise*.

The title slips out naturally in French—for diplomatic is

conspicuously a French science; if the book were to come in the fullness of time from the *École des Chartes* no one would be surprised and all of us would be grateful. Are we not already indebted to that famous tradition for an admirable study of instruments under our minor seals?[1] But we may with propriety watch our balance of payments and ask whether we could not do it ourselves. After all, did not the great Mabillon himself exchange learned compliments with that fierce old non-juror, George Hickes?

Those were the heroic days when Benedictines and Jesuits were hammering out the new science in the heat of battle, and it is good to know that an Englishman was there. Every generation of English historians can show work well done upon this or that question of native diplomatic. Anglo-Saxon charters naturally held the centre of the stage as successive generations of historians re-examined them for constantly changing purposes. Instruments under the great seal were even more abundant and their form was of practical legal importance long after the middle ages ceased. Documents of private origin were apt to be overlooked, save for the purposes of the mysterious art of conveyancing, until Madox produced our first and still our best *Formulare* on historical principles in 1702. Madox was not quite a lawyer, and the contents of his book may have shocked so many legal dogmas that lawyers seem to have kept well away from it. Indeed, it is a characteristic of a historical legal system that practitioners are apt to be afraid of any disturbance of the historical bases of their work, which depends upon a sincere belief in the 'fable agreed upon'. The legislation of the nineteenth century has made those fears superfluous. The time is ripe for a history of conveyancing, which will be a long chapter in that *Manuel*. Diplomatic study has been continuous with us, but the stream has been very slight and has meandered from topic to topic without ever becoming generalized into the broad and noble flood which ought to have refreshed the field of medieval history as a whole.

One attempt was indeed made to treat diplomatic in general terms. That was by Hubert Hall, to whom several generations of commencing historians have been indebted for countless acts of kindness. His *Formula Books* have many merits, but his volume of *Studies in English Official Historical Documents* was starved of space because it included palaeography and a history of the public records as well. Still, it gave to many young students a glimpse of what diplomatic is. He nominally con-

[1] E. Déprez, *Études de diplomatique anglaise* (1908).

fined the *Studies* to official documents, and his interest in them to the language in which they were couched; but the very fact that his treatment takes place within the larger framework of archives and public administration was significant. He realized that diplomatic is barren indeed if it concerns itself only with phraseology and omits to consider a document as part of a transaction in which it is an instrument carefully chosen with a view to its appropriate functions.

And indeed, diplomatic does include the functional as well as the formal study of documents; but these documents function within the general legal system of the place concerned, and so a considerable chapter of legal history is common ground to legal and diplomatic science. We can go further. A general survey of human cultural history would surely have good cause to consider at length the nature of the revolution whereby documents replace real acts. To take your cow to market, find a purchaser, strike a bargain, and come home again with some money instead of the beast, is one of the oldest and commonest transactions in history. But the contract is real, and executed; the seller, the buyer, the cow and the money are present together in one place at the same time. While those conditions were necessary only parochial trade was in contemplation. It was indeed a revolution when it became possible for a sale to take place when the purchaser was on the Continent, the seller a woolgrower in Yorkshire, the money in an Italian bank, and the wool not yet in existence. Such complicated transactions became possible by making very slight modifications in the form of traditional documents.

For some purposes the use of documents began fairly early, especially in connection with transfers of land and the acknowledgement of debts. As soon as their use became common, it was evident that there was a problem—practical as well as theoretical—concerning the relationship of the document to the economic facts which it represented. Is the document merely a memorandum to aid the memory of the parties? Or is it the transaction itself? Since Brunner's famous essay it has become usual to describe documents of the former sort as evidential, and the latter as dispositive.

This distinction was made familiar to English readers by Maitland.[1] It is difficult to find in Anglo-Saxon sources the

[1] F. Pollock and F. W. Maitland, *History of English Law*, ii. 86–7, accept Brunner's thesis that the Anglo-Saxon charter was dispositive; Hazeltine in his preface to D. Whitelock, *Anglo-Saxon Wills*, pp. xiii–xiv, regards it as evidential; for later discussions, cf. *Economic History Review*, vi. 64, and the review of recent literature by A. de Boüard, *Manuel de diplomatique* (1948), ii. *passim*.

answer to this question, for we may well doubt whether contemporaries ever put this question to themselves—in any case, in a form so clear cut. Indeed, that part of diplomatic which is concerned with the functional aspect of documents is generally hampered by the failure of evidence at this critical point. Moreover, the requisite evidence is generally not in the documents themselves. Every scholar who has worked upon them has been impressed by the fact that conventional forms are constantly employed in situations which make it evident that the forms no longer accurately represent either the thoughts or the deeds of the parties.

The patient gleaning of chance phrases has assembled much suggestive evidence upon such matters. When we get our English manual, however, we shall have much more precise information at our disposal. The immensely rich judicial sources available in this country enable us to overhear medieval men discussing, with deliberation and in their own words, the nature and meaning and effect of the documents which they used in the course of their affairs. The *Curia Regis Rolls* are already an imposing series at the beginning of the thirteenth century; the *Year Books*, beginning towards the end of the century, give us an even more intimate glimpse of the function of documents as the courts conceived it. Some samples of this sort of contribution will show the value of rolls and reports for this type of investigation.

At the outset we may note that common language has seemingly pre-judged the matter, for the charter under seal was currently referred to as a *fet, factum*, deed. At first sight this would seem to justify the deduction that the charter was itself the fact, and not merely evidence of the fact. Matters were not as simple as that, however. In 1294 Hertford, J., reminded counsel that 'charters and fines are not deeds, but only evidence of deeds'.[1] That seems to suggest that popular language (even on the lips of lawyers) had run far ahead of the law, and that it was erroneously that charters were called 'deeds'. Such unwarranted use of language was constantly occurring, however; the word 'feoffment' was often loosely applied to the document which narrated the act of enfeoffing.[2]

The doctrine of Hertford was already enshrined in the classic pages of Bracton,[3] and it has been demonstrated that charters founding monasteries may be drawn up many years

[1] *Year Book 21 & 22 Edward I* (Rolls Series), p. 404; note the inclusion of fines in the remark.

[2] Cf. Hazeltine, *op. cit.*, p. xiii, n. 1.

[3] Bracton, *De Legibus*, fo. 169 *b*.

after the first steps were taken. In other words, the gift was effective without the charter, and the charter merely narrated the early history of the process of foundation. Clearly there were practical reasons for that, as Professor Galbraith has shown ;[1] perhaps too there was the legal difficulty of finding a donee for the first gifts when there was no church, no abbot and no monks to take title. Such difficulties long remained, as the *Case of Sutton's Hospital* (1612) well shows.[2]

Apart altogether from the special case of gifts to a proposed corporation, the same sort of question is raised by gifts between natural living persons. The distinction between the fact of the gift and the making of a charter is clearly drawn.

If we pursue that proposition any further, however, we find ourselves immersed in what Maitland called 'the mystery of seisin'. It is not simply the relation of parchment to the events inscribed upon it, but the nature of the event itself which is involved : in other words, a right in land rests upon seisin, and seisin alone. Pen and ink, parchment and wax are irrelevant. The secondary importance of the charter seems therefore the result of the doctrine of seisin rather than of a doctrine of charters. Here are a few cases in skeleton form :

> *A* brings novel disseisin against *B*.
> *B* says 'I entered by feoffment,' and shoves in (*boute avant*) a charter.
> *A* : 'Never mind the charter' ; we were seised and disseised. The assize shall pass.[3] (1292)

Again, a deed made by one not himself seised is worthless :

> *A* brings mort dancestor against *B*.
> *B* says *A* enfeoffed him by charter.
> *A* admits the charter but says she was not seised when she made it ; this issue will be tried by the assize.[4] (1293)

Yet another example :—

> In a writ of ael the demandant alleged that his grandfather died seised.
> The tenant pleaded a charter by that grandfather.

[1] V. H. Galbraith, 'Monastic Foundation Charters', *Cambridge Historical Journal*, iv. 205. As to witnesses *ex post facto*, see Sir Cyril Flower's *Introduction to the Curia Regis Rolls* (Selden Society), lxii. 281, and cf. the remarks of Brunel in *Bibliothèque de l'École des Chartes*, lxxi. 606–7.

[2] Coke, *Reports*, x. 1.

[3] *Year Book 20 & 21 Edward I* (Rolls Series), p. 184.

[4] *Ibid.*, pp. 456–8.

Held: the charter does not matter, and the plaintiff may prove that the grandfather died seised.[1] (1302)

In all three of these cases the defence put in a charter from the demandant or his ancestor, and in all three the defence was told that, even assuming the genuineness of the charter, it will not help him; his only defence is to prove or disprove some alleged fact of seisin.[2]

So far, so good. The cases give us a clear and consistent idea of the place of the charter in our law. But turn over a few pages of the Year Book, and you find this:

> Alan demanded by a writ of entry, saying that his mother had disseised him.
>
> The defence put forward his mother's deed with warranty.
>
> Alan protests vigorously that he was seised and disseised.
>
> *Judgement:* Alan must answer the deed.[3] (1302)

This time the rule is completely reversed, and we therefore seem to catch our ancestors stating two mutually inconsistent theories about the nature of a deed. The situation is far from simple. We must remember that these apparently discordant decisions were made after due deliberation by judges of the highest eminence, Hengham himself among them, and that keen intellectual analysis of legal decisions was constantly going on at the hands of teachers and students in the law schools at this very moment. Woolly or untidy thinking about the law was very much at a discount, and there is abundant evidence that lawyers were deliberately searching for rule and logic and principle. We may be sure that the contradiction in our cases is not the result of ignorance or muddle, but is rather an example of rule and exception. But which is the rule, and which the exception? And, however we answer that question, what was the disturbing factor which made an exception necessary?

I shall not be so rash as to prejudge the conclusions of our new Manual on the first question, but on the second I may venture to hazard a few guesses.

Looking again at the four cases just mentioned, it will be noticed that the first was an assize of novel disseisin, the second an assize of mort dancestor, and the third an action of ael (which is a variant of mort dancestor). The fourth—the discordant case—was an action of entry.[4] That circum-

[1] *Year Book 30 & 31 Edward I* (Rolls Series), p. 2.

[2] In the second case the further point was made that the charter presumes that *A* was seised since the ancestor's death; that in itself would exclude *A* from bringing mort dancestor.

[3] *Year Book 30 & 31 Edward I* (Rolls Series), p. 12.

[4] Sir Cyril Flower first made this distinction: Selden Society, lxii. 358.

stance suggests a reason for the divergent rules, and seems to indicate that the ' disturbing factor ' which we have postulated may be the petty assizes of Henry II. If this is true, we have an explanation for the conjecture put forward a moment ago, that our treatment of charters was based primarily upon a doctrine of seisin rather than upon a doctrine of charters as such.

The framework of Henry II's assizes was so rigid, and wording of the writ was so clear, that for a long time courts refused to allow parties to depart from the strict tenor of the writ. The peremptory question in novel disseisin was whether the plaintiff was seised, and whether the defendant disseised him; in mort dancestor and aël, whether the ancestor died seised and whether the demandant is his next heir. These actions make no pretence of getting to the question of rights between the parties; they merely concern themselves with the affront to public order when a disseisin or an abatement takes place. From that point of view it becomes clear that charters are irrelevant, and that they contribute nothing to a case: charter or no charter, the sole question was whether the defendant had committed (or profited by) a disseisin. The defendant is therefore not allowed to plead that he has title (by a charter or otherwise), but must show that he has not committed a ' tort '.

The razor-edge of Henry II's assizes grew blunt with the years and took astonishing twists and turns when finally deeds were pleaded, until in the end we find the invention of the curious doctrine of ' colour '; but that is a later story.

Our fourth case, however, is not an assize but a writ of entry. That brings us to a very different part of the law. We are already mounting the ladder which leads to the writ of right, although this particular specimen is still very low down. It is permissible in this action to introduce matter which trenches upon the right, as distinct from the barest and most recent seisin. By the early years of Edward II it had become a commonplace that if you talk about your ancestor, or put in a charter, you have embarked upon a discussion of the ' right '. This was logical and inevitable. Yet even here, the role of the charter is not quite what one would expect; the doctrine of seisin still seems to get in the way of the charter. Let us look at some cases:

> Entry to recover land after a lease had expired.
> Tenant says he was enfeoffed in fee during the term.

Neither the term nor the fee was witnessed by a charter. Issue taken on the feoffment.[1] (1292)

Neither the lease nor the feoffment are any the worse for being made without a charter. But in a similar action when the alleged term was without deed, the tenant produced a charter of feoffment; the demandant was put to answer the charter [2] (1293).

We have already noted that a descent will introduce some element of right, even into mort dancestor, and have seen a case where the demandant seemingly answered a deed put forward by the tenant.[3] Here is another example, where the answer is particularly notable: the tenant in an assize of mort dancestor pleaded a charter in fee simple; the demandant admitted that it was his father's charter, but said it was in fact conditional upon the tenant marrying the demandant's sister within a month—which he failed to do [4] (1292).

This raises a very important question: if a charter says one thing, can one plead that it meant something else? In particular, if the charter is in common form, can one allege that in fact there were conditions annexed, which are not expressed in it? The practice of doing so was very common, and many a lease for years was accompanied by a charter of fee simple as an additional security, especially when the transaction was essentially in the nature of a mortgage. It is only slowly that our courts came to the conclusion that you cannot aver to the jury facts which would modify the terms of a deed. When the Year Books begin, that process is already well advanced, and the tendency is unmistakably in the direction of casting more and more emphasis on the charter in real property cases.

Once again, causes can be detected for this development. Changes in the attitude towards seisin may account for much. Henry II's policy roughly thrust aside the charter and concentrated on the most recent seisin. Edward I reversed that policy, and his legislation deliberately shifted attention to questions of right rather than mere possession, and assumed (even where it did not prescribe) that transactions would be carried out by deed and not simply by word. The petty assizes thus grew less common among well-to-do litigants,

[1] *Year Book 20 & 21 Edward I* (Rolls Series), p. 314.

[2] *Ibid.*, pp. 430–2.

[3] *Supra*, p. 145, n. 4; the defendant professed to use the charter to abate the writ, not as a bar.

[4] *Year Book 20 & 21 Edward I* (Rolls Series), p. 258: the judge held (but with obvious difficulty) that the father died seised, notwithstanding the charter.

who resorted instead to the writs of entry. Pressing in the same direction was the widespread use of clauses of warranty in charters. Warranty worked simply and naturally in the old days before *Quia Emptores*; but an unforeseen effect of that statute was to separate warranty from feudal lordship. When subinfeudation was the rule, it was obvious to the countryside who owed the duty of warranty, for your neighbours knew perfectly well who your feudal lord was. After *Quia Emptores* there was no bond of tenure between the vendor and purchaser of land, and if the vendor had given a warranty it was essential to have it expressed by deed, for the country might easily lose memory of a relationship which was not regularly and publicly made clear by such means as homage or suit of court or other feudal services. A charter thus became essential.[1] Once again, however, we must observe that the position and nature of the charter are being modified by extraneous forces, and not by the conscious development of a doctrine of charters as such.

So far, I have only dealt with charters of land. It must be remembered, however, that the bond under seal was universally used in connection with the loan of money. Its great effect was that compurgation was not a defence to a bond, although it was a defence to a simple debt.

At a later stage, in the fifteenth century, the courts reached a very precise answer to the problem of the relation between the bond and the debt. Thus, suppose that *A* lends *B* ten pounds. At that point *A* is entitled to an action of debt against *B*, in which *B* would be entitled to defend himself by wager of law—compurgation. Subsequently (while the debt is still outstanding) *B* gives to *A* his bond under seal for ten pounds. The situation is now changed: *A*'s remedy is an action of debt on the bond, and *B* will have to defend himself before a jury. Later still, *A* loses the bond. *A*'s remedy is gone for ever for he cannot sue on the bond without producing it, and the law regards the simple debt as having been discharged by the making of the bond.[2] Such a doctrine has at least the merit of being consistent with itself: it regards the debt and the parchment as being the same thing. No debt exists apart from the parchment.

Suppose the debt is finally paid. The only safe discharge is for the debtor to get his parchment back. In one case

[1] The process had already begun in 1267 with the statute of Marlborough, c.9 (cf. my *Legislation of Edward I*, pp. 63 ff.). The need for a charter lay at the root of the *quo waranto* controversy, and was reinforced (though not in express terms) by *De Donis*.

[2] Y.B. 1 Henry VI, Michs. no. 31; cf. Y.B. 22 Henry VI, Pasch. no. 32.

when this happened the debtor, yielding to human weakness, kept his old bond—perhaps to gloat over it. The former creditor, knowing this, contrived to get possession of the bond again and brought his action. The debtor must pay again.[1] Similar troubles were caused by the lost bond, the lost acquittance, and the special case where a party tried to plead a deed which was in the hands of his adversary. It would seem that the common law grew stricter as time went on, and that it was only with the rise of equity in the chancery that relief against this rigorous operation of a deed could be obtained.

It remains to say something of seals. We have little as yet to place beside the numerous continental monographs upon seals, their form and their legal effect. But ample material exists wherever the nature of deeds is questioned. The seal, in fact, is the essence of the deed and not mere corroborative detail. Thus an indented acquittance was not a sufficient discharge of a specialty debt, because it bore no seal—the judge appealed to the creditor to act in good faith, but there is no evidence that he did do the honest thing.[2] A writing without a seal is therefore not a deed. Conversely, we can say that a seal without writing is a deed: thus a deed between *A* and *B* bore also the seals of *C* and *D*. Thereby they were held to become parties to the deed although their names were not mentioned in the operative part of it.[3] Again, take the case of a tally with a seal attached to it. The maker might protest that it is 'only a piece of wood', but the court held that the seal had made it a deed.[4] The unauthorized use of a person's seal might have disastrous results therefore, and the loss of a matrix caused great concern, among others, to Isabel de Forz.[5] The matrix itself became a mighty thing; the king might impound the seal of a marcher lordship,[6] and the statute of Carlisle tried to enforce upon religious houses certain rules for the custody of their seal.[7]

There is abundant material for the legal effect of seals, but not all of it is clear. Thus we are told that Howard, a serjeant, demanded a view of a deed proffered by his opponent. It seems that the deed was shown to him folded up, with the seal hanging outside, and that Howard looked at the

[1] *Year Book 11 Richard II* (Ames Foundation), pp. 12–14, and my commentary, *ibid.*, pp. xliii–xlvi.

[2] *Year Book 30 & 31 Edward I* (Rolls Series), p. 158.

[3] *Year Books of Edward II* (Selden Society), vii. 9; xx. 122.

[4] *Ibid.*, vi. 154.

[5] N. Denholm-Young, *Seignorial Administration*, p. 18.

[6] E. F. Jacob in *Transactions of the Royal Historical Society*, 4th series, x (1927), 27.

[7] 35 Edward I; cf. Dom Berlière, *Revue Bénédictine*, xxxviii. 288 ff.

seal only, but dared not look at the writing inside. Unfortunately the Year Book does not explain the reason for this timidity, which is all the more puzzling because Howard was very well acquainted with the contents of the deed, which he proceeded to discuss in detail.[1]

That, however, is a very minor matter compared with the serious and fundamental questions of the nature and operation of deeds under seal. In its broadest aspect, the subject-matter of diplomatic is the relation between documents and facts. English sources are abundant for the study of this problem which becomes more impressive as time goes by—are we not all of us filed on cards in the Ministry of National Insurance ? That of course would make a very long story ; for the moment I shall be more than content if I live to see a *Manual of English Diplomatic*.

[1] *Year Book 20 & 21 Edward I* (Rolls Series), p. 66.

VIII

THE IMPEACHMENTS OF 1376

NEARLY ten years ago I ventured to lay before you some speculations upon the origin of impeachment, and to suggest that the classical view of its nature was not a sure guide to its historical origins.[1] In its developed form it could be reasonably described as a trial by the lords of a person whom the commons had indicted (or nearly so) of high crimes and misdemeanours. Thus linked up with the age-old criminal procedure of the common law, the parliamentary impeachment could cast a decent veil of legality over the political realities which too often disgraced it, and could pose before the world in the reassuring robes of justice.

That being so, the events of 1376 had to be considered. They were obviously impeachments, and the general shape of the proceedings was easily recognizable, albeit with some technical refinements lacking. Consequently some have been tempted to say that even as early as 1376 it would already have seemed to contemporaries plausible to regard the commons as the grand inquest of the nation.

The line of argument looks tempting, but the conclusion to which it leads is far from convincing. There was a good deal of novelty in the proceedings of 1376, and it would be natural to endeavour to make them seem regular, or at least defensible, by linking them with familiar procedures in criminal law of undoubted legitimacy. Trial upon indictment seemed the most attractive analogy to the seventeenth-century lawyers, but was it equally obvious in the fourteenth century? The answer to that must clearly be, No. An examination of a number of cases in the earlier fourteenth century seemed to show that the problem was

[1] *Trans. R. Hist. Soc.*, 4th ser., xxiv. 47–71.

then conceived in rather different terms. The point that gave most trouble was whether a man could be brought to a legal trial for serious crime otherwise than by indictment, appeal of felony, or original writ.[1] It was then thought that he could. There survived still the ancient notion that ill-fame and notorious suspicion were potent factors in criminal law. There had been a time when they operated an instant conviction, without further proof of specific offences. That stringent rule had been almost abandoned, but there still survived the principle that ill-fame, notoriety or public clamour were sufficient to put a man on his trial without the formality of an indictment.

The cases previously considered seem to show the gradual intrusion of that notion into parliamentary proceedings. There is nothing remarkable in the fact that these cases were in parliament, or that the magnates exercised judicial or quasi-judicial functions. From the earliest times the wise, or the great, assembled in the royal presence, had been called upon to deal with offenders whose deeds had imperilled the king or had threatened the public peace and welfare. The cases more worthy of remark are indeed those in which so important a matter as a state trial is entrusted to some other or subordinate tribunal. They occur but rarely in this period. Our business is therefore to examine the impeachments of 1376 in order to see whether they rest upon the principles which have been extracted from the earlier cases.

The sensational trials of 1376 have not lacked commentators. Stubbs[2] gives a cautious narrative which refrains from speculation upon the legal aspects of the cases. Stephen[3] notes a few legal points but does not consider origins. Holdsworth[4] puts forward a few guesses at their origin in the general conditions of the age, but does not consider the medieval cases. Miss Clarke[5] accepts the old view of Hale[6] that the commons presented indictments in 1376,

[1] The statutes mentioned by M. V. Clarke, *Fourteenth Century Studies* (1937), p. 246, do not agree, and do not always succeed in giving an exhaustive list of lawful procedures; the expression 'due process' in some of them may be an attempt to meet this deficiency by using a general term to cover those omitted.

[2] *Constitutional History* (1875), ii. 430.

[3] *History of Criminal Law*, i. 148.

[4] *History of English Law* (1922), i. 380.

[5] *Fourteenth Century Studies*, p. 242.

[6] *History of Pleas of the Crown*, ii. 150.

and suggests that the indictments were developed out of the common petition, perhaps in Ireland. Professor Wilkinson[1] dealt with these matters only as incidental to his inquiry into the structure of parliament, with special reference to the relations between the council and the lords. The administrative and political aspects (the latter being peculiarly complicated) have received attention from Tout[2] and Mr. Steel.[3] With these issues, interesting in themselves, we are not now concerned, and still less with the guilt or innocence of the accused; the crux of the matter is the procedure, and we must endeavour to find out precisely what happened when a man was impeached in the Good Parliament of 1376.

For that purpose we are exceptionally well served by a parliament roll of unusual bulk, by a St. Alban's chronicler[4] who had access to good information and who served it up piping hot and richly spiced with malice, and above all, by that *Anonimalle Chronicle*[5] which stands alone in its vivid portrayal of what went on among the commons. This last has the additional merit of giving a chronology of events which seems generally convincing, in spite of occasional small lapses. The parliament roll, on the other hand, has classified its material and does not profess to be a daily journal. After formal preliminaries[6] it passes to the grant of supply,[7] then to the general grievances of the commons and the remedies provided,[8] then to the state trials,[9] and finally to the common petitions.[10]

The Good Parliament was due to open on Monday, 28 April 1376. The chancellor read the speech from the throne on the 29th and on Wednesday the 30th there began those debates among the commons which the *Anonimalle Chronicle* has made famous. Here it is important to distinguish the private confabulations of the commons from their formal and public appearances in the parliament; it is the latter only which can furnish the procedure—whatever it was—which constituted an impeachment, and so much of it as seemed significant to the clerk must be sought on

[1] *Studies in Constitutional History*, p. 82.

[2] *Chapters in Administrative History*, iii. 286 ff.

[3] *Richard II*, pp. 23 ff.

[4] *Chronicon Angliae* (R.S. no. 64), pp. 68 ff., 391 ff.

[5] Edited by V. H. Galbraith (1927).

[6] *Rotuli Parliamentorum*, ii. 321 (1–8).

[7] *Ibid.*, ii. 322 (9). This must not be taken as evidence that supply preceded redress.

[8] *Ibid.*, ii. 322 (10)–323 (14).

[9] *Ibid.*, ii. 323 (15)–330 (47).

[10] *Ibid.*, ii. 331 (52)–360 (212).

the parliament roll. The roll gives no dates, but the chronicle shows the commons still debating on 9 May when finally they agreed to enter the parliament, and asked for a group of magnates, named by their Speaker Peter de la Mare, to be assigned as a liaison committee. This seems to be the incident in item 8 of the parliament roll. The king's express assent was obtained by the members of this group, which was formally appointed on Monday, 12 May.

That same day, or probably soon afterwards, the commons made a second solemn entry into parliament. This time the Speaker dealt with the removal of the staple from Calais, which he said was contrary to statute (he had the book ready in his pocket),[1] and contrived by Lord Latimer and Richard Lyons for their private profit. He alleged that these two had engaged in fraudulent transactions and asked that Lord Scrope and the bishop of Exeter (both ex-treasurers) be permitted by the king and his council to give sworn information to the commons. It will be observed that these are extraordinary proceedings which the commons admitted to be beyond their competence; they therefore sought and obtained royal approval at several stages, and especially for the remarkable step of examining a peer and a prelate upon oath. Indeed, formal messengers were nominated by the commons to keep the king informed, and all the declarations of the commons were couched in language which implied that they were acting in his interest, on his behalf, and with his authorization.

As originally framed, the request of the commons seems to contemplate that the two ex-treasurers would be examined by the commons in their own house,[2] but in fact the examination seems to have taken place in the parliament with John of Gaunt presiding,[3] and as the story came out, other witnesses were called, sworn and examined. According to the chronicle, this brings us to 19 May. The parliament roll gives what seems to be the Speaker's opening speech, but none of the evidence, in items 15 and 16 (except the last four lines); but it is to the chronicle that we owe the concluding scene of the day's exciting work:

[1] One would like to have seen that book; there is no statute on the subject, although the commons did petition in 1373 for the staple to be at Calais—to which the king gave an evasive reply: *Rot. Parl.*, ii. 318 (17). See Professor Galbraith's note in *Anonimalle Chronicle*, p. 183.

[2] *Ibid.*, p. 88.

[3] *Ibid.*, p. 89.

And then all the commons cried with one voice, 'Sir Duke, now you can see and understand clearly that Lord Latimer and Richard Lyons have acted falsely in order to have advantages for their own use; and so we pray remedy and redress, and that Richard may be arrested and kept under guard until our lord the King and the council of parliament shall have declared their will concerning him.'[1]

It is not necessary to believe that the commons had prearranged this formula and had declaimed it in unison. It may merely be that the Speaker spoke those words 'amid loud cheers' as modern reporters would say. But it is surely safe to conclude that there was a good deal of noise. We may even call it 'clamour'. It was a good curtain, and Peter de la Mare took leave of the lords with his customary formula: 'that is all for to-day'.

Having demanded the arrest of Lyons, the commons turned to another matter. On 24 May the lords sent for them, and the commons demanded the reform of the council and the removal of Alice Perrers; the lords communicated this to the king on 26 May and he 'benevolently' agreed.[2] The result is the new ordinance for the council in items 10 to 14 on the parliament roll.[3]

This first example of a council named and sworn in parliament marks a turning-point in the history of the council, as Baldwin[4] has noted. There is a further fact of significance, however. The names of the nine newly-created councillors are almost the same as those of the group of twelve prelates and magnates of the liaison committee between the lords and commons set up in the early days of the parliament. This suggests some very competent staff-work which from the beginning had directed the operations of the commons. Baldwin has suggested that the Black Prince was the brain behind it all. He was certainly the figure-head whom the public regarded as the leader, but it may be doubted whether the Prince, who had long been desperately ill, and died at this critical moment, could have planned so skilful a parliamentary campaign. The dramatic transformation of the liaison committee into the new sworn council suggests that the planning had been done by that group. Among them the earl of March is conspicuous, and the intrepid Speaker, Peter de la Mare, was his steward. The

[1] *Ibid.*, p. 90.
[2] *Ibid.*, pp. 90–1.
[3] *Rot. Parl.*, ii. 322–3.
[4] J. F. Baldwin, *The King's Council*, p. 120.

planning may well have been inspired in the March circle and elaborated by the astute and experienced manager of the Mortimer estates.

Furthermore, the swearing-in of the new council was of crucial importance for the matter of the impeachments. The commons were present on the occasion in parliament, and Peter de la Mare addressed the assembly in a speech which left no trace on the parliament roll save the last four lines of item 16. From the *Chronicle* we learn that he reminded the lords (meaning possibly the new council) that they were set up in order to hear and amend the defaults in the realm, that he had mentioned many such defaults concerning Latimer and Lyons which so far have not been dealt with, and said that now he would go further. Addressing himself particularly to the case of Lord Latimer, he introduced a completely new accusation which was not financial but military, namely, his responsibility for the loss of Bécherel and St. Sauveur:

> Wherefore we pray and require you on behalf of the king and the council of parliament that the said lord Latimer be arrested and kept safely for all the said trespasses and forfeits, until he has made satisfaction to the king for his misdeeds; and that the said Richard Lyons be judged as he deserves upon the points and articles put against him, which he cannot reasonably deny.[1]

Here then are the impeachments. Much had been said in the last few weeks in denunciation of Latimer and Lyons, but this time the proceedings take on an air of greater formality. The demand is not for a trial but for punishment and judgement. De la Mare seems to think that no further proceedings are necessary and that no defence is possible; moreover, he is emphatic in saying that he is acting on behalf of the king and the council of parliament. Finally, we observe that the proceedings are only oral.

Latimer was thereupon called and arraigned, and prayed the lords to give him the charges in writing, to allow him counsel, and to give him time to answer. In effect he demanded a trial. This crucial question of principle was argued at some length. William of Wykeham opposed it. Latimer replied.

At that point the chronicle breaks off, but fortunately the roll of parliament now becomes very full. Items 20 to 29 all deal with

[1] *Anonimalle Chronicle*, p. 93.

Latimer's case. Item 20 at once puts the whole matter into focus by saying that 'William, lord Latimer, was impeached and accused by clamour of the commons.' Essentially, this implies that impeachment was not a jurisdiction of the lords, nor a mode of trial, but a means of initiating criminal proceedings, basing them not upon indictment, or information or appeal of felony, but upon 'clamour'.

We are particularly fortunate in having the *Anonimalle Chronicle*, for without it the nature of impeachment and its roots in the past would have been obscured. The debate between William of Wykeham and Lord Latimer is indeed a turning-point of high importance, for it set impeachment upon a new course at the very outset. The view of Peter de la Mare, seconded by William of Wykeham, was conspicuously old-fashioned. Peter claimed to arraign Latimer 'on behalf of the king and the council of parliament'; he asked for no trial, but only that Latimer be taken in execution forthwith. This seems to mean that the clamour of the commons entitled the king to treat Latimer as immediately convicted—in short, it is the old theory of conviction by notoriety with the sole difference that it is the Speaker instead of the King who asserts that the misdeeds are notorious. William of Wykeham concurred and urged that 'no one knew his own deeds so well as the culprit himself'; he was apparently ready to let Latimer make a statement, then and there and without preparation, notice or counsel, but nothing more.

Who else spoke in this debate (for debate there must have been) we do not know, but it is clear that de la Mare and Wykeham lost their point. A momentous decision was taken, for Latimer in effect secured a trial. At the outset, therefore, impeachment was diverted from the antique courses suggested by de la Mare[1] and became not only a mode of arraignment but in effect a mode of trial.

The mode of trial can be gathered from the parliament roll. Whether Latimer succeeded in getting the charges reduced to writing (and thus susceptible of treatment like an indictment) may well be doubted. The roll is mainly in narrative form. The fact that it embodies the text of one 'bill' (a list of monies corruptly received by Latimer's underlings) seems to indicate that this was

[1] As early as Glanvill, xiv. 1, a traitor could be taken, although there were no certain accuser; his trial would then be by inquisition and ordeal.

the only document in the case;[1] de la Mare's prodigious memory and fluent tongue was apparently the sole basis of the rest of the proceedings which the roll merely reports. There was indeed a letter 'called Ragman' under the seals of many Breton lords which the commons wanted to see, but it had mysteriously disappeared. That did not prevent its contents being discussed, and Latimer's defence to it was not that the letter was not produced, but that it emanated from the king's enemies and so deserved no credence.

As for evidence, the commons asked for the examination of two of the underlings mentioned in the 'bill' but there is nothing on the roll to show that they were produced.

The opening speech for the prosecution was evidently long, and at several points it refers back to previous more detailed accusations; the roll does not say who delivered it, but there seems little doubt that here, as throughout the proceedings, Peter de la Mare was the spokesman. The prosecution concluded with the assertion that Latimer had 'notoriously accroached royal power'.[2]

Thereupon Latimer made his defence. He had asked for written charges, time to prepare, and for counsel. He did not get the first, but evidently got the second and the third. As in criminal cases then, and for long afterwards, the accused himself made such points as seemed likely to help his defence, but although he was not represented by counsel there is everything to show that his remarks were based upon legal advice given to him behind the scenes.

Items 26 and 27 on the roll contain the substance of Latimer's defence—once again, the roll contains a narrative report, and it is clear that nothing in the nature of common law pleadings took place. After reserving his rights as a peer, he professed himself willing to answer any accuser who cared to come forward. This went straight to the point, and raised the question by what authority he was arraigned and put to answer. Now was the time

[1] In his defence, *Rot. Parl.*, ii. 326*a*, Latimer answers that 'bill', but makes no allusion to any other. There seems no room, therefore, for the supposition that [written] petitions had become a [written] indictment. The impeachment as a whole was not embodied in a document; if it had been, the parliament roll would certainly have taken the easy course of reproducing it, instead of compiling a narrative of the lengthy proceedings.

[2] There is an excellent history of 'accroaching' in Clarke, *Fourteenth Century Studies*, p. 247. On the continent the idea was as old as 1066: F. Kern, *Kingship and Law* (tr. S. B. Chrimes), p. 93.

for the theory of impeachment to be stated in clear language, and for the commons to explain that they regarded themselves as the grand inquest of the nation, that they had found an indictment against Latimer, and that he must answer it. In fact nothing was said of this analogy, so obvious to later lawyers; no such notion occurred to them. There seems to have been an interval, perhaps for discussion, for the roll continues—

> And then afterwards, forasmuch as no particular person would openly accuse the said lord of the said matters in parliament, but the commons wanted to maintain the said accusations in common, the said lord Latimer, as a personal excuse and in defence of his good fame, said . . .

Does it need much imagination to guess that an awkward pause had compelled the commons to think of a hasty answer? Latimer's objection was not altogether novel; ex-Chief Justice Willoughby had made it a generation earlier in 1341.[1] It would have been possible to give the same answer to Latimer as had been given to Willoughby—'the king is informed by the clamour of his people'. That answer would have been consistent with de la Mare's previous insistence upon 'clamour' and his assertion that the proceedings were technically on behalf of the king. If there had been the will or the time to search for precedents, that logical principle might well have been restated; but the tense atmosphere of the Good Parliament did not favour research into legal history. Taken perhaps unprepared, the commons on the spur of the moment stumbled upon a novel answer to Latimer's demand for an accuser: they would all maintain the accusations, in common.

Once again, therefore, a critical decision was taken which determined the future course of the history of impeachment. The function of 'clamour' had been to put the person defamed upon his defence, and Lord Latimer's opening speech in his own defence was a 'declaration of his fame'. The clamour of the commons had accomplished its object. The commons could well have left the matter there, relying on the crown to take over the prosecution as it had done in Willoughby's case. It may have been the peculiar circumstances of the year 1376 that caused a change of plan. Edward III was hardly capable of action even if he had been

[1] *Trans. R. Hist. Soc.*, 4th ser., xxiv. 65–7.

willing; the Black Prince had died, and John of Gaunt had been conspicuously omitted from the new council. Neither the king nor his kinsmen were likely to undertake a vigorous prosecution, in spite of the pointed insistence of the commons that their impeachment was at the suit of, and in the name of the crown. When Latimer demanded to see his accuser, therefore, no one stepped forward—not even the newly named council. The affair might have been smothered at that moment had not the commons boldly taken up a new function. They had already clamoured and denounced: now they were to maintain their accusations in common and become prosecutors.

Startling as was this innovation, the commons still maintained that they prosecuted on behalf of the king, and from the roll we learn that the king was consulted frequently. The trial was long and difficult. The question whether Latimer was responsible for the misdeeds of his lieutenants was referred to the sages of the law. Much evidence taken by the commons in the course of their investigation was treated as part of the trial; further evidence was taken in parliament, at such length that the enrolment cuts the story short:

> whereupon many other speeches and arguments having been made both in full parliament and otherwise before the prelates and lords only, both on behalf of the king and on behalf of the said lord Latimer, and many examinations having been made thereupon, both in private and in public, and after long deliberation thereupon had, judgement was rendered in parliament against the said lord Latimer in the words following . . .

Such was Latimer's trial. That the commons 'maintained their accusations' with great pertinacity we may well believe; every time Latimer put in a defence, 'the commons replied' to it. The roll persistently refuses to peer behind the collective fiction and mention names; although we may feel sure that de la Mare took the lead, he is never mentioned once the impeachments are started.

The Latimer case is exceptionally important because we have so much information about its successive stages. Moreover, it seems to have been almost the first in point of time, and therefore the occasion of decisions upon procedure which were naturally followed in other cases. For there were many others in this same parliament.

Lyons' case has already been mentioned. 'Impeached and accused by the said commons' of 'notoriously assuming royal power', Lyons made his defence in parliament, pleading guilty to some counts, and as to others that he had authority from the king and council. Some lords testified that the king, only yesterday, had disowned Lyons; so he was condemned. A little later he was recalled by the lords on the ground that the sentence was too light. He submitted to total forfeiture and the record concludes with an order to inquire into his extortions. The decision to find out the facts after he had been twice sentenced sounds curious. Yet it was in a way logical; when it came to making restitution to his victims, then detailed inquiry was needed.

William Elys was 'impeached and accused in divers manners'. First of all by the commons, to whose charges he pleaded not guilty. To this the commons indignantly retorted that the day before 'in their common assembly in the chapter house of Westminster Abbey' he had confessed,[1] and to clinch the matter they brought in two of his victims who were examined in parliament. Elys could answer that, and said that he took the money pending a decision by the king, that by order of the king he had restored it, and produced an acquittance from the attorney general of the Scottish merchants. This time the prosecution had obviously broken down. The commons having failed, the two victims impeached him another way, that is to say, by a bill (which is enrolled). It tells a lurid story of their arrest on a trumped-up charge, in order to prevent their coming to parliament to complain; Elys alleged that they planned to rob him and that he had written to that effect to the king. The lords seized upon that and convicted him under the statute 37 Edw. III, c. 9. This tendency to entangle impeachment by the commons with proceedings at the suit of parties became stronger as the parliament continued. It produced remarkable results, for on this occasion the lords condemned Elys in 20*l.* damages and costs.

The next case, of John Pecche, one of the earliest cases on monopolies, carries this a stage further. Instead of separate proceedings by the commons and the parties we now see the commons impeach on behalf of the king and of the injured parties simul-

[1] The same situation arose in Nevill's case when a witness in parliament did not maintain what he had previously said the day before to some of the commons; he was committed to prison.

taneously. Nor did the injured parties proceed by bill, but orally, it would seem.

It will be noticed that as the cases proceed, they involve more and more questions of law. Whatever the situation at the beginning, it is clear that before the cases were over a good many lawyers must have appeared on the scene (or rather behind the scenes). As I have suggested, impeachment in its origin derives from legal folklore rather than legal science, but half a dozen cases in as many weeks gave lawyers the chance to exert an influence upon their conduct. In Nevill's case the lords construe a penal statute with becoming strictness; Alice Perrers was dealt with by an *ad hoc* ordinance; Medbourne was in effect accused by a Prior of packing a jury, but the roll refuses to say he was impeached, and the Prior was told to bring his bill.

This investigation seems to suggest, therefore, that the Good Parliament made considerable progress in settling the forms of impeachment upon legal and modern lines. The roving commission assumed by the commons to search for scandals in its early weeks, soon turns into preparing material for a trial. Their early assumption that clamour and notoriety were equivalent to a conviction was soon destroyed as a result of the sturdy stand by Latimer. The absence of written charges is conspicuous at first, but the later cases show an unmistakable preference for written bills. Further, the principle of clamour was not even allowed to be an exception to the common law rules of procedure; Latimer again scored a point for posterity by demanding an accuser, and so the commons were compelled to manage the prosecution (although protesting all the time that they did so on behalf of the king). Consequently the proceedings took the familiar form of a contest between a prosecutor and an accused, with a steadily increasing legal atmosphere. All this is development, and development in the right direction, although the political situation was far from favourable. It is sometimes said that the Good Parliament left no permanent results, but I suggest that its best and most permanent work was in rationalizing impeachment.

IX

STATE TRIALS UNDER RICHARD II

WITH the accession of Richard II, the political plot thickens. Crisis follows crisis, and each time there is a spectacular state trial. At times there is an air of good humour, even indulgence, in the conduct of these affairs, but as the reign proceeds they become more grim, ending in such savagery as is rare in our political history. Modern historians have contributed much new material to the study of this reign, and yet the result is not an increase of clarity; the more we learn, the more obscure the whole story becomes. There seems an unmistakable likeness between the successive crises and their accompanying state trials, and yet it is hard to define it in terms of politics. They seem to be all of them variations—one might say Enigma Variations—upon an undisclosed theme which still eludes us.

This is not the occasion to pursue that major quest. The stresses within the royal family and the convolutions of London politics must be laid aside, and Richard himself must be left in the dim light of the psychiatrist's consulting-room where Mr. Steel has put him. The much more modest object of this paper is to examine the procedure of the state trials which are so conspicuous in the reign. The principle had by now been accepted that parliament was the proper jurisdiction for the trial of eminent or official persons who were accused of misconducting public affairs. It still remained to settle the proper course of proceedings upon such occasions. The precedent in all men's minds was the great Latimer case in the Good Parliament of 1376 in which the outlines—very rough outlines—of impeachment had been hastily drawn in the heat of a moment of great political excitement. Even in that case, however, the presence of the lawyers soon made itself felt, and during the reign of Richard II legal opinion is conspicuously invoked on all sides, and notably by the king himself in the famous questions to the judges. Violent as their proceedings often were, politicians felt the prick of a civic conscience, and were uneasy until an appearance of legality had been cast over their actions.

From Latimer's case[1] it would seem that the process of impeachment consisted of oral accusations based upon the clamour of the commons and upon the notoriety of the facts. These charges were put forward by the commons professing to act in the king's name and nominally at least in consultation with him. The demand by the commons that their charges admitted of no defence was rejected; consequently, the impeachment led to a trial in which the judges were the whole body of the lords in parliament. The trial procedure was flexible and governed by no clearly stated rules. Latimer was not formally represented by counsel, in spite of the fact that the charges against him did not amount to treason or felony, but it is clear that informally he received professional help. The proceedings took the form of alternate speeches of accusation and defence. In some of the other cases in the Good Parliament there was frequently introduced the unwritten recollection of evidence collected by the commons in the course of their preliminary investigations, and occasionally when witnesses were heard at the trial itself, they were confronted with their earlier statements.

That was as far as development had gone when the new reign opened, but the first incidents in Richard's first parliament threatened to divert procedure into other channels. Thus, two captains were arraigned by Sir Richard le Scrope (steward of the household) before all the lords at the king's command for having surrendered certain fortresses, and were sentenced to death. The commons took no part in the proceedings, and they are nowhere called impeachments in the careful record compiled, we are told, by a clerk of the crown, Geoffrey Martin.[2]

A month later in the same parliament, the lords commanded the steward of the household to put divers articles to Alice Perrers; she was allowed to call witnesses and a regular trial by

[1] Discussed in *Trans. R. Hist. Soc.*, 5th ser., i. 153–64.

[2] *Rotuli Parliamentorum*, iii. 10 (38)–12 (40).

witnesses, sworn and examined in Parliament, ensued. She was sentenced to forfeiture, having been found guilty on the articles 'contained in the same impeachment', and the record was drafted by 'Edward Brudenell, clerk of the crown assigned to do this by the clerk of the parliament'.[1]

Brudenell's language was less precise than his colleague's. Whatever the name of the procedure, it is clear that the commons took no part. The two captains were prosecuted by the steward of the household on the king's behalf, and Alice Perrers by the same steward at the command of the lords. The spectacular prosecution of Latimer by the commons must have seemed to many serious observers a very dangerous precedent with quite incalculable implications for the future. We need feel no surprise that the three state trials which opened Richard's reign all take care to say nothing of the commons, and place the conduct of the prosecution in the hands of an experienced household officer. Prudent ministers may well have felt that criminal prosecutions should be firmly controlled by, or in the name of, the king. The lords naturally clung to their vaguely judicial role.

But the commons were not to be so easily eliminated. Their exploits in 1376 were remembered, and were enrolled; the roll moreover naturally says nothing of who pulled the strings and in fact kept the proceedings firmly in hand. Besides, there were the lawyers in the background, testing and criticizing and trying to reduce it all to an orderly procedure. In Richard's second parliament they even ventured to bring proceedings in error to reverse the judgement of the first parliament on Alice Perrers with all the implications of a minute and technical scrutiny of the record.

Then there was a lull until the trial of the bishop of Norwich in 1383. This militant prelate had entered into indentures by which he undertook, in consideration of notable sums of public money, to conduct a campaign in Flanders for one year. He sailed with only a small part of the agreed army, failed to reach his objectives, received (it was said) 18,000 gold francs from the enemy, and brought back the remnant of his force in less than six months. That view of his campaign being commonly expressed among the commons, the bishop asked the king for an opportunity to clear

[1] *Ibid.*, iii. 12 (41)–14 (43). It is notable that she was to forfeit lands held by others to her use.

himself in parliament, whereupon evidence was given about the gold by the bishop's clerk, not on oath, but charged upon his allegiance.[1] This took place in parliament, the chancellor, Sir Michael de la Pole, presiding; some further evidence was heard and then the chancellor 'on the king's behalf' adjudged the bishop's body to prison until he should pay over the gold received in such peculiar circumstances. A proclamation[2] called upon all others who had received gold from the enemy to explain their conduct to the chancellor; several persons did so, and were similarly dealt with.

These proceedings might seem at first sight to have been in the nature of preliminary investigations, were it not for the fact that they concluded in judgements. They are nowhere called impeachments, and although they took place 'in parliament' the lords are not associated with them. Even the commons are only represented to have 'requested' them, and as far as the roll of parliament is concerned, it was the chancellor alone who directed affairs 'on the king's behalf'. There is one casual reference to the presence of the king (who was then sixteen), but even that is perfectly consistent with the supposition that all this took place, during the parliament, but before the council.

If that is so, there may well have been some misgivings about their propriety, and the assembled lords may well have been surprised at being left out. As for the commons, their sentiments towards the bishop were of sorrow rather than anger, and they seem never to have pressed their case; in so far as there was a prosecutor, it was the chancellor himself.

Whatever the reason, the enrollment of these proceedings is immediately followed by a further trial, introduced by the words: 'Item, Henry Bishop of Norwich was impeached in this parliament of many things, but especially of four articles shown to him by the Chancellor of England in the presence of the king himself and of my lord of Lancaster in full parliament.' Here then we have a formal 'impeachment'.[3] It merits attention on several grounds. First, the conspicuous absence of any action, or even mention, of the commons. Next, the complete control of the proceedings by

[1] *Rotuli Parliamentorum*, iii. 152 (15). Archbishop Stratford had similarly asked for a trial when he was defamed among the commons in 1340: *Trans. R. Hist. Soc.*, 4th ser., xxiv. 68.

[2] *Rot. Parl.*, iii. 153 (16).

[3] *Ibid.*, iii. 153 (18)–155 (20).

the chancellor, who throughout professes to be following the king's directions. As in the preliminaries, the prosecution is conducted by the chancellor without the slightest reference to the commons. The four articles seem at this stage to be in writing, and although they are described as 'notorious' the bishop was allowed his trial. This took the form (as before) of an altercation between the chancellor and the bishop. No evidence was heard although the bishop offered to bring it; his despatches were discussed but not produced; the trial in fact consisted entirely of alternate speeches for the prosecution and the defence. Finally, the chancellor announced that the king had heard the proceedings and had deliberated thereupon with the lords temporal and sages of his council. Their conclusion was that the defence had failed and that the bishop must be in the fine and ransom of the king.

That was not the end of the matter. Shortly afterwards, the bishop moved for a new trial, and got it, on the grounds that he had been much interrupted in his defence by captious questions, that he had got flurried, and forgot much that would have helped his defence. This astonishing indulgence of a re-trial is not easily matched in the state trials of any reign, and is singularly incongruous in that of Richard II. The enrolling clerk, who had already told the sorry story twice over, contented himself with saying that this time the defence was much as before, save for the additional matter which he now records. The chancellor then gave judgement for the third time, 'by assent of the earls, barons and other temporal lords'. Remarking that the bishop had been telling people that the peers never really assented, the chancellor reminded the bishop that this was not a matter of peerage but merely a question of contract, of a soldier who had broken the terms of his indenture with the king.[1]

That was true. The story of the gold francs corruptly received was not pursued against the bishop, but against his underlings, although he was held civilly accountable for the money. The case was in fact more suitable for the now rising court of the constable and marshal, but in view of its political importance the king seems to have allowed it to proceed as an impeachment, but a strangely attenuated impeachment. The commons took no part whatever; the lords were merely consulted as a matter of grace. On behalf of the young king, the government of the day had

[1] *Ibid.*, iii. 155 (22)–156 (23).

clearly captured the new weapon of impeachment and had openly adapted it to use as a procedure for prosecution by the crown, instead of by the commons.

The bishop's underlings were similarly dealt with, save that the lords were not consulted upon their fate—unlike the bishop they had no claims to peerage. Their defence was too curious to pass over although it is not relevant to my theme. Briefly, they protested their complete honesty in having taken the gold, not as a bribe, but as the proceeds of perfectly honest trading with the enemy in military stores; the French had received, so they alleged, very nearly the full value of their money in good horses.[1]

From that mild beginning in 1383, the pace quickens. In 1384 a demented Irish Carmelite denounced the duke of Lancaster as a traitor, but the matter never got as far as the parliament roll.[2] A much more serious affair, however, does figure on the roll of that same parliament at Salisbury. This was an attack upon the chancellor (still Sir Michael de la Pole) by John Cavendish, a London fishmonger 'first before the commune of England in their assembly in the presence of some prelates and temporal lords then and there being,[3] and afterwards before all the prelates and lords being in this parliament'. Cavendish said his life was in danger and sought sureties of the peace from the chancellor. Two earls mainprised the chancellor, and then Cavendish told his story alleging that the chancellor, through his clerk, had demanded and received a large sum of money from Cavendish to favour him in certain proceedings in the court of chancery. The favour was not forthcoming, however, and the chancellor paid for a large gift of fish and cancelled a bond which was part of the transaction. Cavendish was a thoroughly disappointed man. The chancellor made his defence 'first before the prelates and lords in parliament, and secondly before the lords and commons', with the result that the fishmonger abandoned most of his complaint. Since the chancellor was himself party, there was no escape this time, and the lords had perforce to play the role of judges; but only for a moment.[4] Finding that the defence had succeeded, the lords committed the fishmonger to the judges with power to proceed as the lords could

[1] *Rot. Parl.*, iii. 157*b*. [2] Higden, *Polychronicon*, ix. 33–40.

[3] Perhaps one of those liaison committees of lords appointed at the request of the commons which are frequent during this period.

[4] *Rot. Parl.*, iii. 168 (11)–(13).

have done if time had permitted. The judges fined him 1,000 marks for defaming the chancellor.[1]

The roll is careful not to call this an impeachment, and that is an important point; the distinction between proceedings at the suit of a private party and those at the suit of the commons, or the crown, or both, was now becoming settled.

Two years later, de la Pole, now earl of Suffolk, was indeed impeached, and with great solemnity. 'In this parliament [1386] all the commons assembled in a body with one accord came before the king, prelates and lords in the parliament chamber, grievously complaining of Michael de la Pole, earl of Suffolk, lately chancellor of England, he being there present, and accused him in an oral declaration (*par demonstrance de bouche*) as follows'. Seven articles followed, 'of all which articles the commons demand judgement in parliament.'[2] We note immediately the spectacular part of the commons, for the first time in the new reign, although their speaker is not named and no indication is given as to who conducted the prosecution on their behalf.

Suffolk began his defence by protesting at the absence of the king, and at the refusal of the lords to allow Sir Richard le Scrope, his brother-in-law and an ex-chancellor, to conduct his defence;[3] he was given leave, however, to amend his defence if necessary, as his counsel should advise. Clearly, there were lawyers very close at hand although the actual presentation of the case for the defence had perforce to be by the earl's own mouth.

The earl stated his defence to the seven articles one by one, the commons replied, demanding the judgement of parliament upon each article; the earl answered the replication of the commons and was seemingly allowed the last word. At that stage the earl was committed to the custody of the constable of England and mainprised forthwith. A long and complicated judgement followed.[4] It is not stated who delivered it, but casual phrases ascribe it to the king and lords in parliament. Clearly, a deliberate effort had been made to follow the precedent of Latimer's case of 1376. The

[1] The judges made a record (*ibid.*, 169 (15)) in common-law form convicting Cavendish of *scandalum magnatum* under 2 Ric. II, stat. 1, c. 5.

[2] *Rot. Parl.*, iii. 216 (6).

[3] *Ibid.*, iii. 216 (7); Scrope was eventually allowed to recount Suffolk's long career of public service: *ibid.*, iii. 217*a*.

[4] *Ibid.*, iii. 219 (13).

frigid tone of the record is increased by the anonymity which the draftsman imposed. The earl indeed was there and spoke, but for the rest 'the commons' are credited with long and intricate legal arguments which, seemingly, no natural tongue delivered; even the judgement is stated impersonally without any suggestion as to who pronounced it. We lose the drama, but we perceive the growing atmosphere of the plea roll, for although the record is in French, its structure and the course of proceedings can be matched by those occasional common law cases where normal pleading was inadequate and argument and counter-argument was the substance of the record. In short, the whole affair is a very lawyerly piece of work.

There followed the remarkable commission of government,[1] and then the questions to the judges.[2] Our older historians were profoundly shocked at this incident. First it seemed like an attempt to corrupt the bench, and secondly, how could such 'servile' answers come from men who were the authentic predecessors of Lord Somers, Lord Camden and the high priests of whiggery?

In truth, judges in the fourteenth century were accustomed to answering questions from the king, the council, the lords in parliament, and quite probably private persons as well. Their summonses to parliament were not yet a curious anachronism, for there was real work for them to do there. There was nothing improper in the king consulting his judges. The questions were startling, however. Not technicalities of feudal or fiscal procedure, but the most burning question of contemporary politics was laid before them: the lawfulness of the commission. To Richard II, or to someone in his intimate circle, there had come a novel thought, namely, that what seemed to be a purely political crisis might be expressed in terms of law, that the position of the monarch was itself a legal question to which lawyers must give an answer. Someone had dimly foreseen that there might be such a thing as constitutional law.

Both sides had searched for precedents. As soon as parliament had met, the king's enemies reminded him of the 'old statute' by which Edward II was believed to have been deposed; the judges, a year later, in their answers to Richard II's questions, seem to

[1] *Rot. Parl.*, iii. 221 (18); stat. 10 Ric. II, c. 1.
[2] *Ibid.*, iii. 233 (August 1387).

have been inspired by the Statute of York of 1322. At the present moment, however, it is only the eighth question which concerns us: '. . . whether the lords and commons, without the will of the king, can impeach in parliament the king's officers and justices for their delicts, or not? To this question the judges unanimously replied that they could not . . .'

There can be no doubt whatever that this question was provoked by the trial of Suffolk in 1386 in which for the first time the commons repeated their performance at Latimer's trial ten years earlier. In the intervening years, as we have seen, determined efforts had been made by successive governments to capture the impeachment procedure and make it a strictly crown proceeding. The judges now set the seal of their authority upon the dogma that impeachment is properly brought at the suit of the crown and only with the consent of the crown.

That decision was a heavy blow to the baronial factions. No longer could they put ministers on trial without the concurrence of the crown, simply by inciting the commons to 'clamour' and to 'impeach'. They seem to have felt, as had the king, that the question was indeed a legal one, but that the judges had decided it against them. A new solution of their problem was urgently needed, and their own lawyers soon found it for them.

This was the appeal, and it was singularly suitable for their purpose. It was of great antiquity and firmly embedded in the common law. Whereas the novelty of impeachment, and the fewness of the precedents, left its very nature in doubt, there was no doubt at all about the appeal, which was surrounded by a body of law as ancient and as well known as that of the indictment itself. Above all, it was undeniable law that an appeal was a criminal proceeding at the suit of a party and that it needed no authorization from the crown. So independent was it of royal justice that an accused who had been acquitted in an appeal could still be brought to trial again by the crown, and an accused who had been tried on indictment and found not guilty at the suit of the crown, could still be subjected to an appeal by a private prosecutor.[1] This was exactly what the baronial factions were looking for—a criminal procedure over which the crown had no control.

A further merit of the appeal was the fact that it could be used

[1] The last and most famous example is *Ashford* v. *Thornton* (1819), 1 B. & Ald. 405.

for treason[1] and felony—and indeed had once been commonly used for trespass also. The one shadow of doubt was which court could entertain the proceedings. The courts of the justices in eyre, and of the king's bench, were certainly very familiar with the appeal, and under Richard II the court of the constable and marshal incurred the displeasure of the commons for entertaining appeals of treason and felony committed within the realm.[2] For appeals of treason in parliament there was as yet no precedent.

The lords appellants have left their own considered view of their proceedings upon the parliament roll.[3] From this we learn that Gloucester, Arundel and Warwick first brought their appeal at Waltham in November 1387 before the commission of government set up in 1386, the appellees being there present. The commissioners informed the king and arranged a meeting, and shortly afterwards the appellants repeated their appeal before the king and his council; the king reserved the matter until parliament should meet some two months later. Meantime, at the tower of London after Christmas, new parties were joined: Derby and Nottingham also became appellants and a third time the appeal was made. On the 3rd of February 1388 in parliament the lords appellants 'appealed and said' the thirty-nine articles which occupy six folio pages of print. Most of the appellees when called did not appear —they had had ample time to escape abroad—whereupon the appellants demanded judgement against them.

At this point the lords felt the need of legal advice and consulted the judges, serjeants and common lawyers, together with the experts in civil law. These reported (with pacific intentions no doubt) that the appeals were invalid both by common law and civil law, giving no reasons, however. Thereupon the lords overruling their experts made the famous declaration that the civil law had no place at all, and the common law only a restricted place in the kingdom, and that above it was the law and course of parliament, and by that law the appeals were valid. Once again it is to be remarked with what anxious diligence the law was searched,

[1] Appeals of treason are listed in Pollock and Maitland, *History of English Law*, ii. 507, and in L. W. V. Harcourt, *His Grace the Steward*, p. 349 *n.*

[2] The constable's jurisdiction over appeals of treason and felony committed abroad was not contested: Harcourt, *op. cit.*, 362 ff., *Rot. Parl.*, iii. 65 (47). Cf. the statute 13 Ric. II, c. 2.

[3] *Rot. Parl.*, iii. 229–38.

English, foreign and fabulous, and how concerned the lords were to find a theory for their decisions in a matter where precedent failed. It seems to have been a decision of the king himself to transfer the appeals to parliament[1]; thereby he gained time, evidently, but he also helped the appellants over their biggest difficulty of finding a way into parliament. The lords were not loath to accept this tribute to their position in the constitution.

That position was not only legal, but political. A substantial portion of the lords was without commitments to the small but turbulent factions which manufactured these crises, as we may infer from the sensible attempt to quash the appeals. When that failed it needed the astonishing flattery of the '*lex parliamenti*' theory to induce the lords to continue the hearing. The natural moderation and reluctance of the lords as a body, coupled with the king's genuine sense of law, were further outraged by the demand of the appellants that the defaulting accused should be treated as immediately convicted. This proposition was unheard of in English law. Even trial in absence had no place in our criminal system, and if the accused could not be found there was only one possible course—outlawry.

The king and the lords together rejected the revolutionary demand of instant conviction. But pressure of some sort had forced them to yield so far as to conduct a trial in absence. It was no pretence: for nine days the lords investigated the articles 'so that they might give a judgement in this case which would be to the honour of God, of the king and of the realm' and 'using every means to inform their consciences.' The defaulters were found guilty of treason and sentenced. The *lex parliamenti* had done its work, but there is nothing to show that the lords were at all proud of the novel doctrine that had been thrust upon them.

Different problems were raised, and received different treatment, in the cases of Brembre and Tresilian who had been captured and appeared in person for their trial.[2] Brembre at once pleaded not guilty and offered trial by battle 'as a knight should do'. At this point we are surprised to find an intervention by the commons who are here mentioned for the first time in the roll. They seem to say that they would have accused the appellee

[1] A. Steel, *Richard II*, p. 138, regards this as 'his first really intelligent move in the whole crisis'.

[2] *Rot. Parl.*, iii. 237*b*–238.

'which thing pertained to them to do', had not the lords appellants forestalled them. The point of this remark is not clear, and the lords proceeded to rule out trial by battle. Instead, they would inform their consciences by all possible means, as they would answer before God. They found him guilty and he was hanged forthwith. As for Tresilian who had been tried and sentenced *in absentia*, he was captured and brought into parliament. A brief *allocutus*, and the previous sentence was carried out without further ado. The proceedings ended with a remarkable declaration that the king had had nothing to do with all this owing to his tender age and the innocence of his royal person.[1] He was in fact just over twenty-one.

That is far from the complete tale of the deeds of the Merciless Parliament, but we have reached the point where new and desperate courses were being tried. There was real ground for the belief that impeachment was slipping from the grasp of opponents of the court, and the introduction of appeals into parliament was surely meant to be the answer. True, the king persisted in taking part in the proceedings in spite of the fact that he was virtually the appellants' prisoner, and this rather spoiled the picture of the traditional appeal of the common law. The appellants tried to put things right again by their curious declaration exonerating the king from the whole affair. If they succeeded in establishing a criminal procedure independent of the crown it was only by the barest margin.

The parliament roll is a workmanlike record from the Appellants' point of view of what lay behind the cloth of gold and all the picturesque chivalry which the chroniclers describe. The Merciless Parliament has long been credited with its flight into political theory, but on that some reserves must be made. Nevertheless on the lower plane of law and procedure it is clear that much technical thought had taken place. The hand of the lawyers is visible everywhere, and above all it is necessary to observe that both the king and his opponents appealed to the law. Nor was their thought entirely confined to the technical side of law. The roll frequently refers to 'conscience' and to the need of using every means to inform their consciences in order to reach a right judgement. This alone is enough to show that some of those concerned felt anxious about these proceedings. Politically no doubt

[1] *Rot. Parl.*, iii. 238.

the appellants were engaged in recklessly vindictive acts, but they felt the need of clothing them in the ancient vestments of the law. Even if we say that the king, or his opponents, or both, were deliberately insincere in their actions, it still remains to observe that their hypocrisy was the homage which vice renders to virtue, and that their manipulations of procedure impressed upon all beholders the simple fact that legality was part of the nation's traditions.

X

IMPEACHMENT AND ATTAINDER

THE early history of impeachment lies crowded in the eventful years immediately following 1376. From the Good Parliament to the Merciless Parliament, and thence to the Parliament of 1397, is a short span of merely a score of years, yet those years are full of development—so full, that we can discern not only the development of impeachment as a legal procedure, but also a struggle for the right to the exclusive control of the most powerful weapon in the political armoury, short of civil war.

Richard II, when he took the remarkable step of submitting a political crisis to the scrutiny of judges and professional lawyers, elicited from them an opinion which revealed the technical point at which the new device ran counter to the main current of the common law, namely, that it seemed to consist of a procedure for criminal prosecution in which the crown was not a party. The cases, in spite of some obscurity, show a trend in that direction, and the judges not unnaturally condemned that proposition, and in their reply to the king's enquiry asserted that impeachment without the king's consent was illegal.[1] That opinion brought impeachment into line with the general law of the land.

But it did more than that: it robbed politicians of their new-found device for attacking the king's ministers. This was felt to be a severe blow, and the judges eventually paid a high price for their stand upon legal orthodoxy. Opposition leaders who seem to have felt that politics was a dull game unless the stakes were high, cast around for some new method, and found it in the ingenious application of the primitive appeal of treason or felony which was now transplanted from rustic thievery and burglary to

[1] *Rot. Parl.*, iii. 233*b*.

the splendid setting of parliament. The ancient issue of an appeal of felony was trial by battle, and the lords appellants probably contemplated that possibility with satisfaction. The common law judges for centuries,[1] however, had generally succeeded in preventing the parties from engaging in mortal combat, and the assembled lords in parliament seem to have followed the same policy. In this they were aided perhaps in some obscure way by the intervention of the commons when Brembre betook himself to wager of battle.[2] It was ruled that battle did not lie.

The lords appellants may well have felt some disappointment. Appeals had promised so much spectacle and violence, and yet in the end they had been reduced to the much less chivalrous level of a mere trial. If that were to be the case, then impeachment was just as good—if (and that was the point of substance) it could still be maintained that the crown was not necessary as an active party in the proceedings.

The opinion of the judges alone stood in the way, and so, as soon as the appeals had been disposed of, the judges who had given the opinion (which also condemned the extraordinary commission) were attacked by the very procedure of impeachment which they had declared to be an exclusively royal proceeding.

And so, on Monday 2 March 1388, the judges and serjeants who had subscribed to the opinion 'were brought into the same parliament at the request of the commune of the said parliament, and by all the commons there assembled for all the counties, cities and boroughs of England, were accused and impeached'.[3] The record is drawn with great particularity and admirably drafted, but there was no document of accusation; the only document mentioned is a copy of the opinion, which the accused were called upon to admit or deny. There is nothing in the whole process which could suggest that the crown was in any way associated with the proceedings. The accused in turn made speeches in their defence, the commons made a general reply and prayed for judgement, and thereupon the lords announced that they would consider their judgement. The commons then impeached two underlings, Blake and Usk, who rested their defence on the single proposition that everything they had done had been at the express command of

[1] Cf. Bracton, fos. 102, 137.

[2] *Rot. Parl.*, iii. 238*a*.

[3] *Ibid.*, 238*b*. This insistence, in judicial proceedings, upon the representative nature of the commons is notable.

the king.[1] This famous point (which later was determined in Danby's Case) the lords did not venture to resolve; instead, they took the view that the accused knew very well that the king was acting under the influence of the appellees and not of his own will.

In all this, there is no indication of who presided at the trials, nor are we told who presented the case for the commons; if it were the speaker who undertook this difficult and conspicuous task, the roll is discreetly silent. The king is introduced into this record for the first time when the grim business of sentencing the accused was reached: the assent of the king is alleged to the sentence on the two underlings Blake and Usk, and when the judges were brought back, the lords gave judgement by assent of the king. When the bishops interceded for the judges and the king spared their lives, the announcement was made by the chancellor. The impression left by the record is that the part assigned to the king was the barest presidency of the tribunal, the lords assuming all responsibility for its conduct and decisions.

After the judges, the king's confessor, the bishop of Chichester, was impeached,[2] and while the lords were considering the special complications of his position, the roll proceeds to a solemn recital of sixteen articles headed 'The accusations and impeachments made by the commons of the realm' against Sir Simon Burley and others.[3] The roll is not entirely unambiguous, but it is hard to escape the conclusion that these articles were in writing when the trial opened and so constituted the basis of the proceedings. The knights made no special defence but pleaded not guilty and offered to acquit themselves like knights—a hint of trial by battle; the commons joined issue and so the matter was left to the lords. This remarkable introduction of common law pleading into a tribunal which had announced[4] that it did not feel bound to follow the law of the land, added to the delicate matter of the bishop of Chichester, evidently occupied the lord's deliberations from 12 March until the 18th, when parliament was adjourned for three weeks over Easter.

When parliament reassembled the knights were brought in and told that the lords had found them guilty 'by information and examination'.[5] The roll is obscure, and seems to imply that the determination of their guilt was reached in their absence, as was

[1] *Ibid.*, 240. [2] *Ibid.*, 241*a*. [3] *Ibid.*, 241*b*. [4] *Ibid.*, 236*b*. [5] *Ibid.*, 243*b*.

also the decision that the articles (or some of them) were in law treason. The last item of this part of the roll[1] records that the commons asked the king to reward their common clerk, John Scardesburgh, as the Appellants likewise commended to the king's bounty Geoffrey Martin, clerk of the crown. This almost suggests that the principal officer of the commons for these proceedings was their common clerk.

The ten years which followed, with their fairly quiet orderly government, have proved as mysterious to the historians who have searched them as the spectacular crises which distinguish this reign. Fortunately this is not the occasion for a general commentary and interpretation of Richard II's personality and politics: procedure alone is now in question.

The next crisis, that of 1397, differs from the others in one notable respect. From the Good Parliament onwards, the experiments in impeachment and state trials generally had been engineered by opposition groups who often found themselves compelled to improvise machinery to reach ministers and others near to the king. Now the tables were turned, and it is worth watching how Richard II, with all the resources of the prerogative as well as the common law at his disposal, proceeded to deal with his enemies.

The approach of the storm was heralded by Haxey's case.[2] He was clerk of the rolls of the court of common pleas and had received much ecclesiastical preferment from the king. In 1397 he was proctor for the abbot of Selby[3] in parliament, and seems to have thought it his duty to introduce a bill or memorandum into the commons' house (of which he was not a member) enumerating a number of political questions of the day, and among them the suggestion that too many bishops and ladies were living at the king's expense at court. Deeply offended, the king discussed this with the lords, and a few days later the lords declared that it was treason for anyone to excite the commons or anyone else to reform the household. Two days later Haxey was brought in before the king and lords. There is no original record of the pro-

[1] *Rot. Parl.*, 245 (21).

[2] Recited in his subsequent pardon, printed from the patent roll in *Rot. Parl.*, iii. 407–8.

[3] *Chichele's Register*, ii. 657; Margaret Hastings, *Court of Common Pleas*, p. 275.

ceedings on that occasion save a brief narrative on the patent roll. From this it would appear that the Steward of England (John of Gaunt) prosecuted, and that the lords adjudged him a traitor. The procedural details are meagrely recorded, but evidently the steward of England is doing much the same thing as the steward of the household had done in the first parliament of the reign. Haxey's trial must have been merely *in terrorem*; had it been meant seriously, it would certainly have been recorded upon the parliament roll. Perhaps it was an experiment in new procedure, and not much liked. The surprising view of the nature of treason which the lords propounded seems to follow from the general idea contained in the answers of the judges.

As for Haxey personally, he was soon pardoned and restored. The king seems to have taken the view that he was a well-meaning and worthy official who had been a tool in the hands of some magnate who was forming a conspiracy, of which rumours were already current.

The king struck while there was no parliament in being. Of the original lords appellants, several had made their peace with the king and were in favour and office at court, but Gloucester, Warwick and Arundel chose to be irreconcilable; it was believed that they were engaged in some dark design. All three were arrested.

These were executive acts, which a few weeks later were cast into legal form. At a solemn council, presided over by the king wearing his crown, the earl of Nottingham (an ex-appellant) with several other lords put in a bill of appeal against the prisoners, his old colleagues, cautiously reserving the right to amend their bill.[1] They mention their 'counsel' in this connection, and manifestly the whole operation had been carefully settled by their lawyers. Following precedent, the appeal was first launched before the king himself, but without reference to any judicial body; indeed the bill to the king concluded with a prayer that any writs or orders whatsoever issuing out of any court which might prejudice the appeal should be quashed and annulled. Four knights were named as pledges to prosecute. It is difficult to see what sort of interference by the law courts could have caused so much anxiety to the new appellants, but they had doubtless been advised to take the precaution just mentioned.

[1] *Rot. Parl.*, iii. 374 (2).

That bill was duly embedded in a covering note and further accompanied by elaborate articles when a new parliament opened on 17 September 1397 to hear 'pleas of the crown before the lord king in his parliament'—the forms of the common law were being scrupulously followed. The bill and articles were read and the gaolers were ordered to produce their prisoners. At the trials which then ensued, John of Gaunt as Steward of England presided over the lords. Arundel's case[1] was taken first, and when he pleaded various pardons made to him in times past he had the short answer that this present parliament had just repealed and annulled them 'as by the statute thereof made plainly appears'. Arundel refused to continue his defence any further. The king commanded Clopton, C. J., to explain the consequences of this, which he did, but Arundel remained obdurate and refused to enter into the merits of the case. The appellants prayed judgement, and the Steward of England, 'by command of the king and all the lords temporal, and of Sir Thomas Percy having sufficient power of the prelates and clergy of the realm of England', found him guilty of treason and pronounced sentence.

Gloucester's case[2] was taken next. A writ tested 21 September was sent to Calais where he was confined; on the 24th his gaoler (the earl marshal) returned that his prisoner was dead. Thereupon some startling things happened. First, the appellants prayed that Gloucester, though dead, be adjudged a traitor as one who had waged war against the king's person. Then the commons intervened (it is the first mention of them in the record of the trials, and we are left to surmise that they may in fact have been present all the time).[3] They introduced a point not hitherto stressed in the case against Gloucester, namely, that his appearance in warlike array at Harringay and levying of war against the king was 'notoriously known to the king and all the estates of parliament and all the realm', and upon that basis they prayed for judgement. The lords (and the lay proctor of the clergy) were then examined, whence it appeared that the fact was indeed notorious. They therefore found him guilty and the forfeiture of his estates was declared.

The proceedings were certainly curious. The appeal against Gloucester manifestly failed for he was dead. In order to reach

[1] *Rot. Parl.*, 377*a*. [2] *Ibid.*, 377*b*.

[3] The chronicles show them as excited spectators.

his property, a new proceeding was therefore instituted by the commons who harked back to the primitive legal notions of conviction by notoriety which had been the basis of Mortimer's trial in 1330, and it was expressly upon that principle that the deceased Gloucester was found guilty. Carefully distinguished from that condemnation, which was pronounced on 24 September, were the events of the morrow, the 25th. On that day there was introduced the written confession of Gloucester taken before Rikhill, J. No legal consequences were based upon the confession, which seems to have been introduced merely 'for information'.

Clearly, a new problem had arisen. The common law was of old familiar with the problem of the accused who has taken to flight, and had elaborated the law of outlawry to deal with it. An accused who killed himself likewise presented no problem, for he was a *felo de se* and the coroner's verdict was sufficient to warrant the escheat of land and forfeiture of chattels. But the government, no doubt for sufficient reasons, observed the extremest reticence upon the circumstances of Gloucester's death, albeit they made no suggestion of *felo de se*. Hence they had to revert to the principle of notoriety in order to have a mode of proof, and to resort to an innovation in order to reach his property. It will be observed that the forfeiture is dated as from the 13 November 1387 when the act of treason was committed; this was already becoming an established principle and had been enacted in this present parliament, although it was to be greatly complicated with the development of the notion of attaint.

Then it was Warwick's turn.[1] He was produced by the Constable, and the Steward of England arraigned him at some length. The earl at once pleaded guilty, whereupon the Steward by command of the king and the temporal lords and of Sir Thomas Percy gave judgement.

That disposed of the appeals, which in formal words were directed against Arundel, Gloucester and Warwick only. The long set of articles, however, named and implicated several lesser persons as well who were not yet in custody. The appellants prayed for the arrest of Sir Thomas Mortimer to answer them on the appeal. He was not produced, but the commons impeached him in his absence as a fugitive, guilty of notorious treasons. The outcome was curious: the dead Gloucester had been condemned

[1] *Rot. Parl.*, iii. 379 (8).

to total forfeiture, but Mortimer the refugee 'in the highlands of Ireland' got nothing worse than a proclamation to the effect that he should be held convict and attainted if he did not surrender within three months.[1]

Sir John Cobham was also impeached of the matters contained in the appeals, especially of sitting on the commission which condemned Burley. In defence he alleged that he sat by the king's order (and the king then and there admitted it, but protesting that he was not his own master at that time, as Cobham well knew). The commons then used words which had first appeared in the preceding case, praying that Cobham be 'convict and attaint'—and so it was pronounced in due course by the Steward of England.[2] One last case was left over to be dealt with by the famous committee to which the parliament had delegated all its powers. This was neither an appeal, nor an impeachment. The king proceeded upon a sort of information that Sir Robert Plessington, deceased, had been a party to the treasons of the duke of Gloucester. There was not even the allegation that the facts were notorious. The process simply recited Plessington's complicity, adjudged him guilty, and imposed total forfeiture.[3]

The growing insistence on legal technicality which has already been remarked is still more apparent in these cases, especially in the matter of minutely defining the nature of the forfeitures inflicted upon the culprits; of that I shall speak later. Indeed, we are confronted not only with legal tactics at the trials, but also with legal strategy preceding them. There were in fact serious legal obstacles to be removed before these state trials could be begun with any hope of success, and their removal was carefully thought out beforehand.

Thus the very first item of business after the presentation of the Speaker was the consideration of the position of the lords spiritual in state trials. This was an old problem. The lords spiritual insisted upon enjoying the privileges of the magnates —already commonly described as 'peers'; yet they also insisted upon their clerical privilege of taking no part in judicial proceedings which might involve the shedding of blood. Moreover, Thomas Despenser (soon to be created earl of Gloucester) was petitioning in this very parliament for the reversal of the condemnation of his great-great-grandfather, and among the docu-

[1] *Rot. Parl.*, 380 (9). [2] *Ibid.*, 381 (10). [3] *Ibid.*, 384 (13).

ments which he produced was an earlier reversal in which it had been solemnly held to be error that 'the prelates being there, who were peers of the realm, did not assent'.[1] This awkward decision of 1322 could hardly have been dragged into daylight at a less opportune moment. The clergy in this present parliament would beyond all doubt withdraw when the serious business of the trials came on, and (according to the rule of 1322) the judgements of the remaining temporal lords would be invalid. The solution was now found in a most carefully drafted document whereby the lords spiritual conveyed to Sir Thomas Percy their plenary power.[2] This power was formally recited in the subsequent judgements.

The second preliminary was the repeal of the famous commission and—still more vital—the repeal of the pardons which the contrivers of it had subsequently obtained:[3] that provided in advance the answer to Arundel's defence. These two weighty matters were disposed of on the first day; clearly there was excellent staff-work somewhere.

Two days later, the commons ostentatiously yielded to the king one of the points made in his favour in the opinion of the judges, by formally seeking his leave to bring certain impeachments.[4] Finally, they joined with the king and the lords in redefining the law of treason, and extending the scope of the forfeiture.[5] Only after all these preliminary operations was the field clear for the principal matter in hand, the trials. The trials themselves, if we can trust the chroniclers, were noisy and unseemly performances; but it is probably true to say that the decorum and solemnity of judicial proceedings is a habit of fairly recent growth. The rough and tumble of medieval litigation, which seems to have lasted as late as Elizabeth I, if we read Sir Thomas Smith carefully, must not mislead us into underestimating contemporaries' keen sense of technicality in the matters which seemed to them essentials. However much we deplore these proceedings of 1397, we must admit the powerful desire of those concerned to proceed with the most scrupulous (albeit tortuous) legality.

The fact that these proceedings were designed to punish the

[1] *Ibid.*, 365*a*.

[2] *Ibid.*, 348 (9). This was a great improvement upon the earlier device of 1388 in *Ibid.*, 236*b*.

[3] *Ibid.*, 350 (13). [4] *Ibid.*, 351 (14). [5] *Ibid.*, 351 (18).

king's enemies, that the king was completely master of the whole machinery of state at this moment and desirous of making a spectacular display of his powers, and yet used procedures so indirect as these, is a paradox which merits consideration. Sovereigns, like subjects, are surely entitled to the elementary right of self-defence, and must have and use powers to repel internal as well as external attacks upon their safety. That Richard II intended to do so, there could be no doubt; and yet how indirect and artificial were the courses forced upon him. Impeachments and appeals were essentially opposition weapons for use against ministers and favourites, and so there was inevitably a logical tendency to remove them as far as possible from royal control; to those procedures, nevertheless, Richard had to turn in order to crush his enemies. Instead of directly bringing a charge against them, a group of magnates had to be organized to go through the motions of an appeal of treason; or, alternatively, the commons had to be inspired to pray the king's leave to impeach his enemies. Still more curious is the use of both procedures simultaneously against the same accused.[1] The truth seems to be that there was no direct royal procedure available to the king to initiate the trial for treason of peers and ministers.

As we have seen, there was a time when the king's personal record of a man's guilt was sufficient to work an instant conviction —so perished Henry of Lancaster and others under Edward II. But that principle had since been rejected. The close association of the idea of peerage with that of trial meant in practice that state trials became especially connected with parliament, where the commons could obviously attest the 'notoriety' of great public crimes. The use of these methods by opposition parties naturally produced attempts to prevent the crown from frustrating the proceedings, and so the crown lost the formal initiative. There was also a notion contributing a theoretical reason for separating treason trials from the crown. Bracton shows good enough reasons for holding that the king himself cannot try treason, for he would then be judge in his own case; trouble begins when Bracton uses the same principle to disable the king's justices also, on the ground that they bear his *persona*. Bracton's solution is to associate peers with the justices, and the suggestion may have been deliberately followed.[2] All things conspired, therefore, to rob

[1] *Rot. Parl.*, 351 (19).

[2] Bracton, fos. 119–119*b*.

the crown of a direct method of putting an alleged traitor on trial.

If Haxey's case had been meant to fill the gap, it failed. The procedure was not enrolled, and in any event would not have served as a precedent for the trial of a magnate.

I had intended to say something about acts of attainder, but a week ago there came to my hands a study which enables me to be briefer than I hoped. This is the introduction to the 24th volume of the Selden Society's *Year Book Series* which will be published in a few months. In it, Mr. J. P. Collas of Queen Mary College undertakes a penetrating examination of the subtle stages by which the word 'attainder' became a term of art among lawyers. It is a salutary warning that we must beware of treating this word, on sight, as necessarily being anything more than the conversational use of a common and natural French word. Later lawyers, when searching for a richer vocabulary to denote the numerous consequences of a criminal trial, unluckily took a fancy to the word 'attaint' and its derivatives—unluckily, because the old law-books had constantly employed it in a variety of popular senses which made it extremely difficult to extract any consistent technical meaning from it. It is probably not unfair to say that lawyers were so plagued by the use of the word in their older books that they never succeeded in making the word a useful word of art. This can be seen as late as the nineteenth century: the member for Tipperary had been convicted and sentenced for treason-felony —but was he 'attainted'? If so, he was disqualified from sitting in the House of Commons. What promised to be a pleasantly endless debate on the difference (if any) between conviction and attainder was cut short by the Forfeiture Act (1870) which abolished attainder.[1] That was all to the good, but the historian is left heir to the lawyer's unsolved conundrums, and will be well advised to treat the word 'attaint' and its derivatives with great caution.

That is one necessary preliminary to the study of attainder. There are others. Thus the extent of the property subject to forfeiture and the moment at which forfeiture arises raised difficult questions. By a statute of 1361, the king agreed not to exact forfeiture for treason in respect of persons who had not been attainted or judged in their lifetime, unless they were forfeitures of war.[2] This statute therefore rules out the possibility of convict-

[1] O'Donovan Rossa's case: 33 & 34 Vict., c. 23. [2] 34 Edw. III, c. 12.

ing, and getting a forfeiture from, a dead man, unless he had been killed in battle against the king. Further, the common law rule of forfeiture dated from a simpler age when property was almost universally held for an estate of fee simple, but by the later fourteenth century that had long ceased to be the case, and parliamentary condemnations ventured sometimes to subject newer estates and interests to forfeiture. Thus Alice Perrers[1] forfeited not only her fees simple but also lands held by others to her use in 1377, and in 1397 the statute of treason[2] which prepared the way for the new trials enacted the forfeiture of the traitor's fees tail as well as fees simple, and also of lands held to his use. Miss Clarke[3] some twenty years ago suggested that the condemnations in parliament in 1388 had imposed the forfeiture of entails before the statute had made them forfeitable, and in so doing had brought us near to the fifteenth-century bill of attainder; but the evidence seems to me to show that entails were in 1388 preserved.[4] However, the case of Alice Perrers still remains with its forfeiture of uses, and is sufficient as a warning to scrutinize these forfeitures rather closely if we seek the origins of the bill of attainder. The forfeiture of equitable interests was probably less significant at a time when they were imperfectly protected even in chancery.

Another preliminary question which needs attention is the modern view that an act of attainder purports to achieve a judicial object by means of a legislative form. Such a criticism would have been unintelligible in the middle ages. They were indeed familiar with the analysis of governmental powers into three or more categories, but the idea that each power should be exercised by a separate authority, and that it was perilous for one body to exercise two powers, is typical of modern, not medieval, thought. The further refinement that certain procedures are judicial and others legislative would not have been felt of great consequence. Nor must we put too much emphasis on such incidents as one of the acts of the parliament of 1397 which said that all the judgements of this parliament should be held and declared to be statutes.[5] The thought behind this is hard to catch, and certainly far from precise; it may serve to remind us that we are not clarifying an attainder by the converse process of calling

[1] *Rot. Parl.*, iii. 14 (43). [2] 21 Ric. II, c. 3.

[3] *Fourteenth Century Studies*, p. 143.

[4] *Cf.* Holdsworth, *History of English Law* (3rd. edn.), iii. 116.

[5] *Rot. Parl.*, iii. 354 (32).

it a statute which pretends to be a judgement. Again, what are we to say of the case in 1459 when among the common petitions in parliament is a list of articles 'of all which matters done and committed by the said Lord Stanley, we your said Commons accuse and impeach him . . .'? Perhaps we ought to call that an impeachment, but the royal response is in the time-honoured words: *Le Roy s'avisera.*[1] Can we also say that the king had rejected a bill of attainder?

The difficulties of an enquiry into the development of the bill of attainder are thus considerable, and there seems to be little if anything in the period before 1399 (which alone is my concern) which throws light upon it. The answer evidently lies in the fifteenth century, where the state trial was very prominent and produced several novelties in our law.

The growing infrequency of parliament provoked experiments with the court of the constable, and the creation of the court of the lord high steward—and on the latter we have a monograph of outstanding merit.[2] Appeals were removed from the jurisdiction of parliament;[3] impeachments continued until the middle of the century, but by its close bills of attainder become common. They might follow conviction and even execution[4] under other jurisdictions and so were not necessarily a mode of trial; the growing complexities of property law are possibly the reason.

The crown was still faced with the problem of finding a direct procedure for putting its enemies on trial instead of resorting to the make-believe of bellicose appellants or querulous commons. The Tudors here seem to have made a startling and characteristic discovery: they simply used the common law—an indictment and a special commission of oyer and terminer. But the long history of special commissions still awaits investigation.

What has already been said about the earliest cases of impeachment is enough to show how little precise law there was, and how various the precedents were. The revival of impeachment under James I was an astonishing feat of antiquarianism, and yet it was essential in the new age when once again there was an opposition

[1] *Ibid.*, v. 369–70.

[2] L. W. Vernon Harcourt, *His Grace the Steward* (1907).

[3] 1 Hen. IV, c. 14.

[4] Thus the earl of Warwick, tried and executed in 1499, was attainted in 1503.

strong enough to put ministers on trial. Once that resolve was made, impeachment or attainder was the only method at their disposal, and impeachment was almost completely under their control.

The savage weapons of the fourteenth and fifteenth centuries now came to be wielded with such consideration and decency, however, that a most unexpected result ensued. Hanoverians and Jacobites were less bloodthirsty than Yorkists and Lancastrians, with the result that even the law of treason itself was softened. People were conscious of the turn of the party wheel and foresaw that it might be their turn next. So we had the extraordinary enactment of 1696 (which is still law) that a charge of high treason cannot be brought more than three years after the event;[1] the prisoner was given a copy of the indictment before the trial, and also the panel of the jury; his witnesses could give evidence on oath, and the court would compel their attendance; he was to have counsel throughout the trial. The astonishing liberality of these provisions appears when it is remembered that the ordinary man on trial for felony is not yet protected by any lapse of time; that he could not have his witnesses sworn until 1702, and had no counsel until 1837. It is indeed astonishing that our state trials, after so much reckless savagery, should have finally led the way in the humanizing of our criminal procedure—but it is a satisfactory result, and provides a more or less happy ending to an otherwise depressing series of addresses.

[1] 7 & 8 Will. III, c. 3, if committed in England or Wales, and if the charge was not one of designing or attempting the assassination of the king.

XI

CHAUCER'S ESCAPADE

The entertaining article by Mr. P. R. Watts on this subject (63 L.Q.R. 491) is a salutary warning that the mediaevalist ought to include in his general equipment some knowledge of legal history. It also shows that the investigation of an apparently simple incident can reveal serious gaps in our knowledge of the older criminal law. There are two points on which I would venture a comment.

First, the position of Goodchild and Grove. Mr. Watts maintains (though with evident difficulty) that they were somehow accomplices in Chaucer's adventure. To me it seems more likely that they were loyal friends who lent their financial credit to get the poet out of a scrape. It must be remembered that although many deeds were enrolled, the large majority of deeds were not enrolled; the documents printed therefore do not tell the whole tale. The course of events may be reconstructed, I suggest, as follows:

(a) Chaucer and Cecilia quickly came to terms, and Cecilia's enrolled release of May 1, 1380, disposed of the matter between them. Evidently Cecilia wanted money, and got it, but the poet was not in a position to raise a large sum at short notice. Failing cash, he could have given her his bond; but the lady being indignant (or repentant, or just hard-headed) would have no further dealings with him; perhaps she wanted a better security. That security was provided by the friendly Goodchild and Grove. It seems evident that these two became bound to Cecilia in the sum required by their bond (which was not enrolled, and is not extant). This sort of operation was an every-day affair in the middle ages. For their indemnity, they may have taken a bond from Chaucer; at this date their chances would have been very slight without one.

(b) The two friends had been generous and prompt, but the burden was evidently heavy, and some re-financing was needed. Cecilia was persuaded to accept a new security, and on June 28, by deeds enrolled she released to Goodchild and Grove, and they released to Chaucer. To replace that arrangement Grove alone by an enrolled recognisance became bound to Cecilia in ten pounds. At Michaelmas he paid. It may be presumed that Chaucer gave his bond to Grove, and the sale of his house may be due to his determination to meet it. There seems nothing to indicate that these two men had any connection with the affair as accomplices in whatever crime had been committed. It seems more plausible to read the documents as showing that they used their credit (and Grove's ten pounds) to give the poet rather more than twelve months' respite in which to meet what was evidently a heavy claim.

Secondly, there is the much more difficult matter of what were Cecilia's rights. Mr. Watts' interpretation of *raptus* must be accepted. (If only abduction had been involved, then the release would have proceeded from the injured party, *viz*., the feudal lord, parent, husband or employer of Cecilia.) The criminal remedies of a victim of rape were appeal, and indictment. We may eliminate appeal for the reasons stated by Mr. Watts, in all probability, and still more because the release Cecilia gave did not extend to an appeal. As for indictment, we must distinguish. If she convicted Chaucer of felony she would have secured revenge, but could have got no *solatium* because of the resulting forfeiture. Alternatively, she might have indicted him for trepass. It is sometimes forgotten that both Bracton and Marowe hold that all felonies are trespasses, although not all trespasses are felonies. Consequently, whatever the Statute of Westminster II, c. 34, may have said, rape could be indicted as a trepass instead of as a felony; such cases have been printed in Miss Putnam's volume in the Ames Foundation. But this raises several points. In the first place, a grand jury could present an offence on its own initiative, although in most cases no doubt it acted upon the initiative of the injured party. Secondly, although compounding a felony was a crime, compounding a trespass was probably not; but this does not mean that Cecilia's release could be pleaded in bar to an indictment of trespass. It is therefore difficult to believe that the release diminished her criminal remedies.

It remains to note that most indictable trespasses could also be treated as torts giving rise to a civil action for damages. This, in combination with the fact that some felonies could be indicted as trespasses, ought to have raised the problem whether the injured party could be allowed to bring a civil action upon facts amounting to a felony, either before or after the felony had been prosecuted to a conviction, or at all. In fact there is no mediaeval authority on the point, the modern law on the matter going no further back than the seventeenth century. As practically nothing has yet been printed from the plea rolls of Richard II it is difficult to say whether a civil action existed corresponding to the indictable trespass of rape; but if it did, then it would have to be considered whether it was extinguished, or postponed, in consequence of the felonious element. Cecilia seems to have had skilled advisers, and the terms of the release seem to show that in their opinion she had a civil remedy for rape, and that her release was effectual to bar it.

Finally, we must be fair to Chaucer. Rape is a brutal crime and implies a degree of depravity which should make us cautious in fixing such a charge. There is really no evidence for it. That he seduced Cecilia we may well believe; that she was angry with him, and still more with herself, is extremely probable. She may have honestly thought that because it all happened against her better judgment, that therefore it was without her consent. Her scandalised family would naturally treat that as an irrebuttable presumption. But there is nothing to suggest that Cecilia could have convicted Chaucer of felony. The single word on the close roll is the only word anywhere suggesting crime of any sort in this affair, and we must bear in mind that no one incurred legal responsibility for its use in that document, or undertook to prove its truth. Doubtless there was some angry recrimination at the moment and hard words were used. It was unlucky for Chaucer's memory that one of them was engrossed in chancery.

XII

THE CASE OF THE MISCREANT CARDINAL

IT is difficult to suggest a reason why so striking and picturesque a case as that of the Miscreant Cardinal in 1382–1383 should have remained in print for four hundred years in a well-known repository of law reports without exciting a single word of comment from the lawyers and controversialists who have sought argument and precedent within the famous pages of Fitzherbert's *Graund Abridgement*.[1]

Taking the story as it stands in Fitzherbert (for there are no other independent published reports of this portion of Richard II.'s reign),[2] we learn that the king brought an action of *Quare impedit* to recover the right of making a presentation to an unnamed church in the diocese of Durham, the defendant, or, as they said then, the impedient, being the parson *de facto,* whom our report simply designates as "P". The tale the king's sergeant told was that the church was of the patronage of the bishops of Durham, that the pope had put in a certain cardinal (unnamed in our report) by provision, and that this cardinal became a miscreant, the church thereby falling vacant. Moreover, since this vacancy occurred while the see of Durham was likewise vacant and its temporalities in the king's hand, it was for the crown to exercise the prerogative of presenting for that occasion in the right of the vacant see. Hereupon there occurred a remarkable debate, in the course of which several notable observations were made which will claim our attention.

Before going into the law of the case, however, it will be interesting to try to identify some of the persons involved, and to pierce the veil of anonymity with which Fitzherbert's report enshrouds them. In the library of Lincoln's Inn there is a manuscript Year Book[3] which gives a report of this case in almost the same words as Fitz-

[1] A paper read at the meeting of the American Historical Association at Columbus, Dec. 27, 1923.

[2] *Triall,* p. 54. The report in Bellewe, p. 325, is merely a reprint of Fitzherbert.

[3] MS. Hale 77. I have used the rotograph facsimile in the Harvard Law Library.

herbert, with the valuable addition for us of the full name of the impedient, and so we learn that "P" is a certain Peter Galoun. From this one fact all the rest can be derived. From the patent rolls it appears that in the year in which the case closed, this Peter Galoun obtained the king's ratification of his estate in the church of Wearmouth[4]—a frequent mode of settling actions of this sort. Wearmouth is in the diocese of Durham, and so is the church concerned in our case.[5] From the same source we learn that the king made several prerogative presentations to this church in July, 1381,[6] from which it is clear that their failure of success provoked the king to bring this action which occupied the next year, 1382,[7] while in March, 1383, Galoun received the ratification of his estate. Finally, it is equally certain that Thomas Hatfield, who had been bishop of Durham since 1345, died on May 8, 1381,[8] the see remaining vacant until the following October,[9] the king in the meanwhile having attempted to exercise his prerogative in favor of Lynton, Packington, and, in 1382, Trofford.

As for the Miscreant Cardinal, neither Fitzherbert nor the Lincoln's Inn manuscript discloses his identity, but the industry and erudition of the county historians have provided us with a partial list of the incumbents of Wearmouth, from which we learn that at least twice in the fourteenth century it had been honored with a prince of the Church as its rector; Simon, cardinal of St. Sixtus, occupied it from 1370 until he resigned in 1372, and he was succeeded—almost immediately, it would seem—by the Lord Robert of Geneva, cardinal priest of the Basilica of the Twelve Apostles, who is mentioned as rector in Bishop Hatfield's register under the date 1375.[10] Robert's abilities were so considerable that the larger stage of European politics claimed all his attention, and the rich, perhaps, but remote parish in the north never saw its illustrious rector. Perhaps he felt little love for England since another of his English benefices—the treas-

[4] *Calendar of Patent Rolls, Richard II.*, II. 237.

[5] It is later called Bishop Wearmouth to distinguish it from Monks' Wearmouth, which was not in the gift of the bishop but of the dean and chapter. Surtees, II. 11; Hutchinson, II. 511.

[6] Thomas Lynton was presented on July 18, 1381 (*Cal. Pat., Rich. II.*, II. 28), the patent being subsequently surrendered; William Packington was presented on the 28th (*ibid.*, p. 31); and William Trofford on July 17, 1382 (*ibid.*, p. 154).

[7] The date is given as Mich. 5 Ric. II. (1381) by Fitzherbert, and as Mich. 6 Ric. II. (1382) by MS. Hale 77; the litigation may well have extended over both years.

[8] *Dictionary of National Biography* (reissue), IX. 155.

[9] Rymer, VII. 333.

[10] Surtees, I. 231; Hutchinson, II. 512; Hatfield's register has not been printed.

urership of York—was wrested from him by a royal favorite in 1375.[11] However, greater things were in store for him. Allied by birth with many of the royal and princely houses of Europe,[12] and remarkable for his personal bravery and military skill, he nevertheless possessed as well those qualities which made him an astute and successful figure in ecclesiastical affairs. Preferment fell upon him rapidly; lord of Geneva, bishop of Thérouanne, chancellor of Amiens, bishop of Cambrai, cardinal, legate in Lombardy—these were only some of the titles of the rector of Wearmouth, until in 1378 he reached the zenith of his fortune. It was on the 20th of September, at Fondi, that the cardinals who had elected Pope Urban VI. repented of their choice, declared that they had acted under fear of their lives, and set in his place the Cardinal Robert of Geneva, who took the name of Clement VII. and reigned at Avignon until his death in 1394.[13] Antipope is a word our Year Books refuse to utter, and so the courts of England know him simply as the miscreant cardinal.

These then are the characters hidden beneath the cautious reticence of the reports, which must now receive a more detailed discussion. The text of the Hale manuscript here reproduced is collated (as to the more material variations) with that in Fitzherbert's *Abridgement,* and accompanied by a translation, for the first time it is believed.

MS. Hale 77, f. 189.

[14] Le Roi porta quare impedit [14] vers [15] P. Galoun [15] clerc dun esglise deinz le Eveschie de Duresm et counta coment levesque qui mort est presenta un son clerk et le clerc murust et [16] lappostail et noma qui etc. fist [16] collacion a un Cardinall et noma son non et par cause de mescreantise et sismatise lesglise se voida esteant les temporalties en la mayn le Roi. Issint appent a Roi a presenter.

Burgh [17] [18] defendit tort et force et demanda jugement si le court voet conistre quar [18] il ad counte

Translation.

The king brought *Quare impedit* against P. Galoun, clerk, of a church in the diocese of Durham and counted how the late bishop presented one of his clerks, who died, and the pope (and he said which) collated a cardinal (and he told his name), and because of misbelief and schism the church fell void while the temporalities were in the king's hand. And so it is for the king to present.

Burgh denied tort and force and demanded judgment whether the court would take cognizance for he

[11] Le Neve, III. 160–161. He was also archdeacon of Dorchester; *Calendar of Papal Registers, Letters,* IV. 188.

[12] Noël Valois, *La France et le Grand Schisme,* I. 81.

[13] Eubel, I. 367, 166, 38, 26, 21.

[14] Quare impedit par le Roy. F.

[15] Un P.— F.

[16] Cap' fuit. F.

[17] Brugh. F.

[18] Omitted in F.

dun voidance del esglise par cause de mescreantise dun Cardinal al court de Rome quel chose nest pas triable [19] cy et demanda jugement ut supra.[19]

has counted of a voidance of the church through miscreance of a cardinal at the court of Rome which thing is not triable here, and he demanded judgment as above.

BELKNAP. Ieo vous die pur certain que lę court auera conistre de ce plee et ceo ieo provera par resoun quar tout le court christien est un court et si un home en le Arche cy en ce terre soit arette dun certein cryme pur que il est privable et post il appelle al court de Rome et est prive la [20] ce privacion est triable en le court le Roi auxi bien come [21] sil ust este prive en lez Arches quant tout est un court. Et si un [22] home soit aherdant as enemys le Roi en France sa terre est forfaitable et sa enherdance serra trie lou la terre est come il ad este sovent foitz fait [23] de aherdance [23] as enemys le Roi en escoce. Et [24] si un [25] home soit mescreant sa terre est forfaitable et le seigneur [26] auera par voie deschet et resoun le voet quar si un [27] home soit hors de la [28] foy [29] son lige seigneur [30] sa terre est forfaitable ergo [31] a multo forciori lou [32] un home [32] est [33] encontra le soveraign [33] dieu et ce jura BELKNAP pur ley. Pourquoi, *Burgh*,[34] respondez.

BELKNAP, C. J. I tell you the Court will certainly have cognizance of this plea, and I will prove it by reason, for all the Court Christian is one court, and if a man in the Arches here in the land be charged with a certain crime for which he is deprivable, and appeal to the court of Rome and be deprived there, then that deprivation is triable in the King's Court just as if he had been deprived in the Arches, for it is all one court. And if a man be adherent to the king's enemies in France his land is forfeitable and his adherence shall be tried where the land is, as has often been done in the case of adherence to the king's enemies in Scotland. And if a man be miscreant his land is forfeitable and the lord shall have it by way of escheat; and reason requires it, for if a man be out of the faith of his liege lord his land is forfeitable, therefore *a multo fortiori* where he is against the sovereign God; (and BELKNAP swore that this was the law). And so, *Burgh*, answer.

[35] Et post *Burgh* dit que [35] lesglise se voida en tems levesque qui mort

And afterwards *Burgh* said that the church became void in the time

19 cieinz, par que jugement si la court voille conustre. F.

20 de la. F.

21 Om. F.

22 Om. F.

23 des adherauntz. F.

24 sir, par ma foy—added in F

25 Om. F.

26 ceo—added in F.

27 Om. F.

28 Om. F.

29 de—added in F.

30 Roy—added in F.

31 Om. F.

32 il. F.

33 hors de foy de. F.

34 Brugh. F.

35 Brugh, sir. F.

est, et nous fumus parson enparsone en tems mesme cesti Evesque del provision [36] Gregoire le XIe [36] etc. saunz ceo que lesglise se voida par mescreantise le Cardinall ut supra esteantz les temporalties en la mayn le Roi. Prest, etc. Et alii e contra pro Rege. Et venire facias agarde al viscounte [37] de visneto [37] ou lesglise fut et nient al evesque de Duresme ne a son Senescal ne baille. Et dit fut que mescreantise serra trie lou lesglise est, et privacion fait al [38] court de Rome auxi, etc.[39]

of the late bishop and we were parson imparsonee in his time, too, by provision of Gregory XI., etc., without this that the church became void by the miscreance of the cardinal *ut supra* while the temporalities were in the king's hands. Ready, etc. And the others for the king said the contrary. And *venire facias* was awarded to the sheriff of the vicinity where the church was, and not to the bishop of Durham, his steward or bailiff. And it was said that miscreance shall be tried where the church is, and deprivation at the court of Rome similarly, etc.[40]

First of all let us examine the chronology of the king's claim. His title could only arise while the see was vacant and the temporalities in his hands—that is, between May 6 and October 23, 1381. If Wearmouth church did not become or continue to be vacant during this period, then the king's case falls immediately. The cause of the vacancy he alleges, however, took place three years previously, for Robert was elected pope September 20, was crowned on October 31,[41] and was excommunicated and declared a heretic in December, 1378.[42] If his miscreance caused the vacancy of the church then it had occurred before the beginning of the new year, 1379. But the see of Durham (patron of the living) did not fall vacant until two and a half years afterwards: only if Wearmouth church remained unfilled either by pope or bishop during those two and a half years could the king claim a presentation. On the face of it, this is extremely unlikely. The impedient's story, on the other hand, is simple and consistent. He asserts that he has been parson imparsonee ever since his provision by Gregory XI.[43]—who died March 28, 1378, more than

36 le Pape. F.

37 del counte. F.

38 del. F.

39 et ceo appert par cest ple icy par le jugement etc. quod nota. F.

40 and this appears from this plea by the judgment, so note well. F.

41 Eubel, I. 26.

42 Raynaldus, VII. 362.

43 As early as 1363 and 1366 Peter Galoun was petitioning the pope for preferment in the diocese of Durham (*Cal. Pap. Reg., Petitions,* I. 434, 520). But I have been unable to find the provisions of Cardinal Robert and Peter Galoun to the church of Wearmouth in the *Calendars.* From these documents we learn incidentally that Peter was *alias* "de Castro", and a master of arts. A certain Gervase de Castro had been bishop of Bangor from 1367 to 1370, on the appointment of Urban V. (not Urban III., as Le Neve, I. 99).

three years before the temporalities of the see of Durham fell into the king's hands. The Year Book tells us nothing of the verdict, but from the fact that Peter Galoun received a royal ratification of his estate in the church, it would seem that the crown experienced some difficulty in establishing so uncertain a claim, and so compromised the action.

What of the law? A number of interesting and important points are raised, which, however, are not so easily solved. First of all, what was the nature of the vacancy alleged by the crown?

To answer this, it is necessary to refer once more to general political history. Selden once remarked (more in jest than earnest) that Urban VI. was the only pope with a parliamentary title,[44] for at the Parliament of Gloucester the king laid the facts of the Great Schism before the assembled prelates and magnates, who after due deliberation passed a statute acknowledging the title of Urban, and enacting that all the benefices of the rebel cardinals—Clement and his party—were to be seized into the king's hands and the fruits paid to him until further orders.[45] Moreover, the statute was immediately enforced, for we read that two cardinals received restitution of their goods and benefices taken under the statute when they had convinced the government of their adherence to the right side in the schism.[46] So far all is clear, but it must be added that the motives of the government were not unmixed. England was at war with France: Clement was the nominee of the French faction among the cardinals, and so England had naturally supported Urban and proscribed Clement. Then, too, there is abundant evidence that the crown had been accustomed to derive considerable income from the benefices held by Frenchmen during times of war. The statute, it is true, covers its clauses of confiscation with a decent cloak of religion and denounces the Clementine cardinals as rebels and schismatics,[47] but the royal letters patent which soon afterwards appeared show that a different view could be taken. Now Urban VI. had declared Clement and his supporters to be deprived of their benefices, and had appropriated two-thirds of their income to the papal *camera* and the remainder to the improvement of the benefices. Already, then, the king's statute and the pope's bull were in conflict over the disposition of the spoils, and an obvious opportunity existed for the king

[44] Selden, *Table Talk*, CVI. 9.

[45] Stat. 2 Ric. II., st. 1, c. 7. For the text of the manifestos issued by the rival parties, see Walsingham, I. 382 ff., who implies (*ibid.*, p. 380) that their respective nuncios came to the Parliament.

[46] Rymer, VII. 208.

[47] The Commons in the Gloucester Parliament, however, were most concerned at the vast sums of ecclesiastical revenue sent abroad. *Rot. Parl.*, III. 46 (70).

to show his devotion to the true pontiff—and it is here that the more immediate motives of the king find frank expression. Letters patent issued July 6, 1379, recited the statute of the Parliament of Gloucester, and further related that the king had followed the practice of his predecessors in the matter of benefices held by adherents of his enemy of France and had confiscated them to the treasury (*Aerrario nostro fiscali jussimus applicari*); nevertheless, Urban had sought to apply their revenues to his own and the churches' needs, and so the king, moved by the extreme poverty of the Holy Father, conceded his request, and, although by the law of the land these sums were notoriously confiscated, yet the king graciously allowed the papal agents to collect them until Michaelmas of the following year.[48] In short, the statute had hastily assumed that the fruits of ecclesiastical benefices forfeited for schism would go to the crown: Urban's bull appropriated them to the requirements of the papacy; and in face of that claim the king felt a change of front necessary if he was to retain the spoils. Consequently we find the insistence that the Clementine cardinals are not only schismatics but also adherents to France. The attempt of the pope to secure the profits for himself is set aside and it is only by way of charity that he is permitted to collect them for just twelve months—a period which was subsequently extended for similar short terms,[49] although at times a particular benefice would be excepted from the concession and retained in the king's hand.[50] Finally, the letters patent seriously misrepresent the statute of the Gloucester Parliament by alleging that it extends to all benefices held by Frenchmen.[51]

We can now examine the vacancy alleged by the crown with a view to determining its nature. The simplest course would have been to plead that the vacancy was by deprivation; but there were difficulties there, for the very bull containing the sentence also contained the reservation of the profits to the papal *camera* (which the king had so brusquely set aside), with the understanding doubtless that when the benefices were ultimately filled it would be by papal provision. Moreover, it would have been extremely awkward for the crown to have to prove a voidance by the production of a papal bull, seeing that subjects were stringently forbidden to bring papal documents into the king's court.[52] Clearly, then, deprivation by papal

48 Rymer, VII. 222.

49 *Ibid.*, pp. 271, 303, 346.

50 *Ibid.*, p. 289.

51 This was the petition of the Commons, but the king's reply to it only dealt with those held by the rebel cardinals. *Rot. Parl.*, III. 46 (70, 71).

52 30 *Lib. Ass.* 19.

sentence is not the line the royal sergeants will take. The statute of the Gloucester Parliament is even less promising, for it does not go to the length of depriving the rebel cardinals but only seizes their profits into the king's hand—and in our particular case the king wants not the income of the benefice but the opportunity to confer it upon his nominee, for which purpose he must first establish the fact that it has become vacant. Only one course was left, and that was the one that the crown took, namely, to ask the Court of Common Pleas to try whether the antipope Clement VII., rector of Wearmouth, was a miscreant; and if so, to hold that his church was thereby vacant *ipso jure,* and that all these matters lay within its jurisdiction. If this could be done, then the way was clear for the crown to establish its claim to a prerogative presentation in the usual way, if sufficient grounds for such a claim ever existed.

Such an extraordinary suggestion as this must have been received with a vigorous protest, and it is unfortunate that we have only the merest summary of Burgh's plea to the jurisdiction, with the result that it is impossible to say with certainty on what grounds he relied most: did he mean that the Common Pleas cannot try the question of misbelief? Or that a cardinal is beyond their reach? Or that the alleged miscreance would have been triable had it not been laid outside the realm?

The reports available throw no light upon these questions, but it is clear that whatever Burgh's arguments were, they failed to convince the court, and on the contrary, drew from the bench an emphatic assertion of its authority over the present matter. Belknap, C. J., declared that he would prove the jurisdiction of his court from " reason ", *i.e.,* from general principles rather than from precedent. He first laid it down that " all Court Christian is one court "—which we may take as the common law's deduction from the canonical dogma that the pope is universal ordinary.[53] From this Belknap draws the corollary that the deprivation of a clerk is equally within the cognizance of the Court of Common Pleas whether the sentence was given in the Court of Arches in London, or in the court of Rome: there is, moreover, some plausibility in his view, for even appeals to Rome were often tried within the realm by papal delegates.[54] Now it has already been remarked that the crown did not allege a deprivation by sentence, but relied on the general rule of the canon law that heresy and schism involved *ipso jure* loss of benefice.[55] Chief Justice Belknap meets this situation by assuming that depriva-

53 Bracton, f. 412.

54 Maitland, *Canon Law,* p. 105.

55 As to the truth of this assumption, see *post,* note 57.

tions whether *de jure* or *de facto* are equally within his principle that the Court of Common Pleas will take cognizance, wherever the cause of deprivation may have been—"for all Court Christian is one court".

The second step in Belknap's argument is to establish the analogy between heresy and treason[56] when these crimes have been committed outside of the realm. He asserts that the trial of treason in such a case will be at the place where the lands of the accused are situated, and from this draws the conclusion that miscreance should likewise be tried where the heretic's benefice lies.

And so Belknap uses some very general principles as a basis for his claim that the Court of Common Pleas can take cognizance of the voidance of Wearmouth church by reason of the misbelief of its rector. There are several points in his speech which invite discussion: his theory that "all Court Christian is one court" and his remarks upon the trial of treason committed outside the realm both deserve investigation, but they would lead us too far from our present subject, and so must be reserved for a more appropriate occasion. Our immediate purpose is best served by calling attention to the fact that even assuming that the miscreance of a clerk involved *de jure* deprivation in canon law,[57] yet the Church most emphatically denied that any trial of such a matter could take place before a lay judge, or that the *de jure* forfeiture of goods could be actually enforced without a *sententia declaratoria* by the ecclesiastical authority.[58] These points of canon law are significantly absent from Belknap's treatment of the situation.

Nor is this all, for not only the Church but Parliament also stood between the king and Wearmouth church, for in 1350, as the result of a petition of the bishops in Parliament,[59] a statute was made enacting that "whereas the said prelates have prayed remedy because the secular justices accroach to them the cognizance of the voidance of benefices *de jure,* which cognizance and discussion belongeth to the judge of Holy Church and not to lay judge; so the king willeth and

56 This analogy is familiar in canon law, and has played a large part in the development of heresy; c. 10, X. 5. 7.

57 The canons seem to inflict degradation rather than simply deprivation as the immediate penalty upon clerical heretics, but commentators go further; *haeretici enim non possunt possidere rem ecclesiae* is the comment of the archdeacon upon c. 1, Dist. VIII.; and Lyndwood, p. 293, gl. *d,* says, *nec possunt* [*haeretici*] *aliquid beneficium ecclesiasticum obtinere.* Degradation and the milder deposition both involve deprivation and must be performed by ecclesiastical authorities. See Zanchinus Ugolinus, *De Haereticis,* c. xviii, § 7.

58 Lyndwood, p. 293, gl. *confiscata*; c. 19, VI. 5. 2.

59 *Rot. Parl.,* II. 245.

granteth that the said justices from henceforth receive such challenges made or to be made by any prelates of Holy Church in that behalf, and moreover shall do right and reason thereof ".[60] The meaning of the statute we believe to be clear: the king concedes the trial of voidances *de jure* as within the province of the ecclesiastical courts.[61] The alleged voidance of Wearmouth church is *de jure* and so clearly falls within the statute, and should therefore have been tried by the certificate of the ordinary. But nothing of the sort took place; "*venire facias* was awarded to the sheriff" without, as far as we know, any protest by the party or the ordinary. This case is therefore the first of a slender line of authorities extending into the seventeenth century which agree in flouting the statute, which does not seem ever to have been applied—an injustice which the Church resented as late as the reign of Queen Anne.[62]

So clearly was the temper of the bench revealed in Belknap's speech that Burgh refused further controversy, and in accordance with the peculiarly complex pleading appropriate to this action[63] proceeded to set up his own title—" the church became void in the time of the late bishop and we were parson imparsonee in his time, too, by provision of Gregory XI."—by way of "inducement"[64] to his special traverse of that of the king—" without this that the church fell void by the miscreance of the cardinal *ut supra* while the temporalities were in the king's hand; ready ". The issue having been duly joined by the king's sergeants, process issued for the summoning of the jury and the report remarks that, although the cause of action lay within the palatinate of the see of Durham, yet the *venire facias* was sent to the sheriff and not to the bishop. The reason is evident—the king will sue in no court but his own, and where he is party his own officers and not those of any subject's franchise will return the writs. As for the jury's verdict nothing is known, save what may be conjectured from the ratification of Peter Galoun's estate which followed.[65]

60 25 Edw. III., st. 6, c. 8.

61 It is only fair to state that Maitland, *Canon Law*, pp. 156–157, has interpreted this statute differently, and that the present writer has given reasons for holding the view expressed in the text in "*Execrabilis* in the Common Pleas: Further Studies ", which appeared in *Cambridge Law Journal*, I. 71.

62 Gibson, *Codex Juris Ecclesiastici*, tit. XXXIV., cap. 1.

63 See Booth, *Real Actions*, p. 235.

64 For the forms of special traverse, see Stephen, *Pleading*, pp. 188–192. The necessity of setting up a title in the impedient is explained in the judgment in Elvis *v.* Archbishop of York and others, Hob. 320–321.

65 Ratification might even follow a judgment for the king; *Registrum Brevium Orig.*, f. 304b.

As we have seen, the statute of the Gloucester Parliament made some show of confiscating the goods as well as of sequestrating the benefices of the Clementine cardinals on the ground of their rebellion against Urban VI. True, the crown receded from this position later, when the manifold inconveniences of such a step became apparent, but all the same it has been forever put upon the statute roll that the king had presumed to confiscate the goods of certain exalted heretics. Due allowance of course must be made for the fact that these heretics were also alien enemies and that the Commons were mainly interested in this aspect of the case, but, as we have shown from the subsequent letters patent administering the provisions of the statute, the crown was not unwilling to make the charge of schism—if only in a preamble. Moreover, in the matter of Wearmouth church the crown saw fit to base its claim upon that misbelief and schism of which the *fama publica* accused its rector. And so Chief Justice Belknap was moved to make some remarks upon the general question of the loss of property for heresy, with the discussion of which we will conclude this paper. We willingly concede that they are *obiter dicta* and that strictly they are immaterial to the question involved in the case, but nevertheless they still remain of very great interest. The miscreant's lands are forfeit and the lord shall have them as his escheat; such is the case in treason, and all the more does it apply where the treason is against the Sovereign of all earthly lords. This is Belknap's dogma, and the surprised reporter tells us that he swore it was the law. Can it be that the justice's vehemence must be referred to the lack of better authority?

On the Continent the loss of goods and chattels for heresy was no novelty by the time of our case.[66] Gratian stated the principle and vouched St. Augustine for it,[67] and legislation of the emperors enacted it.[68] Provincial councils, especially in the south of France and other regions where heresy was prevalent, systematized the law with every refinement which the greed of secular and clerical lords could devise, with the result that their combined ferocity laid waste the richest and most flourishing province of France. By the time of the fourteenth century therefore there had accumulated a large mass of case law upon the subject, considerable legislation, and several

66 See Havet, *Oeuvres,* II. 117–180; Lee, "Confiscation for Heresy", in *Eng. Hist. Rev.,* II. 235–259; Pollock and Maitland, II. 544; Tanon, *Histoire des Tribunaux de l'Inquisition,* pp. 523–539.

67 Gratian, c. 4, C. 23, q. 7.

68 For Justinian, see *Cod.* 1. 5; *Cambridge Med. Hist.,* II. 107–108; *cf. Summa Rolandi* (ed. Thaner), p. 96; for Frederick II.'s famous constitution *Commissi,* see *M. G. H., Leges,* II. 196, 281, etc., and c. 18, VI. 5. 2.

treatises in which the law and procedure applicable to heretics were expounded with admirable clearness and skill.

In England things were vastly different. Until the rise of the Lollards the country had been conspicuous among the realms of Europe for its devotion to the Faith. Such misbelievers as did exist were few and insignificant and their possessions too poor to be worth the trouble of dispute. Consequently there is no trace in England of the bitter conflict over the spoils between the secular and ecclesiastical authorities which was so striking a feature of the Continental situation. The few slight references to heresy in English records are soon told. In 1166 the Assize of Clarendon ordered that the houses of all who harbored Patarini should be plucked up and taken outside the town and burnt.[69] There is no suggestion that there were native Patarini in England and this penalty is imposed on all who sheltered them, without alleging that such persons were not themselves orthodox. A few scattered cases occur of condemnation for heresy and on one or two occasions the death penalty was exacted,[70] but we find no mention of the fate of the miscreants' lands and chattels. Hale[71] asserts that in two cases of the reign of Henry III. heretics have been condemned to the loss of goods, and as the rolls he refers to have been printed since he (and later Maitland) discussed them it is now possible to speak of them with more confidence.

The first case is that of Ernald of Périgord. On June 11, 1236, a mandate issued to the warden of Boston Fair for the arrest of all the wines and chattels of Ernald within his jurisdiction, the king having learned that he had been convicted of heresy. They were to be valued by good and lawful men and the wines delivered to John Colemere or his attorney to be held by him to the king's use and at the king's orders, "notwithstanding anyone who might claim on behalf of the mayor of Bordeaux or anyone else that the aforesaid wines and chattels were his, or offer to warrant them as his, more especially since the goods of condemned persons which are found within his realm and power are due to the king". Somewhat similar orders were given to the sheriff of Norfolk and Suffolk, while John Gisorz, citizen of London, was ordered to withhold a debt of ninety-six pounds which he owed to Ernald, and to keep the money to the king's use and subject to the king's commands. Finally instructions were given to Colemere to serve the mandates and to dispose of the wines according to instructions to be sent him later.[72] It should be stated

69 For Continental analogies, see Tanon, *op. cit.*, p. 519.

70 Pollock and Maitland, II. 547–548.

71 Hale, *Pleas of the Crown*, I. 394.

72 *Calendar of Close Rolls, 1234–1237*, p. 359; *cf. ibid.*, p. 294.

that Colemere was keeper of the king's wines and that the Close Rolls bear many memoranda of his official activities, one of which throws fresh light upon the case which was not available to Hale and Maitland. On July 24 following, Colemere was ordered to pay the freight upon ninety casks of wine, the property of "Ernisius de Peregord convicted of heresy and detained at Bordeaux".[73] Ernald is therefore at Bordeaux and we may conjecture that his conviction took place there also. It must be allowed, however, that it was perfectly possible for a heretic to be condemned in his absence [74] and that no legal considerations would prevent a court in England from convicting him of heresy while he was in Bordeaux. The facts that he was from Périgord and that the mayor of Bordeaux was expected to claim his goods strongly indicate that his conviction was in Bordeaux too. But in any case we believe that to be immaterial for our purposes, for the records show beyond all doubt that the king claimed to be entitled to the chattels of a heretic irrespective of the place of his conviction; it is sufficient for the chattels to have been found within the realm and power of the king—a truly remarkable doctrine. At first one is tempted to explain it by the fact that Henry III. was not only king of England but also duke of Aquitaine, but there are difficulties in the way: it seems that a proportion of the forfeiture in Aquitaine went not to the duke but to the mayor of Bordeaux, for how else can we account for his claim? Towns frequently substantiated such rights against their feudal and ecclesiastical neighbors in France.[75] But, taking it as it stands, we believe that the king's position is in perfect accord with canon law, for that system had very peculiar views upon the matter. The so-called forfeiture for heresy is in reality no forfeiture at all in the usual sense of the word. It is not a penal sentence enacted by an avenging sovereign and declared by its courts. Its nature is much more subtle than that. Readers of St. Augustine will recall the mystical sense in which he uses the word "justice" and the endless controversies throughout the Middle Ages on the nature and basis of property. And in Gratian [76] we find that it is this very idea which is responsible for the peculiarities of the law of heresy. The passage from St. Augustine's *Epistles* there preserved argues that the heretic cannot possess the Spirit of Justice, but is completely severed from the divine source of all law and order. Property exists solely in virtue of this principle. The moment a man has become a heretic his own rebellious thought has put to flight the

73 *Ibid.*, p. 293.

74 Zanchinus Ugolinus, c. ix.

75 Lee, in *Eng. Hist. Rev.*, II. 241 ff.

76 C. 4, C. 23, q. 7.

Spirit of Justice and he is left without a single point of contact with society. He has no rights, no property,[77] no family.[78] And so the *dominium* of ninety casks of wine at Boston Fair vanished as soon as Ernald entertained a heretical thought, and the sovereign of the place became entitled to them.

General considerations therefore support the king's contention against the mayor of Bordeaux. But the *non obstante* in the royal mandate is not confined to claims by the mayor but applies to claims of all other persons, even those who are willing to "warrant" the goods as their own, that is to say, who can prove their title according to the law and custom of fairs. In other words, the king claims the forfeiture notwithstanding the claims of *bona fide* purchasers for value in open market. Once more we must think of the condition of a man whose heresy has bereft him of the Spirit of Justice. Clearly he is so completely outside of the Divine order of things that legal relations with the just are impossible. He can make no contract,[79] can give no title. Even if his heresy is so well concealed that not a soul in the world suspects him, nevertheless he has lost *dominium*, and all his transactions are void. He may have died to all appearances a true Catholic, yet even after his death the inquisitor may try him and find him guilty, and then the declaratory sentence will authorize the application of the logical results of this doctrine; all the property of the heretic will be forfeit into whosesoever hands it may have come and by whatever means.[80] And so with Ernald's wines. Even if they have changed hands several times so that the last owner can vouch to warranty the one from whom he bought them, it will not avail against the inexorable metaphysic of the canonists.[81] Fortunately for such purchasers Ernald finally purged himself of heresy and so in due course the king superseded his mandates and allowed him to continue his business.[82] One thing is clear from the case, and that is that the king was well acquainted with the canon law of for-

77 "Statim commisso scelere, id est cum incidunt in errorem seu heresim, perdunt ipsi omnia sua bona", Zanchinus Ugolinus, c. xviii, § 4; consequently a heretic cannot be subjected to a money fine, *id.*, c. xix, § 1.

78 Gratian, cc. 7, 8, C. 28, q. 1.

79 "Fiunt infames et intestabiles active et passive, nec habent alicuius rei commercium", Zanchinus Ugolinus, c. xviii, § 3.

80 *Id.*, c. xxiv, § 1.

81 Certain of his wines in fact were arrested although in the hands of purchasers; *Cal. Pat., 1232–1247*, p. 149.

82 *Cal. Close, 1234–1237*, p. 485; *Cal. Pat., 1232–1247*, pp. 175, 193. It will be of interest to note that Ernald was a man of note in his own country; he was one of a commission who received half of all the rents and issues of Bordeaux as security for a debt of 6000 marks, for five years. *Cal. Pat., 1232–1247*, p. 49.

feiture for heresy, and was prepared to take advantage of it in England if he could find the goods of heretics within his realm.

The second case mentioned by Hale occurred a few years later and concerned another merchant from the south of France. The slight details that we have correspond closely with the case of Ernald, and so further discussion is unnecessary.[83] Enough has been said to show that there is a certain amount of precedent for the forfeiture of chattels in England for heresy. Belknap however does not mention the loss of chattels, but asserts that the heretic's lands will escheat to his lord, and of this proposition we know no earlier statement in English law. Indeed until now it has been believed that the first mention of forfeiture of lands for heresy was in the statute of 1414;[84] this dictum of Belknap's will therefore carry the history of the penalty a generation earlier than the statute.

It is such questions as these, then, which are raised by a consideration of *Triall 54* in the *Graund Abridgement* of Sir Anthony Fitzherbert, and it is surely not without interest to tell the story of how the rector of Wearmouth became cardinal, pope, and miscreant, how a sheriff's jury was summoned to say whether his church was thereby vacant—in spite of canon law and royal statute, and how Chief Justice Belknap more than thirty years before the famous statute of Henry V. declared from the bench that a heretic forfeited his land, "and swore that this was the law".

83 *Cal. Close, 1237–1242*, p. 368.

84 2 Hen. V., st. 1, c. 7; Hale, *Pleas of the Crown*, I. 394; Makower, *Const. Hist.*, p. 188.

XIII

ELLESMERE ON STATUTES

THE publication of the first English treatise on the interpretation of statutes deserves more than a passing notice; and when we learn that the treatise is in the youthful hand of Thomas Egerton, later to become Chancellor and Lord Ellesmere, our attention is deeply engaged.* In addition it must be recorded that the Huntington Library, who are the owners of the manuscripts and the publishers of the present volume, have made a very attractive book of it, and that the editor, Professor Thorne, of Northwestern University Law School, has carried out his difficult task with great skill and has prefixed an introduction which can be regarded as the most authoritative and most richly documented discussion as yet upon the problems of statutory interpretation from the later fourteenth century down to the death of Ellesmere and the age of Coke.

The editor evidently means us to construe his title-page strictly : it is '*A Discourse . . . with Sir Thomas Egerton's Additions*'. Who, then, wrote the *Discourse*? Who had the first inkling that here was a great legal problem, and who had the skill, the originality and the courage to make this pioneer attempt to deal with it? Professor Thorne's remarks are extremely guarded. He has evidently thought about the problem, but in his introduction he never explicitly discusses it; he is careful to avoid language which might imply Egerton's authorship of anything save the additions; only once does he confess that the author is unknown, and even then no reason is adduced. There is an air of mystery in Professor Thorne's discretion which has enticed us into the pleasant game of speculation.

The manuscript situation is fairly simple. There is an earlier and fuller version in English (called *E*, and here printed), and also a later and condensed version in French (called *F*, and here collated with *E*). *E* is in Ellesmere's early hand, *F* is in his commonplace book. As for the dates, the editor puts the composition of *E* between 1557 and 1567, remarking that the copy in Egerton's hand may be assumed to be subsequent to 1559 when he began his law studies.

With that dating we must agree, as far as certainties are concerned; but there are also some possibilities which are worth considering. We must bear in mind the fact that two dates are involved, (1) the date when the *Discourse* was composed, and (2) the date when young Egerton first copied it. According to the editor, the *Discourse* was composed soon after 1557, and copied soon after 1559 but before 1567 (and the narrowness of the margin is significant). We venture the suggestion that the date of composition may be somewhat later (and the margin consequently still narrower), for the following reasons.

The *Discourse*[1] mentions 'a statute made in the time of Queen

---

* A Discourse upon the Exposicion & Understandinge of Statutes: with Sir Thomas Egerton's Additions. Edited from manuscripts in the Huntington Library by Samuel E. Thorne, Northwestern University School of Law. San Marino, California: The Huntington Library, 1942. \$5.00.

[1] P. 155.

Mary'; such language would only be natural in one writing in a subsequent reign, that is to say, after Mary's death on November 17, 1558. So 1557 seems too early; and so is all save the last few weeks of 1558. Moreover, the *Discourse* contains the following passage [2]:—

> 'Phyllpotte, that was burnt for heresy, when that he was called to his answer, showed that his words which he had spoken were said in the convocation house; and for so much as by a laudable custom of the realm the parliament was a place of free speech, and that also was a member of the parliament, he therefore desired the freedom and liberty of the house. Howbeit, it was to him by the Lord Rich and Lord Windsor then said that though they came by a writ of summons of the parliament, that yet notwithstanding they were no parcel nor member of the parliament'.

This remarkable case is not to be found in the law-books, but it occupies scores of pages in Foxe's famous *Book of Martyrs*.[3] The author of the *Discourse* was beholden to Foxe for the facts, but they present an interesting chronological problem. Archdeacon Philpot's trial and death [4] in fact were the subject of Foxe's first essay in protestant martyrology, and he published a pamphlet on the subject at Bale of which no copy now survives.[5] The *Acts and Monuments* first appeared in Latin in 1559, and in English in 1563. Now which of these three versions did the author of the *Discourse* use? At this point we must observe that he occasionally touches ecclesiastical questions, but always in a tone of complete detachment. Only a protestant zealot would be likely to have the pamphlet, published, as it was, abroad during the reign of Mary. If he used the Latin version of Foxe's great work (which is dated at Bale, September 1, 1559) he could hardly have done so before the opening of the year 1560. The general resemblance of the language, however, makes it much more likely that our author used the first English edition of what is popularly called the 'Book of Martyrs' [6]; and the date of that is 1563. So within the limits of 1557 and 1567 set by Professor Thorne, the period from 1563 to 1567 seems especially likely as the date of composition of the *Discourse*.

So much for the date; but there is another circumstance which invites comment, and that is the fact that the first version is in English. The native language of our law is French, and there is abundant evidence that a common lawyer who had had time to get himself really immersed in his profession, naturally expressed himself (at least on paper) in that curious notation, law-French. Technical books addressed to the professional reader were in French; if any other language were used, we may conclude that the author had the lay public in mind—but even then, the author's first draft might be in French; thus, St. German wrote his *Doctor and Student* in French before translating it first into Latin and then into English. Old libraries afford many a scrap of hasty notes written in the lawyer's natural medium of French. So technical and professional a piece as this *Discourse* certainly ought to have been in French, and if further confirmation is needed, we can

---

[2] P. 109.
[3] John Foxe, Acts and Monuments (ed. Josiah Pratt, 1870), VII, 605—714.
[4] Philpot was burned December 18, 1555; Foxe, VII, 682.
[5] Dictionary of National Biography, *sub nom.* 'Foxe'.
[6] The relevant passage is Foxe, VII, 629—630.

point to the fact that Egerton himself eventually translated it into workmanlike, lawyerly French. But the fact remains that the author first wrote the *Discourse* in English—in the naturally fluent and idiomatic style, moreover, of a man thinking freely in English and not merely translating.

The next question brings us another step nearer the central problem. How did Egerton come by this *Discourse*, so learned and technical, yet so unaccountably couched in the vulgar tongue? At times, no doubt, the author of a manuscript might abandon it, and chance might bring it into the hands of someone who would continue the abandoned study. Again, the papers of a deceased lawyer might come into the hands of other practitioners who would add them to their own stores of learning. And of course manuscripts circulated freely among the profession in the sixteenth century. These possibilities must be considered in connection with the dates. The original *Discourse* was composed after March, 1563, if our conjecture on Philpot's case is correct; and Egerton had copied that original before 1567. It was not an old, forgotten bundle of papers which he had got hold of, but a new and very recent essay. It is indeed curious that Egerton gives no indication of the author's identity, which he must have known since the text was so recent.

Unburdened as we are with editorial responsibility, we venture the suggestion that the simplest and most plausible solution is to ascribe the *Discourse* in its entirety to Egerton himself. If that be so, then Egerton's early career can be reconstructed on lines such as these.[7] Born in 1540, he was a member of Brasenose College from 1556 to 1559, when he entered Lincoln's Inn. He was called in 1572. Born under Henry VIII, a schoolboy under the protestant Edward VI, an undergraduate under the Catholic Mary, and a law student under Elizabeth, he evidently entered on his legal studies with the determination to keep clear of theology. At Oxford his reading included the classics and much logic; he certainly had a taste for letters, patronised poets, and won Ben Jonson's approval as an orator. That such a man should write English[8] as clear and vigorous as we find in the *Discourse* seems only to be expected. By normal modern standards he was certainly precocious. He was conspicuously successful at Oxford and came to the law with a mind already trained to scholarship. There seems no inherent improbability that such a man, after four years or more of law study, could have written this *Discourse*. He had acquired a good deal of book-learning and had heard or read a number of law readings—'all that gear' is his blunt appraisal of these performances, for which he has all the lofty contempt of a young man from Oxford pouring scorn on dullness and unintelligent pedantry. The *Discourse* is incontestably the work of a keen young mind, which has not yet been broken in to the discipline of Lincoln's Inn learning, and can speak of the ancients of the inns with studied irreverence. If young Egerton is

[7] For biographical details see Campbell's Chancellors; Foss' Judges, and the Dictionary of National Biography. The Huntington Library acquired a large mass of Egerton's papers, and there is ground for hoping that Professor Thorne's researches in them will produce further studies.

[8] There are of course quotations from cases and statutes in French; and the chapter titles are in French.

indeed the author, it should not surprise us that he devoted himself mainly to chancery business (and this in an age when specialization was hardly thought of), where he found a new young system in which pedantry had as yet no place, and whose practitioners thought and wrote in English. In short, it all fits in, and the hypothesis of Egerton's authorship explains and illuminates both the man and the work.[9]

The *Discourse* itself needs no long description. It is pithy, clear, erudite and lively. It begins with proclamations and parliament (using the *Modus Tenendi Parliamentum*) and pronounces fearlessly on many debatable topics—the presence of privy councillors in Parliament, the convocation of the clergy, the immunities of Ireland, of ancient demesne and of aliens. With chapter 3 we come to preambles (and mis-recitals therein). Chapter 4 contains a case 'in the Arches' which has unfortunately resisted all attempts at identification: it seems to hold that a person under a statutory duty (in this case, an ordinary to grant letters of administration to certain persons) is free to disobey the statute if he prefers to pay the statutory penalty.[10] The succeeding chapters contain many succinct examples of the rules of interpretation current in the mid-sixteenth century, sometimes stated in vigorous language. Thus, to those who say that there is no need to know what the law was before the statute 'since it is certain what the law is now by statute', the author replies 'yet are they much deceived . . . for they shall neither know the statute nor expound it well, but shall as it were follow their noses and grope at it in the dark'. Nearly as bad is the rule ('much in use among the readers') which presumed that the common law was the opposite of what the statute provides; against this, too, the author makes a pungent protest—'guessing at the common law, although it be much and almost altogether in use among the Readers, yet hath it caused them much to be deceived'. In a significant passage on intent the *Discourse* raises the psychological difficulty that the Legislature is many-headed and therefore many-minded—thus showing that the day has passed when a statute was truly the King's statute and therefore attributable to his will alone; nevertheless, the author thinks intent a useful conception even now that

[9] There seems little in the Discourse to suggest a contrary view. The fact that manuscript *E* distinguishes between the text of its prototype and the marginalia need not mean that they were necessarily of different authorship, for like Littleton our author seems to have tried to keep the text as clear and short as possible; thus successive accumulations of references stayed in the margin. At only one point (page 130, n. 80) does the margin criticize the text, and that on a matter which the year book expressly doubts. It is the sort of mild correction which a conscientious author would add to the margin of his own book.

A point of minor interest is that the Discourse shows no sign of Plowden's influence until after his reports were printed in 1571, when references to them were added in manuscript *F*. The fact that the primitive text is independent of Plowden confirms our view that the author was too young a man to form part of the circle of senior lawyers among whom Plowden's work circulated in manuscript before it was printed.

It is proper to add that since the above was written, we have seen Professor Radin's article in the Illinois Law Review, vol. 38, pp. 17—18, suggesting that the author is 'probably not Egerton', although 'so far as the substance goes there is nothing that contradicts Egerton's authorship'; the absence of Plowden's influence in manuscript *E* seems to tell against Radin's suspicion that the Discourse may be Jacobean rather than Elizabethan.

[10] This curious point would have interested Mr. Justice Holmes: see his Collected Papers, 173: '. . . what is the difference between being fined, and being taxed a certain sum for doing a certain thing?'

statutes are the product of the Parliamentary mind instead of the King's, and says that in his day 'those that were the penners and devisers of statutes have been the greatest light for exposition'. In another interesting passage the author refuses to allow that a statute can fail for non-user, for obsolescence or because it has never been applied; he sticks to his theory, but his cases go so strongly the other way that he has to say that some words even of Magna Carta are 'void'; on the same page he comments on words that 'seem to have escaped idly and were put in of no purpose of them that were the statute makers'.

The *Discourse* inevitably cites numerous statutes and cases, and their identification has clearly been a most difficult and arduous task; that Professor Thorne has reached the impressive score of ninety-nine out of a possible hundred (which our calculation suggests) is due to his unsurpassed knowledge of the year books and other early sources.[11]

The editor has done more than provide an impeccable edition of a very technical text, for he has prefixed an introduction covering the history of statutory interpretation from the middle of the fourteenth century down to the end of the sixteenth. This is a broad and general study in a hundred pages by a master of the subject, and all who have a general or a specialized interest in the history of law, the nature of legislation and the development of political theory, will find it most interesting and illuminating.

That we are in for a lively debate is clear from the first sentence: 'the history of statutory interpretation begins in the sixteenth century' after the close of Henry VIII's outburst of legislation. As opposed to this, 'the currently received theory' which speaks of statutory interpretation as having existed during the Middle Ages (a) tacitly assumes a 'developed sanction' behind acts of Parliament so that strict adherence to their terms would be the norm, and (b) ascribes the observed deviations from that norm to a 'power wielded by the judges' which authorized them to depart at times from the legislative dictates. Professor Thorne objects to the 'current theory', first, that there was no compulsion to follow a statute strictly during the Middle Ages, and that the extension of a statute was no usurpation by the judges of the Legislature's functions; and hence he objects, secondly, that there is no need to postulate 'powers' in the judges of the year book period. This portentous dogma is something of a shock to one who has been accustomed for many years to write about what he fancied was the 'interpretation of statutes' in the Middle Ages. As a statement of the practice of a later age, Professor Thorne seems to profane those *arcana* of the law which ordinarily are not discussed; but since the matter is now raised, we may venture to ask what is the sanction behind statutes at the present day? Is there any compulsion upon a Court to interpret a statute in a particular way? (Similarly, what sanction compels a Court to regard

---

[11] *Philpot's Case* (*supra*, n. 3) is the only addition we have been able to make; a very few alternative identifications have occurred to us after a close examination. On page 111, line 7, Egerton's 'they' possibly refers to 'those of Ireland' (although actually 'them of ancient demesne' were the last mentioned); if this is so then the 'statute of York' would be not 9 Edw. III, st. 1, but 12 Edw. II (which in fact does mention Ireland in the preamble), and it is c. 5 of this statute which is involved at p. 118, n. 38. A few textual points: on p. 105 'the face of a statute' suggests the emendation 'force'; on p. 130 should not 'uxori' be 'uxoris'?; on p. 167 'Gloucester, ca. 8' seems a misprint for 'Gloucester, ca. 3' (as in n. 199).

certain precedents as binding?) What can we say of such sanctions (supposing them to exist) if we must also postulate a 'power' wielded by the judges permitting them to depart from the legislative dictate?

Clearly it is useless to talk of 'powers' in any sense adverse to the Legislature in England,[12] and we are not aware that anyone has used such language of our mediaeval law; the whole burden of the present writer's contributions to the subject has been that mediaeval dealings with statutes were unfettered by theoretical considerations. True, the judicial attitude slowly changed—and it is changing still,[13] and at no time was it logically consistent; but of a theory of interpretation there is little trace until the doctrine of the separation of powers became fashionable. Professor Thorne associates 'the currently received theory' which he criticizes with the present writer, 'though it is not usual to find the assumption that lies back of it so explicitly stated' as he himself has revealed it. Our defence may be stated very shortly: the omission to state the assumption is due simply to the fact that no such assumption was made.

All this arises on pages 4 and 5; the clue to the difficulty does not appear (or did not appear to this reader) until reaching page 62, and so it may be helpful to draw attention at once to a remark which does much to illuminate the author's position. The author there adopts the word 'interpretation' in the peculiar sense in which some sixteenth century writers used it: 'as enactments acquire formal rigidity their words must be saved by regarding departures from them as "interpretations" made by the judges'. This use of the word introduces the atmosphere of fiction and make-believe which certainly did become prominent in later times, and in this sense the word does imply a somewhat disingenuous evasion of a lawful command. The toleration of such a practice by the Legislature, and the language sometimes used by the Courts, combine to create the impression that the Courts are exercising some sort of 'power' to interpret statutes. But that is not the ordinary sense of the word to-day, and the fact that a modern book or article is entitled the 'interpretation of statutes' does not mean that the author accepts all the implications that the word held four hundred years ago.

There is indeed a difference between the fourteenth century and the sixteenth century attitude towards statutes, and Professor Thorne is assuredly right in thinking that the change is in the statutes—we have often felt that the Statute of Uses is typical of the new age, with its elaborate drafting methodically dealing with every possible aspect and detail of its general plan. The Legislature there took up the burden, which former ages had left to the Courts, of working out the detailed consequences of a legislative policy. We would venture the suggestion that the last years of the fifteenth century saw a change in parliamentary procedure which facilitated this development. Instead of a prayer by the Commons in general terms for a particular legislative remedy, we find the famous petition *formam cuiusdam actus in se*

---

12 In America, of course, the position is different, for the judges there have the 'power', and indeed the duty of applying not only statute law but also the fundamental constitutions.

13 At the moment the tendency seems to be 'back to Edward II'. *Watkinson* v. *Hollington*, [1943] 2 A. E. R. 573, speaks with the authentic voice of Bereford (although he would have been less apologetic to Parliament).

continens. As a result, Parliament considered not merely the general policy, but the exact wording of the proposed statute; and that wording had most often been settled in Government offices. The lawyers in the Commons, the judges in the Lords, and the council, which kept a close watch upon the proceedings, were all dealing with specific and carefully drafted texts. Under this improved and businesslike procedure it was inevitable that the words of a statute should acquire a new significance from the fact that they had been so often examined and finally adopted after prolonged deliberation. Legislation, in fact, was no longer the Government's vague reply to vaguely worded complaints, but rather the deliberate adoption of specific proposals embodied in specific texts emanating from the Crown or its officers. When the time came for lawyers and judges to apply these statutes, they perforce approached them with the knowledge that not only their general drift, but also their detailed wording, was the result of careful thought. Documents prepared by such a procedure inevitably invited the reader to think that they meant exactly what they said, and nothing else. In short, we are inclined to think that the new attitude towards statutes, and the new spirit within the statutes, was primarily the result of more businesslike methods of Parliamentary procedure.

The above suggestion is put forward as an explanation in part, at least, of the unmistakable change in thought upon which Professor Thorne rightly insists. The principal issue involved is that in our view the change in attitude towards statutes was not the outcome of changing political thought; instead, we believe that the change in attitude was the product of procedural and administrative processes. The new attitude towards statutes was not the result of new doctrine, but finally it did in its turn influence political thought. Having acquired the habit of setting great store upon the express wording of a statute, it became all the easier to accept an enhanced estimate of the nature of legislative authority. It is inevitably very difficult to find words which truly define that estimate. The author uses several phrases such as the 'inviolability' of a statute, the 'developed sanction' behind Acts of Parliament, or the 'compulsion to follow Acts of Parliament'. Taken literally, all these expressions seem to us too precise, more especially since the author himself insists upon them, and balances them against the correlative 'powers' which are implied in his use of the word interpretation. For our own part, we are inclined to believe that the greater reverence for Parliament and its statutes was primarily a matter of judicial sentiment rather than of theory. As for the 'powers' of interpretation, it is hazardous to use this word to mean more than the practical possibility of deciding a contested point of interpretation one way or the other—a possibility which will be wider or narrower as the sentiment of reverence for the *ipsissima verba* of Parliament varies.

The largest part of the introduction, however, is concerned with the interpretative technique of the Elizabethan age. In spite of national peculiarities there was still a cosmopolitan body of learning—grammar, rhetoric, philosophy, civil and canon law—some of which was known beyond a doubt to the university-bred Egerton, and several of Professor Thorne's most illuminating pages are based upon it. The specifically English contribution was provoked by the developments outlined in the two preceding paragraphs. The drafting of Henry VII's and Henry VIII's statutes set a standard far above that reached by older legislation; was it possible henceforth to construe the laws of Edward I, many of them still of vital importance in the daily work of the Courts, by the same methods as those of the Tudors? How could the older cases on interpretation, which in practice had settled the scope of Edward I's laws, be reconciled with the newer attitude? It is to this problem that Egerton addressed himself, and it is clear that he and others who attempted it found themselves in insuperable difficulties. To find a common formula which should include Dyer's attitude to the Statute of Uses as well as Bereford's treatment of the Statute *De Donis* was indeed beyond the wit of man. From the mass of expedients and subterfuges there emerged one concept which became of general importance; this was the 'equity' of the statute. Its rise and changing content is one of the many illuminating passages in Professor Thorne's introduction upon which it is tempting to comment.[14] Enough has already been said, we believe, to show that this edition is a work of ripe scholarship, concerned with problems of fundamental importance in the history of legal thought, and very well worth the reader's serious consideration.

---

[14] Several other aspects of Egerton's Discourse, Sir Christopher Hatton's little book on the same subject, and Professor Thorne's introduction, are learnedly discussed by Professor Max Radin, 'Early statutory interpretation in England', Illinois Law Review, vol. 38, pp. 16—40.

XIV

BONHAM'S CASE AND JUDICIAL REVIEW

I

BY an old and universal custom the reports of Sir Edward Coke are referred to simply as "The Reports," and no more striking tribute could be paid to their unique position in our legal literature. Partly, no doubt, this is due to their didactic character, combining as they do the elements of report, treatise, legal history and general criticism, thus becoming not only a repertory of decisions for the practitioner, but also a textbook for the advanced student, who finds in them elaborate discussions of every branch of English law. That alone would have made these eleven volumes a truly remarkable achievement, but for their own age they possessed yet another aspect, which must here receive our attention. Their author was something more than a lawyer with an extraordinary knowledge of the arcana of the common law; more, too, than an antiquary of great distinction, even in an age of such amazingly erudite scholars as William Prynne, John Selden and Sir Robert Cotton; for to all this he added the character of political philosopher. Urged by a presentiment of the coming conflict of Crown and Parliament, he felt the necessity of curbing the rising arrogance of both, and looked back upon his country's legal history to find the means. This instinctive appeal to history for guidance was characteristic, and the choice of a legal rather than any other solution was amply justified by the remarkable continuity and stability of English law during the vicissitudes of the seventeenth century. His attitude is aptly expressed in one of his own picturesque phrases: "Let us now peruse our ancient authors," he wrote, "for out of the old fields must come the new corne."[1] So it was in this spirit that he labored at the ancient patrimony of his profession, those short, thick folios of black-letter Year Books,[2] and from their forbidding mass of obsolescent technicalities raised a harvest of political theory which was destined

---

[1] 4 Co. Inst. 109.

[2] The collected uniform edition associated with the name of Sergeant Maynard did not appear until nearly half a century after the death of Coke.

to be the food of far-distant states to which he had never given a thought.

The solution which Coke found was in the idea of a fundamental law which limited Crown and Parliament indifferently. What that law was, its nature and its contents, were questions as difficult as they were insistent — and, as subsequent events showed, capable of surprising solutions. The nearest we find to an explicit definition of this fundamental law is the assertion of the paramount law of "reason." For the rest, the common lawyer's "reason" is left in as much uncertainty as he himself ascribed to the Chancellor's equity.[3] Moreover, Coke was prepared to advance mediaeval precedent for his theory, and in so doing has drawn upon his head the criticisms of later investigators. Just as these criticisms are, from the point of view of modern scholarship, it is only fair to the Chief Justice to insist that his view of history was not ours, and that it is only by the standard of his own day that a true evaluation of his learning and intellectual honesty can be formed. Although it must be confessed that even then he cannot be found altogether faultless, yet it is believed that a sufficient explanation will be found to establish his *bona fides*. His doctrine is certainly based largely upon mediaeval precedents and the extent to which they justify it is an interesting subject for investigation. But if we reach a different estimate from his of the Year Book authority for his dogma, this must not be taken as necessarily involving a severe censure of Coke. He himself has told us that though the fields are old, the corn is new.

His theory reaches its final expression in *The Case of the College of Physicians*, commonly called *Dr. Bonham's Case*, of which we have two reports, one by Coke himself, who presided at the trial as Chief Justice of the Common Pleas;[4] the other by Brownlow, who was present at the later stages of the case in his capacity of Prothonotary of the court.[5] Brownlow reports earlier proceedings than Coke, while the latter naturally preserves his own judgment at greater length. Taken together, the two sources enable us to reconstruct the arguments in the case with considerable detail

---

[3] For "reason," see Sir Frederick Pollock, *History of the Law of Nature*, in ESSAYS IN THE LAW (1922) 157.

[4] 8 Co. 114a (C. P. 1610); the pleadings are at f. 107a.

[5] 2 Brownl. 255 (C. P. 1610).

and fair certainty, although as we shall see later, the accuracy of Coke's reports has been attacked.[6]

In April, 1606,[7] Thomas Bonham was summoned to appear before the President and Censors of the Royal College of Physicians, who examined him, and finding that he was deficient in medical science, imposed upon him a fine of a hundred shillings and forbade him under pain of imprisonment to practice physic until he had been admitted by the College. Bonham continued to practice, however, and in October was resummoned. This time he defaulted, and was sentenced in his absence to a fine of ten pounds, and a warrant was issued for his arrest. Early in November he appeared and refused to submit to reëxamination, on the grounds that he was a Doctor of Medicine of the University of Cambridge, and that the Royal College of Physicians had therefore no jurisdiction over him. Thereupon the Censors (without the President) committed him to prison in the Counter of Fleet Street, whither he was conveyed by the servants of the President and Censors. Bonham now brought an action for false imprisonment against the leading members of the Royal College of Physicians.

The pleadings of the defendants set forth that letters patent dated 10 HEN. VIII had incorporated them as the Royal College of Physicians, with powers to fine practitioners in London who were not admitted by them, and further general powers to govern all the physicians in London and district with fine and imprisonment — in all cases one-half of the fine was to go to the King, and one-half to the College. This patent was confirmed by the statute 14 & 15 HEN. VIII, c. 5, which in turn was confirmed by the statute 1 MAR. c. 9, with the addition of a general command to all gaolers to keep such persons as the President and College shall commit to them, without bail or mainprise. It was in pursuance of these statutory powers that the College claimed to have committed Dr. Bonham.

Protracted argument followed, particularly on the question whether graduates of the universities were under the jurisdiction of the Royal College,[8] for as Sergeant Doddridge argued, "the Statutes of this Realm have always had great respect to the Grad-

[6] *Infra*, p. 51. [7] 8 Co. 115a.

[8] *Ibid.* 116a; 2 Brownl. 256–57.

uates of the Universities, and it is not without cause," he adds sympathetically, " for *Sudavit & Alsit,* and hath no other reward than this Degree which is Doctor." [9] The details of these discussions, which lasted for several terms, need not detain us, for finally the case came up for a formal argument among the judges themselves. In the course of the lengthy disputes which took place upon the bench, we find an interesting confession of faith in Tudor paternalism by Walmesley, who deduced from the preamble of the letters patent that: " it is the Office of a King to survey his Subjects, and he is a Physician to cure their Maladies, and to remove Leprosies amongst them, and also to remove all fumes and smells, which may offend or be prejudicial to their health, as it appears by the several Writs in these several Cases provided, and so if a man be not right in his Wits, the King is to have the Protection and Government of him . . . " [10] — a notable example of a new political theory being read into the venerable texts of the *Registrum Brevium.* Walmesley, indeed, could not see any possibility of objection to a despotism so enlightened. " It is a marvellous thing," he asserted, " that when good Laws shall be made for our Health and Wealth also, yet we will so pinch upon them, that we will not be tryed by men of Experience, Practice and Learning, but by the University, where a man may have his Degree by grace without merit, and so for these Reasons he concluded that this Action is not maintainable." [11]

Then came the judgment of the Chief Justice, Sir Edward Coke.[12] He took up the challenge of Justice Walmesley, and delivered a glowing eulogy upon the University of Cambridge, of which he was later to become Lord High Steward, while of the Crown he used an extravagant form of words almost certainly adapted from the famous claim of Richard II to bear the law in his breast: " the King hath had extraordinary care for the health of his Subjects. *Rex enim omnes artes censetur habere in scrinio pectoris sui.*" [13]

He then rehearsed the whole history of the case, and with the

---

[9] 2 Brownl. 258.

[10] *Ibid.* 260. The care of the public health is still ascribed to the Crown as *medicus regni.* (1909) 25 L. Q. Rev. 291. We very probably have here a minor result of the Reformation — the Crown succeeds the Church as supervisor of the medical profession.

[11] *Ibid.* 262. [12] 8 Co. 116b; 2 Brownl. 262. [13] 8 Co. 116b; 2 Brownl. 264.

concurrence of Warburton and Daniel,[14] concentrated his attention upon two points which he regarded as decisive in support of the action. In the first place, the College did not possess the powers they claimed over unlicensed (as distinct from incompetent) practitioners; and secondly, even if they did, they had not pursued them aright. It is the fourth of the five reasons adduced in support of the former of these propositions that has since become so famous.[15] He points out that the Royal College of Physicians were to receive one-half of all the fines, and are therefore not only judges, but also parties in any case that comes before them, and it is an established maxim of common law that no man can be judge in his own case.[16] "And it appears in our books that in many cases the common law will controul acts of parliament and sometimes adjudge them to be utterly void: for when an act of parliament is against common right or reason, or repugnant [17] or impossible to be performed, the common law will controul it and adjudge such act to be void;" — words which challenged both Crown and Parliament, and provoked controversies which have continued to our own day. We shall have to consider how far the authorities cited by Coke support this contention; what light recent researches into early Year Book law have thrown upon the subject; the reception accorded to the doctrine by contemporaries; its gradual abandonment in England; and its results in America.

---

14 As to this, see *infra,* p. 51.

15 8 Co. 118a; 2 Brownl. 265.

16 For more than a dozen exceptions to this maxim, see 2 ROLLE, ABRIDGMENT 93 and the numerous citations in Quincy, 525 (Mass. 1865). One of the cases cited by Coke has the following: "*Rolf:* I will tell you a fable. Once upon a time there was a Pope who had committed a great offence, and the Cardinals came to him and said *Peccasti,* and he said, *Judica me.* And they said *Non possumus quia caput es ecclesiae; judica teipsum.* And the Pope said *Judico me cremari,* and he was burnt. And in this case he was his own judge, and afterwards he was a Saint. So it is not inconvenient for a man to be his own judge." Y. B. Hil. 8 Hen. VI, 6. The reference must be to Saint Marcellinus, but the story here is not quite the same as that in general circulation. His legend appears in the Breviary, where his feast is April 26. See the notes by Sir Frederick Pollock in (1895) 10 ENG. HIST. REV. 293, 536.

17 The meaning of repugnant is not clear; it would almost seem that it meant no more than distasteful to the court; there is no evidence to show what Coke meant by it precisely. In United States v. Cantril, 4 Cranch, 167 (U. S. 1807), it is used in the peculiar sense of "self-contradictory." Elsewhere Coke uses it in the sense of "contrary to common law." 1 Co. INST. 206b; *cf.* Sullivan v. Adams, 3 Gray, 476 (Mass. 1855).

II

The first of these questions has already received some attention, and the significance of *Tregor's Case*,[18] which is one of Coke's principal authorities, has been the subject of considerable discussion. It will be sufficient to summarize here the results which have been reached by the present writer in an earlier study.[19] In the first place, Coke has seriously misquoted the Year Book thus: "Herle saith some statutes are made *against law and right*, which those who made them *perceiving*, would not put them into execution." The italicized words are interpolations by Coke which do not appear in the original, and introduce an idea of some superior "right" which Herle certainly did not entertain. The only meaning which Herle's words can reasonably be made to bear is that sometimes the legislator has repented of a hasty piece of work and has been content to allow it to become a dead letter. Secondly, whoever reads the whole of Herle's remarks can see that he did not regard the statute then under discussion as falling within this category; on the contrary, he suggested a perfectly obvious and straightforward interpretation of it, in which Hilary concurred. It cannot be denied that Coke's first authority is far from convincing.

His second instance is the anonymous case printed by Fitzherbert from an inedited Year Book as *Cessavit* 42, which also has been discussed elsewhere.[20] It goes much further to support his thesis than does *Tregor's Case*, and recent discoveries have increased its historical value. In the *Graunde Abridgement* of Fitzherbert it occupies but two lines, and they not altogether intelligible, but in Coke's telling the story gains an aunt and a niece as well as considerable clarity — all derived from an unspecified and unidentified source. However, even in the form in which it appears in Fitzherbert, it is plain that the judgment was in complete accordance with that in an earlier case, *Copper v. Gederings*,[21] which is much more fully reported, and for our knowledge

---

[18] Y. B. Pasch. 8 Edw. III, 26.

[19] Plucknett, Statutes and their Interpretation in the 14th Century (1922) 68–70.

[20] *Ibid.* 66.

[21] Y. B. 3 Edw. II, 105. All three of the MSS. report the case as in the text, but

of which we are indebted to the Year Books of the Selden Society. The details of the earlier case need not detain us here: suffice it to say that the Statute of Westminster the Second enacted that the right of action in *Cessavit* should descend from a lord to his heir; but when an heir brought his writ, Chief Justice Bereford refused to maintain it, on the ground that if the action were allowed, certain general principles of the common law would be disturbed. It is true that upon several occasions Bereford had the hardihood to embody his own distinctly original views upon legal problems in his judgments,[22] but in this case the same decision was given half a century later in the case *Cessavit* 42 quoted by Coke, and was duly enshrined in the books of authority as the final law upon the subject.[23] Here then is no mere caprice of one particular judge but a *catena* of authorities extending from the middle of the fourteenth century down to Coke's own day. The statement of Sir Frederick Pollock [24] that "no case is known, in fact, in which an English court of justice has openly taken on itself to overrule or disregard the plain meaning of an Act of Parliament" must be taken subject to this exception (and others will appear later), which the publication of the Selden Society's Year Books has brought to light. The courts in these cases did undoubtedly "disregard the plain meaning of an Act of Parliament;" but in telling the story Lord Coke has made the important addition of the words "because it would be against common right and reason, the common law adjudges the said act of parliament as to that point void." There is no such judgment as this in the report; the statute is not held void; it is just ignored. To this fact Coke has really added an explanation and a theory all his own — an addition that was to be of immense importance in subsequent history.

The third great precedent cited by Coke is another case in Fitzherbert — *Annuitie* 41. A better report, however, is translated

---

as the record has not been clearly identified, there may be some doubt as to exactly what happened. Even assuming that Maitland found the correct record, there is no great inconsistency. The plaintiff may well have sought leave to retire from the writ in view of an inevitable judgment that the action was not maintainable.

22 Plucknett, *op. cit. supra* note 19, at 129–31.

23 Natura Brevium (1553) clvii *d;* Fitzherbert, Natura Brevium (Hale's ed. 1755) 209; *cf.* 2 Co. Inst. 402, 460.

24 Pollock, First Book of Jurisprudence (3d ed. 1911) 264.

below [25] from the earlier and very rare *Abridgment* of Statham, where it appears as *Annuitie* 11. The Statute of Carlisle, first put forth in 1305 and finally enacted in 1307, had much to say of ecclesiastical affairs, and notably of a legal problem which had long been prominent in the courts. Many of the smaller religious houses did not possess common seals, but contented themselves with the personal seal of their head. Thus questions inevitably arose as to whether a particular document under an abbot's seal was his personal deed binding only himself, or the deed of the ecclesiastical corporation of which he was the head. To do away with this fruitful source of confusion the statute orders all such religious houses to have a common seal for their corporate acts, and (unless such is the case already) to place this seal in the custody of the prior and four worthiest brethren who shall keep it secured under the abbot's private seal, so that the abbot cannot use it without the knowledge of the convent. By this means it was hoped that the presence of the conventual seal would be an infallible proof of the concurrence of the convent in the act of its head. Was this statute in direct conflict with Church law? The general idea that temporal regulations could be made specifying the mode of authentication required to give validity to the temporal acts of spiritual bodies is reasonable enough, and one can heartily sympathize with the common lawyers' fervent desire to devise a means of knowing exactly when an act was that of the corporation, and when it was only the personal act of its head. But the means adopted involved grave interference with the internal economy of ecclesiastical bodies, which was already the

[25] " Pasch. 27 Hen. VI. One Rous brought annuity against an abbot and showed a deed of annuity made by the abbot's predecessor and sealed with the convent seal, which annuity was of certain bread, beer, robes and other things &c. *Pole.* The Statute of Carlisle said of Cistercians and Premonstratensians and Austens who have convent and common Seal, that the common seal shall be in the keeping of the prior (who is under the abbot) and four others, the wisest of the house; and that any deed sealed with the common seal which is not in such custody shall be void. And we tell you that at the time when this deed was sealed, the seal was out of their custody, and the opinion of the COURT was that this statute is void for it is impertinent to be observed, for the seal being in their custody, the abbot cannot seal anything with it, for when it is in the abbot's hands it is *ipso facto* out of their custody. And if it were observed, every common seal would be defeated by a simple surmise which cannot be tried &c. *Vide, quia bene debate et plusours excepcions pris al ple &c.*"

Miss Klingelsmith in 1 STATHAM (1915) 114, has followed the traditional view and translated " impertinent " by " impossible."

subject of canonical legislation. The Church's law placed the custody of the common seal in the hands of the head alone, and afforded as yet no effective means of ensuring the concurrence of the members in the act of their sovereign.[26] However, we find in 1366 that in his visitation of a priory which had suffered from an autocratic head, the Bishop of Lichfield ordered that the common seal should be kept in a chest with three locks, one for the prior and the others for two canons to be elected by the whole house.[27] This is clearly in the spirit of the Statute of Carlisle, but it seems to have been not the normal arrangement but a special discipline for a spendthrift abbot. Canon law still charged the head of a house with the duty of keeping and honestly using the common seal, and inasmuch as the statute professed to relieve him of this duty, it was certainly trespassing upon ecclesiastical territory.[28] If the statute could have simply insisted upon conventual acts bearing the conventual seal, there would probably have been little trouble, but it went further and proceeded to invalidate acts bearing even the conventual seal if it had not been kept in the custody of the prior and four brethren as laid down in the act. This was a necessary step, and the intention was clearly to modify the rigor of the statute and to protect convents against abbots who applied the conventual seal without the knowledge of their convent.

---

26 "Unusquisque [prelatus] per se illud [*sc.* sigillum] custodiat, vel uni soli de cuius fide confidat custodiendum committat, qui etiam iuret quod illud fideliter custodiet, nec ad sigillandum aliquid alicui concedet nec ipse etiam aliquid sigillet inde ex quo possit praejudicium alicui generari, nisi quid dominus eius prius legerit et viderit diligenter et sic praeceperit sigillari." CONST. OTTONIS (1679) 69 (enacted in 1236). The delegation of the seal here contemplated is that which was customarily made to officials who relieved their principals of much routine work, and is quite distinct from the compulsory delegation of the seal to subordinates in order to insure their constitutional control over their head.

27 STRETTON'S SECOND REGISTER (8 Salt Soc. Collections (N. S.) 1905) 114. At an earlier period the Pope himself might prescribe such an arrangement where the case necessitated it: Innocent III, for example, imposed it upon the spendthrift abbot of Bourgueil in 1198: "praecipimus etiam ut duo fratres bonae vitae et maturae aetatis sigillum capituli custodiant nec ideo aliquid nisi de communi assensu sigillent." Register I, ep. 311 (MIGNE, PATROLOGIA LATINA, CCXIV, 271).

28 It is interesting to note that a similar device was in use (voluntarily, it would seem) in some lay communities; for example Coventry in 1424 kept its common seal in a bag which in turn was sealed by four citizens, while in 1421 the common seal was kept in the common chest of which the mayor and three others held one key each — the number of keys rising to five by 1445. COVENTRY LEET BOOK (1867) 22, 73, 218. Probably the sealed bag was kept within the common pyx.

Nevertheless this provision was obviously impossible to work, unless, perhaps, the close and cordial coöperation of the Church could have been secured,[29] and the common law courts were therefore still in the same dilemma of having to settle disputes between abbots and their convents without being able to impose any regulations upon them, or to obtain any reliable facts as to their participation or otherwise in acts which purported to be conventual.

This difficulty is clearly brought out in the case before us, which arose in 1449 — over a hundred and forty years after the passing of the statute. A convent invoked the aid of the statute to defeat a deed charging them with an annuity, on the ground that at the time the deed was made their common seal was not in the proper custody specified in the act. The opinion of the court was twofold. There was the famous piece of dialectic which demonstrated that the statute could not be obeyed, for if the seal was kept by the prior and four brethren, how could the abbot use it at all? This was followed by the more convincing reason that if the latter part of the statute was to be applied, a convent could virtually avoid any of its acts by simply alleging that the seal was not in the proper custody — a fact that the lay courts had no satisfactory means of trying.

Several points require attention. First, we are told of no judgment, but only the "opinion" of the court, and this does not necessarily mean more than that the reporter believed that the court inclined to one side rather than the other. Judgment is not reported and may never have taken place. Secondly, we do find the word "void" used of a statute, though it is unfortunate that we have no access to any document earlier than about forty years after the event, and that the arguments, which we know were very full and interesting, are no longer extant. Thirdly, Mr. Brinton Coxe's conjecture [30] that the decision was influenced by considerations of canon law is less convincing (although the statute certainly was an interference in purely ecclesiastical matters), since it was the abbey which sought to maintain the validity of the statute, and the lay judges who held that it was void. Finally, the excuse given by the judges for their opinion is not the impossi-

[29] Where a convent alleged that an act had been sealed "furtively" without their knowledge or consent, canon law permitted the sworn evidence of the brethren to be taken: c. 5, X. 2. 19. (1187–1191).

[30] Coxe, Judicial Power and Unconstitutional Legislation (1893) 158.

bility of applying the act, as stated by Coke [31] and Blackstone; [32] for the court still had spirit enough to call the statute " impertinent," although it is very significant that it was thought prudent to accompany this with a piece of ratiocination making out a superficial impossibility. The inference is irresistible; the court was feeling distinctly nervous at such a step, even if only expressed in a mere opinion, and the contrast with the earlier cases in which statutes were brushed aside without apology and almost without comment, is very striking.

How far, then, is the case authority for the thesis which Coke builds upon it? In the first place, there are the very serious objections that the report is scanty and only tells of the debate upon one point, although we know that many other questions were raised and discussed in the case. Consequently it becomes all the more necessary to insist that the passage that we have in the *Abridgment* is not a judgment, but what the reporter believes to be the " opinion " of the court on this one point that happened to interest him. Probably no judgment was given at that hearing, but only an adjournment to a later term, by which time the court may well have changed its opinion, or counsel have shifted their arguments to other and less controversial grounds — a frequent occurrence in Year Book cases. In the report as we have it there is no discussion whatever of the proposition that the statute was void, but merely Pole's plea, immediately followed by the court's opinion. In view of this drastic suppression of the arguments *pro* and *contra,* which we know were numerous, it would be very hazardous to assume that we can accurately reconstruct the court's sentiments upon the subject, seeing that all information as to the divergent points of view of the various counsel, which is equally necessary for a correct interpretation of the case, is completely lost. In addition to this it is impossible to tell what weight (if any) this point had in determining the court's judgment (if such there was), for other points were debated. Historically, therefore, the case contains far too many unknown factors to be used with any degree of confidence or safety.

But this was manifestly not the point of view from which Sir Edward Coke and most of his contemporaries would have regarded the case; and so it is only fair that we should try to divest our-

---

[31] 2 Co. Inst. 587–88.

[32] 1 Bl. Comm. 91.

selves for a moment of the critical habits of the modern historian, and see the case as it would have appeared to a seventeenth century lawyer. It is printed clearly and intelligibly in a famous and authoritative folio, with all the pomp and circumstance of Law-French and black-letter. The text is therefore assumed to be satisfactory enough. True, we have only an " opinion "; but since it has been in the abridgments for over a century, the " ancients and sages " of the law surely must have valued it highly. It may certainly be presumed to have the approbation of that much respected judge, Sir Anthony Fitzherbert, who set it there; consequently its authority is undeniably high. As for the subject matter and the actual grounds for the decision, they are brief enough to be quoted *verbatim*; and so one can shift the burden of interpreting them on to the learned reader, who at least cannot deny that " the opinion of the Court was that the statute is void." The diversity of the reasons assigned for the decision is more apparent than real, for our old lawyer will refuse to admit that the dialectic we speak of so slightingly is not a very palpable difficulty — even something of the same nature as the well-nigh impossibility of trying the issue so confidently authorized in the act. The word " impertinent " is not so clear as it might be, but broadly speaking, " impossible " seems to get the meaning well enough. Treated in this way, the case takes a rather different aspect, and if we say, as we surely must, that it is much less convincing to us than to Coke, we must also add that the difference is due to the centuries which separate us from his age and thought.

The last case to which Chief Justice Coke gives extended notice, approaches the problem from a different angle. In early Year Book days the king was " prerogative." That is to say, there was a certain point beyond which the ordinary law of the land did not apply to him — in much the same way, for example, (though to a much less extent) as " one cannot use the law of the land in all its points against a merchant."[33] What will happen then if a statute conflicts with this prerogative character of the Crown?

Such a situation arose out of the vast overturning of legal titles due to the suppression of religious houses and chantries at the Reformation. In consequence of various statutes large numbers of landed properties were deemed to be in the seisin of the Crown,

---

[33] Bereford, C. J., in Y. B. 4 Edw. II, 154.

and remained in that condition until they were granted out to subjects by royal letters patent. Many of these lands were subject to complicated incidents and obligations which the statutes attempted to adjust. For example, many lands not only supported their ecclesiastical owners, but had also been subjected to various rent charges and rents sec, payable to laymen who were in no way connected with religious foundations. Clearly these people should not be made to lose their incomes merely because the lands upon which they were secured had been confiscated; so the act explicitly provides that such rents shall be saved to all manner of persons. Consequently the seisin of the king, and that of his patentee if the lands had been granted out, made no difference, and rents of this class were duly paid by the king and those deriving title from him. So far there was no difficulty. But some of the lands were subject to a peculiar burden known as rent service, and here complications arose. Rent service is a rent reserved at the time of making a feoffment, and is due to a lord from his tenant in virtue of their feudal relationship and the fealty which it involved. It is not a charge, but a feudal service, and the lord can exact it by distress (even though there be no clause of distress in the feoffment to authorize it), for although the land is held by the tenant in demesne, yet it is also held by the lord in service, and a lord can distrain within his own fee. When land subject to this type of rent came into the king's hands, it suffered a change. The king is prerogative and cannot stoop to perform services to any man, and therefore these rent services are extinguished immediately the lands come into the king's seisin. The statute for the suppression of the chantries, however, in its endeavor to be as just as possible, contained a general saving of all peoples' rights to rents (including rent services) due from chantry lands.[34] Here, then, is a conflict between the prerogative and the statute; the one extinguishes these rents, and the other protects them. Which shall prevail? A group of Elizabethan cases which Lord Coke cites[35] gives us the answer. The first is anonymous, but dated 1572.[36] The report is brief: "*Memorandum,* That it was resolved by the opinion

[34] (1547) 1 Edw. VI, c. 14, § 17. At the suppression of the monasteries, this concession was deliberately refused, not only to rent services, but also to rents sec. (1539) 31 Hen. VIII, c. 13, § 4.

[35] 8 Co. 118b.

[36] 3 Dyer, 313 (K. B. 1572).

of the Court in the Bench, That the seigniory and tenure of obit land, or chantry land, is extinct by the possession of the King, by the act of 1 *E.* 6. [c. 14] notwithstanding the saving in the act; *propter absurditatem* &c." So we have here yet another sort of defect which has been suggested as fatal to an act of Parliament; to " impertinence " and, apparently, impossibility, we must now add absurdity. At first sight the decision sounds drastic, but the report goes on to explain that even if the tenure is extinguished (and of course it can never be revived afterwards), nevertheless the rent services which were part of the tenure can still be exacted by the lord from the king's grantee by means of distress and avowry. The situation is curious: the court, greatly daring, refuses to recognize the express words of the statute in favor of rent services, and roundly declares them extinct *non obstante* the act; but what it takes away with one hand, it prudently restores with the other, for it concedes that the quondam lord — we may no longer call him lord after the king's seisin — may still exact his rent by way of distress. In fact, the court's temerity had no practical result whatever beyond the change of one single word, as we may learn from *Strowd's Case,*[37] in which the matter was finally settled thus:

> " If a man has lands which were once parcel of the possessions of a chantry, and which came to the King under the Statute of Dissolution at the time of the dissolution, and were formerly held of someone else by rent and fealty [*i.e.,* by rent service] or by service which is chivalry, the King's patentee shall now hold the tenements according to the patent [i.e., of the King] and not of the former lord and his heirs, and by the services by which they were anciently held, save that the same rent that was formerly rent service, he shall pay as a rent charge distrainable of common right only by the said person who was formerly lord and his heirs. And thus was the saving in the said statute expounded by the Justices of the Common Bench."

The question is now displayed in its right proportions. The decision is identical with that in the anonymous case which we have just mentioned, but without the rhetoric. The ostentatious judgment " notwithstanding the saving in the act " is now reduced to its proper place as being merely an expounding of the statute.

---

37 1 And. 45 (C. P. 1575); 3 Leon. 58 (C. P. 1575); 4 Leon. 40 (C. P. 1575).

The act saves these rents, and so did both of the judgments. The only difference was that the statute still called them rent services, although the judges, for technical reasons bordering upon pedantry, preferred to call them rent charges. In the former case the court adopted this terminology with a pretentious flourish; in the second, it soberly described its action as simply exposition.

One need only quote the words of Coke in this connection to show clearly how much he has magnified the importance of these cases: "So the statute of 1 E. 6. c. 14 gives chauntries, &c. to the King, saving to the donor, &c. all such rents, services, &c. and the common law controuls it, and adjudges it void as to services, and the donor shall have the rent, as a rentseck, distrainable of common right, for it would be against common right and reason that the King should hold of any, or do service to any of his subjects, 14 Eliz. Dyer 313. and so it was adjudged in . . . Strowd's case."[38] Nowhere does Coke's dogma of a controlling common law appear in the reports of these cases, and the voidance of the statute on those grounds is certainly not "adjudged in Strowd's case."

Finally, Sir Edward Coke concludes this portion of his argument with an imaginary case: "So if any act of parliament gives to any to hold, or to have cognisance of all manner of pleas arising before him in his manor of D., yet he shall hold no plea to which he himself is party; for as hath been said, *iniquum est aliquem suae rei esse judicem.*"[39] His argument began with the proposition that letters patent could not make a man judge in his own case, and as a result of the subsequent discussion, he reached the position that an act of Parliament of this nature was equally ineffective.

We have now taken Coke's authorities as he presents them, and it remains, first, to assess the value of his arguments from the point of view of contemporary scholarship. *Tregor's Case* proves nothing; *Cessavit* 42, on the other hand, is a strong precedent in his favor; *Annuitie* 41 would have looked strong also, although it

---

[38] 8 Co. 118b.

[39] This "manor of D." is, of course, none other than the manor of Dale which figures so often in the imaginary cases propounded by common lawyers. CORWIN, THE DOCTRINE OF JUDICIAL REVIEW (1914) 69, however, finds a new precedent in this "case arising in the manor of Dales [sic] where it was held" etc.

is, in fact, of doubtful import; while *Strowd's Case* is valueless. To his fellow justices, therefore, Coke was able to present a fairly convincing case in which the weak points were by no means obvious to an uncritical mind, while there was at least one clear and incontestable precedent in his favor. If, however, we apply modern scholarship to the problem, and make use of sources which were not available in his day, the result is rather different. As we have already indicated, the facts alleged by the Chief Justice can even be confirmed in some cases by newly published Year Books; but on the other hand, the theory which he believed to be their legal foundation must be credited to his own political thought rather than to that of his mediaeval predecessors upon the Common Bench. In discussing *Copper v. Gederings,* which anticipated the judgment in *Cessavit* 42, we pointed out that although the court deprived an heir of a right of action explicitly granted to him by a statute, because such an action if allowed would seriously disturb the general law on such matters, yet the court did not inquire into the authority of the statute, nor even the conflict of it and the common law. It simply quashed the writ on a plea to the action. The constitutional question was never discussed, nor even raised. The nature of statutes was not questioned, and there is certainly not the faintest suggestion of declaring a statute void. The judges did indeed prefer in this case to follow the common law rather than the statute, but they tell us nothing of their inherent right to "control" legislation in its name. A few more instances are extant of this strange habit of quietly ignoring a statute without assigning any constitutional grounds for doing so, or specifying what powers the court claimed to possess in that behalf, and they have already been discussed elsewhere.[40] Finally it must be insisted that these cases are comparatively early, and are not to be found in the later Year Books. Coke's work is therefore in the nature of an antiquarian revival of obsolescent law with a view to applying it to current needs, an attitude towards history which was characteristic of the age, and which can be illustrated from the controversial literature of all parties.

It may be of interest to examine here a few other cases which have been alleged in support of the theory by Sir Edward Coke

---

40 PLUCKNETT, *op. cit. supra* note 19, at 60, 66–71.

in other parts of his *Reports* — for *Dr. Bonham's Case* is not the only place where these high powers are attributed to the common law judges.

We will begin with the famous *Sheriff of Northumberland's Case* [41] which figures largely in the arguments of *Calvin's Case* [42] and later in *Godden v. Hales*,[43] and which has not yet been thoroughly examined. There is a short note upon the case by Coke,[44] but the fullest treatment of it is from the pen of his life-long rival, Lord Bacon, in his *Maxims, regula* xix.[45] These maxims were apparently written earlier than 1597 although they were not published until 1630; so there is a possibility of their being known to Coke while he was preparing what we have preserved to us as the twelfth part of his *Reports*. Lord Bacon's remarks are as follows:

> " So if there be a statute made ' that no sheriff shall continue in his office above a year, and if any patent be made to the contrary it shall be void; and if there be any *clausula non obstante* contained in such patent to dispense with the present act, that such clause also shall be void; ' yet nevertheless a patent of a sheriff's office made by the king for term of life, with a *non obstante,* will be good in law, contrary to such statute which pretendeth to exclude *non obstantes*: and the reason is, because it is an inseparable prerogative of the crown to dispense with politic statutes, and of that kind; and then the derogatory clause hurteth not."

Reference to the Year Book shows clearly enough that some such case arose, but we are told most definitely that " forasmuch as this was the first time, the Justices, Sergeants, and King's Attorney agreed that they should study the matter well, and then be heard; and what they said counted for nothing, since they wished to retain their freedom to say what they liked, and to consider what they had said up till now as nothing." With these words the report concludes and nothing is known of the later history of the case. There is, moreover, in Brook's *Abridgment* another

41 Y. B. Mich. 2 Hen. VII, 20.

42 7 Co. 1a, 14a (C. P. 1608).

43 2 Shower, *475 (K. B. 1686) (reported more fully in Bacon, ABRIDGMENT, tit. *Prerogative,* D7).

44 12 Co. 18.

45 7 BACON, WORKS (Spedding ed. 1879) 369–72.

report of the case[46] which is still more emphatic; "and the matter was let drop on this day and nothing was adjudged," we there read. There could hardly be a more explicit warning against using it as a precedent, or regarding it as adjudging or deciding upon any point of law; and yet in defiance of this disclaimer in the report itself, we find it quoted in *Calvin's Case* as "agreed." It was all to no use that the authority of the case was afterwards denied, for in *Godden v. Hales* the court apparently felt that if there was no such decision in *The Sheriff's Case* there ought to have been, and so they proceeded to raise the case posthumously to the dignity of a precedent after the lapse of two hundred years by adjudging "that the case of sheriffs in the second year of *Henry the Seventh,* was law, and always taken as law."[47] So much, then, for the authority of the case. As for the substance of the arguments reported in the Year Book, still further comments will have to be passed. As both Coke and Bacon remark the report alleged that the statutes 28 EDW. III, c. 7, and 42 EDW. III, c. 5, forbid any sheriff from serving more than a year in his office, even if his patent should contain a clause *non obstante* this present act; and that Henry Percy claimed to hold office under such a patent appointing him Sheriff of Northumberland for life notwithstanding the statute. There are two facts which are very material to the discussion, but which do not figure in the Year Book report at all. The first is that the statutes quoted contain no such provision forbidding clauses of *non obstante.* The second is that this provision does occur in another statute, *viz.* 23 HEN. VI, c. 7, which is not mentioned in the arguments, but this very act contains also an express saving of the rights of those sheriffs who held office for life. Percy's patent is therefore perfectly valid under the statute.[48] We may suggest a reason why the novel debate in the Year Book was never resumed; when the judges and sergeants and the king's attorney eventually "studied the matter well" they must have discovered the existence of this

---

46 Tit. *Patentes,* 109.

47 2 Shower, *478.

48 Percy was sheriff until the death of Richard III when he was superseded by Sir Robert Maners; he was restored in 1488 — immediately after this case — when he rendered accounts from the beginning of the reign, including the whole of Maners' term.

statute of Henry VI and the saving it contained in favor of shrievalties in fee. Once this statute was found, further argument became unnecessary. Finally it will be observed that the situation discussed by Coke and Bacon of a patent attempting to dispense with a statute although the statute itself forbids it, did not arise in this case at all.

The Prior of Castle Acre v. The Dean of St. Stephen's [49] is sometimes quoted as an example of the limitation of the powers of the legislature. The case is much too complicated for full treatment here, but the material point is that a priory which was "parson" of a church was suppressed and vested in the Crown by virtue of an act of Parliament. Did the Crown thereby become "parson" of the church? Chief Justice Frowyke summed up after protracted argument:

> "As for the other matter, whether the king can be parson by the Act of Parliament, as I see it, it is not a great matter to argue, for I have never seen that a temporal man can be parson without the agreement of the Supreme Head. And in all the cases which have been put, *sc.* of benefices in Wales and benefices which laymen have in their own use,[50] I have seen the matter, and the king had them by the assent and agreement of the Supreme Head. So a temporal act without the assent of the Supreme Head cannot make the king parson."

At the end of the report we find a significant "*Quaere*" which becomes all the more explicable when one remembers the words of Justice Kingsmill who had said, "We cannot make any temporal man by our law to have spiritual jurisdiction, for no one can do this save the Supreme Head," and that the Act of Supremacy was less than thirty years ahead. From our point of view, however, the case is less important, for the fact that a statute could not operate in the ecclesiastical sphere proves no more than does the fact that it could not operate in any other foreign jurisdiction.

---

49 Y. B. Hil. 21 Hen. VII, 1–5.

50 Coningsby had argued that "infants and laymen can and do hold prebends which have no cure of souls, and so the King can be parson, as any layman can, for there is an endowed vicarage with the cure of souls"; and the King has divers benefices in Wales which are continually in his hands.

III

Such then were the grounds upon which Coke built his imposing theory. We must now describe the reception which his contemporaries accorded it. For the time being, Coke was dominant, and consequently we find his point of view expressed repeatedly in the courts. True it is that Bacon was influential enough to secure the promotion of his rival to the more dignified but less lucrative post of Chief Justice of the King's Bench on the death of Sir Thomas Fleming in 1613, yet his successor in the Common Pleas, Sir Henry Hobart, was a staunch upholder of Coke's view of the common law, as may be seen in *Day v. Savadge*.[51] Savadge, on behalf of the City of London, had exacted certain wharf-dues from Day, although the latter claimed that by the custom of the City he was not liable. The issue reached was that there was no such custom, and the question arose as to how its existence could be tried. The City claimed the ancient privilege, confirmed to them, it was alleged, by a statute of 7 Ric. II,[52] which authorized their Recorder, by word of mouth, to declare what were the customs of the City — to which it was objected that such a procedure would make them judge in their own case. The judgment of Chief Justice Hobart dealt with a number of points, and in discussing the so-called statute he declared that "even an Act of Parliament made against Natural Equity, as to make a Man Judge in his own Cause, is void in itself, for *Jura naturae sunt immutabilia* and they are *leges legum*."[53] A noteworthy feature of the case, which is reported by the Chief Justice himself, is that no authorities are cited for the proposition that an act of Parliament against natural equity is void, and that no reference whatever is made to *Bonham's Case* as establishing it. Clearly, then, in Hobart's opinion, the truth of its doctrine was beyond dispute, and although it was already possible to refer to

---

[51] Hobart, 85 (K. B. 1614).

[52] There is room for discussion as to the exact nature of this confirmation; for our purposes, however, the question is immaterial, for the court undoubtedly believed that it was dealing with a true statute. See Historical Charters and Constitutional Documents of the City of London (1884) xxviii–xxx, 70–73, 314.

[53] This is a rather serious misquotation of Bracton, f. 4, who had written that "jura enim naturalia dicuntur immutabilia quia non possunt ex toto abrogari vel auferri; potuit tamen eis derogari vel detrahi in specie vel in parte."

Coke's report of *Bonham's Case,* which was published in 1611, it is highly probable that Hobart's natural caution warned him against too open a tribute to one whose fortunes had already begun to decline.

That Hobart was a thorough believer in Coke's doctrine, however, can be seen just as plainly in his judgment in *Lord Sheffield v. Ratcliffe* [54] where he claims wide power of judicial review: "if you ask me, then, by what rule the judges guided themselves in this diverse exposition of the self same word and sentence? I answer, it was by that liberty and authority that judges have over laws, especially over statute laws, according to reason and best convenience, to mould them to the truest and best use. . . ." [55] Coke had claimed that the common law was fundamental, and it was an inevitable corollary of this theorem that the bench, as the sole repository of this common law, should regard itself as thereby endowed with authority to treat statutes with the widest discretion. It is impossible to deny that Hobart's doctrine is implicit in that of his predecessor.

Coke's removal to the King's Bench in 1613 was the prelude to still sterner measures, in view of the fact that he was soon to give still more offense; in June, 1616, he was suspended from his office and ordered to "correct" his *Reports.* In the following October there was a schedule of five questions which were put to the Chief Justice by the King, apparently on the suggestion of Bacon and the Solicitor-General, Yelverton, the fourth of which demanded an explanation of the dictum in *Bonham's Case* that the common law will control acts of Parliament. Coke's written reply is preserved for us,[56] and shows his complete confidence in the historical basis of his theory. "The words of my report do not import any new opinion," he wrote, "but only a relation of such authorities of law, as had been adjudged and resolved in former times, and were cited in the argument of Bonham's case; and therefore the words of my book are these; 'It appeareth in our books, that in many cases the common law shall control acts of parliament, and sometimes adjudge them to be utterly void,'"

---

[54] Hobart, 334a, 346 (K. B. 1615).

[55] These words were quoted by General Varnum in the course of his argument in Trevett v. Weeden. See *infra,* p. 66.

[56] 6 BACON, WORKS (1803 ed.) 405.

(quoting the long passage from his report containing the mediaeval precedents which we have already considered in detail), "which cases being cited in the argument of this case," he continued, "and I finding them truly vouched, I reported them in this case, as my part was, and had no other meaning than so far as those particular cases there cited do extend unto." Here as elsewhere Coke refused to acknowledge any substantial error in his writings, and boldly met his accusers by repeating the offending passages word by word as he first wrote them. He had been suspended from office some months earlier and commanded to correct his *Reports,* but the only defects he would acknowledge were a few trifling slips which he protested were extremely few, considering the magnitude of his work.[57]

An even more serious attack upon the judgment in *Bonham's Case* has been attributed to the Chancellor, Lord Ellesmere, who, it is said, prepared a set of criticisms upon the *Reports* which remained in manuscript until the early part of the eighteenth century.[58] Besides accusing the Chief Justice of trampling upon the Act of Parliament of 14 and 15 HEN. VIII, "having no precedent before him, but many judgments against him," it is further alleged that this was "in triumph of himself, being accompanied by the opinion of one Judge only for the matter in law, where three other Judges were against him." In his report Coke claims the concurrence of Justices Warburton and Daniel, and also the extra-judicial support of Sir Thomas Fleming, Chief Justice of the King's Bench;[59] while Sergeant Hill in a manuscript note in his copy of Ellesmere acquits Coke of this charge on the independent evidence of Brownlow, who implies that Coke had a majority on the bench.[60] It would seem that the Royalist party did not regard this point as easy to establish, for it does not appear in the list of five objections which Coke was ordered to

---

[57] But in at least one case Coke has been found guilty of reporting exactly the opposite of the actual decision in a case. WALLACE, REPORTERS (4th ed. 1882) 174; *cf.* Beale, Southcott v. Bennett (1899) 13 HARV. L. REV. 43.

[58] THE LORD CHANCELLOR EGERTON'S OBSERVATIONS ON THE LORD COKE'S REPORTS. London folio, n. d. [?1710 — British Museum Catalogue]. For its authorship, see 5 HOLDSWORTH, HISTORY OF ENGLISH LAW (1924) 478 n. 1; (1920) 36 L. Q. REV. 4.

[59] 8 Co. 117a, 121a.

[60] This note is printed in 4 Co. (Thomas and Frazer ed. 1826) 375, n. c.

meet. It is very significant, too, that even Lord Ellesmere in his address to Chief Justice Montagu, commending those judges who do not declare statutes void for being contrary to reason and common right, makes one exception — "I speak not of impossibilities or direct repugnances." [61]

Upon the fall of Coke, his doctrine naturally suffered an eclipse, which, however, was not total, for we find Justice Berkeley announcing "that in some cases the Judges were above an act of Parliament." [62] Experiments were indeed made during the Commonwealth, notably in the *Instrument of Government*,[63] in the direction of establishing a fundamental law, but with little success. It was not until the Restoration that we find it again in the reports, and then it is strangely twisted to the advantage of the Crown. In the famous case of *Godden v. Hales*,[64] it was argued whether the Crown had the prerogative of dispensing with "laws of government," for, said Sergeant Glanvil, "there's a great Distinction between the Laws of Property and those of Government" — and if we would express in one compendious sentence the difference of outlook between modern and mediaeval political thought, it would be hard to improve upon this. To the middle ages they were all one.[65] Sir Thomas Powys "urged that the King's Prerogative was, and is as much the Law of England as any Statute." Much was made of the *Sheriff of Northumberland's Case* [66] although Northey vigorously denied its authority. Finally the "Lord Chief Justice took time to consider of it, and spake with the other Judges, and three or four Days after, declared that he and all the Judges (except *Street* and *Powell*, who doubted) were of opinion, that the kings of *England* were absolute sovereigns; that the laws were the king's laws; that the king had a power to dispense with any of the laws of government as he saw necessity for it; that he was sole judge of that necessity; that no act of Parliament could take away that

---

[61] Moore, 828 (K. B. 1616).

[62] 2 [JAMES GRANT], LAW AND LAWYERS (1840) 212.

[63] See JENKS, CONSTITUTIONAL EXPERIMENTS OF THE COMMONWEALTH (1890).

[64] 2 Shower, *475 (K. B. 1686); BACON, ABRIDGMENT, tit. *Prerogative*, D7.

[65] Compare Bacon's observation quoted *supra*, p. 46; and for examples of the mediaeval attitude towards public law, see Plucknett, *The Lancastrian Constitution*, in TUDOR STUDIES PRESENTED TO A. F. POLLARD (1924) 163 *et seq.*

[66] Discussed *supra*, p. 46.

power; that this was such a law; that the case of sheriffs in the second year of *Henry the Seventh,* was law, and always taken as law; and that it was a much stronger case than this; and therefore gave judgment for the defendant. The prerogative is undoubtedly part of the common law of the land, and if statutes cannot alter the fundamental law, then surely the prerogative is beyond their reach. Coke's doctrine is already bearing strange fruit. The fact that the decision has ever since been the subject of severe condemnation on political grounds must not be allowed to obscure the legal and historical basis for it. In the words of Mr. Brinton Coxe:[67]

> "According to now prevalent American ideas, if the constitution of England had been written, and such a prerogative right had been constitutional, the court ought to have done precisely what it did. Moreover, had the decision been one in favour of a popular right instead of a prerogative right, the assertion of a judicial competency of deciding a questioned statute to be contrary to binding right, might have been, perhaps, very differently regarded. . . .
>
> "Trevett *v.* Weeden[68] was a case in which a statute, made under an *unwritten* constitution, and destroying the popular right of trial by jury, was judicially rejected as unconstitutional and therefore void. In the interests of popular rights, an American court flatly refused to obey a clearly worded statute. Godden *v.* Hales was a case in which an English court, also proceeding under an *unwritten* constitution, did likewise in the interests of royal prerogative."

However much the judgment may be esteemed as a striking application of Coke's theory, there is no denying that politically it created an intolerable situation, from which there was no escape save by the Revolution settlement safeguarded by Section XII of the Bill of Rights. As a practical issue in English constitutional law, the Revolution of 1688 marks the abandonment of the doctrine of *Bonham's Case,* and the realization of the futility of seeking permanence in a legal system which was suffering change as inevitable as it was radical. The attempt to check the divergent careers of Crown and Parliament by subjecting them both to the dead hand of the ancient common law, only revealed the disconcerting fact that the Crown had everything to gain by an appeal

---

[67] Coxe, *op. cit supra* note 30, at 166–67.

[68] This famous Rhode Island case will be discussed *infra,* p. 65.

to antiquity, and that it was the common law itself, of which the prerogative was a part, which was the source of offense. The so-called vacillation of Coke himself must be attributed much more to this inherent weakness in his position, than to insincerity or lack of courage. Even believers in Coke's dogma, had they seen the events of James II's reign and the Revolution, could hardly have escaped confessing that the sovereignty of Parliament was more tolerable than a fundamental law of which the Stuart prerogative was so legitimate a portion.

In its earlier stages, the exponents of the theory did not define their " fundamental law " any too closely, and sometimes we find it described as a controlling common law, sometimes as reason, sometimes as natural equity. The Revolution showed that the common law was a dangerous basis to select: the Bill of Rights, moreover, had boldly overthrown several portions of it, and had created a situation which was virtually an *impasse* on any other theory than that of a supreme legislature, for there was no possible middle course between James II and William III, between the inalienable, irreducible and unalterable prerogative, and the statutory Bill of Rights which abolished notable portions of it. Nevertheless, people continued to argue that the legislature was limited by reason, or perhaps even, by natural equity, and it is in this form that we find the last traces of the influence of *Dr. Bonham's Case* in England.

In the *City of London v. Wood*,[69] the City sued in the Court of the Mayor and Aldermen against Wood for a fine due to them under a London by-law for refusing the office of sheriff, the by-law in question specifying that the fine may be exacted in any City court of record. It was argued *inter alia* that this was bad, as they were judge in their own case, and on these and other grounds the judgment was reversed on error. The judgment of Lord Chief Justice Holt shows clearly how perplexed he was by the questions involved in this position. " So in this case it is plain," he observed,[70] " he is guilty of a wrong in not obeying the act of common council, for it is a law in *London;* and every by-law is a law, and as obligatory to all persons bound by it, that is, within its jurisdiction, as any act of parliament, only with this difference, that a by-law is liable to have its validity brought

[69] 12 Mod. *669 (Mayor's Court, 1701).

[70] *Ibid.* *678, *687.

in question, but an act of parliament is not; but when a by-law is once adjudged to be a good and reasonable by-law, it is to all intents as binding to those that it extends to as an act of parliament can be." But this perfectly sound modern doctrine is accompanied by a reminiscence of pre-Revolution teaching: "But THE TRUE GREAT POINT is, that the court is held before the mayor and aldermen, and the action brought in the names of the mayor and commonalty; . . . and this cannot be by the rules of any law whatever, for it is against all laws that the same person should be party and judge in the same cause. . . . And what my Lord *Coke* says in Dr. *Bonham's Case* in his 8. *Co.* is far from any extravagancy, for it is a very reasonable and true saying, That if an act of parliament should ordain that the same person should be party and judge, or, which is the same thing, judge in his own cause, it would be a void act of parliament; for it is impossible that one should be judge and party, for the judge is to determine between party and party, or between the government and the party; and an act of parliament can do no wrong, though it may do several things that look pretty odd; for it may discharge one from his allegiance to the government he lives under, and restore him to the state of nature; but it cannot make one that lives under a government judge and party. An act of parliament may not make adultery lawful, that is, it cannot make it lawful for *A.* to lie with the wife of *B.* but it may make the wife of *A.* to be the wife of *B.* and dissolve her marriage with *A.*" In the course of the fourteen folio pages which this judgment occupies, then, Lord Holt wavers helplessly between two incompatible opinions. Thus he assures us that the validity of an act of Parliament cannot be questioned; but that all the same, it may be void if it enacts an "impossibility"[71] — that is to say, something contrary to the axioms of natural justice in all laws; that acts can certainly "do several things that look pretty odd," although, finally, it is to be believed that they can do no wrong![72]

---

[71] For this peculiar use of "impossible" in the sense of "unbecoming," compare the "impartinent" of Annuitie 41, *supra* note 25.

[72] It may be remarked that 12 Mod. is not very highly estimated as an example of law reporting; see WALLACE, REPORTERS (4th ed. 1882) 355–56, 389–90. A few years earlier, Holt had declared it to be the judges' daily task to "construe and expound Acts of Parliament, and adjudge them to be void." King v. Earl of Banbury, Skin. 517, 527 (K. B. 1695).

Such is the sad state of wreckage to which Lord Coke's stately theory had been reduced after the successive hurricanes of the Great Rebellion and the Glorious Revolution.

Only fragments remain. In *The King v. Inhabitants of Cumberland,*[73] an indictment had been found against the county for not having repaired a bridge, and was removed into the Court of King's Bench by *certiorari* at the instance of the prosecutor. The defendants objected to this procedure as the statute 1 ANN. c. 18, § 5, enacted that such matters were to be determined in the counties where they arose and not elsewhere, " 'and that no presentment or indictment for not repairing such bridges . . . shall be removed by *certiorari* out of the said county into any other court.' " No statute could be clearer, but this is what Lord Chief Justice Kenyon said about it: " The words of this act of parliament are very general: but if in the construction we were to read them in their full extent, it would introduce a solecism in the law; for it must be remembered that in these cases the defendants are the inhabitants of a county, and if the indictment cannot be removed by *certiorari,* and a suggestion entered on the record that the inhabitants of the county are interested in order to have the trial elsewhere, the indictment must be tried by the very persons who are parties in the cause. This, I believe, would be an anomalous case in the law of *England.* However, this question does not rest on that general observation. If this were *res integra,* we should consider whether the extensive words of this statute ought not to be narrowed in their construction, in order to arrive at that point, which is the object of all laws, the attainment of justice." The Chief Justice then went on to examine a long series of precedents where *certiorari* had issued and not been challenged — some of these cases being only one year after the statute. " Therefore on the authority of all these cases," he proceeded, " whatever might have been our opinion if it had been *res integra,* (though in forming an opinion for the first time on the subject we should have been anxious for reasons of substantial justice to have controlled the extensive operation of the general words of the statute of *Anne,*) we are of opinion that the *certiorari* was properly issued." Briefly stated, although Lord Kenyon contemplated the possibility of having to consider

[73] 6 T. R. 194, 195, 197 (K. B. 1795).

whether the principle of *Bonham's Case* might not be applicable, yet he was obviously glad of the opportunity for avoiding such a delicate discussion by sheltering behind the long series of precedents which he enumerates to the length of two folio pages. Indeed, Lord Kenyon had availed himself of the same device only a few years earlier in *Leigh v. Kent* [74] when he refused to make absolute a rule to stay proceedings against a clergyman for non-residence, on the objection that an affidavit had not first been filed that the offense was in the county where the proceedings were brought, this being the requirement of the statute, 21 JAC. I, c. 4. His judgment, in which Justices Buller and Grose concurred, was that "I think no such affidavit is necessary; it has never been usual to take that step. And though, where the words of an act of parliament are plain, it cannot be repealed by *non-user,* yet where there has been a series of practice, without any exception, it goes a great way to explain them where there is any ambiguity." In short, the courts reserve the right tacitly to ignore a statute, if they can show that it has never been followed.[75] A very similar case on a different statute is that of *Stewart v. Lawton* [76] where Sergeant Cross objected to the statute 8 ANN. c. 9, that it required the plaintiff to be examined on oath in his own case — which (at that date) was "repugnant to common right" within the meaning of the rule in *Bonham's Case,* which he quoted at length. Without definitely accepting or denying this proposition, Justice Park based his judgment on that of Lord Kenyon in *Leigh v. Kent,* for here, too, the custom had been not to comply with the act.

It is worthy of note that about this time the courts were prepared to treat statutes with scant respect, but without giving any constitutional justification, in a manner which forcibly recalls the

---

[74] 3 T. R. 362 (K. B. 1789).

[75] For traces of such a doctrine in the fourteenth century, see PLUCKNETT, *op. cit. supra* note 19, at 143–44; *cf.* Quincy, 51 (Mass. 1865). Another remarkable example of this strange notion occurs in 1287. The Statute of Gloucester, c. 3, had recognized a form of action, but when a party tried to use it, his opponent pleaded that "although the statute is as the plaintiff says, yet so far there has never been issued out of the king's chancery a writ of entry upon the statute; and he prays judgment." Judgment was accordingly given that the plaintiff had no remedy by a writ of entry and must bring a writ of right. CHESTER COUNTY COURT ROLLS (Chetham Soc. 1925) 75, no. 196.

[76] 1 Bing. 374 (C. P. 1823).

early fourteenth century. A striking example was when the mere deposit of deeds was held to operate as an equitable mortgage in *Russel v. Russel* [77] in the teeth of the Statute of Frauds which required all such transactions to be in writing and signed, the decision following an earlier experiment in that direction [78] and becoming in turn the source of a considerable line of development.[79]

Long before this, however, we begin to find cases in which Coke's dogma was openly questioned in the courts. Thus in *The Duchess of Hamilton's Case* [80] we have the words of Sir Thomas Powys who argued that " in *Day* and *Savage* in Hobart, 87 it is indeed said that an Act of Parliament may be void from its first Creation, as an Act against Natural Equity; for *Jura Naturae sunt immutabilia, sunt leges legum*.[81] But this must be a very clear Case, and Judges will strain hard rather than interpret an Act void *ab initio*." It is significant that even the application of Coke's principle is now to be decently veiled under the cloak of " interpretation."

A decisive step in the destruction of the theory was taken in *Parish of Great Charte v. Parish of Kennington*,[82] when it was held that although it was a good principle that a man should not be judge and party, yet if a situation arose in which the only competent judge assigned by statute was interested in the dispute, he could, and ought to proceed notwithstanding. The principle of this judgment was affirmed in *Grand Junction Canal Co. v. Dimes* [83] by Lord Langdale, Master of the Rolls, in spite of the citation by counsel of such cases as *City of London v. Wood, Day v. Savadge*, and *Bonham's Case*. Moreover, judgments become more emphatic as the nineteenth century proceeds: " It is contrary to the general rule of law, not only in this country, but in

---

77 1 Bro. C. C. 269 (1783).

78 Hales v. Van Berchem, 2 Vern. *618 (Ch. 1708).

79 See *Ex parte* Coming, 9 Ves. 117 (Ch. 1803), and 2 WHITE AND TUDOR, LEADING CASES IN EQUITY (8th ed. 1912) 86. At times the government connived at the judicial abrogation of legislation which was found to be imprudent, according to Lord Kenyon in Smith v. Armourers Co., 1 Peake, 148 (K. B. 1792).

80 10 Mod. 115 (C. P. 1712).

81 We have remarked above, p. 49, on this misquotation from Bracton; here (with an additional error) it is, moreover, distinguished in a marginal note as "*Maxim* in Law."

82 2 Strange, 1173 (K. B. 1742).

83 12 Beav. 63, 77 (Rolls Court, 1849).

every other, to make a person judge in his own cause," said Mr. Justice Blackburn in 1866, ". . . though the Legislature can, and, no doubt, in a proper case would, depart from that general rule," requiring, however, that the intention be clearly expressed.[84] Finally, in 1871 we have a categorical denial of Coke's principle. "I would observe," said Mr. Justice Willes,[85] "as to these Acts of Parliament, that they are the law of this land; and we do not sit here as a court of appeal from parliament. It was once said,— I think in Hobart (1),—that, if an Act of Parliament were to create a man judge in his own case, the Court might disregard it.[86] That dictum, however, stands as a warning, rather than an authority to be followed. We sit here as servants of the Queen and the legislature. Are we to act as regents over what is done by parliament with the consent of Queen, lords and commons? I deny that any such authority exists. . . . The proceedings here are judicial, not autocratic, which they would be if we could make laws instead of administering them."

Such, then, is the history of the origin, growth, decline, and fall of Chief Justice Coke's doctrine in the English courts of law. But we cannot leave this portion of the subject without a reference to the celebrated passage in Blackstone [87] upon the matter.

"LASTLY, acts of parliament that are impossible [88] to be performed are of no validity; and if there arise out of them collaterally any absurd consequences, manifestly contradictory to common reason, they are, with regard to those collateral consequences void. I lay down the rule with these restrictions; though I know it is generally laid down more largely, that acts of parliament contrary to reason are void. But if the parliament will positively enact a thing to be done which is unreasonable, I know of no power that can control it: and the examples usually alledged in support of this sense of the rule do none of them prove, that where the main object of a statute is unreasonable the judges are at liberty to reject it; for that were to set the judicial power above that of the legislature, which would be subversive of all government. But where some collateral matter arises out of the general words, and happens to be unreasonable; there the judges are in decency

84 Mersey Docks Trustees v. Gibbs, L. R. 1 H. L. 93, 110 (1866).

85 Lee v. Bude & Torrington Junction Ry., L. R. 6 C. P. 576, 582 (1871).

86 The allusion is to Day v. Savadge, *supra* note 51.

87 1 BL. COMM. (1st ed. 1765) 91.

88 Note that this "impossible" is really the "impartinent" of Annuitie 41.

to conclude that this consequence was not foreseen by the parliament, and therefore they are at liberty to expound the statute by equity, and only *quoad hoc* disregard it. Thus if an act of parliament gives a man power to try all causes, that arise within his manor of Dale; yet, if a cause should arise in which he himself is party, the act is construed not to extend to that, because it is unreasonable that any man should determine his own quarrel. But, if we could conceive it possible for the parliament to enact, that he should try as well his own causes as those of other persons, there is no court that has power to defeat the legislature, when couched in such evident and express words, as leave no doubt whether it was the intent of the legislature or no."

From what has been shown in the earlier portions of this paper, it will be evident that Blackstone underestimates the historical strength of Coke's doctrine, but his conclusion is typical of the best judicial opinion, expressed in such cases as *The Duchess of Hamilton's Case,*[89] *Great Charte v. Kennington,*[90] *Mersey Docks Trustees v. Gibbs,*[91] and others.

The text we have quoted above is from the first edition of the *Commentaries,* 4to, Oxford, 1765, and remained unaltered until the ninth edition. There is an interesting note, said to be in Blackstone's own hand, in the margin of a copy of the eighth edition, published in 1778, which makes the third sentence read, "But if parliament will positively enact a thing to be done which is unreasonable, I know of no power *in the ordinary forms of the Constitution that is vested with authority* to control it." The ninth and all the later editions have this modification. Quincy suggests[92] that the alteration shows that the great commentator had changed his opinion in favor of the theory of judicial review, in consequence of American precedents. This is not very likely, while it may be doubted whether the verbal change necessarily implies any great change of opinion. If it really is significant, however, it will be necessary to stress the fact that the wording is extremely vague, and if taken literally might contain serious implications. For example, if this power is not in the "ordinary forms" of the constitution, where else could it be? Can it be supposed that the constitution contains extraordinary forms for emergency use, whose existence is in the nature of a state secret?

---

89 *Supra* note 80.

90 *Supra* note 82.

91 *Supra* note 84.

92 Quincy, 526 (Mass. 1865).

Or does the sentence contain a veiled reference to such means as were used in America against the Stamp Act? Perhaps it might be helpful to recall the Revolution of 1688, the conduct of which would have been impossible under the " ordinary forms of the constitution; " but even so, there is little profit to be gained by attempting to describe a revolution in terms of constitutional law. The simplest explanation seems to be that the word " ordinary " must not be interpreted too strictly, and that all Blackstone means to imply is that such an act is subject to no control save that of force, whether actually armed, or simply the moral force of public resentment, and that the legal mechanism of the constitution alone is powerless to remedy the situation.

IV

It now remains to describe briefly the career of the doctrine in America. Settlers naturally carry with them the main outlines of their native law, and it is perfectly natural that there should have been some vague acquaintance with the common law in New England, although all of them did not view their legal inheritance with equal enthusiasm. Some had gone forth partly with the intention of erecting a theocracy based not on the common law but on the Bible, and in such communities professional lawyers were long under a cloud, their functions being performed by preachers and laymen administering the Scriptures and common sense.[93] With the economic and political growth of the colony, it became necessary to adopt a more refined system of law to meet the requirements of their prospering classes of landowners and merchants. Then it was that the common law began to revive, and its theoretical application to the colonies as laid down in their charters came to be something more than merely nominal. It is a significant sign of the new tendency that we find the General Court of Massachusetts in 1647 ordering two copies to be bought of *Coke upon Littleton*, Coke's *Reports*, *Coke upon Magna Carta*, the *Book of Entries*, the *New Terms of*

---

[93] See in general Reinsch, *The English Common Law in the Early American Colonies*, 1 SELECT ESSAYS IN ANGLO-AMERICAN LEGAL HISTORY (1907) 367. The Puritan element must not be exaggerated; nor was it present in all the colonies.

the Law, and Dalton's *Justice of the Peace,*[94] while in the year before they had set out in parallel columns [95] their own laws and the "fundamental and common lawes and customes of England" to show that they were keeping as closely as possible to the system of the parent country.

In due course we begin to see the results of this step. Justice Symonds of Boston, Massachusetts (some time later a Deputy Governor), became an open admirer of the common law of England and in the long and ambitious judgment which he rendered in *Giddings v. Browne* [96] we have the first clear example of an act of legislature being invalidated by the judiciary in America. The town meeting had voted £100 towards providing a house for Mr. Cobbet, a minister, and the present case arose out of Browne's refusal to pay. Symonds held that "it is against a fundamentall law in nature to be compelled to pay that which others doe give." That positive law cannot prevail against fundamental law, he supports with passages drawn from Finch [97] and Dalton, and some hearsay precedents in Ipswich and Weymouth.

Political events also directed the colonists' attention towards the English common law, which they came to regard as the palladium of their civil liberties. The vigorous rule of Andros in 1688 set Bostonians thinking about *Habeas Corpus,* while at the same time the abrogation of their charter by James II provoked an outspoken claim to independence, in support of which they were said [98] to "hold forth a law book, & quote the Authority of the Lord Cook to Justifie their setting up for them-

---

[94] HILKEY, LEGAL DEVELOPMENT IN COLONIAL MASSACHUSETTS (37 COLUMBIA UNIV. STUDIES, No. 2, 1910) 66.

[95] 1 HUTCHINSON PAPERS (Prince Soc. 1865) 197–247. Since the above was written, an entirely new construction has been placed upon this document by Mr. Richard B. Morris who has made the first critical examination of it in his article, *Massachusetts and the Common Law: the Declaration of 1646* (1926) 31 AM. HIST. REV. 443–53.

[96] 2 HUTCHINSON PAPERS (Prince Soc. 1865) 1–15.

[97] FINCH, LAW, OR, A DISCOURSE THEREOF (1627) 74, develops the proposition that "Common Law [is] nothing els but common reason," and that positive laws contrary to it as void, as are those contrary to the law of nature. The first edition appeared in 1613 under the title Νομοτεχνια.

[98] *An Account of the Colonys and Provinces of New England in general, More particularly of that of the Massachusetts,* printed from MS. Lambeth 841 in PERRY, PAPERS RELATING TO THE HISTORY OF THE CHURCH IN MASSACHUSETTS (1873) 39, 42.

selves; pleading the possession of 60 years against the right of the Crown."

It was two generations later that Coke's influence bore its most important results, however. His name and authority were used freely in *Paxton's Case* [99] by Otis in his indecisive attack upon writs of assistance but still more so in an even greater cause. The disaffection caused by the Stamp Act very early took a legal complexion: ". . . our friends to liberty take the advantage of a maxim they find in Lord Coke that an Act of Parliament against Magna Carta or the peculiar rights of Englishmen is *ipso facto* void," wrote Lieutenant-Governor Hutchinson, on 12th Sept., 1765.[100] "This, taken in the latitude the people are often enough disposed to take it, must be fatal to all government, and it seems to have determined great part of the colony to oppose the execution of the act with force. . . ." A popular demonstration led to the resignation of the only officer who had authority to sell the stamps which the act required to be affixed to most legal documents; thereby producing an additional complication, as we learn from the Governor-historian Hutchinson's "Summary of the Disorders in the Massachusetts Province proceeding from an Apprehension that the Act of Parliament called the Stamp Act deprives the People of their Natural Rights."[101] He relates that "A committee [of the Assembly] at this sitting [25 Sept., 1765] had reported certain resolves, and among others, one that all courts should do business without stamps and that their proceedings should be valid to all intents and purposes, but the house having spent several days upon it, dropped it. . . . The reason given for their resolve, and since given by the people in general for going on with business without stamps is this, that the stamp officer has resigned and no stamps to be had; but upon further consideration and the many arguments used in the publick prints to support the doctrine, the prevailing reason at this time is, that the Act of Parliament is against Magna Charta and the natural rights of Englishmen, and therefore according to Lord Coke null and void."

The popular and lay view of the legal situation was so firmly

---

[99] Quincy, 51, 401 (Mass. 1761, published in 1865).

[100] 26 MS. Archives of Massachusetts, ff. 153–54 (preserved in the State House, Boston).

[101] *Ibid.* ff. 180, 183.

held that the judges were in due course asked for an authoritative statement. As it was out of term, they were able to postpone their decision for a time, during which period researches were made and an anxious correspondence conducted between Hutchinson and the distinguished Massachusetts Justice, John Cushing, on the situation created by the practical impossibility of getting stamps. "I have been well informed,"[102] wrote Cushing to the Lieutenant-Governor on February 9, 1766, "that Mr. Gridley[103] the beginning of November last was fully of opinion the Court could not proceed on civil matters, but since, on searching authority, judges we ought to proceed. What he has found I know not, and am doubtful whether he can find any in point. It's true, it is said, an Act of Parliament against natural equity is void. It will be disputed whether this is such an Act. It seems to me the main question here is whether an Act which cannot be carried into execution should stop the course of justice, and that the Judges are more confined than with respect to an obsolete Act. If we admit evidence unstamped *ex necessitate,* Query if it can be said we do wrong." As the months went by Cushing's opinions became more settled, and we find him writing to John Adams, "I can tell the grand jury the nullity of Acts of Parliament, but must leave you to prove it by the more powerful arguments of the *jus gladii divinum,* a power not peculiar to kings and ministers;" to which Adams replied,[104] "You have my hearty concurrence in telling the jury the nullity of Acts of Parliament, whether we can prove it by the *jus gladii,* or not. I am determined to die of that opinion, let the *jus gladii* say what it will."

The *jus gladii* spoke with no uncertain voice, but still there remained something to be said when finally arms yielded place to the toga; the Congress had resolved in 1774[105] "that the respective colonies are entitled to the common law of England,"—a statement which their founders would have hesitated to make—and it remained to decide how much weight to allow it in their legal system. From this time onward Coke's influence is obvious, and the practice of judicial invalidation of acts for unconstitu-

---

102 25 *ibid.* f. 55.

103 Jeremiah Gridley was twice Attorney-General.

104 9 ADAMS, WORKS (1854) 390–91.

105 1 JOURNALS OF THE CONTINENTAL CONGRESS (1904) 69.

tionality, which had begun in colonial days,[106] steadily grew. In *Robin et al. v. Hardaway et al.*[107] several persons of Indian descent attempted to vindicate their freedom in spite of a statute of 1682 (and others) which reduced them to slavery. The plaintiffs' arguments were eloquent. " All acts of legislature apparently contrary to right and justice are, in our laws, and must be in the nature of things, considered as void. The laws of nature are the laws of God, whose authority can be superseded by no power on earth. A legislature must not obstruct our obedience to Him from Whose punishments they cannot protect us. All human constitutions which contradict His laws, we are in conscience bound to disobey. Such have been the adjudications of our courts of justice. And cited 8 Co. 118a *Bonham's Case*. HOB. 87.[108] 7 Co. 14 *Calvin's Case*." The defense was learned; Puffendorf was used to prove that slavery was a part of the law of nature, and the dicta of Coke were matched by the words of Blackstone which we have already discussed.[109] This issue, however, was not argued to a decision, for the court eventually found that the obnoxious statute had been repealed in 1705. Nevertheless, the arguments throw considerable light upon the legal thought of the period.

In 1786 there followed the much-discussed case of *Trevett v. Weeden*[110] in the Superior Court of Rhode Island. An act of the legislature had imposed penalties on all who refused to take the state's paper money at its face value, empowering any justice of the Superior Court or the Court of Common Pleas, to try offenders summarily without jury. Upon Weeden being so tried on the information of Trevett, Major-General Varnum, for the defense, argued that as the act took away trial by jury, it was contrary to Magna Carta and fundamental rights.[111] We

106 See Colden's protest, July 5, 1759, in NEW YORK HISTORICAL SOCIETY COLLECTIONS (1869) 204.

107 Jeff. 109 (Va. 1772).

108 This is Day v. Savadge, *supra*, p. 49.

109 1 BL. COMM. 91; Puffendorf, Vattel, and Blackstone were all very widely read in America at this time.

110 No report, save the pamphlet by Varnum (Providence, 1786) who was counsel for the defense. The record is in 10 RECORDS OF THE STATE OF RHODE ISLAND (1865) 219.

111 It should be observed that at this date Rhode Island had no written state constitution, beyond the old charter of Charles II (1663).

will not follow the learned advocate's lengthy disquisition on English history from Egbert to date; as may be expected, he often quotes "that great oracle of the law, Lord Coke," holds that the act is "repugnant and impossible," for the judges cannot proceed "without any jury . . . according to the law of the land" as the act commands, and exhorts the judges to exercise their inherent powers over legislation, as had been done in the reports of Hobart, Plowden, and Coke — with the theoretical support of Vattel.[112] The question of paper money was highly controversial, and it is doubtless in view of their difficult position, faced as they were by a determined legislature supported by the public which was in a state of intense excitement, that the court gave a judgment which has never since ceased to puzzle commentators. Two views are possible. One, expressed by Stiness,[113] emphasizes the fact that in form the court's judgment was simply that they had no jurisdiction to try the case, as they were not the special court erected *ad hoc* by the statute. This is certainly the judgment on the record, but there was much more in it than this. Legally, Stiness' view is incontestable, but politically there is more to be said for the conclusion of Cooley who claims that the judgment held the act to be unconstitutional and void.[114] We do not know what was said from the bench, but according to contemporary newspapers [115] three judges declared the act unconstitutional, one doubted the court's jurisdiction, and the Chief Justice expressed no opinion save that in his judgment as it appears on the record. While it is true that judgment was given solely on the question of jurisdiction, as Stiness contends, it is nevertheless true that a majority of the bench had expressed the view that the act was void. The reason for the court's taking

---

112 I VATTEL, LE DROIT DES GENS, OU PRINCIPES DE LA LOI NATURELLE (1758) iii, § 34.

113 Stiness, *The Struggle for Judicial Supremacy,* in 3 FIELD, STATE OF RHODE ISLAND AND PROVIDENCE PLANTATIONS AT THE END OF THE CENTURY (1902) 107 *et seq.*

114 COOLEY, CONSTITUTIONAL LIMITATIONS (1903) 229; but not void as against the charter, nor does the charter expressly give jury trial as there supposed. For a full and recent discussion of the political environment of the case, which employs much interesting evidence drawn from contemporary newspapers, see Charles Warren, *Earliest Cases of Judicial Review of State Legislation by Federal Courts* (1922) 32 YALE L. J. 15.

115 Quoted by Stiness, *op. cit. supra* note 113, at 108.

refuge in this technicality was soon made plain by subsequent events. The judges were immediately summoned to appear before the General Assembly "to assign the reasons and grounds of their judgment in adjudging an act of this Assembly unconstitutional, and therefore void."[116] The Assembly, then, knew very well the true grounds for the decision; but the judges brought the record with them showing that their judgment was on the point of jurisdiction. The device was successful, and the baffled Assembly had to discharge the judges as no criminal charge was laid against them, voting, however, that "no satisfactory reasons have been rendered by them for their judgment." As a legal precedent, the case proves nothing, but as a fact in the history of political thought in America, *Trevett v. Weeden* is striking testimony to the strength of the Coke tradition.

A few years later a similar doctrine was applied under curious circumstances in the South Carolina case of *Bowman v. Middleton*.[117] Eighty years previous to this litigation two families had disputed the boundaries of their respective lands, and an act of the legislature[118] in 1712 had settled the matter by laying down the bounds and confirming the inheritance to the younger sons of one of the contestants who had died intestate. The court held that no title could pass under this act which was "against common right and *magna carta* . . . That the act was, therefore *ipso facto* void," and "That no length of time could give it validity." The reasons for its voidance were that it deprived the one family of its property without judicial proceedings or trial by jury, and deprived the eldest son of the other family of his inheritance, again without trial by jury, inasmuch as the land was partitioned among his brothers — this latter point bearing upon the important attempt made by the colonists to abolish primogeniture.[119]

---

116 10 Records of the State of Rhode Island (1865) 218.

117 1 Bay, 252 (S. C. 1792).

118 For the interpretation of such private acts, see 2 Bl. Comm. 346, and *cf.* Campbell's Case, 2 Bland, 209, 232 (Md. 1829).

119 Important constitutional points were involved, which, however, do not bear directly on our subject. The main cases are discussed in Hazeltine, Appeals from Colonial Courts to the King in Council (7 Brown Univ. Historical Seminary Papers, 1896), and Andrews, *The Connecticut Intestacy Laws* (1894) 3 Yale Review, 261. It has been held that the common law of inheritance has never pre-

The adoption of the practice of setting up written state constitutions was soon to render Coke's doctrine unnecessary. Common right is vague at the best, and cannot compare with a well-drawn constitution as a check upon legislative action. The fundamental nature of written constitutions was foreshadowed in the states,[120] where Vattel's teaching had tremendous influence, and was laid down in the Supreme Court of the United States by Marshall's famous and much discussed judgment in *Marbury v. Madison*.[121] But Massachusetts has long remained partial to the doctrine learned from Lord Coke in her colonial days, and in 1826,[122] and again in 1850,[123] her courts have mentioned with approval the old English cases in which it is embodied.[124]

V

This is a long story, and all the time Sir Edward Coke plays a dominating part. He took the practice of the fourteenth century — an age when courts and statutes were still something of a novelty — and filled it with a new spirit, the product of his own genius. The result was really a new doctrine although fortified, he honestly believed, with incontestable precedents from the middle ages; for he knew well that without such support it would have availed nothing, although with it, there was a possibility that the new theory might prevent the imminent strife between Crown and Parliament. His personal defects alone could not have sufficed to discredit so remarkable a contribution to political science. Indeed, his views were shared even by the cautious

vailed in Connecticut. Campbell's Appeal, 64 Conn. 277, 290, 29 Atl. 494, 495 (1894).

120 In Holmes v. Walton, 4 Halst. 444 (N. J. 1780), (see A. W. Scott, *Holmes vs. Walton: The New Jersey Precedent* (1898) 4 Am. Hist. Rev. 456); Den v. Singleton, 1 Martin, 42 (N. C. 1787); Kamper v. Hawkins, 1 Va. Cas. 20 (1793). For an able demonstration that the idea of judicial review was quite familiar to the framers and ratifiers of the Constitution, see Beard, The Supreme Court and the Constitution (1912).

121 1 Cranch, 137 (U. S. 1803).

122 Commonwealth v. Worcester, 3 Pick. 461, 472 (Mass. 1826).

123 William v. Robinson, 6 Cush. 330 (Mass. 1850). Both cases approve of City of London v. Wood, *supra* note 69.

124 For the theory that there is an unwritten as well as a written constitution, at the present day, see McClain, *Unwritten Constitutions in the United States* (1902) 15 Harv. L. Rev. 531.

Hobart, who later succeeded in winning the respect of republicans as well as royalists. The weakness lay in the theory itself, first, because its mediaeval basis was always open to dispute, and so it was possible to support the vague feeling that it was a novelty by showing that its roots in the past were not as deep as its partisans alleged. The extent to which the theory was a novelty may be judged from the fact that both its supporters and its opponents did not realize the implications of treating the common law as fundamental; but surely, if the common law had always been fundamental, then the prerogative lawyers would have obtained the judgment in *Godden v. Hales* long before 1686. Coke deserves our respect for the originality of his contribution to the political problem of his day, but it proved too strange and too uncertain to serve his purpose.

Secondly, the Revolution alone could finally settle the problem. The march of events had led Englishmen to look to Parliament and not to the Crown as the embodiment of their national life. Apparently opportunist and fickle, Parliament had nevertheless led the nation in its search for the *via media* and had reflected the varying moods of the people. The nation felt that the political pressure of public opinion expressed through Parliament was a more certain safeguard than the operation of judicial institutions, admirably though they had worked during most of the Stuart conflict. The rise of popular government therefore naturally brought with it the sovereignty of Parliament. Nevertheless, Coke's teaching was not altogether vain. His learning and prestige had made enough disciples on the bench to familiarize lawyers with the outlines of his thought, and eventually the strangeness wore off until it became evident that the new thought could be grafted on to the common law. The Revolution came only just in time to prevent the conversion, and to make it finally clear that there was no place for it in English constitutional law. But the common law was not confined within the four seas. In the American colonies the Revolution meant something different. Parliament was not their hero but a distant and unsympathetic body in whose deliberations they had no part. When it aroused their resentment, therefore, it was natural to remember the teaching of the great Chief Justice, which had not been faced with the problem of the Revolution settlement in American minds. The sovereignty of Parliament was by no means so obvious an implication of the Revolution to people who had not lived in London during the critical years from 1685 to 1688. It is a cardinal fact that to the eighteenth-century American the doctrine of a fundamental common law was familiar, and regarded as quite consistent with the common law scheme of things. Finally there came the reception of Vattel's theoretical discussions which coincided so nearly with the less elegant but equally fruitful dicta from the English judge. It was due not only to that doctrine, but also to the firm faith that "what my Lord Coke says in Bonham's Case is far from any extravagancy" that we owe the bold experiment of making a written constitution which should have judges and a court for its guardians.

XV

THE GENESIS OF COKE'S *REPORTS*

It is not the object of this paper to describe the incomparable richness of Coke's Reports, nor to assess their profound influence upon the literature, and indeed the substance, of English law; still less is it concerned with estimating the place of their illustrious author in the political, constitutional, and judicial history of his country. Nor can it enter upon those teasing but recondite questions of the credibility of certain reports, serious though those questions certainly are. The sole concern of this essay is to inquire into the immediate origins of the reports—a much more modest field of investigation, but one which lacks neither interest nor difficulty.

These origins may be considered under several aspects. First, we may regard the long series of English law reports as a literary phenomenon, and study the work of Coke in the light of those who preceded him; since reporting did become eventually a vast co-operative enterprise between successive generations of authors, extending over several centuries, this approach is legitimate and significant.[1] But we must remember, secondly, that an author—even the humble author of a law-book—is something more than a mere point in the stream of literary history; and so we must ascertain, if possible, Coke's own thought upon the venture of publishing his reports. Thirdly, we must trace the sources he used, and the way in which he handled them.

There are quite a number of reports in print at the present day to which we are accustomed to look for cases of the Tudor age extending from Henry VII to Elizabeth. We naturally regard them as a chronological series, and consequently as being in some way earlier than Coke's Reports. In subject matter and in date of composition this is true enough; but in date of publication nearly all of them are later than Coke. Thus Keilway, whose matter is mainly from the years 1496 to 1531, was not printed until 1602. Likewise Brownlow and Gouldsborough only appeared in 1651-2, Gouldsborough in 1653, Popham in 1656, Leonard in 1658, Croke's Elizabeth in 1661, Benlow also in 1661, Moore in 1663, and Anderson in 1664—to name only the best known. The lawyer who bought the first edition of Part I of Coke's Reports in 1600 was not adding a new volume to a lengthening series such as these

[1]For the general course of law-reporting see WALLACE, THE REPORTERS ARRANGED AND CHARACTERIZED WITH INCIDENTAL REMARKS (1843; 4th ed. 1882); Van Vechten Veeder, *The English Reports 1537-1865* (1901) 15 HARV. L. REV. 1, 109 [partly reprinted in 2 SELECT ESSAYS IN ANGLO-AMERICAN LEGAL HISTORY (1908) 123]; WINFIELD, CHIEF SOURCES OF ENGLISH LEGAL HISTORY (1925) 183; HOLDSWORTH, HISTORY OF ENGLISH LAW (3d ed. 1922) v. 355, 461.

names would suggest. In fact, his shelf of reports of every kind was still hardly full. Coke himself has given us a summary glance over it.[2] The series began with the year books, made-up sets of which were common enough, for the influence of Tottel had produced some measure of uniformity in size and foliation. Coke speaks of nine volumes being normal. To these add the abridgements, Plowden and Dyer, and the tale is complete. Apart from the year books and abridgements, therefore, Coke stands very early in the great procession of printed reports, occupying the third place in order of publication.[3]

Of Coke's predecessors, the nearest to him in date of publication was Sir James Dyer, who lived from 1512 to 1582. In 1557 he became a justice, and in 1559 the Chief Justice, of the Court of Common Pleas.[4] His reports were not printed until 1585, after his death, and so their publication may not have been in accordance with his wish. It would seem that his nephews made public (at the desire of members of the profession) a selection from the abundant mass of reports which the Chief Justice had accumulated in the course of his career. If most of the cases were reported from the direct knowledge of Dyer, others certainly were not, for the book has cases as early as 1513. The reports are evidently in the year book tradition in language, mode of expression, and in method.

Much more original and significant is the work of Edmund Plowden.[5] His reports were printed earlier than Dyer's, and were also the first to be printed in the author's lifetime. We must therefore recognize in him the first lawyer who deliberately put his reports before the public in print, under his name, and of set purpose. The reasons which led him to take this unheard-of steps are stated in his preface. It is impossible to read that preface without being impressed by the candor and sincerity of a singularly engaging personality. He tells us that he began at the age of twenty (that

---

23 Rep., preface. The latest editions of all the reports mentioned in this article are reprinted in English Reports, complete Reprint. On the gallant part played by the publishers, see Anon., *The English Reports* (1931) 43 JURID. REV., 96; and for some necessary amendments to the chart accompanying the reprint, see Glanville L. Williams, *Addendum to the Table of English Reports* (1940) 7 CAMB. L. J. 261 clearing up several difficulties in the older form of citations. Most unfortunately the Reprint omits the prefaces, which often contain information necessary for assessing the value of a given reporter; the prefaces must therefore still be sought in the older editions. It is interesting to compare the English Reports Reprint with the prophetic scheme proposed by WALLACE, *op. cit. supra* note 1, at 40.

3In Wallace's work Coke appears as fifteenth in chronological order (of cases dealt with, that is to say).

4For his life, see the memoir prefixed to his REPORTS (Vaillant's ed. 1794); Foss, JUDGES OF ENGLAND (1870); and the DICTIONARY OF NATIONAL BIOGRAPHY.

5The only life is that in the DICTIONARY OF NATIONAL BIOGRAPHY. For appreciations of his reports, see WINFIELD, *op. cit. supra* note 1, at 187; 5 HOLDSWORTH, *op. cit. supra* note 1, at 364.

is to say, in 1538) to frequent the courts for the purpose of legal study. Since his memory was unreliable, he wrote down the notable things he heard. With the deepening of his legal knowledge, he realized that a special importance attached to arguments upon special verdicts and demurrers; thenceforward he abandoned his old and somewhat indiscriminate collection in order to concentrate upon that type of case. Upon such cases he lavished infinite care. He studied the pleadings before coming into court, so that he knew as much about the case as did the counsel engaged in it;[6] he submitted his report to the judges and serjeants who had taken part in the debate, in order to clear up difficult or doubtful passages. Only then did he enter the case in his "book." At first his report tended to be verbatim, or something approaching it. But from *Throckmorton's Case*[7] (1555-6) onward he eliminated much repetition by condensing all the arguments upon a particular point into one statement.

Such was the *modus operandi.* The result of so much diligent and intelligent labor could hardly fail to be remarkable. Surveying his work toward the end of his career, when the nature and implications of the collection had become apparent, its author described it as being, in the first place, a book of entries, "more sure and safe to be relied upon and followed than any other book of entries." This somewhat unexpected remark is nevertheless justifiable upon consideration of the development of pleading in Plowden's age. The mediaeval book report shows us in the majority of cases how serjeants and judges collaborated in settling the pleadings of difficult cases. Their task was to find pleadings which would embody the relevant facts of a case, and raise issues of law or fact which would fairly determine the rights of the parties. When the parties had agreed upon their respective pleadings, the result of the case was generally evident. Reports of such debates were useful enough while lawyers still practiced under such a system, but in Plowden's day the system was almost extinct. Instead, pleadings were prepared and exchanged by the parties' advisors before the case came before the court. If an issue of law had been reached, it was then argued and determined. If the issue was one of fact, then the roll was made up by entering the pleadings, so that there was a formal record upon which a verdict could be taken at *nisi prius.* The effect of all this upon the books of entries then current[8] is shortly expressed by Plowden: such books, he

---

[6]He often states that a case was argued by certain named serjeants "and an apprentice at law"; the latter must mean himself.

[7]Plowd. 145.

[8]In Plowden's day there were already in print: INTRACIONES (published in 1510 by Pynson), a different book with the same title and likewise anonymous (published in 1546 by Smythe), and RASTELL'S ENTRIES (published in 1566 by Tottel). Any of these three works might be called "The Old Book of Entries." See WINFIELD, *op. cit. supra* note 1, at 305.

says, contain copies of records, often concluding to an issue of fact, the forms being settled by the parties without submitting them to the criticism of the court. The fact that both parties agreed to treat the pleadings as sufficient is no guarantee that in law they were proof against criticism. Such forms were therefore misleading guides, and one who followed them might find an opponent who could detect the flaws and take advantage of them. Clearly, this recent and topical problem greatly worried our author, until he was driven to the conclusion that no set of pleadings could be trusted as a precedent unless it had been fully considered and approved after argument in court. Such consideration was most generally had when demurrers were argued, or special verdicts returned; so it was that type of case which Plowden considered most worthy of his pains and the reader's study.

Although Plowden regarded his book as primarily a book of entries, each case supported by argument and decision, he admitted that it was also a collection of reports. From this point of view, too, his book was shaped by the new pleading. Under the old style, the year books often recount "sudden sayings of the judges upon motions" and other occasions when a matter might be imperfectly presented and hastily determined. Nothing of that sort was to appear in Plowden's book. Every case in it was a full-dress debate upon pleadings which judges and counsel had fully studied at leisure before the argument began. And so, he concludes, "In my humble apprehension, these reports excel any former book of reports in point of credit and authority." The tone of deep and unaffected modesty which pervades the preface lends greater emphasis than ever to these high claims for his entries and reports. Plowden was humble, as a genuine student must be; but he knew when he had done a really fine and solid piece of work, and was not embarrassed to say so.

Plowden began to report, like some other eager young lawyers of his day, as soon as he began the serious study of the law. Only slowly did he find a method and discover a sure rule for testing his material. Like all collectors, he made mistakes, and sometimes he was unlucky. After terms or years of argument a case might evaporate without ever reaching a decision, thus rendering the reporter's labor fruitless. In the cause of science he could be stern: in that precious book of his nothing should be entered which was not perfect.

We must believe him when he tells us that all this labor was for his own private satisfaction. He was in fact using the method constantly recommended to the students of his own generation, the only difference being that he pursued it more persistently, more conscientiously, and much more intelligently than his fellows. To print the work would change its meaning and significance. To Plowden himself, the book was part of his arduous self-education in the law; to the casual purchaser of the printed volume, however, it represented something different and less personal. What had been the ripe fruit of one man's toil became instead a ready-made tool for office use. Such a perversion of his cherished book was undoubtedly shocking to the gentle Plowden. He had allowed a few selected friends a sight of it; their clerks surreptitiously copied it. Worst blow of all, they misunderstood its very nature, and tore the heart out of it by omitting the pleadings. In self-defense Plowden was forced to print an authorized version, presenting the book as he conceived it.

It is difficult now to realize the full significance of this, the first printed law report. Plowden was an innovator much against his will. Publication seemed to reverse the natural order of things. The traditional attitude was that one learned while reporting, and learned much more than one could get down on paper. To publish ready-made reports might seem not unlike the illicit circulation of lecture notes which occasionally disturbs academic authorities today. But were there ever such notes as Plowden's, so accurate, so clear, or so completely final in their thoroughness? So he faced the problems of printing—earnestly hoping that no professional reputation would suffer from his disclosures, just as Dyer's nephews expressed anxiety lest that worthy's reports should contain hidden slanders of title. A very curious passage of his preface impresses once again upon the reader how novel the volume was: Plowden was hard put to find a title for his book. The word "report" was hardly worthy, for it savored too much of the "sudden sayings" of the year books. So he decided to call it his "Commentaries or Reports" for (no doubt like Caesar's Commentaries) it recorded both deeds and words.[9]

Published on October 24, 1571, Plowden's Commentaries or Reports embarked upon a strange new life, as books sometimes do when they leave the hands of their authors. The legal profession slowly began to discover its worth, and in 1578 a new edition appeared.

At this point complications began to appear. Plowden's publisher was the great Tottel, whose "list" bears striking witness to his vast enterprise as well as to the liveliness of the market for law books.[10] Tottel had printed both Fitzherbert's and Brooke's Abridgements, and was quick to learn the

---

[9]The full title is: "Les Comentaries, ou les Reportes de Edmunde Plowden un apprentice de le comen Ley, de dyuers cases esteantes matters en ley, & de les argumentes sur yceux, en les temps des Raygnes le Roye Edwarde le size, le Roigne Mary, le Roy & Roigne Phillipp & Mary, & le Roigne Elizabeth." BEALE, BIBLIOGRAPHY OF EARLY ENGLISH LAW BOOKS (Ames Foundation, 1926), 108 (R 484).

[10]His law publications are listed in BEALE, *op. cit. supra* note 9, at 199-206; he also had a large output of general literature.

public's opinion of those two ponderous works. Fitzherbert gave full texts of most of his cases; Brooke gave principally summaries, but much better arranged. One could thus find authority on a given point quicker in Brooke than in Fitzherbert; but having found the case, Brooke's text of it (often merely a summary) might prove inadequate, and in order to see the case as a whole one had to turn to Fitzherbert or the year books. Tottel patiently set to work to disentangle the muddle. Both Fitzherbert and Brooke were fitted out with page references to Tottel's editions of the year books (and they are still precious time-savers);[11] Fitzherbert had long been provided with an index which was meant to make his book almost as handy as the later and more encyclopaedic Brooke—a hope not entirely fulfilled.[12] But there still remained one big problem. Fitzherbert was essential because of his full texts; but Brooke had yet another great advantage—he gave more recent material. Fitzherbert contained nothing later than Henry VII, but Brooke (appearing half a century later) contained many cases of Henry VIII, Edward VI and Mary—reigns in which fundamental legal developments had taken place. So Tottel had the bright thought of getting an obscure Irishman named Bellewe to comb out these more recent cases and put them together for him in a book chronologically arranged.[13] This was the work commonly called Brooke's New Cases,[14] and was published in 1578. The results of these operations become clearer when the successive editions of the books just mentioned (and their subsequent editions down to Coke's day) are listed in chronological order of publication, bearing in mind the range (in point of date) of the cases contained in them.[15]

---

[11]*Cf.* Plucknett, *Bibliography and Legal History* (1932) 26 PAPERS OF THE BIBLIOG. SOC. OF AM., 128 at 139.

[12]The only examination of this table is that by WINFIELD, *op. cit. supra* note 1, at 228.

[13]Bellewe did another similar piece of hack-work in preparing a volume of Richard II's cases collected out of the various abridgements. Bellewe was entered at Lincoln's Inn, but there is no record to show whether he was ever called to the bar.

[14]The original title was "Ascvn Nouell cases de les ans et temps le Roy H. 8, Ed. 6, et la Roygne Mary, Escrie ex la graund Abridgement, compose per Brooke." In 1651 this collection was translated and the cases restored to the original subject arrangement under the headings used by Brooke, and the whole published as MARCH'S NEW CASES. It is instructive to note that there was never a book of Fitzherbert's new cases, although his abridgement contains cases of Henry VII which were very new when the first edition appeared in 1516. Clearly, the reason is that numerous separate editions of the year books of Henry VII were appearing, and so fulfilled the need. The textual relations between Fitzherbert and the printed year books (especially for the later reigns) need investigation.

[15]This table is based upon the works of BEALE and WINFIELD, *loc. cit. supra* notes 9, 1, together with COWLEY, BIBLIOGRAPHY OF ABRIDGEMENTS (Selden Society, 1932), and A. W. POLLARD, SHORT-TITLE CATALOGUE (Bibliographical Society, 1926). In the table, and throughout the article, dates have been converted to New Style. These authors have shown that many alleged editions mentioned in the older lists (especially in the DICTIONARY OF NATIONAL BIOGRAPHY) never existed. This table therefore omits the following editions which can now be regarded as illusory: FITZHERBERT—editions of

Date	Title of work	Edition	Range
1516: Dec. 21	Fitzherbert, Abridgement	1st ed.	c. 1217-c. 1509
1565: Nov. 12	" "	2d ed.	" "
1571: Oct. 24	Plowden, Reports I	1st ed.	1550-1571
1574: Jan. 25	Brooke, Abridgement	1st ed.	c. 1347-1558
1576: Oct. 12	" "	2d ed.	" "
1577: Aug. 20	Fitzherbert, Abridgement	3d ed.	c. 1217-c. 1509
1578: Oct. 15	Brooke's New Cases	1st ed.	1515-1558
" Oct. 20	Plowden, Reports I	2d ed.	1550-1571
1585: Feb. 15	Plowden, Reports II	1st ed.	1571-1579
1586: Jan. 1	Dyer, Reports	1st ed.	1512-1582
" Sept. 29	Brooke, Abridgement	3d ed.	c. 1347-1558
1587	Brooke's New Cases	2d ed.	1515-1558
1588: Oct. 22	Plowden, Reports I	3d ed.	1550-1571
1593: Jan. 1	Dyer, Reports	2d ed.	1512-1582
1594	Plowden, Reports II	2d ed.	1571-1579
1597	Brooke's New Cases	3d ed.	1515-1558
1599	Plowden, Reports I	4th ed.	1550-1571

The first conclusion to be drawn from this table is that there was a sudden boom in expensive law books during the seventies. It took fifty years to absorb the first edition of Fitzherbert; but the twelve years from 1565 to 1577 saw two new editions of Fitzherbert, and two editions of Brooke. Clearly, then, the appearance of the two collections of recent cases in Plowden and in Brooke's Abridgement did nothing to deflect interest from the solid mass of mediaeval cases in the two heavy folios of Fitzherbert and Brooke.[16] Secondly, the trend of publications seems quite consistent with the conjecture just put forward in order to explain why Brooke's New Cases was published at all—and an explanation certainly seems called for. A plan there must have been, for all these books came from the same house.[17] Thirdly, a further element must be considered. The years covered by Plowden neatly continue the period for which Brooke's Abridgement had such novel material. This was doubtless a mere coincidence, but it did suggest the usefulness of a continuous stream of reports, one beginning where the other left off. Now Plowden's first edition was going well, and so it may have provided an additional reason for collecting the "New Cases" out of Brooke's Abridgement and making of them a volume to accompany the second edition of Plowden; in fact, they were published almost simultaneously. Lastly, it is abundantly clear that not only was there a steady demand for what we may call the mediaeval classics, but also a new demand for a novel type of

---

1514, 1573, 1586; BROOKE—editions of 1568, 1570; BROOKE, NEW CASES—edition of 1585; PLOWDEN, PART I—edition of 1584; PLOWDEN, PART II—editions of 1578, 1588, 1599.

[16]Tottel contemplated a fourth edition of FITZHERBERT in 1583, but did not proceed with it. COWLEY, *op. cit. supra* note 15, at xlvi-xlvii.

[17]Except the FITZHERBERT of 1516 (which was published by John Rastell). The PLOWDEN of 1594 came from Charles Yetsweirt, the BROOKE'S NEW CASES of 1597 from his widow Jane, and the PLOWDEN of 1599 from Thomas Wight, all of whom in turn were Tottel's successors in the business.

material, namely, the "new cases." Plowden's book, we suggest, was not planned as a response to that demand; but it did greatly stimulate it.[18] The first edition of the Commentaries in 1571 whetted the appetites of lawyers, and when the first edition of Brooke's Abridgement appeared soon afterwards in 1574, it is a safe inference that the later cases in Brooke were a powerful factor in its amazingly rapid success. The full effect of Plowden's example (unconscious though it was) appears in 1578. That year witnessed a second edition of Plowden, and also the first edition of Brooke's New Cases. The new demand for recent cases could have had no more striking illustration than this dismemberment of Brooke's heavy work. Tottel had divined that there were lawyers who wanted Brooke's new cases but not his old ones.

The unforeseen effect of Plowden's Commentaries was, therefore, the creation of a new class of legal literature, that of "new cases." Plowden would have had us admire his book for its deep learning, its infinite care, its scientific basis in the most fundamental principles of pleading. To his busy, contentious fellow lawyers these qualities were less obvious; to them it was a book of new cases, to which they could soon add the untidy and unscientific reports gleaned by Bellewe out of Brooke's Abridgement. It is curious to note in passing that the crafty Tottel had Brooke's New Cases arranged chronologically instead of under subjects, thus increasing the resemblance (at best, superficial) to Plowden's Commentaries. Even in point of novelty, however, Brooke's New Cases could not compete with Plowden, in spite of their challenging title. Brooke died in 1558, and the cases which Bellewe culled from his Abridgement run from 1515 to 1558. Brooke's most recent case was therefore sixteen years old when it first appeared in the Abridgement, and twenty years old when Bellewe brought out the New Cases. Plowden, on the other hand, consists of an even run of cases from 1550 to 1571. Tottel dated the colophon October 24, 1571, and purchasers who looked over their acquisition during the Christmas vacation would have found that the last case in the volume was barely six months old. Could a case, even today, be much newer than that? Once again, however, we must scrutinize Plowden's preface. He makes not the slightest allusion to the newness of his cases; it is only their quality that interests him. He tells us that he began reporting in 1538. Slowly he found a principle and a method, and by 1550 he had reported a case well enough to put in his book. In 1556 he felt sufficiently sure of his learning and judgment to adopt a shorter method. And so he continued. Clearly, he published his later cases

---

[18]The demand for new material appeared early in Henry VIII's reign, when numerous editions (unfortunately many of them undated) of the year books of Henry VII were published.

simply because he was well satisfied with them, and not because he thought the public wanted "new cases."

Unwittingly, therefore, Plowden created a demand for reports of recent cases. The first reaction was the appearance of the factitious "New Cases" compiled by Bellewe. Soon Plowden himself was caught into the stream, and in 1585 he was persuaded to publish a continuation of his first volume.[19] The cases resume at the point where he had left off, and run continuously from 1571 to 1579. Moreover, the pagination is continuous with the first volume, so that the two could be easily bound together as one book. In short, the consequence was the appearance of still more new cases, although they were not quite so startlingly recent as the last case in the first part.

A further consequence may be seen in the appearance of Dyer's reports in the same year, 1585. Plowden's book rested entirely on its intrinsic merits. Its author was a simple barrister;[20] his firm adherence to the Catholic faith excluded him from the coif and the bench; his friends believed that the Great Seal was within his reach if only he would conform. But Plowden preferred to live and die a simple "apprentice in the law." Dyer, on the other hand, had been for twenty-three years the Chief Justice of the Common Pleas. Yet in spite of the prestige of his high office, Dyer's reports never acquired the renown which sheer merit had won for the Commentaries of the simple apprentice.

We have spoken of Dyer's "Reports." Indeed, it is often said (no doubt following Wallace) that "Dyer is the first book regularly called reports."[21] Such words are misleading as well as ambiguous. As we have seen, the first reports to be printed were Plowden's, and he regularly called them "Reports" in his preface and "Commentaries or Reports" on the title page.[22] Next in order of time (and fifteen years later) came Dyer's book, which certainly came to be called his "Reports" in a few years. In point of fact, however, the early editions of Dyer were published under the title of "Certain New Cases."[23] In name as well as in substance, therefore, our earliest re-

---

[19]The second part of PLOWDEN is strictly a posthumous publication but only by a few days. The colophon is dated February 15, 1585; Plowden had died on the 6th of that month.

[20]He was not a serjeant. WALLACE, *op. cit. supra* note 1, at 145. The writ calling him to that rank, indeed, issued, but abated by the death of Queen Mary; Elizabeth issued no new writ.

[21]WALLACE, *op. cit. supra* note 1, at 131-2.

[22]*Supra,* note 9. The first edition of the second part of PLOWDEN was entitled "Cy ensuont certeyne Cases reportes par Edmunde Plowden puis le premier imprimier . . ."; the second edition was entitled "La second part de les Reports. . . ."

[23]The first edition (1585) was entitled "Cy ensount ascuns nouel cases Collectes per le iades tres-reuerend Iudge Mounsieur Iasques Dyer. . . ." An index separately published three years later, however, adopts the newer terminology—"La Table al lieur des Reports del tresreuerend Iudge Sir Iames Dyer . . ." (1588). BEALE, *op. cit. supra* note 9, at R 483.

ports are Plowden's. The title selected by Dyer's executors is not without significance, for it seems to indicate that in their judgment what the profession wanted was "new cases," and, as we have seen, this thirst for new cases was the result of the first publication of Plowden.

After Plowden and Dyer came Coke.[24] The currents in legal literature which have just been mentioned were certainly well known to him. The first edition of the first part of Plowden came out when Coke had just entered Clifford's Inn as a nineteen-year-old law student. Brooke's New Cases appeared when Coke had just been called and held his first brief in the King's Bench.[25] When Dyer came out, Coke was Recorder of Norwich. By the time Coke's first report was published (in 1600) there had been four editions of 1 Plowden, three of Brooke's New Cases, three of Brooke's Abridgement, two of 2 Plowden, and two of Dyer's New Cases. In short, Coke's vertiginous career—by now he had been autumn reader, Recorder of London, solicitor general, member of parliament, speaker, and attorney general—was passed in the period when Tottel was discovering how eager lawyers were for "new cases." Coke knew it too, and he too was ready to satisfy the demand. In 1600 there appeared "The First Part of the Reports of Sir Edward Coke, Knt."

After the straightforward simplicity of Plowden and Dyer, the Reports of Coke present a strong contrast at almost every point. The natural chronological arrangement of the two elder reporters is here replaced by indescribable confusion. Plowden and Dyer each pursued steadily his own individual method of reporting. The result in each case was a book homogeneous and consistent. Coke, on the other hand, presents us with every conceivable variety of style and method. Such confusion and diversity can hardly have been deliberately planned. Coke had before his eyes the solemn, sober folios of his two predecessors—the only models yet in print. If he did not follow them, there must have been a reason (or at least a cause). Single-handed, Coke doubled the number of volumes of law reports on the shelves of his contemporaries; more than that, his books greatly out-weighed those of his predecessors in their ultimate influence upon legal development. How Coke's books came to be written, and why, is a matter of legitimate curiosity for lawyers.

Even if Plowden had left us no preface, we could easily have discovered his method and guessed his sources. Many of his reports are of cases in

---

[24]For Coke's biography see the lives by H. W. Woolrych (1826), Cuthbert W. Johnson (1837), and Hastings Lyon and Herman Block (1929); *cf.* Lord Campbell, Lives of the Chief Justices (1849) and Foss, Judges of England (1870). For his reports, see 5 Holdsworth, *op. cit. supra* note 1, at 461-6.

[25]Cromwell's Case, (1578-1581) 4 Rep. 12b, at 14.

which he had been professionally engaged; he had the pleadings and drafts of the arguments among his business papers. In court he made notes of the case as it was actually presented, and of the resulting arguments—and in those days the judges were far from silent listeners; they argued point after point backwards and forwards among themselves, as well as with the bar. Such an argument might be spread over several terms or even years before judgment was eventually reached.[26] Then only did Plowden arrange his notes and write up the case in his big book. Necessarily,[27] the order of the cases in that book was the chronological order of judgments.

The first glance at Coke is enough to show that the set of reports as a whole does not come from a chronologically arranged register like Plowden's, and does not reproduce a single series of cases noted down as they occurred. Indeed, no single series of any sort, chronological or systematical, seems to explain the present arrangement of the Reports. The only plausible hypothesis seems to be that the printed book is based upon several collections (which may or may not be the work of the same hand), with the addition of particular cases when there were special reasons for including them.

The range of dates in the Reports is interesting. Almost without exception the cases come from between 1581 and the year of publication. Beyond all doubt, Coke could draw heavily upon a vast reserve of cases coming from those years, and actually did so, in the preparation of every Part of his Reports. The accompanying tabulation will facilitate the study of these points. A vertical column is devoted to each of the Parts I to XI of Coke's Reports, giving the number of cases from any particular year contained in it. The total at the foot of each column is therefore the total number of cases in that Part. The total of each horizontal line of figures will be the number of cases from any particular year printed anywhere in the set of eleven Parts. The horizontal rule at the head of each column will indicate that that Part was first published in the year appropriate to the line next below it. The number of folios in each Part is put on the lowest line of each column; two numbers were needed in Parts V and VII as they each contain a case separately foliated from the rest. Those cases (and their foliation) are distinguished in the table by asterisks. Parts XII and XIII have no place in this discussion; they were published long after Coke's death under circumstances which can throw no light upon Coke's own methods.

---

[26]Thus, Capel's Case, 1 Rep. 61b, was argued for twelve years, 1581-1593.

[27]In Smith v. Stapleton, Plowd. 426, at 438, we see his scruples carried even further. The plaintiff got judgment in 1569, but did not pay the requisite fees for its entry on the roll until 1573. Consequently Plowden omitted it from his first volume (which contains other cases decided in 1569) and printed it only when the record was complete; hence the case appears in the second part among those of 1573. In only one instance did Plowden disturb the chronological order, and that was when he put *Bracebridge v. Clowse,* 1576, immediately after *Bracebridge v. Cook,* 1572, both cases arising upon the same title.

Year	I	II	III	IV	V	VI	VII	VIII	IX	X	XI	Total
1615	—	—	—	—	—	—	—	—	—	—	3	3
1614	—	—	—	—	—	—	—	—	—	—	11	11
1613	—	—	—	—	—	—	—	—	—	9	2	11
1612	—	—	—	—	—	—	—	—	9	11	2	22
1611	—	—	—	—	—	—	—	—	15	1	—	16
1610	—	—	—	—	—	—	—	23	6	—	1	30
1609	—	—	—	—	—	—	—	11	1	3	—	15
1608	—	—	—	—	—	—	1*	9	—	—	—	10
1607	—	—	—	—	—	9	3	—	—	—	1	13
1606	—	—	—	—	—	4	1	1	—	—	—	6
1605	—	—	—	—	3	10	1	—	—	—	—	14
1604	—	—	—	—	6	1	2	—	—	—	—	9
1603	—	—	—	5	4	1	1	1	—	—	—	12
1602	—	—	4	5	2	1	—	—	—	—	1	13
1601	—	3	—	3	11	3	1	—	—	—	—	21
1600	3	—	—	1	5	1	1	—	2	—	—	13
1599	—	1	—	6	12	6	—	—	—	—	—	25
1598	2	1	1	2	9	4	1	—	—	1	—	21
1597	2	2	—	4	8	—	2	—	—	—	1	19
1596	—	2	3	1	9	2	—	—	—	—	—	17
1595	1	1	1	4	1*, 7	3	—	—	—	—	—	18
1594	1	1	1	5	3	4	—	—	—	—	—	15
1593	1	—	—	3	11	1	—	—	—	—	—	16
1592	1	—	2	1	7	—	1	—	—	—	—	12
1591	—	1	1	6	2	—	2	—	1	—	—	13
1590	1	—	—	3	5	—	—	—	—	—	—	9
1589	—	3	1	3	3	—	1	—	—	—	—	11
1588	—	—	—	4	4	—	—	2	1	—	—	11
1587	—	—	1	4	3	1	2	1	—	—	—	12
1586	1	1	—	3	—	—	1	—	2	—	—	8
1585	—	1	—	6	1	—	3	—	—	—	—	11
1584	1	2	3	6	1	—	—	1	—	—	—	14
1583	—	—	1	3	2	1	1	—	—	—	—	8
1582	—	1	—	1	—	—	—	—	—	—	—	2
1581	1	—	—	2	—	—	—	—	—	—	—	3
1580	—	—	—	—	—	—	—	—	—	—	—	—
1579	—	—	—	—	1	—	—	—	—	—	—	1
1578	—	—	—	—	—	—	—	—	—	—	—	—
1577	—	—	—	—	—	—	—	—	—	—	—	—
1576	—	—	—	1	—	—	—	—	—	—	—	1
1575	—	—	—	—	—	—	—	—	—	—	—	—
1574	—	—	—	—	—	—	—	—	—	—	—	—
1573	—	—	—	—	—	—	—	—	—	—	—	—
1572	—	—	—	1	—	—	—	—	—	—	—	1
Total	15	20	19	83	1*, 119	52	1*, 24	49	37	25	22	467
Folios	177	94	91	128	127 41*	80	45 28*	173	142	144	100	1301 69*

If we assume that Coke himself reported all the cases he printed (a statement which is both ambiguous and unproved)[28] then the year 1580 becomes

[28]To say that Coke "reported" a case may mean (a) that he attended the arguments, noted them, and forthwith drew up the final report as printed; or (b) that he heard the arguments and made notes which some years afterwards he cast into shape, possibly enriched by his own later learning; or (c) that having been engaged himself in a case

significant. He printed no cases whatever from this year—we may conjecture that the duties of Reader at Lyon's Inn completely absorbed the energies of the young and comparatively inexperienced lawyer. The three isolated and very early cases of 1572, 1576 and 1579 obviously stand outside the general pattern , and may be set aside as casual intruders. We are therefore left with the large mass of cases drawn from the years 1581 to 1615. The totals in the last column of the table show that after a slow start (3 cases in 1581 and 2 in 1582) Coke began in 1583 to establish a fairly steady pace in reporting.[29] Between 1583 and 1614, both years included, he reported (or obtained material for the reports of) 456 cases, out of a grand total of 467. The average over those thirty-two years is slightly above 14 cases a year, and generally speaking Coke kept fairly close to his average; there were only five years in which he took more than 20 cases, and only once did he take 30 cases. The general picture is undeniably one of steady, persistent effort maintained unflaggingly over thirty-two years.[30]

A comparison with Plowden at once suggests itself. The two parts of Plowden contain a continuous chronological series of 62 cases, covering a range of thirty years. The adjoining tabulation tells their simple story in its simplest terms. Once again, however, we must remember Plowden's preface. He says that he was assiduous in collecting reports from the age of twenty, that is to say, from the year 1538. Of all the cases which he collected in the twelve years 1538 to 1549 not one did he print—silently he suppressed the first quarter of his life's work. We have already said that he was ruthless in the cause of science, and here is further proof; the proof is all the more impressive since it is apparent only after an analysis of dates and figures. His prime still lay before him, and the next thirty years produced the 62 cases which he eventually deemed worthy of publication. Here the contrasts between Coke and Plowden are most striking. Whereas Plowden averaged 2 cases a year, Coke gave us over 14. Plowden's maximum for any one year is 5; Coke's is 30. For six separate years Plowden reported nothing; Coke never gave less than 6 cases in any one year. Plowden's original accumulation may easily have been as large as Coke's grand total[31] of 467; the significant fact, however, is that Coke chose to print seven times as many cases as Plowden. Evidently we have an exacting choice

Years	Cases
1579	2
1578	5
1577	1
1576	4
1575	1
1574	1
1573	4
1572	2
1571	2
1570	—
1569	2
1568	3
1567	—
1566	—
1565	5
1564	2
1563	—
1562	3
1561	1
1560	3
1559	—
1558	2
1557	—
1556	2
1555	1
1554	4
1553	4
1552	1
1551	2
1550	5
Total	62
Folios	567

he made no contemporary report, but later wrote it up from the papers in the case resting in his office; or (d) that he used notes taken by other hands, but revised in the

on the one hand and a wide comprehension on the other, as the broad and general distinction between the two reporters.

So far, we have considered Coke's reported cases in the bulk, as a single mass of material steadily collected in the course of some thirty-two years, and have thought merely of the mounting pile of papers in his study. To do this, it was necessary to compile a tabulation of the material he used, because the form in which he published it (unlike Plowden's) effectually concealed the chronological range of his work. It is now time to approach another aspect of the matter and to examine the method by which Coke published his collection of cases. With Plowden there is no problem at all. It was his regular practice to enter into his book those cases which he knew were of real importance and which he knew he had reported adequately by his own high standards. Then he printed the book. Its chronological arrangement was inevitable.

In Coke's Reports there is a seeming capriciousness and irregularity in the distribution of the material which is deeply puzzling. If it is the result of Coke's deliberate planning, then we ought to try to discover that plan, and with it, the real meaning and significance of a set of law reports as Coke conceived of it. If, on the other hand, the published state of Coke's Reports is merely accidental, then we ought to know that too, and consider its bearing on our estimate of the man and his book and the place of both in the history of English law.

Looking once more at the tabulation of Coke's cases, it is immediately clear

---

light of his own recollection of it, and his own view of the legal points involved; or (e) that he had notes of a case, which he stated with great brevity merely as a text for a disquisition on a portion of law, possibly wider than the matters directly raised by the case. Any of these possible methods may lie behind a case reported by Coke. He sometimes significantly refers to his reports as "Commentaries". 8 Rep., preface.

[29] 1 Rep. preface, xxviii.

[30] The later years even show some acceleration.

[31] Plowden explains in his preface that there are many of his notes in circulation which he asks the public to ignore, as not conforming to his highest standards; and, of course, lawyers exchanged experiences in private conversation as we can see from a passage in Fermor's Case, 3 Rep. 77, at 79 (1602), where Coke mentions "Some's Case in the common pleas in Sir James Dyer's time, as Plowden told me." This is one of possibly many cases reported but not published by Plowden. Coke's total of 467 was reached by counting those cases which had a separate name or title in the text or in the table of cases. It often happens, however, that a report by Coke will contain statements of other cases, but without disclosing whether (a) these are additional cases reported by Coke and added by him to enrich his report, or whether (b) they are merely cases cited in the course of argument in court, and hence appearing in Coke's notes. In many cases only Coke himself could tell into which class a particular citation should be put. If there were many which ought to be put in class (a), that would explain Coke's estimate that he had reported "above six hundred cases." See his letter to the Earl of Buckingham, in Wallace, *op. cit. supra* note 1, at 181. These "cases within cases" are an opportunity for an intricate investigation which might throw more light upon Coke's methods.

that Parts I, II, and III are much alike in structure (their subject-matter does not concern us at this stage). Each part contains few cases—twenty or less—drawn from a period of about twenty years, and fairly evenly selected from that period. Parts IV, V, and VI yield a very different set of figures. Part IV contains four times the number of cases in Part II; Part V, six times; Part VI, two and a half times. The range of years covered is slightly longer—about twenty-three years, with an exceptional range of thirty years in Part IV. Their respective totals of 83, 119,[32] and 52 cases are the highest for the whole set. Part VII has a small total, but it is a very slender volume (save for the separately foliated *Calvin's Case*) and like Parts IV, V, and VI it is evenly drawn from a long range of years. Still a third pattern is revealed in the concluding Parts VIII to XI. Here the totals are dwindling towards the point at which the set began—49, 37, 25, and 22 respectively. The range of years shortens also. Moreover, a new feature appears in these last four parts. We have seen that in Parts I to VII the cases were drawn fairly evenly from the range of twenty or more years covered in each part; now in Parts VIII to XI that distribution is conspicuously abandoned. Instead, we get a marked preponderance of recent cases. Thus, out of the 49 cases in Part VIII, 43 are from within four years of the date of publication. In the succeeding parts the figures are still more striking—31 out of 37, 21 out of 25, and 18 out of 22.

Coke's Reports therefore fall into three clearly distinguishable groups, comprising Parts I-III, IV-VII, and VIII-XI, each group being characterized by its own distribution of material—and, as we shall see later, by other features as well. We are bound to conclude from this that Coke twice changed his policy in the course of his career as a publisher of law reports.

The first group, consisting of Parts I, II, and III, may therefore be studied as illustrating the master's first manner. When he began publication in the year 1600, Coke was already looking ahead, for he entitled his book "The First Part. . . ." How many parts he originally contemplated we cannot say. The example of Plowden suggested but two. Perhaps he meant to cap Plowden by publishing three volumes; if so, that would account for the uniformity of style in the first three parts. Examining once more the tabulated analysis, it is evident that by the year 1600 Coke had accumulated at least 248 cases from the years up to and including 1599. All of these 248

[32]There are two special circumstances here. Prefixed to Part V is a report of *Caudrey's Case* which is separately foliated; *Calvin's Case* is similarly prefixed to Part VII. In calculating the average length of cases in these two parts it was obviously necessary to omit these two exceptional, and in the author's intention, separate cases. *Caudrey's Case* covers 41 folios, and *Calvin's* 28. These two cases are distinguished by asterisks in the general tabulation of Coke's Reports given above, and their folioation is likewise indicated separately with the same symbol.

cases he printed sooner or later (and we may be certain that this stock included a possibly small number of cases which he published elsewhere, or not at all during his lifetime). In order to make up Part I of his Reports, Coke picked out only 12 of these 248 cases, and added to them 3 which had been decided in the very year of publication. From these figures alone it is clear that Part I is an extremely select collection. That conclusion is more than confirmed when we think of the cases themselves: *Archer's, Corbet's, Shelley's, Chudleigh's Cases*—never before had such ponderous masses of law in the raw been assembled in one book of very moderate size. Beyond all doubt, Part I contained the cream of the cream from Coke's collections.

It is curious to note the arrangement of this extremely choice material. In substance it is all concerned with property and conveyancing—and for that matter, so are Parts II and III. As the subsequent Parts were to show, Coke's collection covered much wider ground than that; hence it follows that the consistency of the cases in Parts I to III is due to the deliberate choice of the author. In assembling material for these parts, Coke took not only his choicest cases, but his choicest property cases. Beyond this, there is little indication of deliberate arrangement. Part I opens with a single case from the equity side of Chancery; this is followed by three from the Exchequer, four from the Common Pleas, six from the King's Bench (the last of which originated on the common law side of Chancery), and the concluding case from the Court of Wards. The arrangement of the cases within each of these groups is chronological. The most recent were the *Case of Alton Woods, Digges' Case,* and *Corbet's Case* (all from 1600, the year of publication); the oldest was *Shelley's Case* (1581).[33]

Part I, therefore, was probably intended to illustrate some of the great heads of property law—remainders, uses, powers, perpetuities and the like. Part II is devoted to another aspect of the same wide subject. Of the first three cases, two deal with the deed of an illiterate grantor, and the other with a deed wrongly dated. The rest of the volume is devoted to cases on feoffments, fines, covenants to stand seised, bargains and sales, conditions, attornment, and kindred topics.[34] By way of confirmation of all that this implies, we read in the preface that a great part of the legal troubles which come into court can be laid at the door of amateur conveyancing by "parsons, scriveners and such like imperites."[35] In short, Part II is a collection of

[33] *Shelley's Case* is also the longest report in the book (the greater apparent length of the *Case of Alton Woods* is due to exceptionally verbose pleadings). In 1581, when *Shelley's Case* was decided, Coke was reader at Lyons Inn; the length and style of the report almost suggest that Coke possibly combined his original report with notes of a heavy course of lectures on the questions involved. *Cf.* note 41 *infra.*

[34] Three of the cases deal with tithes.

[35] 2 Rep., preface. A century later country clergy are still found "drawing bills,

cases on conveyancing. The internal arrangement of the volume is not according to the courts concerned (as it was in Part I), nor yet according to the type of conveyance under discussion, but is chronological throughout save for a single exception.[36]

Part III, as we have said, is still a book of property cases, and on this basis, as well as upon the other grounds mentioned already, belongs in the same group as Parts I and II. The majority of the cases deal with leases, wills, fines, recoveries, etc., and thus resemble those in Part II. Occasionally the selection wanders somewhat from this subject. Thus three of the cases deal with the escape of persons taken in execution for debt. The arrangement could only be called roughly chronological.

Looking at these three volumes together, we seem to detect our author searching through his notes of nearly three hundred cases, matching his reports with the pleadings (which would often be in his office files), picking out the most considerable from his accumulation of twenty years, and putting them together for his books. From the start, he had at least two volumes in mind, one on estates and interests, the other on conveyancing. There was so much material on the latter topic that it seems to have overflowed—hence Part III (which appeared in the same year as Part II). Speaking generally, the reports are fairly long. For Part I the average is nearly 12 folios; for Part II it is over 4½ folios; for Part III, nearly 5 folios. Taking all three parts together, the average is nearly 6¾ folios to the case.

The significance of all this appears more clearly still when we pass to the second group, consisting of Parts IV, V, VI, and VII. We have already remarked upon the high number of cases they contain. It is now time to note that in spite of this the volumes are hardly any bigger. Parts I to III with their 54 cases, contain 362 folios. Parts IV to VII run only to 386 folios, although they contain 278 cases. The average is therefore less than 1½ folios per case.[37] This is no accident. The difference between 6¾ (the average for Parts I to III) and 1½ (the average of Parts IV to VII) is much too great to admit of any other explanation than a change of plan. The arrangement of Part IV shows the new scheme. It begins (somewhat inconsistently) with the earliest case in the whole eleven volumes (*Vernon's Case,* 1572) which was decided six years before Coke was called. Although

---

bonds, conveyances, wills, etc." as a recognized means of augmenting their slender salaries: Norman Sykes, Church and State in England in the XVIIIth Century (Cambridge, 1934) 206-7. Coke also castigated the parliamentary draftsmen in this same preface, but it is noteworthy that he did not attempt to collect cases on statutory interpretation—that field was pre-eminently Plowden's.

[36]The exception is *Thoroughgood's Case,* which, being the oldest, should have come first instead of third in the volume.

[37]Omitting *Caudrey's* and *Calvin's Cases* (*cf.* note 32 *supra*).

the pleadings are not printed, the report alone extends to five folios. It is followed by *Bevill's Case* (1583), occupying two folios of pleadings and four of report or six folios in all. Both these cases are therefore on the scale of the reports in Part III. At this point the new system appears. Under the general heading "actions for slander" we get 17 numbered cases. These are immediately followed by 25 numbered cases headed "copyhold cases" (and among them is *French's Case,* 1576, the second oldest case in the whole set). After a short diversion of three miscellaneous cases, there comes a third classified group consisting of 13 numbered[38] cases under the heading "cases of appeals, indictments, etc." The volume concludes with 23 cases on a great diversity of subjects, united only by their chronological arrangement and their fairly even distribution over the years. They are also slightly longer than those in the classified groups. Even so, the average length of all the cases in Part IV is just 1½ folios. In this Part, therefore, we find a new policy. Instead of long and very choice cases, few in number but carefully selected, we now get a large number of short cases, more than half of them put under subject headings and the remainder very miscellaneous but fairly recent. The three groups of classified cases rather suggest that Coke was taking whole pages out of his commonplace book.

This impression is deepened by an examination of Part V, which shows the next stage of the new policy. Here we have the shortest cases of the whole set, the average length being merely one folio. The subject headings have increased from three to nine, but the cases within each group are not numbered in the text (although they are in the table of cases). The volume begins with 12 cases in chronological order on "leases." Then come 14 cases on "covenants in leases," again chronological. The next 10 cases are on "executors," followed by 15 cases on "jeofails," both groups being nearly chronological. After these four titles, containing 51 cases, the volume rapidly falls to pieces. Five more subject headings do in fact appear (7 cases on "pardons," 2 on "by-laws," 2 on "usury," 2 on "customs," and 5 on "executions") but they are separated by large numbers of highly miscellaneous cases, to such an extent that the later editions often fail to note where the subject headings cease to apply, and the miscellanea begin.

The first four titles seem to indicate that Coke took many pages out of his commonplace book—a possibility already suggested by the examination of Part IV. Such a book, if it recorded solely those cases which he himself heard argued in court, would inevitably be chronological within each title. It might happen, however, that he occasionally heard of a case from other sources (either written or oral) and added it to his collection. If such a

[38]In the later editions the numbers of this third group have somehow disappeared.

case were not recent, then the result may possibly be to interrupt the chronological order, which would be resumed only when the compiler added fresh cases from his own knowledge. It may therefore be suggested that cases thus appearing out of order may in fact be cases which Coke acquired at second hand. The large mass of miscellaneous cases printed in this and other Parts is equally cogent evidence, however, that Coke's stock of cases was not kept in one planned series. He certainly had at least one commonplace book, but only a fraction of his collections ever formed part of it. The miscellany of short cases may have been kept loose—which would account for the lack of chronological order. The elaborate reports of the earlier Parts suggest still another system, arranged possibly according to courts. So many different arrangements existing simultaneously make it difficult to suppress the suspicion that Coke may sometimes have been drawing upon collections made by other hands than his.

That Part V was not an impressive piece of work seems to have been evident to the author himself, and he took a step which seems to have been designed as a make-weight. This took the form of a report, separately foliated and prefixed to the volume, of *Caudrey's Case,* written up in resounding Latin periods. This case was decided in 1595 and so was ten years old when Part V appeared. The report of the point actually at issue is quite short, but in this pamphlet Coke surveys ecclesiastical history from the days of "King Kenulph" down to his own, in an endeavor to show that the royal supremacy in church as well as state had always been admitted. Whatever one might think of the rest of Part V, this at least was exciting, and in fact it provoked a hard-hitting reply from Father Parsons, S.J., to which Coke made no further answer[39] save a short and frigid homily on literary manners in the preface to Part VI. It was *Caudrey's Case,* therefore, which saved the day, and actually made Part V a very successful book. The first edition had appeared in 1605; a second came out in 1606, a third in 1607, a fourth in 1612, and a fifth in 1624. None of the other Parts had so successful a run as that.

We are bound to ask why *Caudrey's Case* was separately foliated. At first sight it might seem that it was meant to be sold separately from the rest of Part V, but this conjecture is not supported by such library catalogues as I have been able to consult; *Caudrey's Case* does not occur separately, it seems. The only other plausible explanation is that it was an after thought, added to make up in some measure for the scrappy and ill-digested character of the 119 cases which were already in type. To achieve

---

39The later editions of 5 Rep. contain a preface on ignorance which was directed against Parsons.

this purpose, it ought to be conspicuously placed at the head of the volume. That, however, raised problems of foliation; the easiest solution was to foliate it separately. Nearly the same thing happened to Part VII. Here the after-thought was *Calvin's Case,* but the reasons for adding it were not quite the same. The cases in Part VII are rather more substantial than those in Part V, and they might well have made their way (slim though the volume was) without any adventitious help. *Calvin's Case,* however, was of the utmost importance in constitutional law and laid down principles of political theory which at the time, and for long afterwards, were of high concern.[40] Moreover, it was decided in 1608, the very year in which Part VII was published—quite possibly at the moment when the rest of Part VII was already in type. The same solution was obvious: *Calvin's Case* must be printed at once, and printed prominently. Hence its appearance at the head of Part VII, but separately foliated so as not to disturb the rest of the volume. The great difference to be noted, however, is that *Calvin's Case* was urgently needed for legal and political reasons, and had only just been decided; on the other hand there was no urgency about *Caudrey's Case,* and the political theory which Coke injected into his essay (although it touched upon the legal nature of the Reformation) was not essential to the decision. We are thus left with the conclusion that urgency will amply explain the separate foliation of *Calvin's Case,* but will not explain that of the ten-year-old *Caudrey's Case*—which, as already suggested, seems best accounted for as a heavy dose of spice added to an otherwise unattractive dish.

We have already noted that when Coke first embarked upon the publication of law reports in 1600, he could draw upon a stock of at least 248 cases which had been decided down to the end of 1599. In the five Parts so far considered he has been steadily drawing upon that stock—at first with careful discrimination (12 of them were used in Part I, 17 in Part II, 15 in Part III), then dipping into them with both hands and using them lavishly (69 in Part IV, 89 in Part V). With the publication of Part V, therefore, 202 of the stock of old cases had been used; only 46 remained. Of these 46 he was to use 22 for Part VI and 14 for Part VII. The early and middle group of his reports, therefore, accounted for practically the whole of his old stock; only 10 of the 248 cases remained unpublished. This

[40] In the preface to 7 Rep., Coke explains that this was the greatest case that ever was argued in Westminster Hall, that he reported it for his own private solace, that he never meant to publish it because it did not touch matters that would arise in ordinary practice, but that he was "commanded" to print it (no doubt by the king). For this purpose he had to expand his succinct notes. He then suggests that the rest of the cases were added to give the volume some usefulness for ordinary practitioners. Coke is obviously bent on concealing something here, and we feel some hesitation in taking all this literally; but James I may well have been eager to get *Calvin's Case* into print.

simple arithmetical fact had important results. Coke had begun by meeting the demand for "new cases," that is to say, cases later than the latest in Plowden (1579). By 1600 he had built up a stock of material consisting of cases dating from 1581 onwards. In the first seven Parts he had drawn upon it so heavily that little remained. Faced by that situation, Coke had either to abandon further publication or else to rely on current or very recent cases. Rather than stop printing he chose the latter course. Indeed, the situation was temporarily relieved by the fact that Coke had been accumulating a second stock. When he began publication in 1600, he did not give up the practice of law reporting; on the contrary he was steadily making new acquisitions. In the years from 1600 to 1608 (when Part VII appeared and his second group of Reports was complete) he collected 111 cases. These should have helped to replenish the old stock. In fact, they had little effect, for he was using new and old cases with equal prodigality. Of these 111 cases there remained only 15 unpublished when Part VII had appeared in 1608. An examination of Parts VI and VII shows how the pressure of these facts produced the inevitable result. The number of cases falls sharply; if Part V had 119 cases, Part VI had only 52, and Part VII a mere 24. Equally significant, and inevitable, is the changed distribution in point of dates. In Part VI 30 cases came from the new stock (1600 and later) and 22 from the old (1599 and earlier). In Part VII *Calvin's Case* and 10 others came from the new, and 14 from the old. Both stocks, as we have seen, were now well-nigh exhausted.

And so we come to the last group, consisting of Parts VIII to XI. The circumstances already described compelled Coke to a change of policy, and the change was all to the good. The number of cases falls; 49 and 37 in Parts VIII and IX, and 25 and 22 in Parts X and XI. The length of the cases is conspicuously greater, varying from an average of over 3½ folios in Part VIII to nearly 6 folios in Part X. Not only were these cases fewer and longer; they were much more recent. For the first time in his career as a reporter, Coke now published a preponderance of cases decided within four years of the date of publication. The proportion of such cases is 43 out of 49 in Part VIII, 30 out of 37 in Part IX, 21 out of 25 in Part X, and 18 out of 22 in Part XI. Coke was now forced to rely upon current cases for his reports, and it is that fact which brings him nearest our own time. If he had continued this course, he would no doubt have given us a long series of up-to-date reports, and the profession quickly would have learned that "new cases" are not merely those decided within the last generation but within the last three or four years. That was destined not to be. Part XI appeared in 1615; in 1616 Coke was dismissed, and never entered a court of common law again.

We have said nothing about Parts XII and XIII of the Reports. They were not published until after Coke's death, and their nature will be clear from the foregoing study. They could only be the tattered scraps and fragments which remained after Coke himself had picked out all that mattered. Much of their content was probably rejected by Coke several times, as he dipped again and again into his store of material. It may be doubted (in the light of the foregoing analysis) whether any purely legal material of consequence was lost when Coke's papers were impounded. A larger question is raised by Coke's other writings. He was indefatigable as a note taker, and his collections must have been immense. We have already seen that he wrote up some cases in the form of elaborate reports which tended to become essays or lectures,[41] that he kept others in his commonplace books, that still others may have reached him from outside sources, to be cued in[42] hastily when he was short of matter. Besides all this, however, there was much else. It was natural for him, as it is for any active scholar, to make annotations in the margins of the great classics of the law. Thus a large paper copy of Littleton's Tenures was furnished with a bewildering gloss which must have slowly accumulated over a number of years. Another way of keeping notes was to attach comments to a set of statutes, to imitate and modernize Staundford's Pleas of the Crown or Crompton's Jurisdiction of the Courts.

Absence from the courts put an end to Coke's Reports, but printer's ink was in his veins. In 1628, at the age of seventy-six, he not only led the opposition in the House of Commons and penned the Petition of Right, but embarked upon a new series of publications. In that year he published "The First Part of the Institutes of the Laws of England." As with the Reports, so with the Institutes he saw before him an imposing vista of folios. The preface to the First Institute announced that the second and third were already in shape, and the fourth in preparation. The First Part, a "painful and large volume" which achieved fame as Coke upon Littleton, was the only one to delight its author's eyes in print. After his death came the gloss on the statutes (2 Inst.), the notes on criminal law (3 Inst.), and the notes on courts (4 Inst.). To the very end, cases may turn up in unexpected places; thus, a really valuable case of 1600 (*Sir Moyle Finch's Case*) did not see the light of day until 1644, because Coke happened to file it away with his notes on the jurisdiction of courts, so that it is now to be found in 4 Inst. 86.

---

[41] Such a report in longhand would form a book. *Cf.* Holkham MS, 250 (Buckhurst's Case, 1 Rep. 1), described in ROYAL COMMISSION ON HISTORICAL MANUSCRIPTS, 9th Report, app. ii.361 and MS 251 (Shelley's Case).

[42] *Cf.* the anonymous Case of Avowry, 9 Rep. 20 (?1588).

There are many other problems in Coke's Reports. Their accuracy has been debated several times, but with insufficient reference to surviving manuscript material. The sources of at least some of the reports might possibly be traced to other hands, as we have already suggested. There may be some connection with the unpublished reports of Chief Justice Wray.[43] The library of Coke's descendants, the earls of Leicester, at Holkham Hall still contains many manuscripts, some of which belonged to Coke himself; but Wray's reports seem to be in the British Museum. Coke openly stated that he had the original manuscript of Dyer's Reports (he had bought Dyer's estate at Stoughton), and he several times cites cases from the manuscript which are not in the printed edition.[44] These and other matters can only be dealt with when the treasures of the English libraries are once again available to readers. In the meantime, it will have been useful to extract from the text of the Reports some light upon Coke's material, how he accumulated it and used it, and how he came near to publishing a continuous series of recent cases. Most significant of all, perhaps, is the way in which circumstances compelled Coke to do what no one, even in "this scribbling world"[45] had yet undertaken, namely, to report cases expressly for the purpose of printing them shortly afterwards, as he did in Parts VIII to XI of his Reports. Plowden—Dyer—Coke is an imposing line of names, and as Coke is entitled to the third place in the succession of printed reports, so Plowden must have his due, and lead the rest. Of the differences between Plowden's idea of a law report and Coke's, it is difficult to speak shortly. The question is not merely one of length, style, carefulness, or accuracy; more important considerations even than these are involved. Plowden would have made a precedent fundamentally a matter of record—that is to say, a proposition logically deduced from the pleadings enrolled on the record. Although Coke also occasionally uses language to this effect, his practice as a reporter is essentially different. He seems to have drifted steadily away from an insistence upon the pleadings, and in most of his work is more concerned with the "resolutions" of the judges, that is to say, their statements of general principle, making little distinction between those which were the basis of the decision and those which were only obiter. It might be possible to deduce that Coke was thinking (unconsciously perhaps) of the law in terms of substance rather than of procedure, and that would be an important conclusion if it were established. On the other hand, it could be maintained that Plowden was advancing far beyond his contempo-

---

[43] *Cf.* Herlakenden's Case, 4 Rep. 63 (1589).
[44] 10 Rep., preface; WALLACE, *op. cit. supra* note 1, at 126-7.
[45] 7 Rep., preface.

raries and the old Year Book tradition of "sudden sayings" toward something more scientific, while Coke tarried behind with his beloved Quadragesimo. Indeed, if Plowden's view were pressed to its logical conclusion, a single case might become a binding precedent—which, superficially, looks very modern; Coke's interest in "resolutions," on the other hand, places the emphasis upon a body of principles whose authority he seems to derive from their undisputed acceptance over a number of years. In other words, he looks not to the single case, but to a settled policy implied by a line of several cases. These are all weighty matters which someone, some day, may discuss more adequately. The aim of the present article has been merely to tabulate dates and figures, and by their means to watch Plowden entering up his "book," and Coke dipping time and again into his huge store of papers in search of material for his Reports.

XVI

JOHN REEVES, PRINTER

The principal source for the general outline of Reeves' life is the obituary notice in the *Gentleman's Magazine* for 1829, and this is the basis for the article in the *Dictionary of National Biography*, which followed it word for word almost throughout its length. One or two modifications only were made by the *Dictionary*, to which I shall have to refer. The first of them is the description of Reeves as "printer."[1] No doubt it is often difficult to find a single epithet that will accurately describe the whole of a man's activity. I understand that gentlemen of the cloth gave particular difficulty to the editors of the *Dictionary*; not all of them were theologians, few of them were saints. Thus some of them became "theological writers," and the rest merely "Divines." But why a barrister, who finally became a Chief Justice, should be commemorated by the *Dictionary* as a "printer" remains entirely inexplicable. The only case in which such a description seems to me justifiable is that of John and William Rastell, in the reign of Henry VIII, who certainly were equally important in both professions (for as Foss remarks, printing was then "deemed more as a profession than a trade, and was pursued by men of learning and education").[2]

However, the basic facts of Reeves' career shall be recounted so that his various titles to fame may be judged.

A Londoner, born in 1752 or 1753, he was educated at Eton but instead of proceeding to King's he entered Merton and then Queen's College, Oxford; thence he went to the Middle Temple. In 1779 he published his first book, a pamphlet entitled *Inquiry into the nature of property and estates as defined by English law in which are considered the opinions of Mr. Justice Blackstone and Lord Coke concerning real property.*

Within a year of this publication he was called to the bar and made a Commissioner of Bankrupts. This office is variously estimated; in one place it is asserted that the commissioners "fared sumptuously at the expense of the estate";[3] in another it is said that a Commissioner might receive a mere three hundred a year, and that consequently "the commissioners were either young men who might be competent, but who were certainly inexperienced, or old men who were experienced, but incompetent."[4] Since Reeves was well under thirty at the time of his appointment, there is little alternative to placing him in the former category.

---

* Professor of Legal History, University of London.
1. 16 Dictionary of National Biography 858 (Stephens & Lee eds. 1921-22).
2. 5 Foss, Judges of England 534 (1857).
3. 1 Holdsworth, History of English Law 471 (7th ed. 1956).
4. 1 *id.* at 472.

We have no light on Reeves' services to creditors, bankrupts, and bankruptcy law; contemporary evidence suggests that the procedure before the commissioners savored of the bear garden, with a cloak of pettifoggery to give it a legal air. It would seem that the commissioners were addressed upon a variety of different cases simultaneously. Since they were paid a fee for every meeting, it was part of the game to adjourn as quickly as possible, and the older hands managed to hold as many as thirty meetings in one morning. Perhaps Reeves did not enjoy this sort of life, for later he seems to have retired to the quieter atmosphere of a clerkship in the Board of Trade.

One thing is certain, however—Reeves had leisure, and employed it, as he should, in the pursuit of legal history. In 1783, three years after his commission, he published the first volume of *The History of English Law*; the second volume followed in 1784; in 1787 both volumes were reissued in a second edition, and during the next forty years succeeding volumes continued the history until it finally reached 1603.

Reeves' first pamphlet was inspired, as its title relates, by the *Commentaries* of Sir William Blackstone, and the *History* can be traced to the same fruitful source. It was a curious fact that although Blackstone did not profess to be a historian, it was the historical portions of his work that contemporaries found most striking. Reeves started from this fact, and wrote deliberate legal history as an introduction to modern law. This is a point to which I must return a little later.

The second edition of the *History* soon brought recognition to the author: in 1789 he was elected Fellow of the Society of Antiquaries and the following year Fellow of the Royal Society. Soon came the appointment to the highest judicial office it was ever his fate to fill. The connection with the Board of Trade no doubt led to his selection for the post of Chief Justice of Newfoundland when the judicial system of the senior colony was remodeled in 1791. It is true that the population of the colony was little more than ten thousand at the time, and that the great wave of prosperity accompanying the Anglo-French war had hardly yet arrived. Nevertheless, a small colony may have complicated politics, and Reeves' position was admittedly a delicate one, for the mercantile interests were opposed to the court over which it was his duty to preside. He stayed only a year, but it was long enough for his personal virtues of impartiality, firmness, and courtesy to overcome opposition. All this appears from the history of Newfoundland he wrote a few years later, and from the evidence he gave before a parliamentary commission on the affairs of the colony.

His return to England coincided with the outbreak of the war with France and the panic caused by the revolution. He immediately plunged into public affairs. On the 20th of November, 1792, there was assembled in the "Crown and Anchor" tavern "a set of respectable persons" who elected him chairman of a society for the protection of the public against levellers, revolutionaries, and other sorts of radicals.[5] For the future, Reeves must be set down as a tory of the strictest sort. And yet a very curious thing happened. In 1796 we have the odd spectacle of Reeves, the patriot and conservative, being prosecuted for sedition, and by none other than that arch-conservative, Sir John Scott, later Lord Eldon, who was then Attorney General. Radicals of the day could hardly have invented a better jest. The occasion of the incident was a pamphlet, published by Reeves anonymously in 1795 under the title *Thoughts on the English Government: Addressed to the quiet good sense of the People of England.* Such portions of this work as I have examined seem to contain a substratum of sound history. In particular, there is the passage that forms the principal charge in the information:

> In fine, the government of England is a monarchy; the monarch is the ancient stock from which have sprung those goodly branches of the legislature, the lords and commons, that at the same time give ornament to the trees and afford shelter to those who seek protection under it. But these are still only branches and derive their origin and their nutriment from their common parent; they may be lopped off, and the tree is a tree still; shorn indeed of its honours, but not like them cast into the fire. The kingly government may go on in all its functions without lords or commons; it has heretofore done so for years together, and in our times does so during every recess of parliament; but without the king his parliament is no more. The king therefore alone it is who necessarily subsists without change or diminution; and from him alone we derive the protection of law and government.[6]

It would be hazardous to dispute any of these propositions on the grounds of either legal history or constitutional theory. But there are statements, absolutely accurate in every particular, that nevertheless may be most perversely wrong, and nowhere is this so likely to be the case as in statements about our constitutional law.

Reeves' pamphlet was a glaring example of how false a perfectly accurate statement may be. The matter was raised in Parliament, where the commons (or rather, a powerful group of opposition members) affected to treat the matter as one of privilege. Pitt did what he could to smooth things over, but the opposition prevailed. Prominent among them were Fox and Sheridan, and strangely enough, Erskine. We may well believe that Erskine's part in this affair brought blushes to the sensitive cheek of Lord Campbell. It is indeed a surprise to see the defender of Stockdale supporting a resolu-

5. On this momentous meeting, *cf.* Mitchell, *The Association Movement of 1792-93*, 4 HISTORICAL J. 56 (1961).

6. REEVES, THOUGHTS ON THE ENGLISH GOVERNMENT: ADDRESSED TO THE QUIET GOOD SENSE OF THE PEOPLE OF ENGLAND 12-13 (1795).

tion that Reeves' pamphlet was "a breach of the privilege of the House of Commons and that the Attorney General should be directed to prosecute the author for a libel."[7]

In due course the information was tried before Lord Kenyon. Republicans and levellers might well have been daunted, for something like panic had seized the nation. Stones had been thrown at the King's carriage during a state procession, and the Government had replied by passing the Treason Act of 1795,[8] which greatly enlarged the scope of treason, and the Seditious Practices Act,[9] which greatly reduced the right of public meeting, and by suspending the Habeas Corpus Act.[10] John Reeves, however, was no ordinary agitator, and his trial was very different from most of the proceedings that Sir John Scott instituted. Far from being a criminal trial, the proceedings read more like the discussions of the Society of Antiquaries or of the Royal Society in which prosecution and defense exchanged views on questions of archaeology or political theory.

Sir John Scott, accompanied by Mr. Solicitor, and Mr. Law, later Lord Ellenborough, delivered a speech that might easily have been a speech for the defense rather than for the Crown. He offered some learned criticisms, which I think are of some historical interest, of Reeves' view that the term "revolution" is an inaccurate description of the events of 1688. This question, familiar to all candidates in history examinations, he treats at the length of several pages of the *State Trials*.[11] In order to remind the public that they were engaged in a trial, the Crown then called witnesses to prove that Mr. Reeves was the author, although the defense had already admitted it. He then proceeded to give the jury a plain hint of the official view of the affair. It might be that the pamphlet was merely an ill-advised execution of a purpose that was not criminal; if so, they should acquit. If they were to find the prisoner guilty, they would have to be satisfied that he intended to shake the foundations of society.

Our hero was so ably defended by the prosecution that his own counsel had little to do save add a few footnotes. The history of the word "revolution" was further elucidated, and the excellent point was made that on the very day of the trial Parliament was prorogued. Could one imagine a more opportune example of Mr. Reeves' thesis that the King can and does conduct the Government without the intervention of Parliament?

Lord Kenyon continued the same friendly atmosphere in his summing up. To him the most interesting part of the proceedings was its procedural aspect. The prosecution was composed of all the powers of the state: the

7. 31 Hansard, Parl. Hist. Eng. 1087 (1795).
8. 36 Geo. 3, c. 7.
9. 1795, 36 Geo. 3, c. 8.
10. 1795, 35 Geo. 3, c. 3.
11. 26 Howell, State Trials 542-50 (1819).

House of Commons had addressed His Majesty; His Majesty had commanded His Attorney General; the Attorney General prosecuted. All the powers of the state were arrayed against the prisoner. And yet interposed for his protection was a British jury. It was indeed, as his lordship exclaimed to the jury, "a very beautiful feature of the constitution of this country which is exhibited at this moment in your presence."[12] He reminded them of the law as stated by the Attorney General and reminded them that the passage set out in the information was mutilated, and instructed them that they could use every fair leaning toward the prisoner so long as their verdict did not undermine the criminal law of the land.

The result was hardly in doubt, although the jury lent verisimilitude to the proceedings by deliberating for an hour before acquitting the accused. The usual public rejoicing followed, and it seems I ought to present John Reeves before you in the light of a historian who risked fine, imprisonment, and, I believe, the pillory, for his learned opinions.

However that may be, Reeves enjoyed his triumph, and issued three more pamphlets, full of the same sort of "sedition," this time without attack.

And so we reach the year 1800. Reeves was now well into middle age. He published some criticisms on the Hebrew text of the Psalms, and took a lively part in the controversy over Catholic emancipation, maintaining that the coronation oath would prevent the King from signing the bill then before parliament—"an opinion," says the *Gentleman's Magazine*, "which His late Majesty always most conscientiously acted upon." This controversy was long, and so deeply grounded on general principles as to be particularly uninteresting. One point only seems to suggest a touch of humor. The preamble of the bill then before Parliament solemnly asserted as its motive the desirability of having more Irishmen in His Majesty's forces in view of the serious state of the war. Reeves pointed out that the Catholic tests had long failed to exclude Irishmen from the fighting services, a situation that was regularized by annual Acts of Indemnity. Or, as Reeves neatly put it in 1807: "The pretence alleged for the bill of gaining the population of Ireland for the services of our army and navy is certainly without foundation; we already possess it in a very great degree, by the silent operation of forces more powerful than legislation itself"—surely a gracious reference to the Irish temperament.

But we must return to the year 1800. In this year Reeves, with two others, was appointed the King's printer, a lucrative position, for it carried with it a share in the monopoly of printing the Bible and Prayer Book. To this, no doubt, Reeves owed the considerable fortune that he left at his death. At this juncture Reeves displayed once more his business capacity. The Bible trade was perhaps languishing a little, and as a means to stimulate

12. 26 *id.* at 590.

it Reeves had the ingenious idea of founding a Bible Society. Like a skillful advertiser, he addressed himself to very different interests among his prospects. A proposal was issued that embodied his views.[13] Every house in the kingdom ought to have a Bible, not merely a nominal, but a readable and instructive Bible. Such a Bible should attract its owner to read by means that I think will be of interest; not merely because it is the depository of God's word, but also "because it will surpass in price and figure every other volume in the poor man's library."[14] In short, Mr. Reeves proposed to issue a Bible of attractive appearance, at a price so high that the purchaser would never forget it, in order to stimulate Bible reading.

It is not clear whether Reeves' efforts had any substantial result; it is perhaps a mere coincidence that the British and Foreign Bible Society was established this very year, and more probably Reeves had little to do with its establishment. Indeed, its policy of putting cheap editions in the hands of the poorest was very different from his idea of putting costly editions in the hands of the not-so-poor. The real fulfillment of Reeves' wish seems to have come, as the *Gentleman's Magazine* remarked,[15] with the publication of the famous *Family Bible,* which as far as I know exactly represented Reeves' idea of what a Bible should be—and cost.

The remainder of the works of John Reeves are enshrined in the pages of the *Gentleman's Magazine,*[16] and they may well rest there. All that is of importance has been reproduced in the *Directory of National Biography.*[17] Reeves never married, and his financial habits are described in the obituary notice as economical; the *Dictionary* follows exactly save for the substitution of the less gentlemanly word, "parsimonious."[18]

We are now free to examine Reeves as a historian of English law. His reputation rests naturally upon his magnum opus, *The History of English Law.* His *History of the Law of Shipping* was a considerable work in its own day, and went through three editions, of which only two are in the British Museum. But a minor work of his seems to me particularly significant for the light that it throws on Reeves' approach to the subject. It is, in fact, almost his earliest work, and certainly his shortest, for it covers only two sheets of paper. It appeared in 1779 under the title *A chart of penal law, exhibiting by lines and colours an historical view of crimes and punishments according to the law of England, in which the several offences being distributed under separate columns, the origin and progress of the*

13. Reeves, A Proposal of a Bible Society for Distributing Bibles on a New Plan (1805).
14. *Id.* at 2.
15. 99 Gentleman's Magazine pt. 2, at 469, 471 (1829).
16. 99 *id.* at 471.
17. *Op. cit. supra* note 1, at 858-59.
18. 16 *id.* at 859.

law respecting each offence are shown in chronological order and the degrees of guilt specified by a peculiar colour assigned to each.

The idea of a graphical representation of history is not recent, and even Reeves was not its originator,[19] but his example was soon followed by others. The very next year, for example, a chronological table, similarly colored, displaying the years and courts covered by the various law reporters, appeared. The year after that the eminent Charles Fearne, whose essay on contingent remainders occupies a position in the lawyer's library not unlike that of Reeves' family Bible, compiled an *Historical legi-graphical chart of landed property in England from the time of the Saxons to the present Era.*

These charts are worth looking at, especially Reeves', for the history of criminal law really needs some sort of diagrammatic aid if its halting career is to be traced with any ease. His method is beautifully clear. Each crime is represented by an upright column, the top of which represents the earliest period, and the bottom the present age. This column is colored according to a scheme that shows at once whether the crime is a treason, a felony, a capital crime though not a felony, and whether it is clergyable or not. These circumstances naturally varied at different dates in history, and the change in color, as one glances down the column, immediately shows the change. The columns likewise vary in width as the definition of the crime was enlarged or restricted by the huge and disorderly mass of penal legislation that flowed from the sixteenth to the eighteenth centuries. Larceny is an admirable example of how illuminating such a chart may be. At the top, larceny is a broad green column, for it was originally a clergyable felony. As time goes on, it turns red to indicate that certain larcenies are now no longer clergyable—for example, the larceny of pumps from ships in distress.[20] Still, all statutory larcenies were not made nonclergyable, and so even the green band may be broadened at times; an important example is the Perjury Act,[21] which made the thefts of bills, notes, and bonds clergyable larcenies. Another example is the act that placed in the same category the theft of goods from furnished lodgings.[22] Of the statutory nonclergyable larcenies an important group are represented by the pink band, which shows the various statutes dealing with larceny from warehouses, but a tiny green patch warns us that if the warehouse is that of the Plate Glass Company the larceny will be clergyable.[23]

And so on for all the crimes. As can be seen, the haphazard provisions of the criminal law at once became apparent by a glance at this chart, and

19. For the use of charts in economic history, see Funkhouser & Walker, *Playfair and his charts*, 3 ECONOMIC HISTORY 103 (1935).
20. Stranded Ships Act, 1713, 13 Anne, c. 21, § 5.
21. 1728, 2 Geo. 2, c. 25.
22. Benefit of Clergy Act, 1691, 3 W. & M., c. 9.
23. Plate Glass Manufacture Act, 1772, 13 Geo. 3, c. 38.

any student of legal history can consult it with interest and profit, even to this day.

Its significance for us at this moment, however, is the light that it throws on Reeves' character. To me it seems an indication of his great virtues—accuracy and a regard for dates. Some pedagogues have attempted to handle history without those stubborn, elusive little things, dates. It can not be done. The most interesting thing in history is, in fact, this very element of chronology. No fact has historical significance until its date is known. Only then can it take its place in the proper sequence of things, for history is simply human affairs plotted against the time axis. Reeves' chart shows that he understood this clearly.

His great book, *The History of English Law,* has the same merit, and, we can admit at once, the defects of this virtue. It is strictly chronological, and that makes it a most handy tool if one is commencing an investigation.

Reeves had a good deal of critical sense, as Sir William Holdsworth justly remarks.[24] He was the first to have suspicions as to the credibility of the *Mirror of Justices.*[25] He foresaw what later was established by the late Dr. Bolland,[26] that the statute *De Donis*[27] has had a rather crooked history in the courts. Above all, Reeves had a thorough knowledge of the Year Books and the Statute Book, which, with the treatises, formed his principal sources. Out of them he produced a book that Holdsworth finds indescribably dull and terribly technical.[28]

In a sense this is true. But I think something may still be said in Reeves' defense. Let us look at the dates, for that is the only way to look at history. The first edition was in 1783, the second in 1787, the third in 1814, and the final volume in 1829. Clearly, if Reeves or anyone else were to write a history of the law at those dates, he could only write the history of the law of 1829, and the law of 1829 deserved all the strictures that have been passed upon Reeves' book. It was abominably technical; the sterile part of antiquity that Reeves set out at length was largely current law in 1829. Even the courts gave up the attempt to understand conveyancing, and took the word of the most eminent practitioners of that abstruse science. Pleading had reached its most glorious heights of complication and was soon to receive the tribute of Serjeant Stephen's famous essay.[29] The forms of action were then ruling us, not from their graves as now, but from lofty thrones in Westminster Hall. How could a history of such law be anything else than what Reeves wrote?

24. Holdsworth, Historians of Anglo-American Law 62 (1927).
25. 2 Reeves, The History of English Law 232-338 (Finlason ed. 1880).
26. Bolland, The Yearbooks 59 (1921).
27. Statute of Westminster II, 1285, 13 Edw. 1, c. 1.
28. Holdsworth, Historians of Anglo-American Law 63 (1927).
29. Stephen, Pleading (1824).

His book has been described as unreadable and unread; perhaps that is true now, although I think it is an overstatement. In its day it was read, and I myself have read it with profit, although I am ready to admit that this is not a guarantee of its rank as a thriller. As a means of access to the older authorities, Reeves is really most useful, and a useful work of reference need not be a delight or a joy forever.

But Reeves has left us many things besides his *History*, and if you do not relish that learned work, there is always the *Family Bible*.

XVII

THE UNION AND THE TESTS

THERE is no lack of studies upon the Act of Union of 1707; a distinguished list of works extends from the massive folio of Daniel Defoe down to the very useful little volume of texts and comments by Dr. George S. Pryde of 1950. One of these works is of special interest from the eminence of its two authors, the one of them being Albert V. Dicey, the Vinerian Professor of Law at All Souls, Oxford, and the other Robert S. Rait, the Historiographer-Royal of Scotland, and Professor in the University of Glasgow. No more impressive combination of English and Scottish scholarship could be desired for a careful discussion of an Act which means so much to the life of both peoples. True, it contains some peculiarities which might cause surprise. The subdivision of the chapters into 'Thoughts' (each with its appendant 'Comment') could hardly have appeared much later than 1920 when the work was published: the word has acquired a different connotation in these latter days. Even so, its use will have served a good purpose if it reminds us that the Act of Union treats of high matters which can properly be discussed with an air of solemnity matching the earnestness with which thoughtful men in both countries approached the union.

The mere fact that it is an unavoidable question whether Scotland bartered her political independence against commercial advantages,[1] is witness to the difficult choice between political and economic elements in Anglo-Scottish relationships which had to be made by the framers of the Union. Nor was it the only choice. In England the Restoration had been associated with a stringent system of religious tests designed to protect the Church of England, and in Scotland also there was a statutory religious test for various offices designed to protect the Presbyterian Church Government. To unite the two countries and yet maintain the separation of the two churches was no small feat of statesmanship. The sincere attachment of each country to its national church was known to be a factor of fundamental importance in the negotiations, and the commissioners appointed to treat of a union by each country were carefully debarred from dealing with the problem. It was only at a later stage that the respective legislatures of the two countries ventured to pass upon those things

[1] Cf. the remarks in G. S. Pryde, *The Treaty of Union*, p. 54.

which each side regarded as essential to its religious security. Both governments were fully aware of the perils which might ensue from a misplaced step, and both walked with the greatest circumspection.

In so delicate a matter nothing was left to chance. It has been suggested, however, that crafty draftsmanship may have served to gloss over difficulties which prudence wanted to conceal, and that in some places the Act had the appearance of meaning the opposite of what it said. Indeed, Dicey and Rait seem to create the impression that some sort of mystification took place and that if everything came right in the end it was because guile was more potent than force.

No doubt there were those who suspected only too readily the craft and ingenuity which laymen attribute to lawyers; indeed, the passage of the Act and the wisdom of its provisions created a legend in which hidden meanings and paradoxes contributed to the greater glory and wonder of the Union. Dicey and Rait seem to have fallen under this spell, like some of their eighteenth-century predecessors, and quote as illustration a passage in a speech addressed in 1791 by Dr. Alexander Carlyle to the General Assembly on a subject which we shall have to consider:

> The Test Act has enlarged and confirmed the principles of toleration; so far is it from being a remnant of bigotry and fanaticism as the memorial would represent. The Test Act, Sir, has paved the road to office and preferment. The Test Act, Sir, for there is no end of its praises, is the key that opens all the treasures of the south to every honest Scotsman.

A pretty paradox, indeed, maintained so skilfully that to Dicey and Rait it seemed to betoken some hidden truth, and to match the feeling which they had already expressed that the Act and the documents were keeping secrets from the simple plain reader. That feeling was already abroad from the first days of the negotiations. There were some, perhaps, who fancied that they saw some advantage in such a state of feeling; many others were honestly bewildered by the unusual treaty placed before them, and were quite excusably misinformed about the precise legal position in another country than their own. Daniel Defoe was well aware that there were misapprehensions current in Scotland on some points on which, as an English Nonconformist, he was much more accurately informed (as one would expect). The situation becomes perilous when two eminent authors get befogged over what is really a perfectly simple point, and fall back upon mystical speculations of the type already mentioned in order to make their story coherent.

The question of the Test Act occupies a central position in the controversy for it became immediately necessary to determine to what extent, and in what circumstances, Scotsmen might become subject to its provisions. Indeed, upon the answer to that question depended the principal issue whether the Union should pass. The treatment of the question of the tests under the treaty of union is therefore a matter upon which the classic treatise of Dicey and Rait will be examined with especial care.

Their discussion is often in the form of a discussion of the 'Sacramental Test'—a phrase to which we shall return. They refer to the fact that the Commissioners to treat of a Union were not empowered to deal with matters of religion, but they continue with the words:[1]

> The maintenance of the Sacramental Test in regard to the Scotsmen holding certain offices in England, and especially the post of M.P. in the British Parliament, did not fall strictly within the provision which excluded the Commissioners from dealing with the discipline or government of the Church of England or the Church of Scotland, and they did discuss the topic of the Sacramental Test without coming to any definite conclusion . . . probably they foresaw that as regards seats in the British Parliament, the Church of England would take care that the Sacramental Test should be maintained in the British Parliament. The matter was in reality determined by the Scottish Parliament with the tacit assent of the Scottish Church so as not to offend English feeling.

Returning to the subject a little later, Dicey and Rait remind us that each church secured an Act of its national parliament confirming to it whatever protection it considered essential to its safety, and that the 'Act of Security for the Church of England' imposed a sacramental test upon Scotsmen in England, and consequently upon Scottish members of the British Parliament. The corresponding 'Act for securing the Protestant Religion and Presbyterian Church Government'[2] deliberately left Scotsmen (e.g. when a Scottish member of the British House of Commons) liable to the Test Act, and thus to be called upon to receive the Sacrament in accordance with the provisions of that Act.[3] The authors therefore urge that 'particular attention should be paid to the way in which the celebrated Test Act of 1672, 25 Car. II,

[1] Dicey and Rait, *Thoughts on the Union* (1920), pp. 202–3.
[2] The text of both these Acts is printed in Pryde, op. cit., pp. 105–12.
[3] Dicey and Rait, p. 232.

c. 2, was deliberately made by the Parliament of Scotland applicable to Scotsmen who in England [e.g. as Scottish M.P.s in the British Parliament] came within its terms'.[1] The authors never say so, but it is clear that they felt some uneasiness at the implications of their remarks. Were Scotsmen indeed willing to receive the Sacrament according to the rites of an alien Church, 'Black Rubric' and all? Did they tolerate this imposition, moreover, as a condition of exercising the rights, allowed to them under the Union, of sitting as members of the British House of Commons?

The authors are doubtless right in saying that we must carefully examine 'the celebrated Test Act of 1672, 25 Car. II, c. 2'. The historian will first notice that there was no meeting of Parliament between 22 April 1671 and 4 February 1673, and that the Test Act received the royal assent on 29 March 1673: the ascription of the year 1672 to the Act was the consequence of the facts that the date (or rather the fictitious and unhistorical date) of an Act was obtained by considering the first day of the session in which it was passed—in this case 4 February 1673—and that the year 1672 was regarded as still running until 24 March 1673. The result of these elaborate rules was to ascribe the fictitious date 1672 to the Test Act in the *Statutes of the Realm*, in Holdsworth,[2] and in Dicey and Rait.

Much more important than the date of this statute is its contents. It required from all holders of and aspirants to offices of trust and profit under the crown the oaths of supremacy and allegiance, a declaration against transubstantiation, and a certificate and proof of having received the Sacrament according to the rites of the Church of England. The persons liable to this Act, and whose offices depended upon the reception of the Sacrament according to the Anglican rite, were the holders of civil or military office, or the recipients of pay, by patent or royal grant, or the holders of positions of command or trust under the Crown. There were other persons subject to various statutory restrictions, especially those set up by the statute 3 James I, c. 4 (1606)—an Act which contains the first sacramental test in our penal history—but members of Parliament were not among them; nor were members of Parliament affected by the Corporations Act (1662), 13 Charles II, st. 2, c. 1, which imposed a sacrament test upon mayors and certain municipal officials. It is true that the House of Commons

[1] Ibid., pp. 247–8.
[2] *History of English Law*, vi. 199.

might resolve (as it did on 20 May 1661) to hold a corporate communion according to the rite of the Church of England;[1] but this was not statutory, and it was not a test, for in law it neither qualified nor disqualified members of the House from sitting there.

There was, in fact, but one statute only which imposed upon members of Parliament a distinctively religious test, and this was the Parliamentary Test Act (1678), 30 Charles II, st. 2, c. 1. The tests imposed upon lords and commoners by that Act were the taking of the oaths of allegiance and supremacy and the subscription to a declaration of disbelief in sundry religious dogmas.

In the light of the foregoing remarks, therefore, it must be said that the sacramental test was imposed at various times upon different categories of people, but no statute imposed it upon members of Parliament, and that the Parliamentary Test Act (1678) imposed tests upon members of Parliament, but those tests took the form of oaths and a declaration, not of a sacramental test.

That was the state of the law when the English Parliament passed the Act for securing the Church of England as by Law Established, which in due course was incorporated with the treaty and with the corresponding Act for securing the Protestant Religion and Presbyterian Church Government, into the lengthy and composite text of the Act of Union. The English Act specifically confirmed an Act of 13 Elizabeth I, c. 12 (1571) which imposed the Articles of Religion upon the holders of English benefices, and the Act of Uniformity of 14 Charles II, c. 4 (1662). There followed a general confirmation of existing legislation. It therefore did not introduce any new test. To say that the 'sacramental test was, by the Act of Security for the Church of England imposed upon Scottish members of Parliament'[2] is therefore inaccurate, being based upon the misconception that there was a sacramental test upon members of Parliament, and that the general words of confirmation had the effect of importing it into the Act of Union.

Finally, Article XXII of the treaty of union specifies the oaths and declarations to be imposed upon members of the Parliament of Great Britain as follows:

> The oaths of allegiance and supremacy as modified by the statute 1 William and Mary, session 1, c. 8;
>
> The declaration mentioned in the statute 30 Charles II, st. 2, c. 1 (the Parliamentary Test Act);

[1] See the references in D. Ogg, *Charles II*, i. 197.

[2] Dicey and Rait, p. 232.

The oath mentioned in 1 Anne, st. 1, c. 16 (1702), being an oath of abjuration,

and expressly continues the several Acts authorizing the said oaths.

Whence then did these misconceptions come? They are certainly old, and Daniel Defoe expressly mentions the disquiet caused among the people by a pamphlet which asserted that a sacramental test was a condition of membership of the English House of Commons. Defoe[1] relates that this was immediately refuted by several accounts showing that the facts were otherwise. Why so ancient an error should have been revived in the twentieth century is a matter for speculation; the authors certainly realized the difficulty of their position, and were forced to cite with approval the speech by Dr. Alexander Carlyle from which an extract has already been given. They needed great faith to accept the Doctor's paradox that the Test Act has 'enlarged the principles of toleration' and were driven into the suspicion that the documents they used were something other than they seemed.

The immediate cause of the confusion was to refer only to the Test Act of 1673—the Parliamentary Test Act of 1678 is nowhere referred to by Dicey and Rait in their book—and so to perpetuate a confusion which might be excusable only when pamphleteers were dealing with the complicated legislation of another country. Defoe knew better, and from the documents it is evident that the English did not deceive the Scots, that the Scots did not wax mystical about the Test Act until they had had almost a century to forget all about it (in any case it never operated north of the border), and that the oaths, declarations and abjurations which members of the English, and later of the British, Parliament had to perform were all directed against Catholics and Jacobites and could be sincerely taken by Scotsmen who were returned to Westminster. The unworthy suspicion that they would submit to the sacramental test in order to qualify for their seats in the British Parliament has no historical basis and there is no need to share the fears of Dicey and Rait that Scotsmen, as a result of the Union, bowed down in the house of Rimmon.

[1] *Defoe* (ed. Chalmers), p. 341.

XVIII

WORDS

There is a magic in words which the human race seems almost always to have felt. The words for holy things and the words for intimate things, such as family relationships, have in particular enjoyed an unusually strong sentimental reverence. More than one religion has preserved its truths in a language which long ago ceased to be currently used, and in several quarters of the globe at the present day living languages are defended with fierce devotion as symbols of racial or local independence, while dead tongues are resurrected to a new life of struggle in the same compelling cause. With the growth of enquiry into human history, however, the sense of magic and the force of sentiment give place to a somewhat different feeling. It is admitted that words have changed in form, although remaining fundamentally the same in spite of it; the stable element in the word is now regarded as particularly connected with the idea which the word represents, and the changes merely show the persistence of that idea through the chances of the centuries. Hence arises an interest in the history of words which is to be found all through history from at least the classical times. Of course the somewhat uncritical use of history which was the rule until recently, and the absence of a science of philology reduced the process to something like guesswork, which was moreover employed too frequently in the maintenance of controversy, the decoration of treatises with learned ornament, or some other extraneous end. Lord Lochee long ago remarked that "one of the pre-historical ways of philosophising about law was to account for what wanted explanation by some theory about the origin of technical words. This implied some previous study of words and their history, and is an instance of the deepseated and persistent tendency of the human mind to identify names with the things they represent. The Institutes of Justinian abound in explanations founded on a supposed derivation of some leading term."[1] In the hands of an unskilful student, this method almost inevitably results in attributing the contemporary significance

*Assistant Professor of Legal History, Harvard Law School.

[1]Article on "Jurisprudence" 15 ENCYCLOPAEDIA BRITANNICA (11th ed. 1911) 578a.

of a word to its real or supposed historical ancestors, and assuming that this idea is immemorially old because a particular root, with which it is thus arbitrarily connected, is clearly of an ancient date. Nor were Justinian and his commissioners at all unique in their use of linguistic history as an aid to the elucidation of law; our own Coke developed a fantastic philology all his own as part of his institutional teaching.

With the nineteenth century we come to the influence of Darwin, "the greatest historian of modern times," and instead of the preoccupation of earlier ages with the persistence unchanged of ideas and institutions, we find the scholar admitting that change has been almost always an inevitable factor in history. Thus emancipated, philological enquiry was relieved of the necessity of reaching edifying results, while about the same date the study of Sanscrit revealed a new world of philological material.

To the philologists of the early and middle nineteenth century, legal history and legal science owe an immense debt. Organic connections were discovered between languages which superficially and geographically seemed widely separated. The study of comparative philology rapidly grew up, and immediately began to extend its boundaries far beyond the study of language. Investigation of certain words of primary importance had compelled the philologist to study the institutions which they represented, and so we find that the expert in linguistics discovered many things of the highest importance concerning such topics as property, contract, procedure, succession, marriage, and so forth. Finally, out of these broad territories first explored by the philologist, there has now been carved out a generous appanage for the lawyer. It is with good reason that Vinogradoff dedicated the second volume of his *Historical Jurisprudence* to Dareste, who is one of the notable band of scholars who combine philology with legal pre-history; in fact, Vinogradoff was prepared to assert that "the immediate incitement for the formation of comparative jurisprudence was given by the great discoveries of comparative philology."[2] The separation was completed when India reappeared in the story: having started the cycle with its capital contribution of Sanscrit, it completed it by furnishing Sir Henry Maine with the accumulated treasures of its tribal law and customs. Comparative jurisprudence, then, like its big brother, comparative philology, is under a peculiar debt to India.

So far, the study of language has shed most light upon matters of pre-history. There can be no doubt, however, that the services of

[2]Article on "Comparative Jurisprudence" *ibid.* 580, 581b.

philology may very well extend beyond that shadowy and contentious kingdom, and be fruitfully employed in the less speculative realm of strict history. Our own common law has an uninterrupted history of thirteen centuries for which written sources are available, and there is ample room for linguistic development in so long a period. The terminology in every day use by the Anglo-American lawyer is drawn from a variety of sources and has undergone a variety of transformations together with the legal concepts which it denotes, and in the history of these transformations there are valuable clues to the more general topic of legal history.

Within the last year there was issued the last part of the monumental *Oxford English Dictionary on Historical Principles* (1897–1928.) This immense and fascinating work provides the scholar with a summary history of every word in the language, with excerpts from the sources. Lawyers will find within these heavy folios a carefully compiled series of extracts relating to any word they choose, arranged in chronological order, with an analysis of the meanings and a summary of the ancestry of the word and the changes in its form. The amount of material there available is enormous; but it is not exhaustive. The compilers were not particularly interested in legal matters, and most unfortunately did not use the Year Books in searching for specimens. Consequently there are some gaps. But even where they have the material, it is obvious that they did not have the space for any extended discussion of the questions which interest the lawyer most—namely, the relation between changes in a particular word and changes in the law. Investigators of special subjects have therefore been at the pains of compiling for themselves the history of the technical terminology involved where this is necessary, as is generally the case. In this way quite a fair amount of work has been done, although it is scattered among countless books and articles and so is more or less inaccessible. A recent French scholar has made a plea for the systematic study of what may be called "Legal Semantic" in connection with early legal history, and there is every reason to believe that there is room for its extension to historical ages as well.[3] In Germany, where a large number of local jurisdictions existed until fairly recently, it has been possible to create a geography of legal languages.[4] In Italy, on

[3]Mauss, *Questions de Sémantique comparée de Mots concernant les Institutions et la Morale* (1928) 7 REVUE HISTORIQUE DE DROIT FRANÇAIS ET ÉTRANGER 331–333.

[4]EBERHARD FRH. V. KÜNSSBERG, RECHTSSPRACHGEOGRAPHIE (Sitzungsberichte der Heidelberger Akademie der Wissenschaften, Philosophisch-historische Klasse, Jahrgang 1926–1927).

the other hand, a curious incident in the University of Rome serves as warning that the relations of philologist and jurist may sometimes be very strained.[5] In this country where academic life is less exciting there is every reason to believe that the two sciences could work together in amity if only they could be brought into contact with one another. Without making any extended searches it has proved possible to name several studies along these lines which deserve the careful attention of all who are interested in the history of law. Some of these are particularly interesting because they show the commerce in words between several different sciences. An admirable example is the recent study by Judge Dowdall, K. C., of the history of the word "Person."[6] Beginning as a mask worn by actors and serving to amplify the voice and accentuate the features, it passed into Roman law where it served at first as a word for those various types which were of constant recurrence (like the types of character on the stage). Some types were higher than others; slaves had no *persona*, as it were. But the word was still hardly a term of art. In the Byzantine empire it began to acquire some precision, however, and it may be that it came back to the west by way of Sicily, for by the thirteenth century it could be used of a corporation. Here, be it noted, Judge Dowdall finds that the history of the word *persona* is not quite in accordance with the speculations of Gierke. Not until the seventeenth and eighteenth centuries does the word assume its modern significance in law. Meanwhile there had been great play with the word *persona* and *πρόσωπον* (which was regarded conventionally as the Greek equivalent) among the theologians and philosophers from the patristic age down to the present day.

Words and phrases not infrequently serve as a veil which obscures the processes which go on behind it, and the historian must not only pierce the veil in order to discover what those processes were, but must also reckon with it as one of the factors which permitted or even facilitated the introduction of new elements. A remarkable example of the constant reading of new meanings into time honored formulas

---

[5]The controversy is between Professors Carusi and Nallino both of the University of Rome, and involves numerous points of Arabic language and Mohammedan law; see Carusi's very lively book DIRITTO E FILOLOGIA: RIPOSTA DI UN GIURISTA ALLE CRITICHE DI UN FILOLOGO (1925). A learned criticism of the controversy will be found in the review of Carusi's work in (1927) 47 ZEITSCHRIFT DER SAVIGNY-STIFTUNG (ROMANISTISCHE ABTEILUNG) 446–455.

[6]Dowdall, *The Word "Person"* (1928) 106 CHURCH Q. REV. 229–264. It is still another story how *persona* became the "parson" of the parish.

is to be found in the development of the theory of the Papacy.[7] Even quite modern words, however, need historical treatment if their use is to be freed from latent misconceptions. "Capitalism," for example, comes from the year 1850 and already has provided matter for a substantial study.[8]

Political terms are all the more susceptible of curious changes since innovation is bound to come, and conservatives are easiest placated by using old words, although with new meanings. "Wonderful conjuring tricks with a crown or a basket (*fiscus*) may yet be played by deft lawyers" as Maitland has said,[9] and it will require equally deft work by the historian of words if their evolutions are to be thoroughly understood. The curious suggestion has been made that the word "public looks much like a *Respublica* which, to spare the feelings of 'a certain great personage,' has dropped its first syllable." Eighteenth century statutes do not hesitate to state that "the public stands indebted" to the East Indian Company in the sum of four millions odd.[10]

Few words are more interesting than the group "State," "status," and "estate." The early sense of status seems to have been that which we now have appropriated to the Latin form of the word, that is to say, the condition of a person in the eyes of the law. In the Middle Ages this meaning spread to include such vague notions as we now describe as social classes, whether they had precise legal attributes or not. Then by a natural specialisation, this came to mean more particularly the higher and more important classes, and hence *homo qui statum habuit* means a person of high rank, and finally a ruler, or a body of rulers. Hence we read of "Their Highnesses the States of the United Provinces" in Holland. Such potentates have their powers geographically limited, and so "state" acquires a territorial significance, especially in Italy where the ancient use

---

[7]Caspar, *Primatus Petri: eine philologisch-historische Untersuchung über die Ursprünge der Primatslehre* (1927) 47 ZEITSCHRIFT DER SAVIGNY-STIFTUNG (KANONISTISCHE ABTEILUNG) 253–331.

[8]PASSOW, KAPITALISMUS: EINE BEGRIFFLICH-TERMINOLOGISCHE STUDIE (1928). The word "capital" on the other hand is quite old and has a long and complicated history which lies mainly in the field of economics rather than law. See Cannan, *Early History of the Term Capital* (1921) 35 Q. J. OF ECO. 469–481 and the supplementary note Richards, *Early History of the Term Capital* (1926) 40 *ibid.* 329–338. For some very interesting general observations see Wiener, *Economic History and Philology* (1910) 25 *ibid.* 239–278.

[9]In his Introduction to GIERKE, POLITICAL THEORIES OF THE MIDDLE AGE (1900) xxxvii.

[10]MAITLAND, *ibid.*, at xxxvi.

of the word for a feudal residence, or even for property in general, may have helped the transition. This feudal connection is of interest for it perpetuated the medieval idea of feudal dignities within the Empire as being technically offices; "the State, at least *eo nomine*, arises within the Empire, where the theory long survived that all government, except that of the Empire itself, was however effectively sovereign, an office held from the Emperor. It is significant therefore to observe that the words *état*, state, and estate were never used, as *stato* and *staat* were and are, for a *Landschaft*; and that *status* and *stato* were applied to the position of a prince or bishop, but not to that of the Emperor or Pope." In the hands of Machiavelli the word, as well as the idea underwent a notable change: "a word was wanted for the kingdom of a king, the duchy of a duke, the county of a *unmittelbar* count, the *dominium* of an independent lord, and the government of a free city—in fact, for every form of government which exercises *imperio sopra gli uomini*. Machiavelli, by the same stroke, decisively selected, and defined, and proclaimed, the appropriate word; and by explicitly recognizing and naming a general concept suitable for scientific purposes he rendered possible, and indeed himself founded, the modern science of the State." So far, the state was the governor; the last transformation is the inclusion of the governed as well. "*L'Etat, c'est moi*" would have been a pointless truism if it had been uttered in the days of Machiavelli; by the close of the seventeenth century and the beginning of the eighteenth, however, the change begins to appear which will give point to the epigram, and confer upon the word "state" the meaning which is now its principal signification.[11]

This is by no means the whole of the story, although the rest is shorter told. "Estates of the Realm" have been the subject of learned controversy, and the English use or misuse of the words has been described by Sir Frederick Pollock.[12] Lawyers in England have appropriated the word for a peculiar conception of their own, and thereby have developed the idea of an "estate" in land (which in popular use has come to be transferred to the land itself, thus reaching the same position as the old Italian *stato* but by a different route). For the history of this aspect of the word we have the valuable discoveries of Joüon des Longrais, whose study *La Conception*

---

[11]This is summarised from the most interesting article of Judge Dowdall, *The Word "State"* (1923) 39 L. Q. Rev. 98 where he refers to the previous literature of the subject and dissents from the theory of Jellinek, Allgemeine Staatslehre (3d ed. 1921).

[12]Pollock, Table Talk of John Selden (1927) 150.

Anglaise de la Saisine du XIIe au XIVe Siècle (*1925*) is indispensable for a thorough understanding of the history of real property law.[13] It seems that Bracton does not use the term to mean "an estate" in land in the modern use of the word; with him *status* means chiefly the condition of freedom or serfdom. But there does appear in his treatise a phrase *statum mutare* several times repeated in connection with transactions dealing with land. It is clear from the context (as des Longrais observes) that *status* here refers to the person rather than to the land. The nearest modern equivalent is perhaps the familiar "change of position;" thus a donor who remained in seisin after the alleged gift *numquam exivit a seysina, nec statum mutavit in aliquo*—"never gave up seisin, nor changed his position in any way." This is undoubtedly the sense in Bracton's mind, but as the author acutely observes, "half a century later the word *status* in this same phrase would certainly be taken (by an easy transition) in the real or abstract sense: "he did not give up seisin nor change *the nature of* his estate."[14] In the course of time, the vague word "estate" acquires some degree of precision, and so a new term "interest" is employed to carry the vague sense which once belonged to "estate." To the foreign observer there is something significant of English legal thought in this process: "like the word 'estate,' the word 'interest' in use later, will be one of those broad, practical terms whose use seems indispensable to jurists across the Channel. As we shall see, the word 'seisin' for a moment played the same role in the past."[15] The English taste for ill-defined terms is surely reflected in the extremes of *bizarrerie* to which a common lawyer will go, if once he yields to the urge to create a really exact terminology. Recent years have seen some truly fearful and wonderful productions of this sort.

In the more special field of the common law, the references to the history of technical terms are few, and mainly to be found in a few books. The language of the real property lawyer has been carefully studied by Joüon des Longrais, and he has embodied in his work the suggestions of Pollock and Maitland. The "use" has been definitely traced by the latter to the Latin *opus* rather than to *usus*,

[13]Pages 81 to 205 of Joüon des Longrais are an exhaustive examination of English legal terminology so far as it applies to real property; the study of both normal and Bractonian terms and the distinction between the two is of the essence of the author's thesis.

[14]Joüon des Longrais, *op. cit. supra*, at 127 n.4.

[15]Joüon des Longrais, *op. cit. supra*, at 129.

a fact of significance.[16] "Owe" and "own" have been disentangled;[17] and may perhaps be paralleled by the curious use of "duty" in the sense of a debt; [18] "attach" has been historically treated and cleared of a serious misconception;[19] the short career of "epike" has also been learnedly treated;[20] the present writer has raised questions about "lease" which have not yet been answered;[21] the word "parliament" has been traced back to a time when it could be used of a disorderly or unlawful assembly.[22] As late as 1267 Henry III forbade parliaments, conventicles or congregations which might lead to a breach of the peace.[23] Malice aforethought has also been referred to a curious original,[24] and so for that matter, have a number of terms in criminal law, such as "forestall."[25]

By way of concluding this list of examples, we shall refer very briefly to a word whose history seems to have escaped attention, namely "bailiff" and "bailee." The principal meaning of "bailiff" in English documents is the familiar agent of the lord of the manor who has the general management of the estate. The principal descriptions of his duties are to be found in Walter of Henley and Fleta.[26] A recent writer,[27] however, has thrown doubt upon their veracity, especially as to the bailiff, by confronting them with the evidence of the surviving rolls and accounts of many manors: "It is

---

[16] 2 Pollock and Maitland, History of English Law (1911) 228–229, 233–239. It is curious to note that the change from *opus* to the English "use" was a bit confusing to contemporaries; occasionally we find that the derivation is reversed and that a writer who wishes to employ the word "use" in the sense of "usage, custom," will be tempted to put into it a *p* which ought not to be there: "great-great-grandfather is made cousin in Chancery according to their usage (*par lour oeps*)" Y. B. Mich. 19 Edw. III, pl. 15, p. 333 (1345) Rolls Series.

[17] "We cannot rethink the process which lies hidden away in the history of those two words *owe* and *own*." 2 Pollock and Maitland, *op. cit. supra*, note 16, at 178.

[18] In a text of 1461–1483 we read "the claymor shall have execucyoun to levee the dwtie;" 1 Bateson, Borough Customs (1904) 195. (Cf. *ibid.*, at 208).

[19] Fox, Contempt of Court (1927) 56, 101.

[20] See chapter on "The Transformation of Equity." Pollock, Essays in Legal History (Vinogradoff's ed. 1913) 286.

[21] 4 Bulletin of the Institute of Historical Research (1927) 186–187.

[22] Richardson, *The Origins of Parliament* (1928) 4 Transactions of the Royal Hist. Soc. (4th Series) 137.

[23] Richardson, *ibid.*, at 147.

[24] 1 Maitland, Collected Papers (1911) 304.

[25] 2 Pollock and Maitland, *op. cit. supra* note 16, at 469 n.1.

[26] Walter of Henley's Husbandry (Lamond's ed. 1890); Fleta seu Commentarius Juris Anglicani (Selden's ed. 1647).

[27] Bennett, *The Reeve and the Manor in the Fourteenth Century* (1926) 41 Eng. Hist. Rev. 358.

the overwhelming influence exerted by Fleta and other treatises which has confused our knowledge of the actual working arrangements of the mediaeval manor, giving us a Utopian rather than a real version."[28] As against the bailiff, Mr. Bennett would set up the reeve as the more important officer for practical purposes. These are serious charges to bring against a group of writers who have hitherto enjoyed considerable esteem, and we think that they are open to several answers. In the first place, these ancient authors are interested in the scientific management of big businesses, and like modern writers of the same subject they describe the most elaborate organisations of their day; they do not pretend to give us a picture of the average small concern. Then too, there is other evidence available which confirms the statements of Walter and Fleta. A short experience of the Year Books will show that the bailiff has a definite standing in the law courts, and indeed he figures very frequently in particular forms of action, and above all in the assize of novel disseisin. It is a striking feature of the bailiff's position that he can answer such an assize by pleading the general issue without his lord. The appearance of the bailiff is a sufficient answer to a writ directed against the lord. This is derived no doubt from the age when the position of the bailiff was at its highest. Later, it seems that bailiffs *ad hoc* could be appointed; for example if an assize of novel disseisin is brought against a man and wife, it was the common procedure for the man to answer on his own behalf, and as the bailiff of the wife. On the other hand, a bailiff was subject to very stringent laws on the matter of his accountability to the lord. Account seems to be due as an outcome of the relationship of lord to bailiff, and by statute a lord could assign auditors to his bailiff or other such accountant and if he is found to be in arrears the auditors were given power to commit him immediately to prison.[29]

As the middle ages proceed more and more people are admitted into the category of bailiffs, and a case of the reign of Richard II curiously illustrates the tendency.[30] Here we read that a wine dealer deposited wines in a house which he let to the defendant who was a taverner; the dealer then brought a writ of account against the taverner as "bailiff" of the wines. Finally an issue was reached on the question whether the defendant had assented to this bailment which had been made in fact not to him but to his wife who was a merchant

---

[28]Bennett, *ibid.*, at 359.

[29]WESTMINSTER II (13 Edw. I) c. 11 (1285).

[30]Selby v. Palfrayman, Y. B. 13 Rich. II. 79 (1389). This Year Book is in the press and will be published shortly.

in her own right. On reading the French text of this case, it looks very much as though the word "bailiff" is on the point of turning into "bailee." Both words indeed have the same fundamental idea of one person being placed in control of another's property. More curiously still there is the parallel in the legal position of the bailiff and the bailee. The bailee who is dispossessed has the same remedy as his bailor: the bailiff, however, is not to be regarded as seised and so cannot be plaintiff in a novel disseisin, but he can answer in defence of his lord's title and plead to the assize, and this without being furnished with explicit authority such as a power of attorney. The bailiff's importance steadily declines while that of the bailee correspondingly grows. The word "bailee" seems to appear first in 1528 when it is spelt as often as not "baily"—a very frequent form of Bailiff (cf. "Old Bailey").—where it is used of the indifferent person to whom a deed was delivered in escrow pending the performance of certain conditions.[31] In later days, the bailee will most frequently be a carrier, and it is carriers who have provided the occasion for most of the law relating to bailees. This is a point to which we shall refer later. Meanwhile the growing importance of the bailee can be seen in a very significant case of uncertain date (probably Henry VII, 1485–1509) where it was held necessary to say that the defendant was bailiff, but that this was not traversable. In other words, the only way of getting an account from a bailee of goods was to charge him as a fictitious bailiff of a manor.[32]

If we look abroad we shall find that the word has had various fortunes. If in England it has had the queer chance to be applied to the release of a prisoner upon security (he being bailed to the bailees who were responsible for his appearance), in France it came to be the general word for a lease. But most curious of all, if the word is traced to its remote origins in low Latin we find that it comes from *bajulivus*, an adjective formed from *bajulus*, which means a carrier. So the story begins as it ends, with the carrier, although for a long interval the *ballivus* might carry responsibility rather than merchandise, and might be the bailiff of a liberty or the *balio* of a principality.

It would be possible with some searching to collect many more instances of the part which words have played in the history of legal ideas. All that we shall do here is to urge that the study is of great

[31]"Et aprez le bayle deliuer le obligation a cesty a q' fuit fait." PERKINS, PERUTILIS TRACTATUS (1st ed. 1528). The translation of 1642 used by the Oxford English Dictionary renders "bayle" (doubtless a dissyllable) by "baily."

[32]Keilway 114.

interest in itself, and often of value for its side-lights on legal history. Perhaps in some distant future there may be written a legal dictionary. The *Oxford English Dictionary* is a magnificent beginning, and the Institute of Historical Research in London University is doing most useful work in continuing it, but the responsibility rests mainly with lawyers. Less learned professions (according to common repute) have already furnished themselves with historical dictionaries of their technical words. The drapery trade has long had an excellent dictionary of its terminology on historical and archaeological principles; gypsy-talk and tinkers' cant are the subject of a special literature; a certain *Glossarium Eroticum* is now in a well-deserved second edition; but when shall we get a real Law Dictionary on Historical Principles?

XIX

THE PLACE OF THE LEGAL PROFESSION IN THE HISTORY OF ENGLISH LAW

ALMOST exactly thirty years ago Frederic William Maitland delivered before the University of Cambridge his famous Rede Lecture on *English Law and the Renaissance*.

In the course of one brief hour he contributed a new point of view to the study of English legal history, and to-day it is obvious that his lecture has made a permanent and important advance in our understanding of the forces which have moulded the law. This contribution he stated and developed, elaborating it with his immense learning, decorating it with his sparkling wit, weaving it into a composition of such grace and artistry that it can be read and read again with ever-growing admiration and delight.

The theme was the legal profession, and more especially, its struggle with the Doctors of Civil Law under Henry VIII. The gravity of that crisis Maitland vividly described, and the discoveries of the last thirty years have done nothing to impugn his estimate of the situation; on the contrary they have added weight to his words. For example, a good deal of significance attaches to the recent discoveries of the early history of Doctors' Commons, and Wolsey's powerful patronage of that body is now a fairly well-established fact. The circumstance that Doctors' Commons was not merely a professional gild of civilians and canonists, but also a sort of club to which learned men of all professions might be admitted must have made its influence all the more to be feared.[1]

It is Sir William Holdsworth, however, who has made the most dramatic contribution to our knowledge of the crisis. His illuminating discovery of the struggle over the Statute of Uses has shown that the position of the common law under Henry VIII was not only critical, it was desperate. Only by very clever diplomacy in which all parties were unhampered by any considerations save those of their own particular interests, did the common lawyers turn defeat into a really remarkable victory.

---

* An Inaugural Lecture delivered at the London School of Economics on November 11, 1931, the Master of the Rolls presiding.

[1] See the recent collection of essays by several hands, published in the London Topographical Record, XV.

That victory was won at a heavy price which succeeding centuries had to pay. Feudalism with its system of tenures was riveted still more firmly upon the common law; the development of equity was postponed for a century until the Chancery hit upon the expedient of using the trust to replace the use; and finally, the victory was won in the field of real property, and consequently it was the specialists in its ever-increasing complications who reaped the benefits.

The incident which Maitland found most striking was the cessation of the Year Books in 1535—'the height of the Henrician terror' as he put it. Here perhaps the results of later investigations may suggest a redistribution of the emphasis.

We may admit at once that the Year Books, in their rise, progress and decay, have had an intimate connexion with the common law, and that they were not merely books whose contents are of professional interest, but also books symbolic, in a sense, of English law and English lawyers. Chaucer's Man of Law, for example, is depicted with a fabulously long set of Year Books. For nearly two and a half centuries these books occupied a place of special significance in the history and system of the common law. Their extinction in 1535 therefore seemed to Maitland a dramatic omen that the common law was passing through its darkest hour.

Maitland was truly a pioneer in Year Book studies. Although Horwood and Pike preceded him in the task of editing them, it was Maitland who first grasped the intimate connexion between the Year Books and the development of the legal profession. It was he who first realized that there was a problem there at all, and starting from that capital discovery modern investigators have shown that the problem becomes all the more baffling as it is examined more and more closely. The late Dr. Bolland, Mr. G. J. Turner and Professor Winfield have all made notable contributions to the study of the Year Books, but their cumulative effect has been to emphasize the complexity of the questions involved. At the present moment it is more prudent to remember the importance and difficulty of the Year Book problem than to canvass any particular suggested solution.

Keeping this caution in mind, let us return to the critical year 1535. We now know that the year 1535 has also another significance. It is the year of the Statute of Uses, of the triumph of the common law against its professional rival, equity, and against Henry VIII's threats of root and branch reform. It is, in fact, the hour of victory, and the extinction of the Year Books at this juncture is not only dramatic, but deeply puzzling as well. If the common law had succumbed, if every fortune in England had been removed from the jurisdiction of the Court of Common Pleas to be placed under a sort of council of state, half chancery, half Star Chamber, where doctors from Padua would call Henry *Imperator* and administer civil law through administrative forms, then indeed we might see in the extinction of the Year Books a tragic symbol of the passing of the old legal order. But we have seen that this was not the case. The common law won. Its victory was not heroic, its tactics were not edifying, but still it won. Why then should its sacred books suffer an eclipse in the hour of victory?

If light is to be thrown upon this curious situation, it will most probably come from the science of bibliography. So far, only tentative results are available, but enough has been accomplished to show the general trend of events and to entitle bibliographers to the gratitude of legal historians. Their task has been very difficult, and would have been almost impossible if the late George Dunn had not formed that magnificent collection of early law books which is now the most treasured possession of the Harvard Law Library. With that collection as a basis, it is now possible to survey English legal prints as a whole, and to undertake some preliminary investigations into the content and extent of law publications prior to 1600.

There is nothing outwardly attractive in these little volumes. Indeed, it would seem that no type was too battered, no cut too broken, for use in a book of common law learning. And, of course, a title page or colophon may, but need not, have a date. Still, even the progressive disintegration of woodcuts can be used by skilled observers to place a given print within a fairly narrow margin of years, and so as a result of a careful study of hundreds of wretched examples of sixteenth century printing, it is now possible to make a provisional list in chronological order of early English law books. Such a list will show that the ending of the series of Year Books in 1535 is too complicated a fact to be expressed briefly.

In the first place, the Year Books were never published annually like modern law reports, nor were they ever published in the year which they report. All deductions based upon such modern notions must be carefully avoided for they are profoundly misleading. Nor must it be assumed that the most recent Year Book was the one most used by the profession—on the contrary, some of the older years enjoyed an especially high reputation. If lawyers had wanted their Year Books annually, they might have had them, just as they had official prints of statutes at the end of each parliamentary session; but clearly, there was no demand for such a service. Now if we examine this last of the Year Books, we shall find that although it reports cases of the year 1535, yet it was not printed until 1556,[2] which after all is about the normal delay. Again, if we make a list of legal publications which appeared between the years 1530 and 1540, for example, we shall find signs of considerable activity,[3] especially in the printing of Year Books, and this activity continues for quite half a century, the short reign of Mary being particularly fruitful in Year Book editions.

When we say that the Year Book series comes to an end in 1535, it is therefore necessary to add as a qualification that nevertheless Year Books did not cease to be read or to be printed at that date. It seems rather that there was a growing interest in Year Books at that moment, but it was those of an older date. Perhaps it was a natural effect of a conservative victory that thought should turn to the older monuments of the law—just as the Restoration was later to witness the great uniform edition which is still the current or standard one. Then, too, we must reckon with the powerful influence of the printing press which at this moment was in the hands of the Rastells, conservative lawyer-printers, kinsmen of Sir Thomas More and adherents of the old religion, and the fashion they set was exploited to the full by the enterprising Tottell who seems soon to have achieved his object of making fourteenth and fifteenth century Year Books indispensable to Elizabethan lawyers.

The sixteenth century therefore presents us with a curious double phenomenon: the extinction of the Year Books from one point of view, and their survival from another. Where Maitland saw a reflection of the danger to the common law in the events of 1535, we perhaps would see rather its song of victory. The common lawyer of the sixteenth century was notoriously conservative in law, politics and religion, and, having achieved his victory, instinctively fixed his eyes upon the past. While monasteries were being despoiled and blasphemous new titles conferred upon the King, while conciliar Courts were enjoying a wave of popularity and their own were threatened with the public's indignation, common lawyers may well have heaved a

---

[2] There are eight editions of this year by Tottell between 1556 and 1583; the undated print by Middleton is perhaps earlier than 1556.

[3] Taking the lists in Beale's Bibliography of Early English Law Books as approximately representative, we find between the years 1530 and 1539 that there were two dated Y.BB. and twenty-one undated ones (ascribed to this period on typographical grounds); of the more important treatises, we find the following editions: Rastell's Tracts (2); Articuli ad Novas Narrationes (4); Natura Brevium (5); Old Tenures (3); Registrum Brevium (1); Britton (1); Littleton (5).

deep sigh of relief in 1535 as they thought of their triumph, of the transubstantiation of uses into legal estates, of the preservation of the entail, and of their dominant control over the land of England. In 1535 the Statute of Uses must have seemed above all other things a restoration of the mediaeval order in times when all else was being swept away. Think of the Chief Justice, 'the reverend Judge Sir Anthony Fitzherbert,' who on his death-bed in 1538 solemnly swore his children never to accept a foot of monastic land, and yet remembering that his name appeared in the commission which tried Sir Thomas More. It must have been a comfort indeed to turn from the statutes of the Reformation Parliament to the sober, solid pages of *Quadragesimo*, *Libri Assisarum*, and all the other *Ans de la Ley*.

If in this particular our interpretation of the events of 1535 differs from that of Maitland, the rest of his thesis is only strengthened by the results of later investigations. Above all, it is now abundantly clear that the history of the legal profession is an important part of the history of the law, and it is to this deduction from Maitland's paper that we must now turn.

There is one great fundamental difference between the English system of professional organization and that which prevails in the principal continental countries. In France or Germany or Italy, the young lawyer has to choose at the beginning of his career whether he will serve on the bench or at the bar. If he elects the bench, he will serve his apprenticeship in the inferior Courts and will find his reward in promotion from one Court to a higher one. If he elects the bar, his prospects are confined to the emoluments a successful advocate can obtain, but he will assuredly never be called to the bench. There is consequently a deep cleft between bench and bar which inevitably has influenced the spirit of judicial administration. That system is a product of modern times, and if its history were written (apparently it is not) we might expect a good deal of light upon our own as well.

The English method of appointing outstanding members of the bar to sit on the bench of the superior Courts is, in fact, typically mediaeval, and is the product of little more than two centuries' development. The year 1300 may be taken as the turning point; after that date it was the general rule for judges to be appointed from among the most eminent members of the bar. Prior to that date, it was more usual for royal clerks and administrative officials to be raised to the bench. The first typical example of the modern practice was the appointment of William de Bereford to the Court of Common Pleas under

Edward I—and here it may be noted that it was Maitland's keen and sympathetic eye which first detected the human side of Bereford, till then concealed beneath a heavy shroud of seventeenth century black-letter, while the late Dr. Bolland showed conclusively that Bereford's whole life had been spent in legal work. With him may be contrasted John de Benstede, his contemporary, as an example of the older type of career. Benstede passed the greater part of his life as the confidential clerk of Edward I, travelling abroad with him, following him in his wars and negotiating his treaties. For some time he was Chancellor of the Exchequer and finally rose to the position of Keeper of the Wardrobe, which as the late Professor Tout has shown, was then one of the most important offices in the civil service. Here his work was so distinguished that he was rewarded with a seat on the bench of the Common Pleas in 1309 'as a sort of honourable retirement,' it has been said. He sat for more than ten years, but to judge from the Year Books his career was indistinguished. For our purpose his importance lies in the contrast between his career and Bereford's, and in the fact that he was practically the last example of appointment from the civil service to the bench.

The years round about 1300 were therefore critical years, comparable in some respects to the year 1535. Unfortunately, much less is known of the earlier date, and so we are left largely to conjecture. But in spite of all this obscurity, it is certain that this was the moment when the profession of the law was acquiring its permanent organization which was to last all through the Middle Ages, survive the desperate trials of Henry VIII's reign, and endure in large part until to-day.

As we have seen, it became an established custom for the bench to be recruited from the bar; the profession is therefore unified (at least as regards the higher ranks of it). But besides this, it became a rule that the bench should be selected from a particular branch of the bar, that is to say, from the serjeants, and here we come to an extremely important but puzzling problem.

The *narrator*, counter or serjeant-counter is common in the thirteenth century on the continent as well as in England, but nowhere did his career become so brilliant as in this country. The principal reason for this, no doubt, lies in the fact that England had very rapidly become centralized. The royal Courts at Westminster had acquired early in the thirteenth century a preponderant share of the most important civil litigation of the land and so the fortunes of the legal profession naturally grew with the growth of royal justice. The se[illegible] therefore, was clearly destined to a distinguished and luc[illegible] career.

It is in matters of detail, however, that obscurities are [illegible] found. For example, what is the precise implication of [illegible] title serjeant? Its general sense is clear enough—that [illegible] *serviens*, a servant, usually a permanent employee. But if this is so, who was the employer? Was it the client? Perhaps it was in the beginning, but very soon the word serjeant signifies merely a degree in the profession without any further emphasis on the idea of service. In the course of the fourteenth century some highly significant changes were taking place within the order. First of all, it became established that only serjeants could become judges. Then, simultaneously, it would seem, the Crown began to exercise the power of calling men to be serjeants, and by the close of the century the call is peremptory: the future serjeant cannot refuse to take the degree, any more than a gentleman could refuse to be made a knight. Furthermore, as part of this movement, the serjeant now became an officer of the Court of Common Pleas, and had exclusive right of audience there. And finally it appears that serjeants were sometimes summoned by individual writ of summons to Parliament, which again suggests that they are royal officers. This development should perhaps be placed beside the movement to exclude 'lawyers' from the House of Commons; it rather seems that the serjeants had strong monopolistic instincts.

These developments are of the gravest importance, but it must be admitted that the stages in the history of the serjeants can hardly yet be traced in any detail. The main tendency, however, is clearly for the serjeant to become more and more a Crown official. For a long time it had been customary to send prominent counters on circuit under various commissions, especially of assize, and it may have been in this way that the demands of the Crown became emphasized; perhaps we might find here an indication of the origin of the Crown's right of appointment and of compelling acceptance of the onorous degree. Above all, there is the difficulty of establishing a list of serjeants. The existing lists, although furnished with a circumstantial apparatus of dates, must be used with caution for the earlier periods for they are based upon the procedure in acknowledging fines which in later days was a prerogative of the serjeants, but it is begging several questions to assume that this was always so.

Furthermore, it was part of the development of the office of serjeant to copy the outward attributes of the degree of doctor in the universities, and a word must be said of this, for in the end the degree of serjeant thereby acquired a misleading appearance. Late in the fifteenth century Fortescue emphasized the analogies between the two grades, and no doubt in his day there was a good deal of conscious imitation. The long robe and the hood of fur were common to both dignities; the serjeant's coif was equivalent to the doctor's biretta; like the doctor, the serjeant had delivered two public readings, and like him also, he provided a lavish feast and incurred ruinous expenditure. Nevertheless all this seems rather an after-thought than a natural development. Doctors had always been members of teaching institutions, but the legal profession in England only assumed this function very gradually. The degrees in a university marked the scholar's progress from learning to teaching, but serjeants never taught: by a curious contradiction in terms, it was the apprentices who did the teaching, and the serjeant left his inn of court immediately on taking his degree; and this is in accordance with the general trend of his history, for as we have seen his history lies in Court and not in the class-room. It is therefore difficult to escape the conclusion that the external features of the degree of serjeant were consciously modelled on the degree of doctor at some time in the fifteenth, or perhaps the late fourteenth, century.

Serjeants were never numerous. Alone they could never have conducted the vast mass of business recorded on the rolls of the Court of Common Pleas, and so something must be said of the mysterious order of apprentices. The name itself is something of a problem for it would suggest a learner who studies under a master whom he assists according to his capacity; but there is no evidence that apprentices were indentured or otherwise bound to any particular serjeant. Indeed, the name apprentice very soon became an obvious misnomer. The scale for Richard II's poll tax, for example, shows us serjeants and 'chief apprentices' assessed equally at forty shillings; 'other apprentices following the law' (by which I understand in active practice) at twenty shillings; all other apprentices and attorneys at six shillings.[4] Then again, when a commission to enquire into the possibility of legal reforms was appointed in Parliament, its composition was fixed at eight members—two justices, two serjeants, and four apprentices.[5] And obviously there would never have been any serjeants unless there had been apprentices whose means were sufficient to bear the heavy cost of taking the

---

[4] Rot. Parl. III, 58.
[5] Rot. Parl. III, 101.

coif. These apprentices were therefore clearly men of eminence in their profession, competent to give the government useful technical advice, of sufficient substance to be taxed on the highest scale of the profession, and, as we shall see later, fit to be entrusted with the very responsible task of legal education. It is very difficult to tell what the functions of the apprentice were in the scheme of professional organization. We have practically no information whatever on the nature of his work, and even conjecture is difficult until we can say with some certainty at what date the serjeant established his monopoly and the exact nature and extent of the monopoly. The famous writ of 1292 [6] gives exclusive audience to such 'apprentices and attorneys' as the Court may select. This writ does not mention serjeants, no doubt because it does not affect them, but it would be hazardous to say that an apprentice in 1292 could not address the Court of Common Pleas.

Our principal source for forensic history is of course the series of Year Books, but their use as evidence in this particular investigation presents rather a problem. It was forty years ago that Maitland remarked upon the curious predominance in those books of a very few names—presumably of those who were soon to be described as serjeants, and that these prominent lawyers seemed to conduct practically all the vast litigation of the realm. Moreover, they are treated with profound respect by the compilers of the Year Books and their opinions are set down with almost as great regard as those of the judges. When we search the Year Books for references to the apprentices, however, the contrast is striking. Their almost total absence from those venerable pages certainly demands an explanation. We have a few obscure references to the 'crib' which clearly express contempt for the enclosure set apart for the accommodation of student-spectators in Court. Occasionally we find traces of an apprentice raising his voice in Court upon a point of law, but the usual result seems to be a reproof and a recommendation to go back to his books. In short, the Year Books seem to be openly partial to the serjeants.

Another disquieting feature of the situation is the fact that the Year Books during the greater part of their existence seem to have had but little circulation. Manuscripts are most numerous for the reign of Edward II, and more especially for his earlier years, but after his reign they become quite few in

---

[6] Rot. Parl. I, 84. This and a practically exhaustive collection of material on the subject will be found translated and discussed in Cohen, History of the English Bar and Attornatus to 1450.

number, and their textual relationships very intimate, so that it is obvious that they all emanate from one source. As more Year Books of later reigns are re-edited by the Selden Society and the Ames Foundation, I think it will be increasingly difficult to resist the conclusion that the Year Books are peculiarly and intimately connected with the order of serjeants. It is the serjeants' forensic exploits which are there related; the other branches of the profession are systematically slighted or ignored; and so it would seem that the Year Books are a series conducted under the direction of serjeants and for the use of serjeants—all this, moreover, at the moment when the apprentices were undoubtedly a numerous and eminent body of men. The number of the later Year Book manuscripts surviving seems to suggest that they were only destined for use by a very restricted public. If we contrast the textual evidence obtainable from a study of the Year Books with that afforded by other types of legal literature the results will be striking. Manuscripts of registers of writs, collections of statutes, and of the smaller treatises are quite innumerable. There can be no doubt of the reason: these books were constantly studied and used. Fortescue assures us that in his day there was a large student body amounting to some hundreds, and we cannot help believing him. Their demand for law books, added to that of practising lawyers, readily explains the abundance of all types of legal manuscripts in England—except the Year Books. It seems that the only possible inference from the evidence available at present is that the Year Books must be carefully scrutinized before they are used as sources for the history of the legal profession; at present it seems clear that they did not circulate among the profession at large, but were rather a close and intimate manifestation of the work of the order of serjeants, being most probably designed for their especial, perhaps for their exclusive use.

There is one other grave matter which must be mentioned in connexion with the serjeants and their Year Books, which is all the more important since it has not yet been sufficiently discussed. Some twenty-five years ago Mr. L. W. Vernon Harcourt published a book entitled 'His Grace the Steward and the Trial of Peers' in which, among other startling matters, is the suggestion, or rather the demonstration, that one of our Year Books is spurious—nothing more nor less than a forgery. Such a charge if established would be the less surprising in view of what has just been said, namely, that the series of Year Books is the rather close preserve of the order of serjeants, and that if they represent the views and interests of the serjeants, then it would not be surprising if they occasionally reflected (as here) other interests as well. However, there is no need to settle the question of the Earl of Huntingdon's Case in Y. B. 1 Hen. IV at this moment, although it certainly ought to be settled soon; our present concern is merely to note what disagreeable suspicions may be aroused when a historical source is too intimately connected with a small and close professional group. Such, unfortunately, seems to have been the case to some extent with our later Year Books.

The silence of the Year Books as to the apprentices is much to be regretted, but all the same it has not succeeded in completely suppressing the traces of their work. In spite of the propaganda of the Year Books, in spite, too, of the immense influence of the press when those Year Books came to be printed, the apprentices outstripped the serjeants. The order of the coif, after a long decline, is now extinct in England, but every barrister is the historical successor of the thirteenth century apprentice. More than that, the apprentices founded and endowed with wealth and traditions those inns of court and chancery which are among our most precious links with the mediaeval lawyer, while most important of all, the apprentices undertook the heavy burden of legal teaching. The serjeant may well have fancied himself as a sort of doctor, bestowing rings and liveries, and wearing coif and hood and robe, but the men who taught were not the serjeants but the apprentices. How well they taught, Maitland has told us in his Rede lecture.

The first we hear of law-teaching in London is, rather curiously, in a writ of 1234 which purports to close all law schools in the city.[7] It is a puzzling document, but whatever its meaning, it clearly marks not the end but the beginning of law teaching. Sixty years later we get the more illuminating writ of 1292 which seems to deal with a superabundance of law students. The judges were to pick out the most promising learners and to assure to them the facilities of attending Court; all the others, it is implied, had better seek a career outside of the law.

Modestly and quietly these learners organized their student life. They rented rooms, formed dining clubs, listened to the serjeants' display of learning and subtlety in Court, and went over it all afterwards around the supper table. They arranged moots and disputations and followed a sort of case method, which

---

[7] Close Rolls (1234—1237), 26—27.

from that day to this has been especially appropriate to common law teaching. As we have seen, the senior apprentices who became readers and benchers must have had considerable practice, and out of their experience they taught the younger men. Consequently, legal education in England never became the affair of the universities until recently. The civil and canon lawyers of the continent were long accustomed to look to the universities for their training and for the development of the science of law. The common lawyers, on the contrary, were self-educated, so to speak, and looked solely to the profession for the technical development of their system. Law teaching must have therefore been very close to practice. The frequent occurrence on the continent of dissension between the academic supporters of different views, and their divergence from contemporary practice, has no counterpart in mediaeval England. Ours was the contrary fate; all the asperities of practice became embedded in the very fabric of the law. The result was a rigid structure which Henry VIII certainly could not bend, and would have found it very difficult and dangerous to break. In short, the work of the apprentices of whom the Year Books seem so reluctant to speak was strong enough to survive the critical years of the Reformation Parliament.

These then are a few of the more significant questions which arise out of a survey of the history of the legal profession, with its contacts with the judiciary on the one hand, and teaching on the other; the second of these two relationships, however, is particularly germane to present conditions. Maitland has warned us that 'taught law is tough law,' and we must admit that the common law is once again a 'taught law.' In England this is a recent development, but in America it has been a tendency for a hundred years and an accomplished fact for half that time.[8] Blackstone resigned his chair for a seat on the bench, but Story and Kent did the reverse, achieving high distinction on the bench before accepting university chairs. Hence their appointments immediately conferred a dignity upon the profession of law teaching which it has ever since maintained. Its influence is constantly growing, and it has even been asserted that the teachers are conspiring to control admission to the bar. The most significant recent development, is of course, the establishment of the American Law Institute and the preparation of its Restatements—and here the parallel with French legal

---

[8] For a brief survey of the history of law teaching in America, see Dean Pound's contribution to Morison. Development of Harvard University (1869—1929), 472—507.

history is so striking that a word must be said about it. All the histories of French law attach a good deal of importance to the action of Louis XIV in establishing in 1679 a number of regius professorships of current, customary law in the universities. The result of subjecting the old customs of the provinces to the scrutiny of university teachers was most momentous. They analysed and systematized the traditional law, and restated it in logical form, and so for a century and a half they applied themselves, unconsciously no doubt, to their historic task of laying the foundations of the *Code Civil.*[9]

Both in England and America that analogy will prove suggestive, but I must resist the temptation to pursue it further. One last observation may be made as a result of this rapid survey of professional organization and teaching, and of their influence on the spirit of the law, and that is that we are here to-day in what Maitland would have called 'a school of living law.' That is a very serious fact, for you cannot be in intimate and constant contact with a living thing without leaving your mark upon it. Whether they mean to or not, teachers of law will finally exercise profound influence upon the law. Its extent and character is not my concern, but it assuredly will be the concern of my successors in this chair.

---

[9] A. de Curzon, L'Enseignement du droit français dans les Universités (1920).

XX

FREDERICK WILLIAM MAITLAND

In the year 1850, in the years of the Great Peace, was born the illustrious subject of this note. Philosopher, lawyer and historian, his life was passed in what seems now an incredibly rational age when a man could hold opinions without having an ideology, publish them to the world without propaganda, and discuss them with other rational beings armed only with good sense and good manners. It was a singularly happy age for the life of the spirit, and it reaped what it had sown—the splendid harvest of science and letters which made the Victorian age the most fruitful in our history. Of the many bright spirits who made that age memorable, none surpassed Maitland in brilliance, in charm, in solid achievement, or in permanent significance. That the Editors of this Review should have remembered his centenary, in a land which he never saw, and at a moment when the sky is growing darker, is not only an act of piety and grateful remembrance, but also an act of faith and a public assertion of the values which make scholarship a noble thing.

Maitland's vocation to legal history came to him comparatively late. His first university studies were in political science and philosophy; they led him for a short while to international law, and thence to law itself. Law he found to be in a very unsatisfactory state, and soon he fixed the blame upon the law's history—not a very promising introduction, one would think, for a future legal historian. The fact was that legal history, at the very beginning of his studies, brought that 'enlightened scepticism' of which Holmes had spoken so eloquently.[1]

The main outlines of Maitland's mental evolution during this stage can be seen from his *Collected Papers*.[2] His first composition

---

1 Holmes, Collected Legal Papers 186-7 (1920).
2 Maitland, Collected Papers (1911).

was the fellowship dissertation on 'Liberty and Equality'. Already the swift-running sentences foreshadowed his personal style, but it is extremely odd to find in it no indication whatever that there had once been a period called the middle ages. He submitted it in 1875, but unsuccessfully. For his second choice there was the law. He was called to the bar and set seriously about the problem of establishing himself in practice. It was evidently during this period that he happened to pick up and read, in a London club, a recent book—*The Constitutional History of England* by William Stubbs.[3] The deep first impression was deepened by the companionship of later years with that masterpiece. Maitland recognized in Stubbs a kindred spirit. "He had a strong taste for law" he observed thirty years later, and "it has often seemed to me that if he had changed his profession he might have been a very great judge";[4] in short, "Stubbs was just, and to read his great book is a training in justice."[5]

It is germane to note the qualities which Maitland admired in Stubbs' work, for they indicate the values which he prized most at the end of his own career. First he put the augmentation of knowledge; then the complete frankness with which he explained the technique of the historian's craft; next, the "tested facts and sifted evidence" upon which the broad sweeping narrative reposed; he admired too "the mind that was brimming over not merely with facts but with thoughts", and the gift of vivid portraiture which made even the *Constitutional History* "marvellously concrete"; and finally the courage which accepted "the risks that are run" in writing the history of institutions.[6] The young Maitland loved risks, and when he eventually accepted the call to be a historian he immediately volunteered for the dangerous duty of institutional history.

Stubbs was not the only influence which turned his thoughts towards legal history. He had been reading Savigny, and had thoughts of translating him. He must have seen such works as Digby's *History of the Law of Real Property* (1875) which was

3 Stubbs, The Constitutional History Of England (1883-84). [Another imprint: 1887-91.]

4 3 Maitland, Collected Papers 503 (1911).

5 *Id.* at 509.

6 *Id.* at 504, adding, "Would Gibbon's editor find so few mistakes to rectify if Gibbon had seriously tried to make his readers live for a while under the laws of Franks and Lombards?"

one of the first of a great family of books sprung from Stubbs' *Select Charters* (1870), Holmes' *Common Law* (1881), and actually cited *Seisin of the Freehold* (1878) and *Settlement of Real Estates* (1879) both by Joshua Williams, as well as the *History of Criminal Law* (1883) by Sir James Stephen.

It has been necessary to recite these titles and dates because there is a legend, to which much currency has been given, alleging Maitland's sudden conversion to legal history on the afternoon of Sunday, 11th May, 1884 in the course of a conversation with Vinogradoff; indeed, Maitland himself (who loved to pay compliments to learned foreigners) gave some countenance to the story in later years.[7] It is easily disproved by a glance at Maitland's publications *before* the critical date. They begin in 1879 with a long essay on the reports of a committee on land titles.[8] If the first few pages are what one would expect from a conveyancer who was (at least for the moment) also a Liberal, the remainder is a sparkling attack on primogeniture as 'some sort of fantasia or capriccio on the *Leges Barbarorum*', which shows that in the preceding four years Maitland had not only made himself a competent lawyer, but also an erudite historian. He had read and appreciated Brunner's exploration of the ancient *Anglonormannische Erbfolgesystem* as well as the attacks of Bentham and the learned audacities of Joshua Williams. Indeed, he was already so deep a historian that he could see through the 'historical school':

> To any reader trained in the historical school now fashionable our arguments may savour of a narrow and frigid Utilitarianism long since abandoned by all enlightened persons. The law of real property is, we shall be told, an historical institution—the product of social evolution, of national life—and as such it must be criticised; nor must it be rashly condemned if it fail to conform to our notions of practical convenience. Now it is but too probable that we are sadly deficient in the historic sense which it is the pride of this generation to have discovered in itself. It is not unlikely that we are behind an age whose chief ambition is to be behind itself.[9]

One need be well advanced in historical studies to write that. Amid all the coruscations of this essay it is clear where Maitland stood: "If we want barbarism at its best, we can turn to the *Lex Salica*; if we want scholasticism at its best, we prefer Thomas Aqui-

---

7 Fisher, Frederic William Maitland 24-26 (1910).
8 1 Maitland, Collected Papers 162-201 (1911).
9 *Id.* at 194-195.

nas to Lord Coke". Already in 1879 he had made himself a real historian with his eyes fixed on living institutions.

So Maitland turned to 'barbarism at its best'. In 1881 he produced a penetrating study of kindred and blood-feud in the ancient laws of Wales,[10] in 1882 came a paper on the criminal liability of the Hundred which made a point against Stubbs;[11] in 1883 he wove the Year Books and the *Olim* into a history of malice aforethought, as a supplement to Stephen.[12] Before ever Vinogradoff appeared, Maitland had shown himself in print to be an accomplished legal historian, concentrating on the roots of problems, and using a broad comparative apparatus of English, Celtic, Scandinavian, Germanic, Norman and French material. Moreover, he had reached a momentous decision. Already in 1883 he had decided in principle to abandon legal practice and embrace the academic life, for in that year he was a candidate, unsuccessful as it happened, for a Readership at Oxford.

When at length we reach the critical 11th May, 1884, the legend relates that Vinogradoff first revealed to Maitland the incredible riches of the public records, that Maitland took train to London the next day (a Monday) and went straight to the Record Office, where he was shown a Gloucestershire eyre roll for 1221 on which he based his *Pleas of the Crown for the county of Gloucester* which duly appeared in 1884. It is hardly possible to believe this. He had no previous experience of editing medieval documents or of reading old manuscripts; he had before him not one roll but two, and eventually discovered that the well-written roll gave a bad text, and the untidy roll gave a better text; he collated them and established a text extending to 155 large pages of print, wrote an introduction of fifty pages, found a publisher, had the work set up, corrected the proofs, had it printed and bound—all in the remaining seven months of the year 1884, if we are to believe the legend. It is hard to avoid the conclusion that the Gloucester pleas had been on the stocks some time before 11 May, 1884.

The summer of 1884 contains no sudden conversion; but it did see Maitland's abandonment of legal practice and his solemn conversion to a scholar, with his return from Lincoln's Inn to Cam-

---

10 *Id.* at 202-229.
11 *Id.* at 230-246.
12 *Id.* at 304-328.

bridge as Reader in English Law. He did indeed lecture on contract in his first term and discharge the routine duties of a law teacher, but his life from henceforth was devoted to legal history. From this year onwards there comes the astonishing series of books, each of them a masterpiece, each a capital contribution to some fundamental and difficult subject, and each of them inaugurating a new and fruitful line of research to be continued by his successors. The four years of his Readership were mainly concerned with the enormous task of editing *Bracton's Note Book,*[13] which Vinogradoff had discovered, with those matchless tables and indexes which are a perpetual wonder to those who gratefully use them. Not less important was a venture of a different kind, in the foundation of the Selden Society in 1887, whose sole object is 'to encourage the study and advance the knowledge of the history of English law'. There was widespread support among the highest in the land; no one doubted that the object deserved the most distinguished patronage. But good will alone is not sufficient to produce a steady succession of annual volumes, and the subscriptions did not always quite meet the bills. The most serious difficulty, however, is revealed by an examination of the early list of publications. The first volume was by Maitland (1887). The second volume was also by Maitland (1888). Of the first eight volumes Maitland was solely responsible for three, and partly responsible for another two—in other words, for half of the whole output. There were not enough qualified men to do the work. Arduous indeed were the labours of our founder during those early years.

Having carried the Selden Society on his shoulders for two years, Maitland was elected (in 1888) to the Downing chair of English law, and was called upon to deliver the customary inaugural lecture. It is the only thing he ever wrote which publicly reveals the keenness of his disappointment with academic life. He did not go back upon his decision of 1884, but he did tell his audience plainly that his vocation to legal history had led him through lonely and difficult paths, as he examined the question 'Why the history of English law is not written'.[14]

At the root of that problem Maitland found the irreconcilable

---

13 MAITLAND, BRACTON'S NOTE BOOK (1887).

14 1 MAITLAND, COLLECTED PAPERS 480-497 (1911).

contradictions which make it exceptionally hard for a man with the training of an English lawyer to become a historian:

> We are tempted to mix up two different logics, the logic of authority, and the logic of evidence. What the lawyer wants is authority and the newer the better; what the historian wants is evidence and the older the better. . . . The lawyer must be orthodox otherwise he is no lawyer; an orthodox history seems to me a contradiction of terms.[15]

That is a fundamental which is as true now as it was in 1888. The difference between legal and historical thinking was no great obstacle to Maitland himself, and he does not imply that it is a serious difficulty to lawyers generally, although he obviously felt that a warning was necessary. The really decisive reasons why the history of English law was not written seemed to him to lie in a variety of circumstances. For one thing, he held that legal history was strictly annexed to the study of law, and as consideration for this exclusive right, he was willing to forbid the professor of law from trespassing upon the close of the professor of history. Under this rule, legal history was a small part of a very small faculty. The few aspirants admitted under it were still further reduced in numbers by an additional requirement that the would-be legal historian must have spent some time in the practice of the law. That reduced the candidates to an extremely select handful of well-equipped men; most of them ran a serious risk of becoming successful lawyers, and therefore lost to legal history. 'Where then lies our trust? In failure.' Perhaps one or two of the able men who had not drawn prizes in the lottery of practice would turn their attention to the history of the law.

It was indeed a depressing inaugural. This was partly due to the essential wrongness of the diagnosis and the misconception of the place of legal history. To annex legal history to the academic study of law exclusively, was clearly impossible; had not Maitland himself, in this very lecture, stressed the incompatibility of the legal and the historical points of view? And had he not likewise rejoiced at the fact that one can be an excellent lawyer without legal history? Again, his high respect for Stubbs was enough to show that legal history is not confined to barristers' chambers, and the stimulating influence of Vinogradoff was that of a historian who

---

[15] *Id.* at 491.

was not a lawyer. Further, the prohibition to the lawyer from trespassing in the close of history is quite indefensible in view of Maitland's demonstration that in method and outlook legal history is history, and not law. There can be no question of trespass, for the legal historian is treading his own soil when he enters the pleasant fields of history. Fortunately, Maitland himself in later days was to enter boldly and joyously into the very heart of general history—to his evident delight, and to our lasting instruction and enjoyment.

Those reasons for the complete absence of legal history from English academic studies seem to be mistaken. The truly potent one seems rather to have been the incompatibility of method and outlook, so trenchantly stated in the passage which has already been quoted. The completely opposite aims and methods of the lawyer and the legal historian are inherent in the very nature of history and of English law. Here and elsewhere Maitland stressed this point, with the warning that there was always the fatal danger that legal history might be called upon to produce not the truth but some pious legend which should be useful in settling some question of current law. "If we try to make history the handmaid of dogma she will soon cease to be history."[16]

The diversity of mind between the law and legal history in England has become in our own day an even greater obstacle. It is now very frequent for students to begin their legal studies at an early age, with the result that their first (and only) experience of systematic thought has been within the peculiar framework of English law. Prolonged subjection to that influence, to the exclusion of all others, makes it especially difficult for the well-trained lawyer to think like a historian. Maitland certainly underestimated this difficulty, and the reason, obviously, is that he had never experienced it in himself, although he certainly observed it in others. His mind had not been formed in legal studies, and the law was not his first choice. Indeed, he was one of those 'failures' to whom he looked for the salvation of legal history. His first wish was to be a political scientist, and it was only when he missed a fellowship in that subject that he turned to law. The consequence was that he brought to the law a mind exercised in the wide open spaces of philosophy—and how much it chafed at being confined in a conveyancer's chambers is written large in the boisterous and angry

[16] *Id.* at 492.

paper on real property in 1879. Practice soon became intolerable, and a second 'failure' released him once again, this time to roam at large over the wide ranges of legal history, and eventually, of general history.

It was with a heavy heart that Maitland entered upon his professorship; there was so much to do, and he knew that his own life would be short. His answer was an astonishing burst of physical and intellectual energy. More volumes for the Selden Society and the enlistment and training of recruits for it (notably G. J. Turner); plea rolls for the Pipe Roll Society; a parliament roll for the Rolls Series; studies on canon law; a massive set of articles on seisin, and learned letters to Ames about them; another set of very solid and laborious studies on the register of writs—these were merely diversions while he was writing the answer to the specific question of his inaugural: *The History of English Law* was written, and published in 1895.[17] Tremendous fragments left over became *Domesday Book and Beyond*,[18] and *Township and Borough*.[19] Then he returned to his first interest, political science, and his translation of a portion of Gierke's vast *Genossenschaftsrecht*[20] was followed by the brilliant set of articles on corporations, associations and trusts.

This return to the beginning brought a still greater breadth to Maitland's work. He had done his full duty by institutions and technicalities, and now began those happy 'trespasses' against which he had vainly warned himself in his inaugural. Corporations had led him to the crown (which is a corporation sole), and the crown led him to those entertaining 'Elizabethan Gleanings'. Soon he became no mere gleaner in other men's fields, but the harvester of his own rich acres in sixteenth century history, for in 1903 he contributed his famous chapter to the second volume of the *Cambridge Modern History* on the Reformation settlement. Maitland had finally demonstrated that legal history is not to be confined to the faculty of law, and that the legal historian shares the whole realm of history with his fellow historians.

Meanwhile, the Selden Society had begun to flourish. From

---

17 Pollock And Maitland, The History Of English Law (1895).

18 Maitland, Domesday Book And Beyond (1897).

19 Maitland, Township And Borough (1898).

20 Maitland, Political Theories Of The Middle Age By Dr. Otto Gierke (1900).

time to time it ventured upon 'extra volumes' and a devoted band of editors contributed their labour and their learning to its enrichment, always under the watchful eye of its founder and first Literary Director. In this same year, Maitland gave it the new task of editing the year books of Edward II. As usual, he did the spade work himself, found the manuscripts, devised the method, and wrote the famous essay on the Anglo-Norman dialect which philologists still treat as authoritative. He edited the first three volumes of the year book series, and almost finished the fourth.

The Selden Society is the living memorial which perpetuates not only the work but also the spirit of Maitland. The sixty-four volumes which have so far appeared reflect the catholicity of Maitland's mind. Common law, equity, admiralty, commercial law are all represented; all sorts of courts from villages up to the common pleas, king's bench, exchequer, star chamber and council appear by their rolls and files; borough custumals and civilian treatises stand beside the twenty-two volumes of Edward II's year books. The Literary Directors who carried on Maitland's work—Pollock, Vinogradoff, Turner, Holdsworth—have found editors in England, America, Russia, Poland, and have welcomed the collaboration of historians, philologists, librarians, archivists and administrators as well as of lawyers. The texts are almost invariably translated so that the student and the expert are equally served, while the introductions really do introduce the general reader to the nature and significance of the material presented. The work is proceeding actively, and still further variety will be brought to the list with volumes now in preparation which will contain Law Readings delivered before the inns of court, and ecclesiastical causes drawn from the archives of Canterbury Cathedral (both being edited by American scholars). Maitland corresponded regularly with Ames and Bigelow and it is pleasant to see this association continued by the interest of American scholars in his Society. Maitland's high regard for Harvard makes it particularly appropriate that Professor Mark de Wolfe Howe, of the Harvard Law School, should succeed Dean Roscoe Pound as our Honorary Secretary in the United States. The subscribing members (a noble band which sorely needs recruits) have the satisfaction of knowing that their support is given to a splendid enterprise, and when they open their volumes they are opening a window upon the vast historical horizon which Maitland invited his fellow-lawyers to enjoy.

INDEX